CW00671129

"*The Tao of Equus* is a classic. What does that m‹ an entity that gets passed from generation to ϝ_____ time because it continues to function, to give value and meaning, and despite being from a previous age, stays relevant to whichever present it is currently informing. *The Tao of Equus* has taken its place among the classics of equestrian literature and will be required reading for any horseman or -woman of the future in the same way that it is today. Linda Kohanov was one of the first to point out that the horse carries not just the human body but the human psyche, and that the marriage of those bodies and psyches transforms both into the realm of the shamanic, the transformative, on multiple planes. This updated edition of Kohanov's classic work takes the reader and rider even deeper into the realm of myth and insight, with new explorations of the horse as healer, as well as transformer, of the human. A must-read."
— Rupert Isaacson,
author of *The Horse Boy*

"In the revised and updated version of her seminal book, *The Tao of Equus*, Linda Kohanov provides a pertinent scientific framework to elucidate how the sentient wisdom of the horse is whispered back and forth between horse and human. She skillfully weaves neuroscience, the polyvagal theory, and some exciting new research into and between personal anecdotes, healing experiences, dreams, and mythology. The reader discovers how horses and humans have coevolved to reciprocally regulate each other's physiological states and foster mutual growth and restoration. This timely book will inspire not only people interested in horses but all those who recognize the importance of reviving the wisdom of the ancients and restoring our engagement with nature before it is too late."
— Ann L. Baldwin, PhD, Professor Emerita of Physiology
at University of Arizona, director of Mind-Body-Science,
and author of *The Vagus Nerve in Therapeutic Practice*

"This masterpiece invites us to join Linda Kohanov on her extraordinary journey with horses as she harvests a magnificent maturation of her work that she first introduced over twenty years ago. Expect to have an adventure, a trail ride over many landscapes and across time, if you will, traveling deeply into revelations of the depth of our human connections with our horse ancestors and discovering fresh, empowering possibilities for our future."
— Trish Broersma,
author of *Riding into Your Mythic Life:
Transformational Adventures with the Horse*

"*The Tao of Equus* inspired the addition of equine-facilitated learning into our curriculum for medical students and residents. Linda Kohanov's ongoing research as a teacher, trainer, and writer, reflected in this new edition, is an important contribution to the field of integrative medicine and to our center."
— Devorah Morris Coryell, director of Integrative Medicine Elective
Rotation (IMER), Andrew Weil Center for Integrative Medicine

"Linda Kohanov escorts readers through a transformative spiritual odyssey with horses as the guiding spirits. There's an old adage that says, 'When the student is ready, the teacher appears.' If this book crosses your path, my advice would be to open your heart and mind and let it in."   — Warwick Schiller, horse trainer, host of *The Journey On Podcast*, and author of *The Principles of Training*

Praise for the first edition of *The Tao of Equus*

"This articulate, well-researched story brings together many disciplines of learning and weaves a magic carpet for discovery with our horses. *The Tao of Equus* will allow your imagination to take flight, and give you insight into yourself and your equine partner."   — *The Equestrian News*

"Kohanov is a steadfast writer who isn't shy about claiming a strong feminine approach, showing how mythology and history are filled with examples of powerful woman-horse connections. She also has the courage to reveal her paranormal experiences with these intensely emotional and intuitive animals — stories that may sound familiar to anyone who has ever loved and dreamed of horses."   — Amazon.com's Best of 2001

"An exciting, multidimensional work."   — *NAPRA Review*

"This inspirational book would make an excellent gift not only for horse lovers, but for anyone dealing with fundamental questions of grief, sadness, and healing."   — *BookPage*

"This is a new story in which both masculine and feminine are healed, raised to honored positions, and offered a clean slate — a tabula rasa — for the dawning of a new era."   — *Noetic Sciences Review*

"*The Tao of Equus* helps us to experience the exquisite balance between body, mind, and spirit."   — Lynn V. Andrews, author of *Medicine Woman*

"*The Tao of Equus* reveals the transformative, healing power that is implicit in the human-animal bond. It is a startling challenge to anyone wishing to limit consciousness to humans."   — Larry Dossey, MD, author of *Reinventing Medicine*

THE TAO
OF EQUUS

Also by Linda Kohanov

*Riding between the Worlds: Expanding Our Potential
through the Way of the Horse*

*Way of the Horse: Equine Archetypes for Self-Discovery —
A Book of Exploration and 42 Cards*

*The Power of the Herd: A Nonpredatory Approach to Social Intelligence,
Leadership, and Innovation*

*The Five Roles of a Master Herder: A Revolutionary Model
for Socially Intelligent Leadership*

THE TAO
OF EQUUS

A Woman's Journey of Healing
and Transformation through the Way of the Horse

LINDA KOHANOV

REVISED AND UPDATED EDITION

New World Library
Novato, California

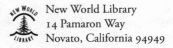 New World Library
14 Pamaron Way
Novato, California 94949

Copyright © 2001, 2024 by Linda Kohanov

All rights reserved. This book may not be reproduced in whole or in part, stored in a retrieval system, or transmitted in any form or by any means — electronic, mechanical, or other — without written permission from the publisher, except by a reviewer, who may quote brief passages in a review.

Text design and layout by Tona Pearce Myers

Library of Congress Cataloging-in-Publication Data

Names: Kohanov, Linda, author.
Title: The Tao of equus : a woman's journey of healing and transformation through the way of the horse / Linda Kohanov.
Description: Revised and updated edition. | Novato, California : New World Library, [2024] | Includes bibliographical references and index. |
    Summary: "Originally published in 2001, *The Tao of Equus* explores the mental and spiritual aspects of the magical bond between horses and humans. This revised and updated edition incorporates recent scholarship in anthropology, psychology, and ethology"-- Provided by publisher.
Identifiers: LCCN 2024009544 (print) | LCCN 2024009545 (ebook) | ISBN 9781608688982 (paperback) | ISBN 9781608688999 (epub)
Subjects: LCSH: Kohanov, Linda. | Horses--Arizona--Tucson--Anecdotes. | Women horse owners--Arizona--Tucson--Anecdotes. | Human-animal relationships--Anecdotes. | Horses--Psychological aspects. | Horses--Philosophy. | Tao.
Classification: LCC SF301 .K64 2024 (print) | LCC SF301 (ebook) | DDC 636.1001/9--dc23/eng/20240314
LC record available at https://lccn.loc.gov/2024009544
LC ebook record available at https://lccn.loc.gov/2024009545

Revised paperback printing, June 2024
First paperback printing, June 2007
First hardcover printing, September 2001
ISBN: 978-1-60868-898-2
Ebook ISBN: 978-1-60868-899-9
Printed in Canada on 100% postconsumer-waste recycled paper

 New World Library is proud to be a Gold Certified Environmentally Responsible Publisher. Publisher certification awarded by Green Press Initiative.

10   9   8   7   6   5   4   3   2   1

For my teachers and companions
on this journey:

Tabula Rasa
Noche
Comet's Promise
Midnight Merlin
Hawk
Nakia and Nakia

CONTENTS

INTRODUCTION

Lightning flashed in the black horse's eyes. A subsonic wave grabbed hold of my heart and stopped the beating, jump-starting a more frenetic rhythm a half breath later. My hands shook as I struggled to remove the halter and head for cover. But there was no time to retreat. I felt the thunder gathering force before I heard it. Bracing for a savage blast of sound, I expected the herd to spook and hoped I could negotiate enough space to avoid being trampled.

No one moved. Our bodies absorbed the massive crash, and though we all seemed to be standing perfectly still, my cells were quivering, spinning, awakening, resonating with deep vibrations that juggled the bones, shaking loose memories submerged and calcified long before my birth.

The feeling was so overwhelming that I was frozen, unable to run for shelter as echoes of that first sonic assault rumbled outward, fading into the distance. The clouds churned and darkened, conjuring a violent downpour. A potent silence hovered over the desert for a few moments, then water gushed through the crack between worlds. Seconds later I was drenched as completely as if I'd been tossed into a pool.

I had often wondered how horses handle Arizona's outlandish summer monsoons. Yet even when I took cover in the tack room during storms that came up too suddenly for me to rush home, I couldn't quite tell what the pastured herds were doing, let alone thinking or feeling. The sound was deafening, and I could barely see ten feet out the window as sheets of rain pounded the landscape. Nearby grazing lands suddenly seemed surreal and distant, shifting in and out of focus like something in a time-traveling dream. Watching vague, lightning-accented visions of the wind practically bending trees sideways, I couldn't fathom how the mesquites and cottonwoods held on to their leaves, let alone how the horses were handling the deluge.

I was therefore completely astonished when the night-haired mare gazed peacefully into my frantic eyes, then gently turned her back to the storm, inviting me to do the same. The other horses gathered round, and over the next hour we moved like a slow carousel as the storm circled us, almost dissipating at times, then coming back for more. Yet no matter how close the lightning, how loud the thunder, I felt safe among them. A force field of protection seemed to strengthen among us, tuning my nervous system to trust the power of presence and deep, ambitionless connection. Civilized thoughts receded. I was vibrating with sensations I didn't have words for, overtaken by primeval memories, flashes of people in strange lands standing with their herds as wind and rain and snow swirled around them.

Thirty-six thousand years ago, ancient artists were standing close enough to horses to memorize subtle facial movements and unique physical attributes. And something more profound: visions of horses *approaching*, unafraid.

The intricate visions at Chauvet Cave do not show herds scattering and hunters throwing spears. Of the more than three hundred images found in this gallery of Ice Age art in southern France — the oldest collection in the world — only one vaguely human figure can be discerned: the lower half of a woman's body. A nearby sketch depicts a human-bison hybrid. The vast majority of the paintings are highly realistic, artistically accomplished representations of animals. Horses are the fourth most frequently depicted subjects, behind lions, mammoths, and rhinos. These early equines are among the most vividly portrayed animals in the cave, clearly showing individual characteristics in striking detail.

One of the most famous sequences captures facial expressions that an artist would only pick up from close, direct observation of living individuals. One horse appears relaxed and engaged with ears forward. Another looks a bit cross, ears pinned in a gesture modern horses use to claim space. Still another, with stallion-like jowls, lays his ears back in a more aggressive, domineering posture. The smallest, most youthful animal has bulges along the bottom of its jaw. This is a classic sign of a colt or filly around two or three years old whose adult teeth are coming in.

In his 2009 book *Cave Paintings and the Human Spirit: The Origin of Creativity and Belief,* David S. Whitley was particularly impressed with how two different horses painted in separate alcoves were purposefully set apart from other animals, creating the uncanny impression that these figures were reaching out to him. They "approach you, slowly, oblivious, and unmoved by the lions, rhinos, and other animals surrounding them," he writes. "They come to you in a stately and unhuried pace."

Reading Whitley's words and staring at photos of these evocative paintings in the oversized art book *Chauvet Cave: The Art of Earliest Times* by Jean Clottes, I was inspired by a compelling possibility. Having lived with herds of horses as colleagues, teachers, guides, and friends — as sentient, empowered beings who made requests, reached out to me, communicated clearly, and quite often had their own opinions about things — it struck me that these prehistoric artists were capturing an ancient invitation, that very moment when a horse looked a human in the eye and stepped closer, hinting at a partnership in the making, one that would profoundly change both species in the process.

The plot thickens ten thousand years after Chauvet when it becomes clear that the artists at Lascaux Cave, also in southern France, were even more obsessed with horses. Out of 915 images at Lascaux, horses represent *over 60 percent* of the recognizable animals, followed by stags at a mere 15 percent, aurochs and bison each at under 5 percent, and felines appearing 1.2 percent of the time. Wolves, generally considered to be the first animal willing to be domesticated, don't even show up in these paintings. And here again, only one human figure abides among a bestiary that scientists now conclude had nothing to do with "hunting magic." According to Whitley, "animal bones excavated from living areas at the mouths of the caves" revealed that "there was little if any correlation between animals painted and animals eaten." Since then, he and a few other scientists have promoted the idea that the paintings were evidence of ritual trance states, that shamanism led to the birth of human creativity.

But what if the explanation was a bit more obvious than that? What if the most detailed paintings were ancient portraits of the artists' favorite animals — and by that I mean individuals with whom these people were forming increasingly trusting, intensely inspiring, transformational relationships? After all, while archaeological evidence of people riding horses doesn't show up for a good eighteen thousand years after Lascaux's artists closed shop, who's to say that these people weren't being called out by the animals themselves, following *their* lead, moving in harmony with ancient herds thousands of years before human beings developed the technology to confine and restrain the horse?

When *The Tao of Equus* was first published in 2001, I hadn't heard of the Chauvet Cave paintings, and Whitley's insightful book had not yet been written. At that time, many people believed that animals, including horses, were instinct-driven biological machines with no feelings, no thought, no opinions, and certainly no individual will. The revulsion some people exhibited when I talked about emotions in horses was striking at times. In the early 2000s, a few audience members actually walked out of lectures and book signings when I broached the subject. I was therefore relieved in 2012 when a prominent international group of scientists made an official statement on the matter. Based on decades of physiological and behavioral experiments with multiple species, "The Cambridge Declaration on Consciousness" stated "unequivocally" that "non-human animals have the neuroanatomical, neurochemical, and neurophysiological substrates of consciousness states along with the capacity to exhibit intentional behaviors. Consequently, the weight of evidence indicates that humans are not unique in possessing the neurological substrates that generate consciousness." The document acknowledges that "neural networks aroused during affective states in humans are also critically important for generating emotional behaviors in animals." This includes "all mammals and birds, and many other creatures, including octopuses."

The record of our fascination with horses goes back well over thirty thousand years. Ancient equines galloped through those Paleolithic cave paintings in France, migrating over time to roam the vast plains of the Eurasian steppes where they were first ridden around six thousand years ago, reportedly in what is now Ukraine. From there, they carried our ancestors through an endless array of foreign lands and new worlds, eventually settling the American West, forever associated with the pioneering spirit.

At the dawn of the twenty-first century, horses began to take on a new identity, breaking out of their roles as beasts of burden or vehicles for ego gratification and moving into a new realm of partnership. Somehow, against all logic, these animals actually became more popular after cars and trucks replaced them as transportation. Statistics from the American Horse Council Foundation's 2017 *Economic Impact Study of the US Horse Industry* showed that equestrian-related pursuits contributed $122 billion to the US economy, with a total impact of 1.7 million jobs. Of the 7.2 million horses in this country at that time, over 3 million were kept for "recreational" purposes, meaning that they were not working in racing, showing, or ranching. A 2023 article by the World Animal Foundation showed that the numbers had increased significantly with over 10 million horses residing in the US, and 60 million estimated worldwide. If the time, money, and effort we spend on these animals can't be entirely explained away by practicality or competition, what are they doing for us?

These days, when a turbocharged SUV harnesses the power of six hundred horses, these animals seem intent on helping adventurous people explore the frontier of consciousness itself, fulfilling a promise foreshadowed in myth and legend. To the Greeks, the Celts, and countless other cultures, horses were magical beings, gifts from the gods, fierce protectors, explorers, and psychopomps capable of carrying a warrior between the worlds as deftly, and as bravely, as they literally carried our kind around the globe.

When I began writing *The Tao of Equus* in 1995, I felt intensely alone — and more than a little crazy. My horses were awakening something in me, something profound and, at that time, indescribable. I could see these animals were having a life-changing effect on other people too. It's just that we couldn't talk about our experiences without sounding far too emotional or mystical — and vague, always much too vague.

So we chattered incessantly about the surface of all things equine: tack, breeds, training methods, lameness issues, therapeutic options, conformation, and competition. Over time, many of us became distracted by those details, losing connection to the powerful yet ever elusive spirit of the horse that drew us to the barn in the first place. As a result, we felt betrayed and frustrated at times, yet we were unable to describe why without sounding whimsical, unrealistic, and frighteningly, embarrassingly irrational. How does the average riding student or instructor express, in polite conversation, that she found her soul in the eyes of a horse, only to lose it in the business of training and competing? What happens when she consciously admits this, even to herself?

My reaction to this dilemma was to ask a thousand more questions and, for some odd reason, to strive to answer them: How do horses inspire us, open our hearts, and enliven our souls? Are there training principles and therapeutic approaches that can enhance rather than suppress this ability? Why would such graceful, regal beings carry our species around the world in the first place, enduring our sometimes violent, sometimes comical moods and infernal shenanigans? Is it because they're lacking significant brain power? Or are they sensitive, highly evolved beings, protecting us, nurturing us, gently guiding us, waiting for us to wake up to the wisdom they so patiently hold while we work through our adolescent fantasies of power and conquest, often at their expense?

In the late 1990s it was laughable, if not dangerous, to ask those questions, at least in public. As my book neared release, many friends and acquaintances distanced themselves from me. Most had experienced mysterious, soul-invigorating interactions with horses, but they weren't willing to formally ally themselves with someone who might actually lecture or write about it. I too was losing my nerve. After the galleys were sent off to the printers and I no longer had any recourse, I would wake up in the middle of the night hyperventilating, convinced that I would be tarred and feathered, burned at the stake, or carted off to the nearest mental ward upon publication. Had I written this same book two hundred years earlier, I most certainly would have experienced one of these dubious fates or at the very least been ostracized.

Instead, when the book arrived in stores and started selling, the reaction was very different from what my fears had predicted. Sure, some readers thought I was a little out there. But many more readers — all sorts of readers, but particularly women riders — wrote to tell me that they too had experienced a connection with these animals that went far beyond rational explanation. They recounted extraordinary experiences, dreams, and coincidences. Then they began joining me to delve deep into their own psyches, with the essential help of these wise equine guides, reaching insights and truths they had buried out of necessity to continue with their conventional lives. They were waking up, both to the true presence of the horses they were partnering with and to their authentic selves.

The popularity of the book you now hold in your hands is evidence that many people are recognizing the transformational power of the equine-human relationship, acknowledging that their love of horses represents more than nostalgia, sentimentality, or recreation.

Because equestrian pursuits have long been identified with conquest, nobility, and competition, much of the horse's innate wisdom still remains untapped. These sensitive, nonpredatory beings respond to the world in ways that are traditionally associated with feminine values, yet many amateur horse owners and a surprising number of professional trainers have trouble grasping these subtler facets of equine behavior. A spirited stallion ten times the size of the average human being inspires feelings of awe and even fear in observers, but first impressions can be deceiving. This kind of horsepower is not effectively tamed through intimidation or coercion. A hundred-pound woman can successfully train an unruly mustang with methods that aren't nearly as flamboyant or forceful as those a burly, six-foot-tall cowboy might employ, yet the horse will respect her more, not less, for her gentle, collaborative spirit.

I originally began researching the intricacies of horse-human relationships in 1993 for an article in a Tucson-based weekly newspaper. I was amazed at how little had been written on the subject. Bestsellers like *The Man Who Listens to Horses* by Monty Roberts and *The Horse Whisperer* by Nicholas Evans emerged a few years later, confirming my belief that many people were fascinated with the subject, but these books barely scratched the surface of the strange and miraculous things that can happen when the two species get together.

Early on, I took this work into the field, observing and interviewing gifted trainers while employing many of their ideas with my own horses. I studied the physiology of the horse brain versus the human brain; I collected myths about horses and compared them with reality. I noticed that some owners experienced increased creativity and intuition as a result of their interactions with these animals, while other riders exhibited only frustration. I slowly began to figure out why. I volunteered at a therapeutic riding facility and saw stroke victims increase mobility, cerebral palsy patients gain balance and muscle control, "unreachable" autistic children speak to their horses. In the process, I stumbled upon some unexpected and extraordinary realizations. First of all, I discovered that horses are more intelligent than we give them credit for, and I mean a lot more intelligent. When allowed to exist in a relatively stress-free environment, a horse's mind is literally swirling with the nuance common in creative geniuses. Just by associating with their equine partners, riders can tap into this stream as well. I also found significant evidence that mankind didn't intentionally domesticate the horse; rather, the species may have chosen to associate with members of early agricultural settlements and eventually lured some of these people into a nomadic lifestyle influenced as much by horse behavior as by human behavior. In the process, I gained perspective on the nature of human intelligence (and our widespread misconceptions about the same) as well as behavioral quirks and historical blunders that led our ancestors down an unnecessarily destructive path.

For general audiences, this is arguably the most valuable feature of *The Tao of Equus:* in order to decipher the myths we hold about these animals, in order to clear the fog of our own preconceived ideas, we are ultimately forced to take a long, hard look at our own species. In the process, we can't help but uncover a few secrets about ourselves, artifacts buried under thousands of years of masculine domination and the accompanying tendencies to emphasize thought over emotion, logic over intuition, territory over relationship, goal over process, and force over collaboration.

As I researched *The Tao of Equus*, I was continually impressed with the powerful bonds women and horses instinctually develop, relationships that emphasize the potent healing qualities inherent in respectful interactions between the two species. The Taoist thread running throughout my book is the unifying factor in explaining how these animals nourish their riders physically, mentally, creatively, and spiritually while inspiring increased sensory and extrasensory awareness in people from a variety of backgrounds and belief systems. Though I originally intended *The Tao of Equus* to be a working title, my editor, Jason Gardner, and I felt it was ultimately the best description of the book's thesis: that horses relate to the world primarily from a feminine, or yin, perspective. As a result, the species is a living example of the success and effectiveness of feminine values, including cooperation over competition, responsiveness over strategy, emotion and intuition over logic, process over goal, and the creative approach to life that these qualities engender. Taoism is unique among both Eastern and Western philosophies in that it offers a sophisticated model of how feminine wisdom operates and how these habitually neglected qualities can be used to temper the more destructive aspects of human nature.

Over time, however, I realized that horses actually do something more sophisticated: they moderate masculine and feminine characteristics with a decidedly Taoist flavor. One of the most famous quotes from the ancient sage Lao-tzu advises people to "know the yang, but keep to the yin," which often translates as "know the masculine, but keep to the feminine." This principle, I discovered, was not only vital in working effectively with my herd, it explained how these animals deftly trained me to bring these opposites into an empowered, compassionate balance, inspiring me to renegotiate my personal and professional relationships with greater ease and satisfaction.

The phrase *the Tao of equus* essentially translates as "the way of the horse," while emphasizing the healing and transformational qualities of this path. Interacting with these animals can be immensely therapeutic physically, mentally, and spiritually, helping people reawaken long-forgotten abilities that are capable of healing the imbalances of modern life. At a time when horses are no longer required to work in our fields and carry us to war, they can do something arguably more important: work on us. The logistics of how horses are currently being employed for this purpose and how we can expand on this model in the future are significant topics of discussion throughout *The Tao of Equus.*

In 1997, I began developing a series of programs based on the concepts outlined in the original 2001 version of this book. These workshops and private sessions employed horses in teaching people of all ages and backgrounds how to achieve a state of greater physical, mental, emotional, and spiritual balance. As I continued to expand my business and tour around the world, I found it necessary to write four more books on the many lessons horses can teach people. What started out as a Tucson-based collective of educators, trainers, coaches, and counselors eventually became Eponaquest Worldwide, with specially trained instructors on five continents serving thousands of people. We still marvel at how talented these animals can be in facilitating the work of human development. Eponaquest Worldwide is one of a growing number of horse-facilitated therapy and experiential learning programs springing up internationally. The field, which has attracted some of the most creative and compassionate people in the equestrian, coaching, and therapeutic disciplines, has amassed powerful anecdotes, inspired numerous books, and resulted in some solid peer-reviewed studies showing horses to be highly effective in helping people integrate mind and body, increase awareness of unconscious behavior patterns, and develop the self-confidence, stress management, and assertiveness skills that lead to increased success in relationships, career, school, and parenting. My colleagues and I have offered workshops and private lessons to women who've suffered from physical, emotional, and sexual abuse, and the results have been impressive. We've helped veterans with PTSD, substance abuse survivors, sex addicts, and adolescents with anger management problems make significant changes through this work. Horse-facilitated leadership and personal development programs have also proved effective for people who want to excel in life and work.

Most equestrian programs remain competition oriented and encourage students to "leave their problems at the gate." While this is a valuable skill to develop for the show ring, the continued suppression of personal issues, which horses tend to magnify, leads to the frustration, tension, anger, and abusive outbursts exhibited by some riders under pressure. Many riding instructors are not equipped to handle the psychological and emotional difficulties their students bring to the stable, and riders at all levels of expertise invariably get activated by the behavior of their mounts. Riding lessons offered by Eponaquest-trained instructors capitalize on the horse's uncanny ability to bring this material to the surface, using time-tested therapeutic methods and mindfulness techniques to help people recognize their own contribution to so-called horse problems and move beyond the challenges that arise when the two species interact. *The Tao of Equus* explores how riders and their trainers can move through these difficulties by treating each and every challenge or setback as an opportunity for personal growth.

The ideas presented in this book will also be of interest to people in the fields of psychology and consciousness studies, as I've found that many of my equine-based experiences support some of the more adventurous scientific observations of mind, emotion, and behavior. To this end, I discuss theories concerning telepathy, human versus animal consciousness, and autonomous, archetypal matrixes of wisdom that make themselves known to receptive members of our species. In my case it's a free-flowing "horse knowledge" I use when training these animals to give me intuitive yet highly specific insights into problems I would have no way of grasping through conventional thought processes. I've shared my experiences with other horse trainers who admit they also feel this force when working, and the anecdotes are amazing. Until I was able to gain their trust, however, I never would have been given this information. Equestrians experiencing this rarely attempt to put it into words. In fact, many avoid doing so, fearing they might be perceived as crazy. It is a significant part of the Big Secret whispered back and forth between horse and human, yet I believe it is possible to demystify the process without taking away from the extraordinary perspective it affords.

My original motivation for writing this book came from a series of seemingly irrational yet ultimately transformational experiences with my own horses. These events motivated me to do extensive research both within and outside the equestrian field, even as I became a trainer and equine-facilitated therapy/experiential learning practitioner myself. In most circles, such experiences would be classified as "psychic phenomena," though I've since come to realize these supposedly supernatural events stem from mostly unrecognized natural processes. My initial reaction was to keep my own experiences out of the book so as not to compromise the integrity of more acceptable studies on horse-human interactions. Then I realized this was exactly what the majority of trainers and equine researchers were doing, even though this unspoken element was a part of the lore historically associated with the "horse whisperer." Once I got over the fear of being condemned as crazy, I set about the task of examining this dynamic. My openness subsequently led me to even stranger territory, but in the long run, I reached the point where I could successfully argue that the so-called sixth sense is a legitimate *natural* phenomenon, with certain parameters and attitudes that foster it, and that horses can kick it into gear, often leaving their owners confused and frightened until they learn to integrate the new perspective into their lives. I also realized that my reactions followed an archetypal pattern of intuitive awakening. That's when I decided to weave the information I had collected into the telling of my own story, allowing readers to take the journey with me, giving them the same emotionally charged sense of discovery I felt when my objective research turned into a desperate search for ways to explain the unexplainable. As I became active in the field of equine-facilitated therapy and experiential learning, I also realized that the most efficient episodes of healing between humans and horses hinged on processes that defy conventionally accepted scientific and psychological theories. I was therefore thrilled to write a revised edition of *The Tao of Equus* so that I could share some new theories and studies that bring deeper insight into key experiences I could not back up with science when this book was originally written over twenty-five years ago.

The Tao of Equus is about horse-facilitated therapy and experiential learning, horse training, and horse behavior, but it's mostly about what these magnificent creatures are ceaselessly, patiently teaching *us*. It's about the courage and humility, focus and flexibility it takes for a human being to listen to those messages. It's about the quiet pools of reflection we experience in their presence. It's about the transformations that await us when we embrace our seemingly irrational sufferings with the same grace and dignity that horses exhibit in the face of adversity.

Human responses to trauma range from an overwhelming sense of fear to feelings of personal failure, denial, resentment, and mistrust in the universe. These and other powerful emotions run rampant in the equestrian arts as the best intentions, aspirations, and preparations are routinely thwarted by unforeseen circumstances and injuries. It's not uncommon for riders to go through horse after horse, trying desperately to find that rare animal physically and mentally capable of fulfilling some lifelong competitive goal. Are they missing something vital as they discard all these "mistakes"? Certain people just seem to attract problem horses. Is it bad luck, bad karma — or is there another, more benevolent principle at work? Is there a light hidden in those moments of darkness we try so often to avoid or ignore?

Lao-tzu observed that "it is upon disaster that good fortune rests," pointing to what is perhaps the most potent Taoist paradox, one that my own herd has brought home to me time and time again. Throughout *The Tao of Equus*, I weave my journey with the odysseys of many two-legged and four-legged teachers who repeatedly reminded me that the mysteries of life, the most potent gifts of existence, quite often arrive on the backs of black horses.

Part One

THE CALL

Enlightenment is not a matter of imagining figures of light,
but of making the darkness conscious.
— C. G. Jung

CHAPTER ONE

RASA

This is the story of a woman and her horse. On the surface, it seems a bit of a cliché. Adolescent girls are, after all, the ones who go horse crazy, lining their bedroom shelves with plastic models of the different breeds and begging their parents for riding lessons. For many, the obsession strengthens with age. *Horse Illustrated* observed that a 90 to 95 percent female entry is not unusual in amateur dressage and hunter-jumper shows. The majority of equestrian magazines also note a larger female readership. Men still dominate the worlds of polo and racing, and a greater percentage of them show and train professionally. To a woman, however, horses often represent something more profound than sport or hobby. Among the picture frames lined across her desk, there's invariably at least one of her four-legged partner, and when she finds the right trainer, she'll often speak of him or her with the reverence usually afforded a guru. A feeling of quiet ecstasy surrounds many female riders and their mounts, as if they've resurrected a lost part of themselves while galloping down the trail, as if all the centuries that men went to war on well-trained steeds seem trivial compared to a single moment of understanding between a teenage girl and her first bay mare.

I've come to realize that women and horses are fully capable of weaving new myths into the future, perspectives based, not on conquest and domination, but on harmony and collaboration. Truly feminine modes of interaction can't help but uncover artifacts of experience buried beneath the preconceived notions of our mechanized world, evidence of a time when horses taught people a thing or two and were respected for their inherent wisdom. Some of these treasures are physical and emotional, like the sensual union of strength and gentleness trotting against the skin, like the rush of clarity and serenity unleashed when one's control of a thousand-pound creature begins to flow from the mind and not the muscle, like the flash of hope rising from the knowledge that the ones who live as prey are fully capable of outwitting the ones who live as predators. Some of these treasures can only be described as spiritual, like mending the separation between mind and muscle, like the promise that the lion shall lie down beside the lamb in paradise. Or should it be the mare?

Perhaps these were the things I glimpsed when I first gazed into the black horse's eyes. She was standing in a box stall smelling of pine shavings, and she spoke to me more eloquently in silence than anyone ever had in words. I'd already been to every ranch and breeding farm in Tucson and was spending the weekend in Phoenix looking for the perfect prospect. I wanted a filly whose spirit had not yet been broken by the saddle and all the baggage that comes with it. I was unconsciously craving the kind of relationship between human and horse that had once been common among members of a distant clan — though at the time I had no idea who my ancestors were or that their ghosts had led me on this quest.

Still, I resisted falling in love with her. I'd dealt before with the problems that can result from buying a horse on impulse, and I wanted to do everything right. I made an offer contingent on a veterinary examination and decided I would walk away from this filly if there was the slightest indication of a problem. A week later, she passed the exam with flying colors. The week after that, she was delivered to the Tucson boarding facility where I kept an unruly thoroughbred ex-racehorse and a previously abused mustang ex–cow horse.

The filly's breeders had christened her Black Beauty at the moment of her birth. She was named after the long-suffering equine hero of the nineteenth-century classic by Anna Sewell, the first book to bring widespread public attention to the tortures endured by horses at the hands of human beings. As a purebred Arabian with Egyptian bloodlines, her name was etched in stone as far as the registry was concerned. The papers that came with my new horse could not be changed, but I wasn't about to refer to the Black Beauty legacy every time I wanted her to come to me. I decided to call her Tabula Rasa — "clean slate" in Latin — or simply Rasa, a term in Indian music for the mood, emotional soul, or innate extramusical image expressed through an extended improvisation. It was my intention to protect the youngest member of my herd from the unspoken fears and injustices I saw hovering behind the eyes of my other horses, traumas I had tried and failed to heal.

They say an elephant never forgets. The same is true of horses, which is why it's important to treat them with the utmost sensitivity and, above all, to strive to do things right the first time. Most of the animals I'd encountered at public boarding stables in Tucson exhibited behavior problems stemming from some form of physical or emotional trauma. The retired cow horse I acquired for my husband Steve was a classic example. Noche initially acted as if I were going to rap him across the head with a two-by-four every time I walked into his stall. Carrots were alien objects, and it took weeks of coaxing before he consented to take a sample from my hand. (The look on his face was one of stunned pleasure, and he's been addicted ever since.) Yet even after we spent months slowly gaining his confidence, Noche's memories of rough handling would suddenly resurface at the slightest provocation. One hot summer afternoon, I arrived at the barn with a handful of apple slices, and the old mustang refused to come near me. In fact, he snorted and raced around the corral as if I were the devil himself. It took me half an hour to figure out what the problem was. For the first time since we'd met, I'd worn a cowboy hat to keep the sun out of my eyes. When I took it off to wipe the sweat from my brow, the frightened horse immediately calmed down. To this day, Noche still expects the worst from people when their heads take on that strange shape.

I was adamant that my new filly would have nothing to fear from the human race, no matter what style of hat was involved. Unlike Noche, who cowered at the back of his stall whenever anyone on two legs looked his way, Rasa was gregarious, curious, affectionate, and always ready for the next escapade, whether it involved sizing up new people, teasing her stablemates, or chasing stray coyotes across the arena. She was a tabula rasa only in the context of adverse human influences. Otherwise, her character was clearly defined, and it was a pleasure to watch her actions and emotions arise out of pure abandon. The challenge was keeping her that way as we proceeded toward formal training.

In the meantime, I made sure Rasa associated me with the good things in life — not just carrots, but adventures. Together, we hiked for miles through the open desert searching for that rare patch of fresh grass. When the rains came and the washes flowed, we splashed around in the rushing water like a couple of kids. Back at the stable, we chased each other around the arena and engaged in mutual grooming sessions. As I rubbed her withers, she massaged the small of my back with her powerful lips. Eventually, she discovered how to use her nose to point to whatever place on her body needed a good scratch, and I was happy to oblige.

My fellow boarders thought I had taken leave of my senses. Some warned that Rasa would lose control and run me over or at least give me one hell of a bite. Others verbally chastised me for treating my horse like a dog. Yet the affection we openly expressed had nothing to do with canine sensibilities. I was encouraging Rasa to treat me like another mare. Still, the line I crossed made everyone nervous. The vast majority of riders I encountered at that time thought horses were incapable of even the most rudimentary forms of discrimination, as if these creatures couldn't help but take a mile if they were given an inch. Some trainers continue to insist that hand-fed horses develop dangerous biting habits, but Rasa never mistook my finger for a carrot, nor did she leave bite marks on my shoulders during our little grooming episodes. Even so, I didn't allow her to nuzzle me the first time I met her in Phoenix or dare her to chase me along the fence line the day she was trailered to her new home in Tucson. We didn't take liberties with each other until we had reached a level of mutual understanding that came about incrementally. Whenever Rasa became careless, the games stopped, and she was returned to her stall. Whenever I did something that made her nervous, she swished her tail as a warning, and I backed off long before she felt it necessary to bite or kick.

I treated Rasa with respect and expected the same from her, and no one was going to make me feel foolish for it. Besides, the boarders who made the most ruckus over my misguided ways were the same people who came out to ride their horses twice a month, smacked them around when the animals showed signs of being barn sour, and took off whooping and hollering into the desert at a brisk, bucking gallop. Barn sour horses become unruly and sometimes even panic when taken beyond sight of their stalls, because they've been confined for weeks on end with little human interaction and sporadic exercise at best. Yet I rarely observed an owner acknowledging his horse's frenetic confusion as a legitimate reaction to being cooped up for too long. Instead, these people would shout and curse as they forcibly tried to restrain their jittery mounts long enough to climb into the saddle and head for the trails. The ones who returned with broken arms and collarbones were the first to shake their heads when they saw Rasa quietly rubbing my neck.

At the time, I wasn't entirely conscious of what I was doing, so I wasn't able to justify my behavior to other riders. My playful excursions outside the boundaries of the stable and its conventions tested a long-standing protocol between humans and horses that other people never seemed to question. Since I couldn't express this to my critics, I simply stated that my goal was to help Rasa feel secure in my presence away from the barn and the other horses before I attempted to get on her back. I felt vindicated when I finally did begin riding her and we had little trouble crossing streams or exploring the trails alone, two seemingly simple feats known to cause horse owners a great deal of trouble.

Rasa's initiation into the world of bits and saddles proved to be a pivotal experience in many ways. I was pushing the envelop on an informal basis, but when it came to helping her accept a rider, I wanted everything done right the first time, and I knew I wasn't the one for the job. Yet of all the trainers I interviewed, those who specialized in "breaking colts" employed methods I was determined to avoid. I didn't feel it necessary to tie an energetic youngster to a fence post and make her stand there for an hour under the guise of teaching self-discipline. I didn't want someone belting her across the face if she mistakenly tried to groom him, and I certainly didn't want some hotshot spurring the bucks out of her for sport. I also knew I couldn't argue my case with trainers who had been in the business for twenty years, especially when they already treated me like a silly, sentimental woman. Still, I sensed there was a better way to relate to these animals as surely as if I carried a hidden blueprint for such an alternative in my blood.

Mirror, Mirror in Your Stall

I had already come to the painful realization that a trainer's confidence, experience, and successful show record did not necessarily justify his methods and that even techniques approved by second and third opinions could be disastrous. My first horse, a beautiful thoroughbred I called Nakia, had been trained at the track and then passed along through a succession of amateur riders. By the time I bought her, the seven-year-old mare had developed a nasty habit of pulling back from the hitching post, breaking the lead rope, and running off. Her previous owner was careful not to mention this to me, even when I asked him about any behavioral quirks she may have acquired. She was a little barn sour, he said, because he was working two jobs and didn't have time to ride her. Though I later learned from a mutual acquaintance that Nakia's fear of the hitching post was the main reason he decided to sell her, the man actually performed some clever ministrations to avoid a scene when we were saddling her up for a test ride.

Crystal Angel was the name listed on her papers. I thought the phrase smacked of New Age sentimentality unbecoming a registered thoroughbred, and it seemed a wholly incongruous image for a willful, dark bay mare. At the time, I wasn't sure what Nakia meant — it was something I had called one of my childhood equine friends — but the strong, lyrical quality of the word seemed to fit the horse's personality. Nakia had definite notions about what she would and would not accept, and I had to come up with some creative ways to get her to cooperate. This proved a bit unnerving at first. I was raised to believe that human beings were higher life forms, but this mare had no intention of indulging me just because I walked around on two legs. I had to gain her respect every step of the way, and I often felt that she was training me. Still, Nakia was a remarkably forgiving creature, even as she remained an intelligent and spirited mare. She took good care of me on the trails, but for all my efforts she remained paranoid about being tied. Nothing I tried, short of giving her a pile of hay to nibble while she was being saddled, seemed to help.

Looking back on the episode, I'm certain that under the tutelage of the right trainer, we could have worked through this difficulty and made an exceptional pleasure horse of her. The problem was I had been adopted by the local cowboy contingent, consisting of several older men who had actually ridden the range and a number of younger adults dressed like Garth Brooks who wished they could quit their desk jobs and rope cattle for a living. While we all had a lot of fun galloping through the open desert, kicking up dust in the moonlight on extended evening rides, and chasing steers around on team penning nights, these men and women discouraged me from enrolling with a talented English riding instructor who was also based at the stable. At the time, I accepted the advice of my friends and suffered immensely for it.

In the meantime, Nakia's habit of breaking her lead rope and running off was becoming dangerous, especially at a public boarding stable where children were a constant consideration. I began seeking the advice of some "trainers" recommended by the cowboys and some clerks at the local feed store. Several came up with the same solution. I was to buy a thick, soft rope about twenty feet long, toss it over the horse's back, and tie a special knot under her girth area. Then I was to bring the longer end of the rope through the gap between her front legs, attach it to her halter in a certain configuration, and secure it to the hitching post. The idea was that eventually Nakia would pull back, expecting unlimited freedom at any moment, and her efforts would be thwarted. She would jerk and rear and twist and squeal until she was exhausted. Then she would be cured forever. The thickness of the material was designed to minimize rope burn and withstand the pressure of the horse's attempts to break free, while the extra length running around her belly and between her front legs would keep her from injuring her neck. No matter how she struggled, I was warned not to release her until she stood quietly for at least thirty minutes.

To say this method backfired would be an understatement. As Nakia pulled with increasing vehemence, the rope stretched until it had the consistency of a thin, hard lasso twice its original length. This made it possible for the enraged mare to lunge around the post, slam into the tack room door several times, and leap into the air with one final, emphatic gesture of revolt, only to fall flat on the ground and moan in pain. The knots had tightened beyond my ability to loosen them by hand. The insides of Nakia's legs were raw, and at first I thought she might have broken some bones.

As she lay there huffing and wheezing, I was overcome by a hauntingly realistic memory that paralyzed my body and kept me from coming to her aid for an indeterminate amount of time. Five years earlier, I had unleashed a similarly violent, self-destructive display of unbridled anger the night I realized I would either have to leave my first husband or continue to experience a long, slow, soul-stupefying death. I had screamed and jerked, twisted and convulsed as I slammed my own body against the walls of the house that had become my prison and finally fell to the ground in a state of shock.

Emotional intimidation is a clever and insidious form of control. My first husband's searing insults and verbal tirades never produced visible bruises. I had no overt excuse to divorce him, no physical evidence of abuse that could bring the justice system to my defense. Even so, my self-esteem and effectiveness in the world were systematically drained. Any time I became too confident in my work, too successful as a writer and radio producer, my husband would reel me back in with a series of sinister comments and sexual games that would leave me thoroughly demoralized. I'd usually call in sick after these episodes and lie around in a catatonic state for hours. I finally reached the point where suicide seemed like it would be a welcome relief, yet some other, more tenacious part of my psyche decided to fight back. My husband could only watch in horror as my quiet pleas for him to take back a particularly cruel remark turned into howls of anguish and screams of rage. I pulled my hair and began to fling myself around the room. I felt like a chained animal willing to chew its own leg to escape captivity, and I succeeded in producing bruises that reflected the hidden scars I had carried around for years.

In a strange, dreamlike state, I found a small knife in the tack room and began cutting the rope that had subjected my troubled mare to this trauma, one I had set in motion with seemingly the best of intentions. For the next week, she was so sore she could barely walk, and when she was well enough to ride again, she had even less tolerance for the hitching post. Both of us were spooked. I'd confirmed her worst fears, and she had brought into focus a painful event I thought I had forgotten. Even more disturbing, however, was the mystery of how I'd managed to acquire a horse capable of reenacting this distressing chapter in my life. Somehow, Nakia had allowed me to watch a remarkably similar emotional explosion from another perspective. Did my husband feel it was his duty to keep me in line? Why was he so afraid of the passionate, independent side of my personality? Didn't he notice that the harder he tried to rein me in, the more I wanted to run away? Having experienced the injustices of forced coercion in my first marriage, why did I subject Nakia to the same rigid, controlling standards? Why did I feel it was necessary to tie the mare if she had such an aversion to it? Couldn't I have saddled her up in the corral or explored some other option? For all my talk about treating horses with respect, I had given in to the peer pressure of my cowboy friends because I didn't want them to think Nakia was getting the better of me. Rather than searching for an unconventional solution that we both could live with, I tied her up with an even stronger rope and expected her to surrender. Suddenly, Crystal Angel didn't seem such an inappropriate name. I didn't like what I saw when I gazed into her eyes, but I was grateful for the reflection.

The stable provided no pleasant diversions for me that weekend as I watched my injured horse standing in the corner of her stall, staring listlessly at rows of horses being groomed for a Saturday evening trail ride. Some were pawing the ground. Others were refusing to pick up their feet to have their hooves cleaned. A twenty-year-old gelding owned by one of the cowboys was sidestepping and tossing his head; it finally took two men to get the saddle onto his back and cinch up the girth. These were the same people who'd told me I had to toughen up and be the boss in my relationship with Nakia. I had been raised and married in a world that emphasized aggressive forms of control and coercion, yet merely recognizing this fact didn't allow me to change my behavior. I had never seen another way in practice and couldn't quite imagine how to proceed or how to repair the damage I had already caused.

This synchronistic event helped me better understand the dynamics of my first marriage. My husband had been taught to dominate, not collaborate. Whenever I asserted my own will and vision, my own creativity and passion, he saw this as a dangerous bid to disempower him. His criticisms of my body and soul weren't designed to be constructive; they were intended to whittle away my confidence and rein me in. People use ropes, whips, and spurs to keep their horses in line, but they often find that words are just as effective in subduing members of their own species. Though he possessed a keen intellect and an acrobatic wit, my husband had no idea how to express his conflicting feelings or discuss his deepest fears in private. Whenever he felt threatened, he would use verbal intimidation and sex to enforce his position. Without warning, a romantic evening would turn into a nightmare. The man would make fun of my figure, insisting that my anorexic physique was still too fat, the insults escalating until I was reduced to tears. An hour after I retreated to the bedroom alone, he would slip under the covers, turn my body and most especially my face away from him, and ride me like a beaten-down horse. For days and sometimes weeks afterward, I would feel dead inside, my heart and spirit broken. From my husband's point of view, however, I was operating at a level of self-esteem he could manage, and our marriage was once again harmonious.

I tell this story not to condemn my first husband. He had many admirable qualities, and his sometimes loving, sometimes demeaning behavior confused me for years. In my work as an equine-facilitated therapy and experiential learning practitioner, however, I subsequently encountered a number of people whose husbands and lovers regularly treated them similarly. And, most importantly, such realizations would invariably emerge when we were working with abused horses. Because these women weren't obviously battered, they couldn't articulate why they felt a vague betrayal and lack of fulfillment in their relationships. In the presence of a horse who had been broken, however, they would equate the image of being tied, saddled, and ridden forcefully with sexual experiences they instinctively knew were about dominance, not connection.

Many equestrians believe it's impossible to form a partnership with an intelligent, vivacious mare or stallion. They feel they must break the animal's spirit to be in control. Acting as my emotional mirror, Nakia inspired me to see this as a cultural phenomenon with parallels in romantic relationships. To a significant number of well-meaning, well-educated, socially upstanding men, being in the presence of an empowered woman conjures up an ancient, nameless fear, one they respond to at a gut level with equally ancient modes of intimidation. The women's liberation movement of the late twentieth century has barely begun to alter the unconscious patterns of male dominance cultivated throughout the entire history of civilization. For millennia, wedding vows obliged wives to pledge their obedience, and the majority of men raised as late as the 1960s were taught to expect it. The fact that my husband and I expunged that line from our own vows ultimately didn't hold any weight. On the surface, we were committed to creating a relationship of equals, yet neither one of us had been given the tools to bring this nice idea into form. His conditioning made it impossible for him to accept my growing creativity and self-actualization as anything but a challenge. He had been taught to dominate. I had been taught to submit. Our life together was ruled by old-world values that crept into our relationship and ultimately destroyed our marriage.

What struck me as so insidious about this cultural dynamic was the fact that when I was "in charge" of Nakia, I had no idea how to change the pattern either. Under pressure, I lapsed into the same controlling mindset that had once shredded my soul at the most intimate level, in a marriage that was supposed to be about trust and support.

Reluctantly, I concluded that both Nakia and I needed a clean slate and a fresh start. At that time, I wasn't skilled enough in the training or the therapeutic techniques needed to process and move beyond the trauma we experienced together, and I didn't know whom to ask for help. Most horse trainers insist that students "leave their problems at the gate" and would have shied away from the intense emotional dynamics the mare and I mirrored in each other. Where would I find a counselor capable of helping me heal my horse? What I needed was a few sessions with an experienced equine-facilitated therapy specialist, but the field hadn't been officially invented yet, and I had no idea the potential even existed. The least I could do was find Nakia a good home. Less than a month later, she stepped onto a trailer owned by a patient older woman who promised she wouldn't tie the mare, and as the two drove away, I promised Rasa, my new filly, that I would never again take a trainer's advice so lightly or use force and intimidation to bend her will.

Blood of the Medusa

After watching several professionals with a most critical eye, I decided to put Rasa's formal education in the hands of an experienced riding instructor who had never actually started a young horse before. Vikki Lindsey's insightful, respectful demeanor in working with intermediate-level horses and riders impressed me much more than the flamboyant techniques of the local cowboys or the high-pressure, somewhat snobbish attitude of trainers I'd encountered in the show and race worlds. What's more, Vikki had a collaborative spirit and was intrigued by the idea of exploring ways of training young horses in a more conscientious manner. The three of us met five days a week as Vikki initiated each new concept with Rasa and then invited me into the ring to try it. After the first lesson, I felt confident I had chosen a humane and sensitive teacher for us both. It was only a matter of days before Rasa knew how to walk, trot, and canter on voice commands given from the ground. She spent an hour milling around the corral wearing the saddle and bridle as if there was nothing the least bit unusual about it, and by the end of that first week, we were riding her around the ring. At first, Rasa moved like a drunken sailor under Vikki's weight. She looked mildly perplexed, as if to say, "These two-legged ones come up with the strangest ideas," but she gave no indication of being offended — no bucks, no kicks, not even a nervous whinny. Rasa was apparently too genteel to act like a rodeo horse. To her, this was just another in a long series of games we'd played during the two months I had owned her; we had simply acquired a coach to teach us some new moves.

Based on my previous experiences with horses, I knew this wasn't the norm. Rasa was intelligent and unjaded. She had been exposed to the habits of human beings in a gentle, progressive manner. These factors explained much of our success with her, but there was something else I couldn't pinpoint. Even Vikki noticed it. "You have an unusual relationship with this filly," she said out of the blue one breezy February afternoon. "It's almost like you're sisters." Someone else, someone who had been in the equestrian field long enough to see a little bit of everything, had felt the force of my connection to Rasa. At that moment, I was more compelled than ever to understand the meaning behind my obsession.

In most books on symbology and dream interpretation, the horse is associated with the explosive power of the instincts and the ability to travel back and forth between the world of the living and the realms of the dead. Yet as

I delved more deeply into myths from a variety of cultures, I realized there was a persistent connection between these animals and aspects of feminine knowledge that were routinely suppressed or demonized in patriarchal societies. Most people know who Pegasus is, for instance, but few realize that he was born from the blood of snake-headed Medusa immediately after she was slain by Perseus. The luminous winged stallion of the Greeks emerged from the life force of womanly wisdom in its darkest, most disturbing aspect, yet poets were said to receive their inspiration from encounters with the flying horse, and many a hero rode to the stars of immortality on his sturdy back.

A feminine psychopomp in the form of a mare took the Islamic prophet Mohammed to heaven on his famous night journey. Alborak, the white winged horse with a woman's head and a peacock's tail, was the vehicle by which the father of one of the world's most stringent patriarchal religions received the holy visions that solidified his spiritual authority. Was Alborak the first night mare? In the guise of a black horse, the night mare was thought to be the punisher of sinners. She was also the destroyer aspect of the Greek mother goddess Demeter. The nurturing qualities of this mare-headed deity were often symbolized by a white horse, but whenever Demeter was particularly frustrated with the arrogance of gods and mortals, she turned into a vengeful creature known as Melanippe, literally "black mare." In the mythology and folklore of old, black horses were almost unanimously feared and spurned. These superstitions affected the species in more tangible ways. I had to pay a couple thousand dollars extra for Rasa because her color was so unusual among Arabian horses. According to some sources, the Bedouin, originators and long-standing caretakers of the breed, were inclined to slaughter black foals at birth because they were perceived as purveyors of bad luck.

The fact that these male-dominated Islamic tribes exhibited a savage fear of dark horses would not have surprised Carl Jung. The Swiss psychiatrist never mentioned the Bedouin in his extensive writings, but his own experience led him to recognize images of black mares as manifestations of feminine wisdom rising up from the collective unconscious. Jung was particularly fascinated by a horse dream of mythical proportions that was troubling one of his clients, a scenario that also involved a magician and a dying king. It seems the sickly monarch was looking for the perfect burial place among a number of ancient tombs scattered throughout the countryside. He finally chose a grave belonging to a virgin princess from an ancestral clan, but when the tomb was opened and the young woman's remains were exposed to the light of day, her bones suddenly changed into a black horse that galloped off into the desert. The magician immediately raced after the enchanted creature. Through a journey of many days and endless trials, he crossed the desert and came to the grasslands on the other side. There he discovered the rarest of treasures, for the mare had led him to the lost keys of paradise.

In not one but three of his books, Jung discusses this dream in detail, using the sudden appearance of the black horse to illustrate the characteristics of the anima, the feminine aspect of the male psyche that is suppressed in most men and, consequently, in our culture at large. *Anima* literally means "soul," but in Jung's theoretical model, this numinous creature has an autonomous identity outside the controls of intellect and societal etiquette. A man's anima can remain dormant for years and then suddenly rise up to cause him all sorts of trouble. To those who make friends with her, she becomes the muse, the source of inspiration and innovation to an artist, musician, or inventor, like Pegasus rising from the blood of the Medusa or mare-headed Demeter calling forth the fertility of spring. To those who ignore her talents, fear her passion for life, or try to overpower her with the forces of logic, she becomes an impetuous and compulsive element, inflicting nightmares, mood swings, and bizarre cravings on a man who once seemed the epitome of good sense and reason. Under these circumstances, the anima takes on a role remarkably akin to Melanippe.

In Jung's estimation, the dream of the ailing king who inadvertently set the black horse free held significance far beyond the personal needs of his client. It was a new myth that had emerged fully formed from the archetypal realm, a vision that predicted the death of patriarchal systems of leadership and pointed to the resurrection of a long-buried feminine principle capable of leading future generations toward a more balanced existence. The fact that the redemptive image took the shape of a black horse immediately struck a chord in my own heart, and I began to wonder what trials might be involved in accompanying this night-haired mare across the desert.

Myths of the Recent Future

In the meantime, Rasa's training proceeded without incident. Two weeks after we started, I felt comfortable enough with the process to bring a guest with me. My friend and mentor from Minneapolis–St. Paul, J. Otis Powell, was coming to town. The poet, philosopher, and arts curator had managed to obtain a grant for a brief residency in Tucson to collaborate with my second husband, Steve Roach, a renowned recording artist in the contemporary instrumental and ambient music scene. The *rasa* of Steve's highly individualistic style had always been tied to the stark, wide-open spaces of the Southwest. J. Otis's proposal involved soaking up the sun and scenery of the desert, translating his impressions into free verse, and recording these spoken-word pieces in my husband's studio with some atmospheric sound worlds composed especially for the occasion.

A heavyset African American with significant dreadlocks and four or five different rings dangling from his ears, J. Otis looked like a stranger in a strange land when he arrived at the airport. I was almost paralyzed by the spectacle we created. People not only stared, they wrinkled their brows and scowled as if our very presence was a threat to their collective well-being. I had always thought of Tucson as an easygoing town. Anglos, Mexicans, and Native Americans had learned to get along, for the most part; mixed marriages were common among these groups. However, the sight of a beefy, Rasta-headed Black guy and a mild-mannered white woman hugging at the baggage terminal seemed to release a churning specter of anger and confusion. *People are afraid of the dark in more ways than one*, I thought to myself as I picked up J. Otis's briefcase, led him to the car, and sped him away under the gentle, welcoming obscurity of mother night.

The next day, I couldn't help but giggle at the sight of J. Otis sitting under a mesquite tree sipping a Coke as Rasa galloped and bucked around the ring, kicking up a cloud of dust that settled into a fine film on the mottled locs of our distinguished guest, producing a misty, earth-colored halo that seemed to hover around his head whenever the sun shined his way. The black horse was particularly feisty, and Vikki took some extra time outlining the attitude needed to stay on a young horse as I stepped into the stirrup and swung my leg over the saddle.

J. Otis was the one laughing on the way home from the stables. Rasa had given me a bit of a scare, though I'd managed to stay on her back. Beyond this mild episode of excitement, however, my citified companion was amazed at how intriguing the experience proved to be from a philosophical and poetic standpoint. Vikki was an effusive yet soft-spoken, practical woman not given to extended reflections on metaphysics. But to J. Otis, her little pep talk had the substance and metaphorical impact of a high-level discussion on the nature of time's relation to transcendental states of human

consciousness. He and I both chuckled at the irony that neither the teacher
nor the student had noticed how profound the entire exchange had seemed
to our observer outside the arena.

"It wasn't just what she said," J. Otis emphasized, "but how she said it.
At one point I was pissed because I had no way to take notes. I mean, who
would have thought to bring a pad and pen along to watch a couple of people riding a horse?"

Essentially Vikki had explained that to avoid being thrown from an inexperienced mount, the rider has to remain relaxed and confident enough
to make the horse feel secure while also conjuring up a state of heightened
awareness in themselves that most people associate with the adrenaline rush
of a crisis. In such a mindset, senses are more acute, and time seems to slow
down, so that the brain can process a wealth of information and make complex decisions in a split second. The trick was not to wait until the horse
started bucking to instinctually trip the switch but to learn how to access
this expanded state of consciousness at will — without the accompanying
nervousness, which would surely set the horse off. Prey animals are extremely
sensitive to apprehension and fear in members of their herd. If I became
tense and ill at ease, Vikki said, Rasa would automatically explode at the
slightest sound or outside movement.

"But how do I get the heightened senses without the nervousness?" I
asked, feeling overwhelmed at the prospect. J. Otis was so delighted with
the response that he memorized the exact wording of Vikki's answer: "Take a
deep breath. Keep your body fully in the present and your mind in the recent
future. Don't let the past get in your way."

At the time, I managed to absorb the meaning of Vikki's words without noticing their resemblance to obscure statements made by monks and
mystics. Then again, I was already on the edge of an altered state. Rasa had
picked up on my confusion and insecurity. She was jerking the bridle and
dancing around like a circus horse. I knew I was about to lose control. Following Vikki's advice as if my life depended on it, I shut out images of
acquaintances flying off rearing horses. I suppressed memories of the sound
of breaking bones. I forced my fiercely beating heart to allow the breath to
flow freely through my lungs, in and out, slower and slower, deeper and
deeper. Rasa began to do the same. As my body relinquished the rigidity of
fear, I felt every twitch of her muscles moving through my legs and up my
spine like an electric current. When a truck sped by on the street beside the

arena, I already knew which way she was going to bolt before her feet left the ground, and I moved with her sudden sideways leap as effortlessly as if we were a single centaurian entity.

J. Otis especially liked Vikki's choice of the words "recent future," a twist of phrase I wouldn't have noticed if he hadn't drawn my attention to it afterward. Normally, one would refer to the "near future" or the "recent past." As a poet, however, J. Otis thought this slip of the tongue provided an intriguing insight into the relativity of time. It implied a state of mind in which past and future could easily trade places and suggested the possibility of seeing what was about to happen as vividly as what had just occurred. To him, what seemed like a mistake in syntax actually offered a more accurate representation of the mental state Vikki was trying to convey. I had to agree. As Rasa moved in a way I would normally consider unpredictable, I sensed what she was going to do as if a part of me had already memorized what had not yet taken place. The black horse had indeed led me to one of the lost keys of paradise; the door to a vista outside linear time had been unlocked. Little did I know just how effective this opening would prove to be.

A few weeks later, I had three dreams that foreshadowed future events in ways I never thought possible. The first seemed silly upon waking, but it left me with a strong sense of foreboding. It was simply a phone call from my mother, who said she had found the perfect wallpaper for Rasa's stall — bloodred. In the dream, a pang of fear shot though my body, yet I agreed that the suggestion was appropriate. Because Rasa was black and didn't show up in pictures very clearly, I said to my mother, surrounding her with such a vivid hue would help define her form and show off her best features.

The second dream was even more disturbing. Rasa and I were enjoying a beautiful day when a menacing thunderhead whirled out of the clearest of skies. We ran for cover under a nearby carport where a large black dog had already sought protection. The storm shrieked and howled, moved to the west, then settled into a potent stillness. Rasa, the dog, and I turned to face the storm as if we were waiting for its edict, at which point it began to shoot out mandala-shaped black clouds that passed through us and eventually combined to create a human skull that hovered over my horse's head. I took this as a threat of death to Rasa, yet rather than be intimidated by the omen, I refused to accept this premonition as an irreversible prophecy. I shouted, "No!" to the skull, grabbed the frightened horse in my arms, and carried her underground just in the nick of time.

The final dream concerned an operation at a local veterinary clinic. A healthy deer was cut up to exchange parts with a sick deer that greatly resembled Rasa. Unfortunately, both deer died in the process.

For weeks afterward, I tried to interpret these visions while shaking off the feeling that something was amiss. Then, a little over a month later, I was riding Rasa in a dry riverbed when I noticed the shadow of a large bird floating in the sand, tracing circles around us as if it were trying to attract our attention. I looked up expecting to see an eagle. Instead, a shudder ran up my spine as I realized we were being trailed by a vulture. Suddenly, a large black dog looking very much like the one in my second dream ran down the bank, snarling and barking at us. This frightened the horse and sent her running at full speed through the thickest part of the wash. It took me a good half mile to bring her down to a walk.

The next day, Rasa was extremely lame in her right back leg. At first, the vet thought she had bowed a tendon from the stress of galloping through all that sand, but when he took an X-ray of her stifle (comparable to the knee in humans), the problem was clear. Rasa had developed a cyst, known as an OCD lesion, in an area where her young bones had not formed properly. The stressful run had exacerbated swelling in the joint and had perhaps caused even more damage. The vet recommended that I take her to a Phoenix surgeon who had some success healing this affliction by extracting cartilage from the opposite, healthy stifle and transplanting it in the wounded area. There was a chance she would become lame in both legs as a result, but even the vets I called for second and third opinions agreed that it was my best option if I ever wanted to ride her again.

It's difficult to describe the downward spiral of confusion, grief, and anger I felt. In beauty, intelligence, and potential ability, Rasa was an exceptional animal; the tacit understanding and affection we shared were even more remarkable. Yet what good was a three-year-old filly that could never be ridden? I didn't have the money to buy another horse of her caliber. Even if I sold Rasa as a brood mare, I wouldn't come close to recouping my investment. If I kept her, I would be shelling out several hundred dollars a month for a thousand-pound pet. I decided I had to take my chances with the surgery. After all, I had paid for both health and mortality insurance. The expensive operation would cost me nothing, and if Rasa died, I would have the money to buy another filly and start over.

Still, every time I went to see my horse, I felt like the angel of death. Two nights before the surgery, Rasa wouldn't come to me, though her lameness had improved significantly since the black dog incident. I practically had to force her head into the halter and drag her toward the arena for a little exercise. As we were standing there in silence — me at one end of the ring and the black horse sulking with her hindquarters to me at the other — a flock of at least twenty vultures landed in the eucalyptus grove on the north side of the fence. Never before and never since have I seen more than nine or ten vultures circling the desert at any one time, yet there they were, two dozen massive black birds with bald red heads, cackling at the tops of those trees, sometimes falling off and squealing as they floated down to a lower level because their feet were too large and cumbersome to balance on the higher branches.

I resented the buzzards' mocking squawks. On the surface, my actions were justified. I had gotten not one but two other opinions, yet the pressure inside me was building, and the only time it seemed to let up was when I momentarily considered canceling the appointment. Steve was the only person I finally told about my dreams, but neither one of us was truly prepared to reject a legitimate medical treatment based on a series of metaphorical visions. As an artist used to the ups and downs of the music business, he was also concerned about spending the next twenty or thirty years feeding a lame horse. Rasa and I seemed to be moving inexorably toward that fateful day, and the vultures were gathering in droves.

The following evening, I invited my neighbor, a horse artist named Judy Delano, to the stable. As a birthday present the month before, my husband had commissioned her to do a portrait of Rasa. I told Judy it would be best for her to come out and get a feeling for the filly before the surgery, in case Rasa lost weight (or died) in the process. Judy asked me about the nature of the operation as she took photographs from various angles. When I told her the surgeon I was using, she became concerned. "I think that's the one my friend is suing for malpractice," she said.

"I can't imagine it would be the same man," I replied. "He's been recommended by three different vets in town as one of the best in the business."

Judy called me later that evening, begged me to cancel the appointment, and gave me the number of the friend who insisted her horse had died unjustifiably at the hands of this doctor. When I called the woman, she described the vet in question as a brilliant yet arrogant man who took chances in the operating room without affording the owner a full understanding of the risks involved. Sometimes it worked out, lending credence to his reputation as an innovator and occasional miracle worker. The luck of the draw was not in her favor, however. Not only was her gelding disfigured by an experimental procedure, the surgeon had allegedly gone out of his way to make the horse colic after failure was established, essentially looking for a standard malady that would kill the horse and get rid of the evidence.

The patient survived only because the owner unexpectedly stopped by the equine hospital's recovery ward, noticed the horse's dangerous condition, and demanded that the surgeon on duty respond to the emergency. Unfortunately, the wound became infected under equally questionable circumstances, and the confused, grief-stricken woman was given the option of putting her horse down or amputating the leg and fitting it with a prosthesis. Feeling that the gelding had already suffered unbearably, she grudgingly chose what she perceived was the more humane option. The only good that could come of his death, she said, was the evidence she had collected for a suit that might save the lives of other potential victims.

I had been given another piece in the puzzle. Finally, I could sense where we were headed: Rasa and I would travel to Phoenix the following morning. She would seem to come out of the surgery successfully, and I would go back to Tucson while she recuperated. In the meantime, the surgeon would realize that both her legs had been permanently damaged and proceed to destroy the evidence. I would receive the call before I was scheduled to pick her up the following week. "These things just happen sometimes," he would say. "It's impossible to predict which horses will develop problems. What would you like to do with the body?" The insurance company would pay up because her death had been the result of some legitimate postoperative complication, and I would be left holding the blood money. Even if some part of me had been influenced by notions that animals were functional possessions, biological machines that lost their value if they were broken, some indescribable force was going out of its way to make sure I got the message: Rasa had to be spared. I made the call first thing in the morning, canceling the surgery five hours before it was scheduled. And just to make sure I acknowledged the supernatural origins of this strange rescue, Judy provided another anecdote that left both our minds reeling. A week later, when I stopped by her house to look at some sketches for Rasa's portrait, my neighbor seemed uneasy, as if she wanted to tell me something, but she kept putting it off. Finally, she took a chance as we headed toward the door.

"You're going to think I'm crazy," she said, "but several days before you called me to see Rasa, I kept having this recurring dream. Some kind of animal was laid out on a table. I couldn't make out what it was, but just as the scalpel was cutting into black fur, I would scream for it to stop. A male voice of considerable authority would insist the procedure was necessary and that everything would be OK, but I refused to believe him. I would shout, 'No' at the top of my lungs and wake up in a sweat. I had no way of knowing your horse was scheduled for that operation until several days after the dream began to possess me. At first I thought it was ridiculous to connect the two, yet as soon as you told me you had canceled, the dream stopped."

I proceeded to tell Judy of my own adventures in the dreamtime. I have no idea how long the two of us stood in the hallway gaping at each other before she found the strength to turn the handle and release me into a daylight so surreal I pinched myself to make sure I was indeed awake.

Melanippe's Blessing

Was the black horse bad luck after all? If I had been raised a Bedouin, members of my tribe surely would have chastised me for courting disaster, and their fears would have been confirmed. Rasa's presence had brought vultures and prophetic nightmares into my life. The sinister whirlwinds that emerged from my own nocturnal imagination conjured up a black dog that literally chased us through the desert with the bald-headed bird of death circling silently above. Perhaps I inadvertently formed an alliance with Melanippe herself when I brought Rasa home. In one emphatic gesture, Demeter the avenger had destroyed all my plans and aspirations for this filly's career as a conventional dressage and endurance horse. Then, for some unfathomable reason, the forces that predicted our fate reached out to protect the black horse, sending a flock of vultures to warn of her possible death, even torturing my neighbor with five nights of recurring dreams. It was difficult to explain the entire drama away as a series of coincidences. I couldn't help feeling there was some kind of intelligence operating behind the scenes, but I wasn't sure if I was the protagonist in a divine comedy or the victim of some cosmic joke. Either way, I eagerly awaited the punch line.

I leafed through my journal looking for clues and turned to a description of the first and most peculiar Rasa nightmare — the image of my mother offering to decorate the filly's stall with bloodred wallpaper. The suggestion had frightened me, but it also foreshadowed a hidden blessing: surrounding Rasa in the color of sacrifice promised to bring the black horse's true character into focus, and by the end of the dream, I agreed to go along with the idea. The painful and confounding events that followed were already working their magic. To understand how a crippled filly could be of any worth, I would have to surrender not only my equestrian ambitions but my most basic attitudes about horses and their relationship to human beings. In order to do that, I would have to follow my heart, not my head. The culture that molded my conscious identity considered animals to be useful possessions devoid of genuine thought or feeling. It was illogical to waste time and money on a beast that couldn't perform its primary function, but I knew I would have to allow Rasa to exist on her own terms if I were to discover the meaning behind our strange alliance.

The sense of gratitude and affection I felt for Rasa grew stronger as I accepted our fate. Somehow, she had awakened a more intuitive, creative, and compassionate spirit in me, one that had been suppressed by the cold cult of reason for most of my adult life. It was, indeed, time for the old king to die. With his imminent demise on the horizon, a new perspective emerged, and it was limping across the desert in the form of a night-haired mare named Tabula Rasa. I sensed that someday the color of sacrifice surrounding us both would blossom into the rich red hue of empowerment, and at that moment I understood why the patriarchal Bedouin tribes were so afraid of dark horses. When feminine modes of wisdom are banished to the nether regions of the collective unconscious, they tend to manifest in disruptive, vengeful ways, but sometimes vultures, black mares, whirlwinds, and savage hounds are exactly what a woman needs to define her form and show off her best features.

CHAPTER TWO

THE LOST ART OF DOING NOTHING

After canceling the surgery, I felt confused and emotionally drained. A puzzling, downright irrational series of events had dictated that Rasa be spared, but what was I supposed to do next? I tried to remain hopeful by discussing the possibilities with just about every vet in town. Some suggested putting the mare on pasture for a year and letting nature take its course. Others thought I was a fool for avoiding the operation. Several told me I had been duped into rejecting the most promising treatment strategy by an unrealistic and hysterical woman whose horse had received the best of care. Unable to accept a tragedy that was beyond human control, she was out for revenge, they said, and would stop at nothing to ruin a man considered by his peers to be one of the best surgeons in Arizona. I couldn't quite bring myself to tell them that a series of dreams had validated her accusations in my mind and that the horse artist across the street could vouch for us both.

In the meantime, I needed to do something to ease my frustration. I considered getting a loan to buy another two-year-old to train from the ground up and sell for a modest profit. My search for this investment horse eventually led me to a breeding farm in a small desert community outside Tucson. I must have impressed the operation's trainer-manager with my enthusiasm, because she ended the conversation by offering me a part-time position helping her start young horses. I would have a dozen colts and fillies to work with, and she would hone my skills in the training arena. A week later I moved Rasa and Noche to this new base of operations and began my apprenticeship in earnest.

I'm obliged to change some of the names and details of this episode because I observed a certain amount of abuse at the facility. Though my experiences were fairly mild compared to the kinds of mistreatment trainers, riders, and grooms from around the country have since brought to my attention, the incidents I witnessed represented a classic dysfunctional dynamic that's widespread in the horse business. The owner of the breeding farm also used a common method for distracting people while disempowering them, an intellectual bait and switch tactic I've since recognized in the workshops of several nationally known horse clinicians.

The trainer, whom I'll call "Susan," was under constant pressure from the owner, "Mr. Wolverton," a successful attorney who would undermine her progress as a way of blowing off steam and asserting his dominance. He fancied himself an expert rider and a sensitive, cultured gentleman, yet his opinions about the proper care and training of horses would change from moment to moment as a way of justifying his erratic behavior. If he was having a bad day, he'd wander down to the barn and ridicule Susan for something he'd praised her for a week earlier. Then he'd saddle up one of the colts we'd just started under saddle and take the animal on a reckless trail ride, which usually made the horse more difficult to manage for a week or two afterward. He even brought a filly home lame from one of his fitful outings. We had to call the vet, hand walk the horse for a month, and practically start all over again as we endured the owner's complaints that the farm was wasting too much time and money on horses that wouldn't likely sell for more than a few thousand dollars. Susan didn't dare suggest that Wolverton was part of the problem, that the process of training these animals would run more smoothly and efficiently if the man would refrain from riding these colts until they had more experience under saddle.

Susan emphasized the importance of diligently yet gently conditioning the equine mind and body. The two- and three-year-olds we worked with were still growing; they needed to be taught the most efficient way to carry the rider's weight so their young bones and joints would not be unduly stressed. They needed to build up the muscle mass capable of supporting those same bones and joints through several weeks of progressively longer periods of exercise on good footing.

One day, when Wolverton was puttering around the barn in a particularly good mood, Susan casually mentioned that "all those people in the neighborhood" who cantered young horses across miles of rocky trails were endangering their "investment." He agreed wholeheartedly, proselytizing about the evils of hacks in the horse business, completely ignoring the fact that he was also guilty of such infractions. For the next few weeks, I heard him reciting this same bit of wisdom to a number of boarders and prospective buyers.

A month or two later, however, he fell into one of those dark states of his and took off on another hell-raising ride, this time with a client. Wolverton divested himself of all responsibility when the other person returned leading a limping, bleeding horse. It was an unfortunate accident, he insisted. Susan narrowed her eyes, and I looked knowingly across the tack room at her. It had been an accident all right, an accident waiting to happen, like so many of the events I witnessed at that farm.

One of the first things Wolverton showed me was how to "safely" beat Flash, his most spirited stallion, with a lead rope if the animal got out of hand. Of course, this only escalated the situation, keeping the horse in flight-or-fight mode rather than calming him and teaching him self-control. Not at all vicious by nature, the exquisite sorrel stud possessed an open, curious disposition. Those of us who took care of Flash daily were continually amused by his antics, yet when Wolverton was around, the same horse turned into a tornado of nervous energy. Still, I learned it was better for the animals if I didn't question Wolverton's authority or even politely suggest other options. In his territory, I was just an apprentice making minimum wage. Wolverton would react to the slightest challenge by becoming more violent, illustrating that these were his horses and he would do with them whatever he wanted, even as he continued to talk to me in a quiet, controlled, condescending way about the "logic" of his training methods.

Wolverton's ability to explain away or completely ignore his own fitful, fearful motivations amazed me to no end. He truly believed he was the benevolent master of all he surveyed, yet his emotions would rear up in the face of his "reasonable" persona as surely as Flash could be counted upon to buck, spin, and try to run off with Wolverton in the saddle.

The image of a man on a horse is often used to symbolize the intellectual and moral superiority of the mind ruling the animal passions of the body. Sigmund Freud saw the relationship between horse and human as the struggle between the id (instinct and raw emotion) and the ego (which he associated with rationality). Every time Wolverton took Flash for a ride, the man seemed engaged in the same mythical battle to conquer his own irrational, unresolved, wholly unconscious feelings. Yet as far as I could tell, the horse — and all he represented — was winning.

To me, the challenges Wolverton repeatedly faced in his interactions with Flash provided a powerful illustration of how violent and delusional the logical mind could be when it tried to divorce itself from emotion and forcefully subdue instinct. My own experiences with horses had brought this lesson home time and time again. I had seen training strategies that sounded perfectly reasonable in theory cause all kinds of problems in the riding arena, while impulses that seemed to make no sense at all often worked effortlessly. As my own mind formed a reciprocal relationship with feeling, instinct, and intuition, my success with horses increased exponentially.

Wolverton, on the other hand, was horrified by emotion. Keeping his feelings on a tight rein, he believed in the superiority of reason despite repeated failures at controlling his baser impulses and unconscious motivations. In effect, his faith in the cult of logic blinded him to the reality of his situation: that the nonrational elements of his world could not be dominated, ignored, or explained into oblivion for long. In refusing to form a partnership with his id and his horse, his ego was constantly at war with life.

Unlike Flash, Wolverton's staff readily submitted to his whims. Their minds had already been well schooled in the bait and switch tactics of logical idealism, a tradition that conditions people to focus all their attention on well-constructed arguments for some noble goal while ignoring the speaker's inconsistent, even malevolent, yet quite often unconscious motivations. Whenever one of these people did raise an objection, the seasoned attorney in Wolverton could easily, if temporarily, mesmerize his staff with rationalistic defenses of demoralizing repression and aggression. Susan was a frequent target, and she acted like she was used to this sort of treatment.

In hindsight, her reactions were similar to those survivors of physical, emotional, and sexual violence I now coach in my equine-facilitated therapy and experiential learning practice. Wolverton instinctively recognized her high tolerance for abuse and used it for his own gratification. During the six months I worked there, I watched him slowly turn up the heat. His eyes reflected a queer sense of satisfaction whenever he broke her composure, though he proceeded to ridicule her all the more. The stress finally reached the point where Susan took to screaming at the horses and the other apprentices, including me, for the slightest infraction. She was most patient with the younger horses, a trait I admired, yet ultimately she lashed out at them as well.

Though I just barely maintained the advantage in my dealings with Wolverton, I still found life at the farm increasingly unbearable. The inconsistent, egotistical decision-making process, as well as the constant abuse of Susan, the horses, and some of the other employees, was taking its toll.

In the meantime, I continued searching for ways to deal with Rasa's problem, and I kept in touch with our first trainer, Vikki Lindsey. We finally loaded Rasa on a trailer one morning and made the hour's drive to a clinic owned by a husband-and-wife veterinary team. Vikki had heard they were open to alternative therapies like acupuncture and might be able to come up with a nonsurgical solution. Both doctors were present at the initial evaluation and brainstormed about options afterward. They made several calls around the country and discovered another approach to managing OCD lesions. They could inject the joint with steroids, which they hoped would prevent swelling and promote cell growth. Rasa would be stall bound for ten days, but then I could start riding her again.

Much to everyone's amazement, the procedure seemed to work, and Susan helped me get my beloved mare back into shape. I was a more experienced horsewoman by then, having studied English riding and jumping with Vikki and basic dressage with Susan. More important, however, was the fact that during Rasa's time off, I had resurrected some of the games I had played with horses as a child because the black mare wasn't able to follow a more conventional equestrian agenda. These naive yet effective impulses solidified the bond between us, creating a greater sense of cooperation in her and a more intuitive, imaginative way of relating to horses in me. I didn't want anyone to see me engaging in these antics, however, so Rasa had to wait until the human contingent left for lunch or called it a day.

Whenever I let down my guard, trusted my own instincts, and wasn't afraid to act the fool, I found Rasa to be more intelligent and adaptable than I had previously suspected. By adopting her postures, gestures, and breathing patterns, I was able to slip into an equine frame of mind. Suddenly, the reactions of all the animals on the property made more sense, and I began to refine some of this horseplay into training and troubleshooting strategies I felt comfortable using during regular business hours. When I tested my simple new methods on other horses at the farm, I discovered they too had more going on upstairs than anyone was giving them credit for. Most of the frustrations and misunderstandings between the two species seemed to arise from the fact that equine motivations, values, and responses were often exactly the opposite of human goals and reactions to the same situations. Rather than fight the equine perception of reality, I decided to work with it. Unfortunately, this also led to increasing differences of opinion between Susan and me, culminating in an episode where she beat a particularly bright and sensitive filly in front of everyone because the youngster was acting favorably toward me and running away from her.

Much later, I realized the horse's reaction could not be attributed entirely to a difference in training technique or philosophy. Rather, the increasing preference for me over Susan among many of the animals at the farm hinged on my emotional congruency. When I was confused, afraid, or uncomfortable with something, I'd speak up and ask for advice. As a trainer in training, it behooved me to be honest about my fears and frustrations. Susan, however, was supposed to be the expert, a position that was constantly undermined by her boss. After weathering Wolverton's relentless insults and devilish games for so long, she was on the verge of a nervous breakdown, and everyone felt it. This made the horses more agitated and flighty in her presence.

The common human habit of suppressing negative or socially unacceptable feelings is notoriously unsettling to a species that survives by being able to gauge a predator's presence and intentions at a distance. A person who is emotionally incongruent, who acts one way while feeling the opposite, appears dangerously out of focus to the equine awareness system. At the time, however, I didn't know what emotional incongruity was, let alone that it bothered the horses. I certainly wasn't capable of discussing it with Susan as a way of explaining why my modest successes with the horses seemed to coincide with her increasing inability to calm them down.

The horses themselves were challenging traditional methods and mindsets. Even though I could see that on her better days Susan still had much to teach me, I wasn't sure how long I would last. It was Rasa who determined the leaving time when she started limping for no apparent reason. The moment she lost her strength, all I wanted to do was find a facility closer to home where we could relax into a period of physical and emotional convalescence. Rasa's lameness had set me up to become a more confident and effective trainer of other horses, something I had never considered a part of my own master plan. The reappearance of her affliction was herding us toward a new adventure.

An Oasis in the Desert

A series of coincidences led to heaven on earth — a private, ten-acre miniranch, two miles from home, built from scratch by an independently wealthy real estate developer. There was no house on the property, just a half-dozen horses, a barn, an insanely comfortable tack room (complete with leather couches, a powerful stereo system, and a refrigerator full of imported beer), an aviary with pheasants and peacocks, two grass pastures, a field of oats, and a four-acre mesquite grove where Rasa, Noche, and a seven-hundred-pound steer named Norman lived the good life for three years. "Timothy Graham" had created this paradise as a hobby. He'd been looking for a few people to help him take care of the animals in exchange for a reduced board rate that barely covered feeding expenses. I saw him ride his own horses twice. Most of the time, he played a grown-up version of erector set, tooling around the place on his tractor, forever coming up with new improvements. When he and his family finally lost interest, he was able to sell the property for three times what he paid for it.

At Timothy's minifarm, I had the time and the privacy to experiment with my horses in any manner I saw fit, and I often gave them the run of the place. They would wander in and out of the stalls, pause in the center aisle to listen to Steve's latest CD, visit the other horses, nibble some fresh oat grass, and stand in the doorway of the tack room demanding carrots and Coronas from whoever was taking a break inside. I did set some minor limits. The horses weren't actually allowed in the tack room, for instance, because Rasa had figured out how to open the refrigerator door. There was nothing to stop me from spending twenty-four hours a day with my four-legged friends, and I gained a new perspective on horse behavior from doing what they liked best — a whole lot of nothing. Because Rasa was intermittently lame during that period, I was once again forced to associate with her on the ground. This time, however, the experience wasn't the least bit traumatic for either one of us. The atmosphere was so rich and nourishing, in fact, that I took to calling Graham's desert playground the Oasis.

There was another, quite unexpected consequence of relating to my horses without a specific agenda: Noche's behavior improved significantly with little effort on my part. He began to trust me at a level I never thought possible, and I actually witnessed startling aspects of his personality rise to the surface. When human beings were around, Noche's eyes would become glassy, his demeanor withdrawn, his movements stilted and machinelike. Of course, he had been acting this way around me for years. I just figured he was a stoic old horse with an occasional tendency to spook around people. I had no idea he came to life only when all the two-legged creatures went home. He didn't show this side of himself to me until I began hanging out in the pasture and acting like another horse.

Over time, I learned that Noche was a wise, compassionate, and powerful leader with a romantic streak, transcending the fact that he had long ago been gelded. He would expertly woo every new mare we put on the pasture and keep the other geldings in check while also forming strong alliances with each individual. He would even protect Norman the steer from Rasa's occasional assaults. This interspecies association became so strong that Noche would actually let Norman mount him in jest, a strange concession to make considering the bay gelding would kick the tar out of another horse for attempting such a feat.

Rasa and Noche had never lived together before I moved them to the Oasis. I watched with fascination the curious relationship they developed under that canopy of mesquite. Rasa's gregarious nature and strangely humanlike presence gave her the confidence to challenge the older, more experienced gelding, and she almost succeeded. Her strong alliance with me was intimidating to Noche, who waited until I wasn't around to deliver the decisive blow. I returned the next morning to find the black mare quietly standing behind the bay horse, wincing from the pain of a large bite mark in the center of her back. Perhaps for reasons related to this bid for supremacy, Rasa was the only mare Noche showed no sexual interest in; he always kept her at a distance, except where human beings were concerned. Whenever a new person or group of people entered the pasture, Noche would step back, shut down, and let Rasa take over, watching her walk up to each individual as if he were depending upon her expert judgment. In this way, Rasa became the ambassador of the herd, the liaison between the human and equine realms, a position she held until her death in 2011, despite the fact that a dozen horses came and went in the interim. Though Rasa and Noche maintained a certain sense of aloofness until his passing in 2005, it was obvious that the old sage gelding grew to value the black mare's talents as well as her presence. Every time I took the mare away to an overnight event or workshop, Noche made it a point to walk directly up to her upon her return and gently lick her face for several minutes. This was a special gesture, something I never saw him do to Rasa in the day-to-day life of the herd.

It was my newfound recognition of Noche as a vibrant, highly adaptable being that motivated me to enroll the two of us in lessons at the hunter-jumper club next door, something I never would have considered when I saw him purely as an ex–cow horse. There I found the trainer I had been waiting for: Cathy Schreiber knew the standard moves inside and out, yet she had also investigated a number of progressive techniques and had devised some of her own methods in the process. She believed in treating horses as collaborators, not possessions, while acknowledging the important differences between our two species. She was also certified in equine massage and had studied with Linda Tellington-Jones, an internationally recognized trainer who developed a series of techniques using the healing and communicative powers of touch in working with horses.

One of Cathy's students and assistant trainers, Julia Standish, bought a horse and boarded at the Oasis. Over the years, we explored new ways of relating to our equine partners. The Oasis became the meeting ground for other open-minded professionals in the city, eventually leading our core group to form Epona Equestrian Services, which later expanded to Eponaquest Worldwide as interest developed internationally. Founded in 1996 by Cathy, Julia, Dana Light, Cathie Hook, Stacey Kollman, Shelley Rosenberg, Paula Frey, and me, the organization initially functioned as a referral service with an emphasis on education and self-empowerment. We sponsored clinics, developed our own lecture series, and acted as a clearinghouse for information on trainers in all disciplines. When someone had a horse or a client they couldn't seem to get along with, we found a better match. Trainers actually shared information and traded students, which was uncommon in the horse business at that time. We also encouraged one another to stand up to the dark side of the industry.

The ego-serving trappings of greed and chauvinism run rampant in the show world, where horses are started too young, pushed way too hard, and discarded when they break down under the pressure. People are equally disposable. Nearly everyone in the expanding circle of trainers associated with Epona had a horror story to tell. A few had experienced physical abuse and even rape on the show circuit. All had seen ethical and legal considerations repeatedly swept under the rug by wealthy horse owners and officials happy to cater to them. The members of our little organization dared to imagine a different life for horses and their people. We made significant changes in our own barns and businesses through an atmosphere of mutual support, drawing inspiration from our namesake, Epona, the Celtic horse goddess who sometimes took the form of a white mare capable of illuminating the future. By the time I moved my herd to a public boarding operation called The Ranch and officially began my equine-facilitated therapy and experiential learning practice in the late 1990s, the Epona referral base also included bodyworkers and psychotherapists who could address the physical, mental, and spiritual issues riders were uncovering in their work with the horses.

Wu Wei

During my two-year stay at Timothy's miniranch, I instinctively developed a therapeutic approach to the equestrian arts by helping a number of amateur riders with so-called problem horses. Capitalizing on the inroads I had made with Rasa and Noche, I introduced many of these frustrated owners to the benefits of relating to their four-legged adversaries as sentient beings worthy of collaboration instead of domination. In the process, I often recommended that they simply hang out with their horses for a few weeks. I had seen how quick-fix training techniques, whips, increasingly severe bits, and other gadgets that try to force a thousand-pound creature into submission would invariably lead to physical and psychological breakdown, not to mention the kind of fear and resentment in a horse that can put the rider's life in danger. Encouraging people to back off, suspend all goals, and set aside time to do nothing with their horses was surprisingly effective in alleviating long-standing behavioral problems and some physical challenges as well. I'm still amazed at how much those "crazy" stallions and "difficult" mares appreciated this seemingly insignificant gesture from the human beings in their lives.

I have since recognized this inclination marking the turning point in films portraying therapeutic relationships between human and horse — and human and human, for that matter. In *The Horse Whisperer*, the main character kneels down in a field with his traumatized subject, waiting patiently an entire afternoon before the horse slowly walks over to him and nuzzles his shoulder. In *Good Will Hunting*, the psychologist played by Robin Williams sits in complete silence with Matt Damon's character for nearly two hour-long sessions, thus encouraging the troubled genius to respond on his own terms. It's this therapist's willingness to do nothing for as long as it takes that leads to a breakthrough. For me, these brief yet powerful scenes reinforced an impulse I discovered out of necessity when Rasa was too lame to engage in conventional equestrian pursuits. To many people, however, the idea of paying a trainer to simply hang out with a troubled horse for a couple of hours, or even advise the owner to do so, seems ludicrous.

In our culture, doing nothing is the slacker's vice. Those who work more, buy more, try harder, and seem busier are the ones we're taught to admire and emulate. The art of not striving has been lost, and we're suffering from a host of stress-related ailments as a result. The entire history of Western civilization is proactive. I actually had to look back to ancient China to find a term capable of defining the constructive aspects of doing nothing: *wu wei*, which more accurately translates as "not doing" (enhanced by deeper meanings related to "not striving" and "not forcing"). This is one of the central principles of Taoism, a system of thought and experiential learning that I quickly realized has much in common with the equine perspective. Horses are, in fact, natural Taoists. In reading the Tao Te Ching (pronounced "dow deh jing"), the most famous work to arise from this three-thousand-year-old philosophy, I found numerous concepts that helped me better relate to these remarkable creatures and explain the more elusive aspects of horse-human interactions.

Taoism is best known in popular culture for the yin-yang circle, its two interlocking tadpole-like symbols representing the balance of opposites in the universe and in the human psyche: white and black, light and dark, creation and destruction, male and female, conscious and unconscious, sound and silence, doing something and doing nothing. To the relentlessly assertive, patriarchal Western mind, the Taoist picture of reality at first appears contrary to everything we believe, because it asks us to consider the opposite of our normal inclinations. One of the most famous quotes from the Tao Te Ching advises us to "know the yang, but keep to the yin," which often appears in translation as "know the masculine, but keep to the feminine." When I was with the horses, I began to live this philosophy. My adventures with Rasa and Noche taught me that when all my best efforts failed, I still had one other potent option, to do nothing, which was often much more effective in the long run than any intellectual solution I could have come up with. They showed me that when logic couldn't make sense of a situation, some completely irrational notion that popped into my head, my heart, or my dreams might lead me to the truth. They repeatedly reminded me that all those things considered feminine — emotion over intellect, intuition over reason, prey over predator, relationship over territory, cooperation over competition, process over goal, compassion over judgment — would prove to be my greatest strengths. Over time, these four-legged sages led me into a nonverbal realm so far off the beaten track that my most basic assumptions about the nature of reality were called into question.

CHAPTER THREE

VOICES FROM THE ANCESTORS

I don't remember when it finally occurred to me that I was being haunted. The feeling had been sneaking up for weeks. The air was charged, full of anticipation, as if something were hovering just outside my view, waiting for me to acknowledge its existence. By October 1996 — two years after my otherworldly experiences with Rasa — the sensation had become such a distraction that I began to search the literature for some kind of precedent.

My own encounters with prophetic dreams suggested that some as-yet-unmapped properties of the mind might be at work, but I was still convinced that people who had authentic interactions with supernatural beings were the minority among a multitude of shysters and wishful thinkers who were simply giving names to their own psychological processes and calling them spirits. Was this ghost following me around some aspect of my psyche screaming to be heard, creating a larger-than-life disturbance to get my attention? Whether I was dealing with an internal or external force, I was reluctant to give way to its influence for fear of being possessed. The pressure was increasing daily, and I could easily imagine it taking over, devouring my identity if I opened the door and let it in.

This fear of losing control stemmed from a similarly disturbing shift in consciousness that occurred during my tempestuous first marriage. Shortly after that explosive protest to my spouse's insults, I was drawn into an affair out of grief, confusion, and spite. My mind and morals suggested this was further proof of the gross character flaws I possessed, yet much to my own surprise, I found myself expanding rather than contracting under the weight of self-examination, and I was momentarily released from the spell of my husband's aggressive criticism. This was not a feeling of romantic love for a new man. The sensation stemmed from the sudden rush of empowerment I felt upon reclaiming my sexuality from the dominance games of my marriage. The person with whom I engaged in the affair had no claim of ownership over me. In that context, I was truly an equal. Perhaps more important, the act of stepping outside well-worn behavior patterns and value systems cracked open the veneer of ordinary perception. I felt blessed and protected; colors became intensely vivid; the features of everyday life seemed extraordinary. I wandered around for three days in a steadily increasing state of ecstasy, imagining I was filled with a lavender light that smelled like roses. My soul was in full bloom.

Other people noticed it too. Complete strangers came up to me in stores and insisted on buying me little gifts. Even my voice had a startling effect. I was working as a classical music radio announcer, and on the day the lavender rose reached the peak of its blooming, the studio phone rang off the hook during my shift. I took one call after another from fans I had never spoken to before who proceeded to tell me the most intimate details of their lives and ask me for advice. As if in a trance, I heard myself counseling them with a level of eloquence and insight I never could have fathomed in an ordinary state of mind. The experience was so exquisite and unsettling that I tried to capture its effect in a few lines from my journal that still convey the intensity of the experience for me:

> *It is ecstasy to fly again, surrounded by the warm lavender light of my first blooming. Strangers give me gifts in exchange for alien words and silent nourishment, for a strange luminosity that feels like the caress of a flower or the kiss of a pearl.*
>
> *I know this new landscape is too fragile to sustain a numinous garden. Too soon it fades and shrivels, leaving fragrant memories. I gather the dried petals into a sacred place and wait for a future rejuvenation fertilized by all this sin and pain and refuse. Now that I've embraced the sky and set my house on fire, your swords will never pierce so deep again. I have tasted the rose. She may be sleeping in her bottomless grave, but I can still hear her dreaming, whispering my name in the night.*

This glimpse of another reality continued to sustain me during the trying times ahead. It took me several years of struggle to finally break away from my first marriage, but the rose that bloomed inside gave me a profound sense of comfort. It also frightened me, for shortly before the feeling subsided, I was tortured by a number of psychic dreams I refused to fully acknowledge. I saw the house I was to buy several years later when I moved to Arizona with my new husband. Of course, I had no idea this was anything more than wishful dreaming at the time. I hadn't even met Steve. I was simply impressed by the vividness of the image and the intense yearning I felt for a home I longed to return to, even though I had never stepped foot in it.

No, what really scared me were simple, downright trivial visions that were reinforced soon after waking. For instance, early one spring morning shortly before sunrise, I dreamed a black cat rushed into my modest Florida townhouse through the patio door. If I were to have such a dream now — after learning the vocabulary of Jungian psychology — I'd be inclined to interpret it as a metaphor for a powerful intuition rising from the depths of my unconscious. This night, however, I felt the urge to get up and call my own camel-colored cat in from the darkness. My pet was nowhere in sight. Instead a shadowy form bounded in when I slid the glass door open — a real, live black cat I had never seen before. I caught the intruder and tossed him back outside, my hands shaking as I stood in the fragrant, balmy air of twilight. I couldn't deny some new perspectives were riding the coattails of my lavender-colored awakening, but I was overcome by the fear that I would see my own death if I let it get any stronger.

At the time, I had no one to commiserate with; my husband's flippant attitude toward anything outside conventional human reason discouraged me from discussing these experiences. I didn't think I was crazy, but I was afraid everyone else would question my sanity if I let the cat out of the bag.

To this day, I sometimes have dreams that come true, and I'm comfortable talking about them thanks to the remarkable series of nightly visions that saved my horse's life and changed my own in the process. The boundaries between the seen and unseen, the logical and the mythological worlds began to blur when I considered both sides of those coins to be equally valuable. An immense river of meaning seemed to flow beneath the circumstances of consensual reality, as if the events that were taking place when I was awake were contributing to a much larger and more intricate drama the creator of the universe had been dreaming into existence since time began. When I saw human experience as a feature of a much larger imagination, I was able to interpret seemingly disconnected and incomprehensible incidents as if I were analyzing the plot of a novel. Sometimes I had to read a little further in the book to understand the implications of what had just happened, but the underlying streams of logic and poetry that nourished my own story would inevitably rise to the surface in the fullness of time.

In analyzing the myth that is my life, a luminous thread connects my brief encounter with an anonymous black cat and my overwhelming attraction to the black horse I sought out and bought seven years and a thousand miles later. The cat — a small predatory being associated with the powers of the collective unconscious — leapt from the twilight mists of dreams and magic into my physical home. I didn't ask for this visitation. It came to me as a thief in the night, and I was so startled that I promptly tossed it out the door. Yet as I became stronger and more confident with my place in the "real" world, I chose to cross the imposing chasm that separates the land of myth from the land of reason. More specifically, some hidden aspect of my psyche had already decided to ride over the precarious bridge between the two on the back of a creature that seemed bound by destiny to take me there.

Bridges to the Otherworld

In legends told throughout the Far East, Central Asia, Europe, and the Middle East, horses were considered mediums between the spirit and material worlds. Certain Celtic tribes, for example, used a white mare as an oracle. Through a series of simple ritualistic movements, the horse would answer yes or no to questions about everything from battle strategies to planting times to lovers' quarrels. Arabic tales exalt the horse's sixth sense. One story tells of a lone rider escaping unexpected attack by acknowledging his steed's nervous whinnies and riding off into the desert hours before his skeptical companions were massacred where they slept. Yet unlike cats, to whom similar extrasensory gifts were attributed, horses were also perceived as carrying riders between the seen and unseen realms or leading people to some form of lost knowledge. Modern Yakut shamans, representing the second largest native group in Siberia, wouldn't dream of visiting the otherworld without the aid of their horses. The animal, its image, or, at times, an object personifying it is always present in the shaman's preparations and performances. The shaman's drum turns into a powerful steed during these rituals, and the leader himself often becomes a horse in episodes of trance while his assistants hold a pair of reins attached to loops sewn onto the back of his sacred robe. The Hausa Bori culture in Nigeria, an urban variation of a pre-Islamic religious system emphasizing interactions with the supernatural, refers to its mediums as horses, as do a number of Vodou sects in Haiti and Jamaica. Through a series of initiation rites, those called to the profession of medium learn to yield to invisible forces that are said to "ride" their human mounts.

As time went on, I found this seemingly mystical dimension of the horse-human connection had some basis in fact and was more prevalent than I had realized. What's more, I was able to use myself as an example. Shortly after I bought my first horse in Tucson, an equine-influenced shift in consciousness profoundly affected my writing style. At the time, I was making my living as a radio announcer and music reviewer. Among many other projects, I was writing the liner notes for Steve's 1993 release *Origins* when the tribal rhythms and primordial drones he was recording inspired something quite different from my usual journalistic style. Suddenly, the narrator in this little piece was not an impassive critic and historian, but a lone traveler trapped in the desert during a raging thunderstorm, forced to seek refuge in a small black hole of a cave.

> *A savage blast of thunder reverberates through solid stone, shaking loose fragments of conversation buried in the dust, incantations in languages that no longer exist, tales of heroes whose bodies nourish the soil. Their spirits linger in the wind. An old man holds a snake. Another shakes a rattle. Sardonic laughter dissolves into cries of existential longing.... Flames burst from the medicine bundle, and suddenly no one can hide in the shadows. We gaze at each other through veils of smoke as sparks fly in all directions and time spirals in on itself, momentarily unwound by the rage of a summer storm. Am I delirious? Or are they dreaming of now, then? Can they really see me, clinging to the walls of the cave, face reflecting in the fire, a specter in torn hiking shorts slipping in and out of focus through their own blurry visions of the future? Am I the one who has been conjured up by some strange primeval rite?*

These words flowed into the computer as if I were taking dictation — no writer's block, no agonizing over ideas; it was as if my husband's music had drilled a hole through my brain and tapped an underground spring of images that flowed down my arms and spilled onto the screen. I thought it was a fluke.

A year later, when Steve completed the companion album to *Origins*, I doubted I would be able to match the experience in writing. Yet sure enough, as we were listening to the final version of *Artifacts*, a familiar sensation came over me. The next day, after a particularly satisfying trail ride, I felt the urge to take out my notebook and jot down a few ideas. The story from *Origins* picked up where it had left off and practically wrote itself as I watched my horses grazing in the distance.

At first, I attributed these bouts of effortless inspiration to the music alone, but I had been writing about tribal-infused styles for years without being affected in quite this way. Then it occurred to me that the emergence of this more creative imagery coincided with the year that I began spending several hours a day in the presence of the horses. Whenever I was with these magnificent animals, I felt connected to a part of myself that seemed more ancient, more mysterious, and more in tune with the indigenous instruments and rhythms that Steve was weaving into his increasingly primal soundscapes, and I yearned to return to a much older form of human awareness.

These ideas came into play as I continued writing in the style I began calling the Voice of Remembering. In the summer of 1995, the liner notes to *Origins* and *Artifacts* gave birth to a book-length project titled "The Black Horse Speaks." As I worked in this mode, I became increasingly adept at entering an awareness somewhere between dreaming and waking, a mildly ecstatic state that straddled the boundaries of this world and the other. Insights from the left and right sides of my brain intermingled as naturally as two streams from opposite directions converge into a much larger river. Using a metaphorical representation of my experiences with Tabula Rasa as a point of departure, I set the stage for a journey through an otherworld that the narrator travels with a lame black horse as her main companion. Along the way, she finds herself having to explain the customs of human thought to creatures who've never been to the logic-laden land they call the Surface. At a pivotal point, she meets a group of amorphous beings called the Ancestors who suggest that she invent new myths and reinterpret old ones to characterize the features of human consciousness and their limited function in a much larger matrix of potential knowledge that gives rise to infinite styles of nonhuman thought and awareness throughout the universe. In the process, she discovers a long-buried secret that actually saves the black horse's life.

Many of the breakthroughs I had in understanding the language and behavior of horse-human interactions came during the writing of this unusual text. The strange places I was traveling in my imagination demanded a deeper understanding of history, religion, mythology, philosophy, psychology, and the workings of the creative process itself. It was as if pages and pages of disconnected insights were digested organically by some unconscious feature of my brain, only to reemerge as an intricate tapestry of ideas woven by the Voice of Remembering. My urge to decipher the strange events of my life set the agenda for my studies.

I wanted to know why it was possible to dream the future, how the logical and artistic impulses of the brain interacted, how intuition fueled discoveries that were later proved by scientific methods, how horses seem to jump-start expanded states of awareness in certain riders, how some people hear voices on the way to the psychiatric hospital while others hear voices and try to explain the phenomenon by writing five-hundred-page books, like Julian Jaynes's *The Origin of Consciousness in the Breakdown of the Bicameral Mind*. I also had to know why a congenitally lame Arabian mare inspired this whole thing to begin with.

During that time, however, I was afraid to tell even Steve of my ghostly experiences. It just seemed too weird to take the whole thing literally. Besides, it was difficult to characterize why I increasingly felt this was an external rather than internal phenomenon. Whenever I tried to interpret the sensation in psychological and mythological terms, the pressure only increased, as if whoever or whatever was following me around was getting impatient with my attempts to explain the whole thing away. As a last resort, I decided to act as if I were dealing with an autonomous awareness, a visitor from the other side. I decided to address this invisible force as if it actually existed.

Nothing dramatic happened. No specters in long robes materialized before my eyes and spoke to me in those lofty yet cryptic phrases that ghosts of legend and literature always prefer. I did, however, sense a nod of appreciation for my reluctant acknowledgment. I was filled with the unmistakable feeling that this whatever-it-was had something important to say and was determined to hang around until I removed the cotton from my ears and took notes.

At that moment, it occurred to me that the Ancestors I assumed I had invented might actually be *my* ancestors, that I had somehow brought them back to life through the simple act of writing about them in an altered state of mind. Or was it their presence that made me write those words to begin with? Perhaps the Voice of Remembering was actually the Voice of Re-membering, an aural wraith presiding over my initiation back into the membership of some ancient bloodline.

Taking the path of least resistance, I continued riding this train of thought backward in time, hoping I wouldn't lose all touch with reality in the process. Who were my ancestors, after all? My mother's side of the family hailed from the Scottish highlands, yet even though I related to many of the symbols and ideals of the early Celtic tribes, I was drawn more emphatically toward my father's roots. I began reading books on Ukraine. My grandparents had emigrated from this tempestuous region in the early twentieth century, and I grew up hearing the melodious sounds of their native language. *Ukraine* means simply "borderland," an appropriate name for a land that lies on the southeastern edge of Europe, on the threshold of Asia, along the banks of the Black Sea and the fringes of the Mediterranean; it sits astride the once important border between the sheltering forest and the vast sea of open grasslands known as the steppes. Power in those places was not concentrated, writes Neal Ascherson in *Black Sea*: "The title of supreme ruler might belong to a man or woman whose family origins were among pastoral steppe nomads, Turkic or Iranian or Mongol. Local government and regulations of the economy might be left to Greek, Jewish, Italian, or Armenian merchants. The soldiery, usually a hired force, could be Scythian or Sarmatian, Caucasian or Gothic, Viking or Anglo-Saxon, French or German."

That my family emerged from such a potent cultural melting pot made perfect sense to me. I had always felt an equal affinity for Eastern and Western philosophies. When I was a music major in college, the delicate strummings of the Japanese koto and the sensuous rhythms of Middle Eastern song were no more foreign to me than the lush symphonic harmonies of my European classical training. These were not opposing viewpoints in my mind, but interlocking threads weaving a more complete picture of human inquiry, art, and innovation. In the true (yet certainly unconscious) spirit of my Ukrainian heritage, I saw no reason to reject the tenets of Western society in favor of Eastern insights. So many seekers of my generation were convinced this was the answer, yet the underlying theme of my life involved a general mistrust of any kind of civilization, no matter which side of the world had given birth to it. I always felt like an outsider, as if the history of the entire human race was some intricate experiment based on a misguided premise and we were headed toward a permanent dead end in our evolution if we didn't realize we were supporting a grossly limited hypothesis. This proved the key to understanding exactly who was haunting me.

Amazon Country

My Ukrainian grandfather was a blacksmith by trade. He might just as well have been a hatmaker for all the good it did me, because by the time I entered the picture, my family had no use for horses. These animals were relics of the preindustrial past. They survived only as expensive diversions for the elite, as far as my father was concerned, so there was little chance of my working-class parents granting their daughter's wish to actually own one. I had to be content with riding a friend's pony, volunteering my services as a groom and horse handler at local shows, and sneaking off to the old horse trader's farm down the street to steal bareback rides on members of his transient herd. For many years, my obsession was considered little more than "that thing young girls seem to have for horses." I was inclined to believe this as well, until I began investigating my ancestral roots at the urging of a ghost.

I never saw the tools of Grandpa's trade. After technological innovations made the working horse obsolete, he was forced to sell his skills to the steel mills for an hourly wage. When he died shortly before my fifth birthday, the only evidence of his former occupation consisted of a few horseshoes rusting in the root cellar. Even less is known of his family history. I've since discovered, however, that blacksmiths in the Slavic lands have always existed along the fringes of mainstream culture. Traditionally, they kept to themselves, because peasant folk considered the ancient art of fire and iron to be a suspicious (if essential) brand of magic. Ukrainian blacksmiths were feared and respected, sometimes enlisted as healers, sometimes accused of sorcery, but rarely invited to enter the village inner circle. The craft was handed down from father to son like a secret, unspoken pact, and the ritual continued over countless generations.

Grandfather Claudius was notoriously antisocial; anyone outside the family was unwelcome and vaguely suspect at best. His behavior seemed ridiculously eccentric to my mother, my sister, and me. Yet it never occurred to any of us that grandfather's intolerance might have something to do with the social conditioning of his age-old vocation. "Your grandpa lived a hard life," my father would say. "He came from the old country, fought in World War I, and struggled during the Depression. It was difficult for him to trust people after all that."

When Claudius Kohanov immigrated to the United States, he was indeed fleeing a long series of wars and famines in his native land. He rarely discussed the details of life in Ukraine; the memories were much too painful. My grandmother, an intensely subservient woman, had fled similar conditions, though she and Claudius had met and married in the New World. The fact that Palahia had been orphaned at the age of four meant that stories of her lineage weren't suppressed by choice; they had simply died with her parents. The only thing we knew for sure was that Grandma had been the daughter of a Cossack. Whenever that word was spoken in my family, it was usually followed by an emphatic silence, underlining the fact that these warriors struck fear into the hearts of peasantry and royalty alike. It was no wonder my grandmother lost her parents before she ever knew them. They were probably killed in some kind of skirmish they helped instigate. Still, I had little knowledge of what being a Cossack actually involved until thirty years later, when I was motivated to investigate the sketchy clues of my ancestry.

As it turns out, my grandmother was descended from a line of ruthless horsemen who ruled the wild kingdom of the open steppes from the fifteenth to the early twentieth centuries. These people were social dropouts who tried to resurrect the romantic existence of a much more ancient horse-based culture that flourished in the region more than four thousand years earlier. Yet according to Ascherson's *Black Sea*, they were never able to claim the glory of those early nomads. The Cossacks were an abomination, a collection of thieves, naïve idealists, and outcasts who used their newfound freedom to engage in violence and treat women like slaves. My grandmother acted like a servant in her own home because she had been raised by a culture that reinforced such behavior under the socially accepted penalty of severe beatings.

By becoming mercenaries to the czar, the Cossacks were eventually seduced back into the rigid Russian Empire they originally sought to escape. "The Cossacks were not capable of acting as partners and protectors" of the steppes, Ascherson concludes, "but instead fell into subjection. Compared to the Indo-Iranian peoples of antiquity, and to some of the Turkic peoples who followed them, the Cossacks were primitive. Force, race, and maleness are seldom values of a stable and traditional society, but rather of bandits.... This was once Amazon country, and the very maleness of the Cossacks is in reality a discord with the past."

Amazon country? I never dreamed my ancestors roamed the same historical landscape that inspired campy television shows like *Xena: Warrior Princess*. I was under the impression Amazons were creations of distorted male fantasies, ancient precursors of Wonder Woman, wild, whip-snapping, ironclad maidens who raced around on horseback in short leather skirts and formfitting bodices. Yet as I read Ascherson's book and other histories on the region, I learned that horses were first domesticated by the peoples of those grasslands between 4500–4000 BCE and 2200 BCE, that the women rode and fought alongside the men if they chose, and that some of these tribes were decidedly matrilineal. Most important, I could see from vague descriptions of their customs that the so-called Scythian and Sarmatian cultures, which came later, were influenced as much by horse behavior as they were by human behavior. The amorphous presence hovering over my left shoulder couldn't wait for me to turn the page.

The first equestrians left no evidence of a written language. The few stories that survive were recorded around 450 BCE by Herodotus, the Greek "Father of History," whose recollections of the Scythians and gossip about the warrior women he called Amazons were considered pure fantasy up to the Victorian age. In the 1950s, however, much of what he wrote was confirmed when archaeologists began excavating the numerous nomad burial mounds that rise above the steppes.

Corpses of horse and human alike lay among a dazzling array of colorful saddle cloths depicting scenes from daily life. These in turn revealed a culture of decorative mane dressing and fantastic crested horse masks. Four-legged members of the tribe were groomed and dressed with as much enthusiasm as their two-legged counterparts. The bodies of both species had been stuffed with many of the herbs recorded by Herodotus in his account of Scythian burial rituals — anise, frankincense, parsley, and assorted marsh plants. In the corner of one tomb lay a fur bag containing cannabis, bronze cauldrons filled with stones, and the frame of a four-foot-high inhalation tent, fully corroborating the Greek historian's tales of how the steppe nomads engaged in what he called a "vapour-bath" of "steam that no Greek vapour-bath could surpass." In other words, the Scythians preferred to alter their perception by sitting in portable sweat lodges and tossing marijuana seeds onto heated stones.

Since the horse tribes had no particular base of operations to maintain, they wore their wealth in the form of exquisite, highly symbolic jewelry and stylish riding clothes. These nomads were even credited with the invention of pants. If there really had been a warrior princess named Xena, she would have worn tight-fitting leggings tucked into leather boots, long-sleeved shirts, and hip-length coats, all of which would have been woven and embroidered with intricate designs. Galloping through the treeless expanse of the open steppe, she would have protected her head from the sun with a cloth hat or, in times of war, an ornate helmet. A thick iron belt designed to shield the groin area was an important element of battle attire for both men and women. According to Renate Rolle's *The World of the Scythians*, however, these "Amazons" were no less aware of their femininity. Their graves are filled with mirrors, scent bottles, cosmetics of various colors, and significant pieces of jewelry. One magnificent gold necklace dating back to the fourth century BCE weighs over three pounds and features three tiers of intricate designs, the top level consisting of mares and cows nursing their young, a fleece being stretched between two long-haired, heavily bearded men, and a ewe being milked by a woman who looked a lot like my grandmother. The middle level is decorated with flowers and spirals, no doubt symbolizing the earth. And underneath these gentle scenes of the pastoral life lay depictions of a mythical underworld in which a number of strange creatures proliferate and interact. The imagery is startling in its affinity with some of the visions I had been conjuring up during the writing of "The Black Horse Speaks."

Most important of all, however, are reports of the nomads' behavior in battle, descriptions that have little in common with the standardized legends of fierce barbarians out to vanquish the sacred innovations of the civilized world. Herodotus tells the story of King Darius I of Persia, later the invader of Greece, who entered Eurasia for the first time in 512 BCE on a punitive expedition against the Scythians. When he arrived at the edge of the steppes, however, none of his officers could figure out how to engage these so-called primitives in combat. Whenever the troops got too close, the Scythians simply dispersed, riding into the grasslands, leading the king's rigidly disciplined military force further and further into the wilderness. For weeks, the horsemen watched from a safe distance, ignoring the king's provocative insults, infuriating him further by breaking ranks to chase a stray rabbit as the Persians made their threatening gestures. The Scythians were sleeping on horseback, drinking mare's milk, and playing games along the way, while the men Darius led were growing weak from starvation and exposure. Finally, the Persians were forced to turn around and march home as the horsemen cheered and chuckled in the distance.

The Scythians maintained their culture and their territory by acting like the horses they rode. Flight before fight was not a cowardly act; it simply made good sense. No blood need be shed over the protection of the herd. Women with children and mares with foals might just as well have vanished into thin air as they hid within the wide-open spaces. Warrior riders and mounts of both sexes simply led the challengers in another direction. The enemy was ultimately irrelevant, because there was no city to defend. It was only when increasingly materialistic members of these horse tribes began trading with city dwellers that they sacrificed centuries of freedom. The more possessions they craved and acquired, the more their belongings weighed them down, the more they became. Greek gold and wine and decorative vases eventually lured the nomads into a gilded cage of cultural amnesia. The ones who refused to forget fled further into the grasslands until civilizations developing to the east and west expanded and overlapped right over their graves. One way or another, the real-life ancestors of centaurian legend were finally corralled by both Eastern and Western opportunists, men who set out to annex and subdue every last scrap of wilderness as if they were on a divine mission.

"Remember it now," the ghost seemed to say.

Gifts of the Nomads

Horses are natural nomads, and the people who discovered how to ride these graceful, fleet-footed beasts did not necessarily domesticate them. Rather, the two species merged into a single herd of mutual influence and cooperation. Recent theories on animal domestication support this view. This did not mean, however, that these tribes were less sophisticated than the people who chose to plant themselves in one place and till the soil. The still-popular notion that agriculture represented a huge innovation over nomadism is based, according to Ascherson and other theorists, on an inherent "terror of peoples who move." This perspective was promoted by the Greeks and later adopted by the increasingly sedentary Europeans. But nomadic pastoralism was not a "primitive" condition. It was, on the contrary, a specialization that developed out of settled agricultural communities, requiring horses and skillful riding techniques. It used the wheel to allow populations to migrate with their herds by cart and wagon, a central leadership able to make quick decisions in an emergency, and many craftspeople and specialists, far more than family subsistence farming needed. The horse tribes even managed to raise some crops without building permanent settlements. They simply planted their wheat in patches of fertile soil and returned to reap the benefits during seasonal migrations.

The assumption that nomads were more violent and destructive than their city-based counterparts has also begun to evaporate in the light of new research. The Danish archaeologist Klavs Randsborg insists it wasn't marauding hordes of barbarians that led to the fall of the Greco-Roman world. Rather, these societies destroyed their environment and in desperation moved out to sublimate the lands and cultures nearby — Celtic, Germanic, Thracian, Scythian — "which until then had led an effective and long-standing existence in harmony in nature."

The Greeks were among the first men to successfully build mental and physical walls between themselves and the cycles of Mother Earth. In their increasing isolation, they imagined they were not only separate from the natural world and its creatures but superior to them. Their urge to distinguish themselves led to the invention of a category for human beings who chose to live by different standards. *Barbarian* comes from an onomatopoeic Greek word designating a foreign language, the sound of an incomprehensible tongue. However, this term soon came to symbolize something a great deal more sinister than a lifestyle choice. In her book *Inventing the Barbarian*, Edith Hall suggests that during the fifth century BCE, the Athenians transferred all they found alien and repulsive from the mythical world of monsters to the actual terrain inhabited by the "barbarian." Previously, there were Cyclopes, Harpies, sirens, and snake-haired Gorgons to symbolize the fearful aspects of the human psyche. Yet as Hellenic consciousness, separated from the wisdom of nature, gave birth to the discriminating mechanisms of Greek logic, the mythological world receded in importance and believability. At the same time, their early cities were suffering from the anxieties of instability resulting from conspicuous consumption and unchecked population growth. Rather than abandon the city, as much earlier agriculturalists had done when settlements became too large for local resources to support, at that time Greeks, Romans, Egyptians, and others from similar cultures chose to expand outward, taking over the territories and resources of other peoples, subjugating them into slavery to provide the labor needed to build new buildings and reap greater harvests. After nearly a millennium of expansion to compensate for repeated economic failure, this process brought city dwellers to the point at which they devastated the whole natural and political world around them.

The duality of civilization versus barbarism, a concept presented as indisputable fact in the public schools I attended, was actually a myth created by settled societies to justify their own aggression, a desperate rage incited by economic peril disguised as a moral imperative. (With the advent of the Holy Roman Empire, it became a religious dictate handed down by God himself.) Barbarians, we learned, were an evil blight that had to be absorbed into a kinder, gentler society — or wiped off the earth. Only this mindset could justify the rampant destruction needed to feed the bottomless pit of consumption at the center of many complex civilizations. Nomads also faced limited resources during droughts and longer-term climate change. Yet when they engaged in similar conquest-oriented behavior, city dwellers demonized their horse-riding neighbors, using this as yet another excuse to take over their territories.

In the last few years, a philosophy known as "nomadology" has begun to analyze and even promote the benefits of this lifestyle for modern people oppressed by the whims of sedentary society. The Polish artist Krzysztof Wodiczko has designed a vehicle for twenty-first-century nomads combining shelter, mobility, and communication. Patrick Wright, a friend of Wodiczko, holds that this "nomadic war machine" is in reality "devoted to survival, intelligence and the avoidance of engagement rather than to battle itself... closer to the hunted animal that learns to coexist with enemies than to the hunter who goes in search of prey... an instrument of manoeuvre as opposed to battle, of mobility and sudden disappearance and reappearance, of intelligence rather than brutal, unstoppable advance."

The first time I read these words, it struck me that the culture of nomadism is based on decidedly equine behavior. "Here is a technique through which the weak become stronger than their oppressors: by scattering, by becoming centerless, by moving fast across space, by all that is nomadism." The ways of horses also seemed to have much in common with the ideals of the original Jesus of Nazareth (not the Christian religion as it was adapted by the Roman Empire and other capitalistic incarnations of the faith). As a Jew, his was a nomadic bloodline. Around the time the civilized world was seeking to eradicate the nonsedentary lifestyle, this prophesied savior of humankind was crucified for encouraging people to give up the seductions of city life, to wander the earth and let God provide for their needs through nature, to avoid combat at all costs. In Christ's vision of redemption, the weak shall inherit the earth, and the lion shall lie down beside the lamb. In such an early stage of human development, however, the savior did not even try to save himself. The king of beasts rose up to kill the Lamb of God and has been on the rampage ever since.

As omnivores, human beings embody characteristics of both predator and prey. It was the predator in humankind that was capable of domesticating the cat and the dog. But according to descriptions of the first equestrians, it was the prey aspect of the psyche that solidified a partnership with the horse. Both carnivore and herbivore philosophies were active in these steppe tribes. Yet outside the persistent checks and balances of nature, the civilized world gave birth to a situation in which the lion became a ruthless, unstoppable killing machine. These days, it's common for the predator side of the personality to devour the prey aspect early in life. People may go to church on Sunday and voluntarily sit through tales of disciples giving up their possessions and turning the other cheek, but when Monday morning arrives, the beast rears its ugly head, and the rabid carnivore is unleashed once again. For change to occur, the human psyche has to accept another matrix of wisdom capable of balancing the violent nature of the predator inside. The lion must lie down beside the lamb. Yet with the entire race teetering on the edge of extinction, it will take a stronger, more compelling symbol to gain the lion's respect. The image of the hunted who outwits a hunter of such monstrous proportions is not likely to be the lamb, a much more innocent symbol of nonpredatory philosophy. But the horse might capture the carnivorous beast's attention as an innovation of this ideal in its maturest, most elegant, most powerful, most regal manifestation. Was this what my ghost was trying to say?

It suddenly became apparent that the desiccation of Native American tribes and the tragedies of African slavery were modern parallels to the civilized savagery that wiped out my own ancestral tribe and many others thousands of years earlier. Once the whole of Europe was tamed and drained of its natural vitality, sights were set on other territories. We're still dealing with the fallout from this last wave of atrocities, not because these cultures were eradicated as they had been in the ancient past, but because their total annihilation was somehow arrested in the eleventh hour. For all their suffering, those of Native American and African descent at least have some of the stories of the elders, the ancient rhythms of the tribe, and remnants of their rituals providing a lifeline to the resurrection of a cultural memory that can sustain them through these difficult times. The only evidence of my ancestors was buried under what's left of the Ukrainian steppes. There are no names, no stories, no detailed descriptions of their religion, only a handful of artifacts scattered about in museums and a few paragraphs written by a Greek who watched their strange ways from a distance. Even so, these archaeological findings have exerted considerable influence on researchers sharp enough to cut through the haze of civilized propaganda, what Ascherson calls "a ruthless mental dynasty which still holds invisible power over the Western mind."

Yet apparently there was another invisible power waiting in the wings, a force that had traveled across the mists of time and halfway around the earth to speak to me at the exact moment I was crazy enough to listen. This courtship culminated in a simple, classic gesture, one that promptly sent me scrambling for a counselor. Like a suitor who wins the attentions of his beloved when he acknowledges the mythology of her soul, my specter reached through the seemingly insurmountable barrier between our worlds to present me with a most uncanny gift: an exquisite, and quite real, lavender rose.

A Genetic Fluke?

Steve and I are bathing Noche on a warm, moonlit night. The old sage mustang, who has suffered such violence, is standing calmly, allowing me to spray cool water over his body as he nickers his approval. Yet it seems he has something important to say. His voice gets louder and more emphatic as he tries to approximate what sounds like human speech wavering and vibrating at the pitch of a whinny. He tries again and again, the words becoming clearer with each effort. Finally, he manages to form a simple question.

"How long have you been lasting?"

The phrase echoed in my mind as I awoke. What could it possibly mean? After the dream, Steve suggested Noche might be asking me how old I was, but this interpretation didn't seem quite right. Something about the words the bay horse chose felt more like a Zen koan than a mundane question. Buddhist monks use such paradoxical inquiries to jolt their disciples out of the habitual thought processes of reason into states of sudden intuitive understanding. Sometimes it takes months of meditating on a single phrase for the lightning bolt of recognition to strike, but when it does, the student is ready to join the ranks of his or her teachers.

A few weeks after this puzzling dream took place, I set Noche and Rasa free to run around the Oasis, spread a horse blanket over the grass, and entered the dream in my journal. I hadn't been able to solve the riddle. I was merely hoping the act of writing it down would lessen its persistent hold over me. Rasa came up, nuzzled my shoulder, and then pointed to her belly, begging for a scratch. Noche was grazing nearby. Normally a rock-solid horse on the trail, he had spooked unexpectedly the previous night. I had dismounted to cool him down on the way home, and we were walking side by side as the last traces of a fluorescent sunset slipped below the horizon. All of a sudden, Noche jumped forward and bolted as if someone or something were literally attacking us from behind. In the three years I had owned him, he had never behaved this way under saddle. His fear of human beings made him unpredictable around strangers at the barn, but nothing else seemed to bother him. Still, if I hadn't maintained control of the reins that evening, he surely would have left me in the dust. When I turned around to see what had caused all the commotion, there was nothing there, just the utter stillness of twilight. A potent chill ran up my spine.

I shuddered again as I remembered the incident in the broad ninety-five-degree daylight of a luminous October afternoon. At that moment, I realized I'd rather be scared out of my wits than go on wondering if my ghost really existed. I challenged the spirit to offer some physical evidence of its existence, to make up a form if it had to; otherwise, I was just going to give up and get on with my life. Sunlight filtered through the mesquite tree above me. Rasa ambled over to greet one of the other horses as Noche stood dozing in the shade. I packed up my books, locked the tack room, threw some hay to the horses, and headed for the car, which I had parked at the main gate several acres from the barn. As I slipped through the outer fence, I saw a splash of color hovering next to my old, beat-up Cavalier. Something was attached to the mirror on the driver's side.

It was a rose, a lavender rose. I was enchanted. I had never actually seen such a flower before. The owner of the barn had planted roses on both sides of the entrance, and I looked to see which bush was producing such remarkable blooms. There were yellow roses, red, orange even, and white, but no evidence of anything close to the rarefied hue of this perfectly formed blossom. It must have been a genetic fluke. But who would have plucked it and left it where I was sure to notice?

I had told my friend and fellow boarder Julia Standish about the original lavender rose incident I'd had in my twenties. She must have been taking a lesson at the riding academy next door, seen that single rose in passing, and attached it to my car. Strange that she didn't come over and talk for a moment, knowing I was around. *Oh, well, she must have been in a hurry*, I thought as I started the ignition and headed home.

I didn't have a bud vase, but the rose managed to fit quite nicely in a thin champagne glass I found tucked away. Steve was equally intrigued by the color when I dragged him out of his office to show him my prize, but we were both even more amazed when I called Julia to thank her.

"Wow," she said. "I wish I'd done that. But I wasn't anywhere near the barn today."

I never did find out who put that rose on my mirror, but as I leaned over to inhale its heady fragrance, it really didn't seem to matter. Even if some acquaintance or secret admirer had wandered by the gate and suddenly been overtaken by the desire to place that particular flower where I was bound to find it, how could he or she have known what such a gesture would mean to me? I was spooked by the synchronicity of the event — and impressed by its poetry. I also felt like I needed some serious help.

Feeling more tortured than ever, I called up Dr. Patricia Hursh, a counselor recommended highly by my riding instructor, Cathy Schreiber. At the time, Cathy, Julia, and I were part of the informal pre-Epona trainer's group that got together weekly to blow off steam about the horse business and life in general. Over dinner a few days before the rose graced me with its presence, Cathy had described her cathartic sessions with Patricia and their effect in helping her deal with a destructive and manipulative relationship. It seemed that even though Dr. Hursh had a PhD in psychology, she was also well versed in spiritual healing techniques. I'd asked for her phone number, thinking she would be the only person with whom I could speak freely if I couldn't figure out what to do with this ghostly presence on my own.

Still, I wasn't quite sure how I would approach the subject as I drove to her office the following Monday afternoon. I figured it might take me a couple of sessions before I was ready to tell her what was really going on — after all, I didn't want to appear crazy, even if I'd already reached the point where I thought I *was* quite possibly going mad. My Midwestern, middle-class upbringing made me wary of sharing these kinds of experiences with people I didn't know. This mistrust stemmed not only from a cultural bias against anything that couldn't be explained through logic but from the fact that my father had been briefly institutionalized, treated with shock therapy, and pumped with drugs for forty years after his release, consequences he experienced when he was overcome with a series of feelings and visions that made it temporarily impossible for him to hold down a job in the early 1960s. He had been cursed with a highly creative, extremely empathic personality in an environment that solely valued making a secure living while suppressing strong emotion. He had also been physically and emotionally abused as a child, though no one knew this was a factor until his second "nervous break-down" in the early 1980s. In both instances, medication was emphasized in a health care system unwilling to invest in therapy. The doctors gave him sufficient Valium to tame his visions, reconstruct the socially acceptable façade of breadwinner, and calm his raw, aching nerves just enough to allow him to return to his compromising position in an architectural firm. The intensely colorful psychedelic landscapes he painted in his spare time became an infrequent outlet as the tranquilizers took hold; his art thereafter remained in a state of arrested development. Would Dr. Hursh respond to my feelings and visions with a similar treatment strategy?

A graceful woman with dark, shoulder-length hair and a smooth, calming voice, Patricia immediately put me at ease. I vaguely touched on the fact that I had some strange things going on in my life that deserved consideration outside standard therapeutic practices, though I also felt more secure with someone who had studied conventional psychology as well. I asked her to describe her background and how she worked. Patricia explained that since childhood she'd been able to see and hear things that others didn't seem to notice. Over the years, she tried to find her place in a world filled with forces beyond her understanding by studying the psyche as Western medicine mapped it and by pursuing intuitive practices to fill in the gaps. She said she worked with a variety of "guides" who oversaw the mechanisms of "universal law" and were capable of assisting in any number of ways.

"So," she said, folding her hands in her lap, "what can I do for you?"

"I seem to be haunted," I found myself blurting out, as if it were a common and legitimate affliction. Patricia didn't bat an eye as she proceeded to ask for details. I told her about the Voice of Remembering and quoted the Ancestor-related passages from my manuscript. I described the increasing pressure in the air around me and how it seemed to want to tell me something. I discussed my fear in opening up to the experience because I wasn't sure what to make of the ghost's intentions.

"I guess I'm not so much afraid as I am cautious," I concluded. "I don't know if it's really possible to be possessed by an outside force, but if stories about ghosts are true, then I have to assume possession is a reality as well. I need to know, first of all, if this whole thing is a figment of my imagination. If it's not, I have to figure out whether I can safely let this whatever-it-is in the door, so to speak. And of course, I'd really like to know who it is and what it wants."

Much to my surprise and relief, Patricia nodded in thoughtful agreement. "You're right to be concerned," she said. "I once let a very disturbing entity into my life, and it was more trouble than you'll ever want to know." My counselor shifted in her chair, uncrossing her legs and placing her feet flat on the floor. "If you feel comfortable with this, I'd like to consult some beings who can assess the situation. I call them by a number of different names, but basically they function as the guardians of universal law. I do this by creating an energy circle around us for protection. I invite these beings of light into the circle, and if they feel whoever is haunting you is not harmful, we can call this entity in as well."

"Sure," I replied, not knowing what to expect. Was she going to start chanting and shaking rattles, close the blinds and light thirteen candles, put on a purple cape and wave a wand in the air? I had no idea. Dr. Hursh simply took a deep breath and closed her eyes. Outside the french doors of her office, the sky was a perfect blue. Birds were singing, and the sun was almost blinding in intensity as it reflected off the shiny leaves of an immense flowering hedge that surrounded the backyard. Patricia created a circle of energy I could not see or sense, merely by voicing her intention to do so. I was struck by how normal the whole process seemed. She spoke to her guides in a respectful yet matter-of-fact tone, nodding as if engaging them in conversation, and occasionally asking them for clarification. Then she opened her eyes and informed me that my ghost was adhering to accepted rules of conduct and had no malevolent intentions toward me whatsoever.

"How are you feeling?" she asked. "Are you comfortable calling this presence into the circle?"

"I'm very cold all of a sudden," I said. "But other than that, I'm fine. By all means, call it in." Patricia handed me an afghan she kept draped across her couch and proceeded to ask whoever was haunting me to step into the circle. Then she started giggling as if the spirits were telling jokes or making lewd gestures.

"I'm sorry," she said, still chuckling. "They're laughing at me because I started counting them. I got up to twenty and realized there were way too many of them to take a formal census."

No wonder the air felt so thick. Addressing this legion, Patricia asked them to choose a single representative who could speak for the group. "Ah," she sighed. "A beautiful feminine spirit. Lovely. It is truly a pleasure to meet you." Then, turning to me, Patricia said I was free to ask about whatever I wanted to know.

I had no idea where to start. I stammered around the issues for a moment, expressing a desire to find out who these people were, where they came from, and what they wanted from me. My interpreter between worlds voiced these desires more coherently and then began to look quite puzzled. "They don't seem to be from anywhere near here," she told me after several moments of silent inquiry. "I don't recognize the place at all."

"Ask them if their homeland is in what is now known as Ukraine, the grasslands along the Black Sea," I offered.

"Yes," she said. "That's it. Very good." Then she opened her eyes and told me that from now on I would be expected to participate in the conversation. "Ask a question, then quiet your mind and see if the answer comes through in some form or other. I will be here to validate, to make sure that we are both receiving the same information."

I wasn't sure what was supposed to happen. Would I hear voices or see the outline of a young woman floating in midair? At first there was only silence. I did pick up a few words that sounded close to the syntax of my own thoughts. Patricia confirmed these phrases were not accurate, that they were in fact wishful thinking. After a couple of false starts, I closed my eyes and actually began to see vague monochromatic images in response to my requests for information. Yet even though she validated what I described, Patricia didn't seem to understand much of what was communicated any more than I did.

When I asked who these spirits were, I saw an M. C. Escher–like design of many interlocking horse heads. "Shall I call you the People of the Horse?" I asked. Patricia said no, that didn't seem to be quite what they were saying. Then I remembered the dream I had about Noche. Was this a message from the ghosts? Yes it was, we both confirmed. What was the significance of the words "How long have you been lasting?" My question was followed by the unmistakable image of a window opening to reveal infinite space.

"I believe they are saying that this question was designed to open me up to a new way of seeing," I explained. Patricia nodded in agreement. As we went on in this fashion, we managed to piece together a few facts. The book I was writing was important to their cause, although they wouldn't say what that cause was. However, they were adamant that I was to speak for them, to resurrect their perspective and communicate it to those who lived in my time. Patricia interpreted it as "a pact or an agreement" that had been made between us. I asked, "Why me?" Patricia explained that once in a while there is someone who has a genetic and emotional configuration suited to such an undertaking, that it was in part an ancestral dictate, but that was all she could make out from what the spirits offered.

The whole process was like trying to speak to an alien life-form that wasn't capable of expressing itself through human language. Perhaps these people came from such an ancient tribe that their thoughts were barely translatable by modern standards. When I inquired as to the best way to converse with them in the future, I saw a very clear depiction of rushing water.

I was growing increasingly frustrated. I took a break, went to the bathroom, and splashed some water on my face. I felt dizzy, depleted. When I finally walked back into the room, Patricia was standing up, seemingly in concentrated meditation.

"I think I've figured out what the trouble is," she said. "We've been assuming all along that these entities are human. They are not. They are horses."

I sat down in shock. Of course. I couldn't believe I hadn't thought of it myself. All this time, I had assumed I was speaking to a tribe of extinct Scythians or Sarmatians. Instead I had somehow summoned the equine side of that ancient intersection between our two species. Horses obviously don't think in words. They'd be more likely to think in pictures and feelings.

"Well," I replied, "that makes perfect sense to me."

"There you have it." Patricia gave me a weary smile.

I finally understood what I was dealing with, and I was grateful to Dr. Hursh. Yet we both knew my work was just beginning. I would have to experiment with creating a channel of communication between two species, one that not only transcended the barriers between the realm of the dead and the world of the living but also somehow united my verbally oriented human mind with a group mind that was immensely different in scope and orientation. To do that, I knew I had to bypass the essence of human language itself. But I had no idea how to proceed. I asked Patricia if the spirits could offer any clues. She closed her eyes one last time and voiced the question.

"Ah-ha," she said, gasping in sudden recognition of an obvious course of action. "It is a shamanic act," she relayed as she stared into space, surveying the parameters of a barely traceable path she knew I would have to walk alone. Her final piece of advice was vague yet emphatic: "You must become the horse."

Tracking the Horse Ancestors

I felt as if I had entered the twilight zone, and I couldn't help but wonder if my counselor was as crazy as I was. Still, the amorphous presence hovering over my shoulder refused to be explained away. In fact, whenever I tried to interpret the sensation in psychological or mythological terms, the pressure only increased. I had no choice but to deal with this force as if it actually existed, hoping all the while that I could find some rational purpose behind this irrational phenomenon.

The Horse Ancestors, as I came to call them, did offer some benefits. They communicated primarily through monochromatic pictures that unfolded behind my closed eyes. What I saw looked like the negative of an instructional film. And the subject was always horses. I could ask general questions about the species or specific questions about problems I was encountering in the training arena.

One feisty two-year-old I was hired to train had trouble learning how to move in circles on a longe line. The longe (pronounced like "lunge") is a valuable tool for teaching voice commands, correct leads, and other controlled movements. It's also a safe means of getting a green horse used to the feel of the saddle bouncing around on his or her body before a rider is added to the formula. The trainer stands in the middle of the arena with a twenty-five-to-thirty-foot rope attached to the horse's halter as the animal moves around her at a walk, trot, or canter on command. This particular gelding would get halfway around the circle, resist the pressure of the rope, then rear and carry on like a maniac. I had never encountered a horse that didn't get the concept after the first two sessions, but this colt was becoming dangerous in his objections to the process.

In frustration, I took a break, closed my eyes, and requested a little help from the Horse Ancestors. The figure of a mare appeared. She stared at me for a moment, as if to acknowledge my question, then began moving her head and neck back and forth from the shoulder area. Her actions puzzled me for quite some time before it finally hit me. This colt was tensing his neck. He didn't understand how to bend and move forward at the same time, only how to go straight, turn, and then go straight in another direction.

Consequently, when he got halfway around the circle, the pressure of the rope felt like a signal to stop, yet he was confused because I continued to push him along with increasingly animated gestures. He was angry that I kept asking him to stop and go at the same time, and he reared in reaction to my impossible request. The moment this conclusion entered my mind, the mare stopped her movement, bowed her head to me, and ran off.

I put the longe line away for a few days and worked on loosening up the colt's neck muscles with some massage techniques. I also got him used to the feeling of bending and going forward by walking beside him with one hand grasping the halter, pulling his head and neck gently toward the center of the ring. The other hand (and pretty much the weight of my entire body at first) pressed firmly against his shoulder to keep him going forward. In this way, he began to realize that different parts of his anatomy could move independently of each other with various results. When we returned to the longe, he continued to be impatient learning new moves, but he trotted around in circles as if it were the simplest thing in the world.

Whenever I resorted to contacting the Horse Ancestors for advice, it really did feel like I was directly tapping some form of equine consciousness. I rarely received words in association with these images, and I didn't always understand the message behind what I was seeing, because the imagery was sometimes so alien to me. On rare occasions when a vision did evaporate into sound, the words and their syntax were usually so strange that I still found it difficult to grasp the meaning. With time, however, the insights always proved accurate. Once I actually had the nerve to consult the Horse Ancestors in the presence of an open-minded cowboy who was having problems with his roping horse. The professional rodeo rider had had a long and fruitful relationship with this gray quarter horse mare when she suddenly became unmanageable for no apparent reason. When I asked the Horse Ancestors for advice, a single horse appeared rearing and pawing the ground in agitation as the image dissolved into the phrase "No more rustling."

The word "rustling" was very clear, yet the cowboy and I assumed that the Horse Ancestors must have meant "wrestling." The man had been thinking of retiring from the circuit and seemed relieved that his horse was objecting to his continued entries in steer wrestling events. Two months later, however, I learned that this same cowboy had been arrested. In order to sustain a growing cocaine habit, he was buying horses on payment plans, trailering them to an undisclosed location, and selling them to other buyers without contacting or paying the previous owners what he owed. "Rustling" was indeed the appropriate word, a term that literally means "stealing" with a decidedly cowboy flavor.

As time went on and I gained more confidence, the Horse Ancestors proved to be quite an asset, sort of like having an interactive computer chip implanted in my head that held a vast encyclopedia of knowledge directly from the horse's mouth. During one particularly potent meditation, the voice conveyed (much to my relief) that what I was dealing with was not necessarily a bunch of disembodied horses from an extinct Ukrainian tribe. This invisible force was, in her words, "the wisdom that gives rise to the form of the horse." As such, what I experienced as the Horse Ancestors was a field of potential that encompassed all horses who ever lived and all horses not yet born. It was the blueprint of the species in all its physical, mental, emotional, and spiritual variations. What continued to unnerve me, however, was the fact that this blueprint seemed to have an agenda, and it was quite displeased with the way the species as a whole had been treated over the last few thousand years.

Much later, I discovered that my interactions with the Voice of Remembering and the Horse Ancestors had a scientific parallel in the work of the biologist Rupert Sheldrake, whose controversial theories involve what he calls "morphogenetic fields" (from the Greek *morphe*, "form," and the Latin *genesis*, "coming into being"). In his book *The Presence of the Past*, Sheldrake writes that the nature of things depends on a collective memory for each species that influences the form of living organisms: "Each kind of natural system has its own kind of field: there is an insulin field, beech field, a swallow field, and so on. Such fields shape all different kinds of atoms, molecules, living organisms, societies, customs, and habits of mind. Morphic fields, like the known fields of physics, are nonmaterial regions of influence extending in space and continuing in time. [When they appear,] they contain within themselves a memory of their previous physical existences."

His theory suggests that when we die, our perspectives and insights do not die with our physical bodies. They are instead retained by the human morphogenetic field. Was the Voice of Remembering my connection to that aspect of the field representing the long-suppressed wisdom of the ancient horse tribes? Sheldrake's research suggests the past in some sense may become present to us directly. Our memories may not be stored in our brains, as we usually assume they must be. "Natural systems, such as termite colonies, or pigeons, or orchid plants inherit a collective memory from all previous things of their kind, however far away they were or however long ago they existed." And what of the Horse Ancestors? In Sheldrake's terms, it seemed I had tapped into the morphogenetic field of horses, which suggested that the morphogenetic fields of different species could influence and inform one another. From descriptions of the ancient horse tribes, I suspected that the morphogenetic fields of horses and humans had been fully interactive in the distant past and as such continued to influence each other. This would explain why the fascination people have for horses endures, even if they've never ridden. The collective memories of horses and humans still intersect in intimate and highly emotional ways, even as contemporary human thought patterns and lifestyles strive to separate people from the rhythms of the natural world and its creatures.

When I first encountered these strange forces, however, I had never heard of Sheldrake or his fields. My only option was to delve further into an experience of them. As the Horse Ancestors kept teaching me how to see and think like a horse, I realized that the most basic problems riders encounter stem from the fact that a horse's natural reaction to stimulus is often exactly opposite how human beings are conditioned to respond. The key word here is *conditioned*. I knew from the customs of the ancient horse tribes that human beings were fully capable of merging horse behavior with their social and religious structures. Recognizing that someone's belief system has a strong impact on his or her behavior, I searched for religious and spiritual traditions still in existence that most closely modeled my experiences with equine "philosophies." Most major faiths promoted aspects of horse knowledge, but Taoism and shamanism turned out to hold the most parallels.

As anthropologist Michael Harner defines it, "Shamanism is a disciplined way of getting knowledge and help, which is based on the premise that we do not have to restrict ourselves to working in one reality, one dimension, when we need assistance." In looking at tribes as geographically diverse as the Huichol of Mexico and the Even people of Siberia, I found a number of cultures that were regularly assisted by an archetypal force taking the form of a deer, a prey animal similar in behavior and symbolic significance to the horse. The Pascua Yaqui tribe of southern Arizona has actually combined this antler-infused brand of shamanism with Christianity: the men of the tribe perform the sacred deer dance of their ancestors as a part of the community's Easter rites.

My interactions with the Horse Ancestors were remarkably similar to the experiences some of these indigenous cultures reported with their deer spirits. What's more, the strange ritualistic techniques I initially used to strengthen my connection with the Horse Ancestors turned out to be text-book examples of shamanism, yet I had never felt compelled to study with a medicine man or woman or to practice the traditions of another culture. The experience itself dictated my actions. As a child, I once used the body language I had learned from my equine friends to entice a wild deer to fol-low me home, and I've read that the trainer Monty Roberts, who wrote the bestselling book *The Man Who Listens to Horses*, had used similar gestures to develop relationships with the wild deer at his California ranch. That's when I recognized it was not simply the wisdom of the horse asserting itself, but the wisdom of the *prey*.

But for what purpose? I found hints in the lives of Christ, the Buddha, and the numerous teachers who gave birth to Taoism, a philosophy that blends the ecstatic insights of a shaman with the thoughtful consideration of a sage. Shamanism comforted me because it embraced the mystery of oth-erworldly encounters even as it explored ways of inducing these numinous experiences for practical reasons. Medicine men and women of old accessed the invisible world to heal the sick or find the nearest herd of buffalo. I was simply engaging in shamanic behavior to solve problems with unruly horses. Still, this wasn't enough for me; I wanted to know how and why these things were possible. Then I came across the lesser-known discipline of Taoist alchemy, a philosophy capable of explaining the mechanisms by which I experienced the Voice of Remembering, the Horse Ancestors, and all those early, seemingly prescient dreams of Rasa. Over time, I realized that the Taoist picture of reality encompassed Sheldrake's morphogenetic fields, author-physician Larry Dossey's description of "nonlocal" states of consciousness, and author-researcher E. Richard Sorenson's theory dividing human awareness into "preconquest" and "postconquest" consciousness. At the same time, Taoism provided the only system of thought — ancient or modern — that valued and defined feminine forms of wisdom that coincide with the behavior of horses and other large herbivores. This combination of philosophy and scientific theory invigorated my own experience with mul-tifaceted layers of meaning, showing me that apparently supernatural events are simply natural processes the current Western paradigm doesn't recognize. I set about expanding that paradigm in the training arena and beyond.

CHAPTER FOUR

MIND UNDER MATTER

With strip malls and subdivisions devouring its desert out-skirts, Tucson is no longer the Wild West by any stretch of the imagination. There is, however, one saving grace: an intricate network of washes that me-ander through the foothills and down into town like nature's own veins and arteries staking a claim for her survival. Most of the year, these snakelike passageways of mesquite, creosote, and cactus are dry, offering sanctuary to a healthy population of coyotes, javelinas, lizards, tarantulas, and rattlers. Yet during the monsoons of late summer, you can predict the severity of a distant storm by how fast the water rises through the floodplains in your neighborhood while the sun still shines overhead.

For Tucson's large population of amateur equestrians, these washes provide the last vestige of fenceless desert suitable for rides long enough to warrant saddlebags. Somehow it's comforting to know that the moment civilization proves too much to bear, I can tack up my horses and, without crossing any major roads, head for the hills, perhaps never to be heard from again. There were, in fact, two years when I was as good as gone, though I managed to limit most of my excursions to the washes within a five-mile radius of my home. By chance, I happened upon Timothy Graham's Oasis, the small gentlemen's ranch where I encountered the lavender rose. Nestled in a mesquite grove, this ten-acre plot of desert heaven provided instant ac-cess to an extensive maze of washes and undeveloped land just minutes from my house. There I developed the courage to conduct my unconventional inquiries into horse-human relationships. I suspect that by the time I finally moved my herd to a facility better suited to training and teaching, the people who lived around that secluded little ranch were not at all convinced of my sanity.

My activities appeared innocent enough at first. I'd saddle up Rasa with provisions to last the day, and we wouldn't be seen again until dark — sometimes well after dark if the moon was full. Together we'd explore some undeveloped stretch of desert, but it wasn't really the riding that intrigued me. After all the time I had spent on the ground with Rasa during her period of convalescence, I found that I often preferred walking beside her even when she showed no signs of lameness. The fact that she could carry water and lunch for us both — not to mention a couple of beers, a blanket, and some writing supplies — made it worth tacking her up, of course, but we both were more interested in finding some shade and a good patch of grass than logging serious miles on the trail.

Something shifted in me during those lazy afternoons. The black horse and I began to move and breathe in sync, to wander across the sweltering cactus forests, through the washes, and into the grass-lined mesquite groves by virtue of a flowing, give-and-take decision-making process, a form of shared leadership best described by the most basic meaning of the word *consensus*: "to sense together." One day, this full-bodied, dual mode of perception blossomed into something even more intimate.

We were wandering through a field dotted with scrub brush, paloverdes, and cholla cactus. Rasa was sauntering along, muzzle to the ground, sniffing casually at old sticks, snatches of coyote dung, and tufts of dried wildflowers. When she discovered a sizable clump of grass, I had nothing to do but prop myself against a rock and wait for her to devour every last blade. I reached over, absentmindedly picked a creosote blossom, and held it to my nose. A chorus of mesquites swayed to the music of heat waves. The Catalina Mountains loomed over the valley a good four-hour walk away. My thoughts expanded to fill the distance and eventually evaporated altogether.

Then, out of the corner of my eye, I noticed the black horse gazing at me with a quizzical expression as a series of decidedly nonhuman notions began to seep into my mind. I wasn't quite seeing through Rasa's eyes, but almost. There were no voices buzzing through my head, no visions parading by on strings of words. It was more like an explosion of subtle perceptions dissipating into a whisper. Sight, sound, smell, and touch seemed to merge and become interchangeable. I took a deep breath. The sensations coursing through my bloodstream filled my brain and were exhaled as conscious thought. I realized why Rasa was so perplexed. After years of traveling together in so many ways, the black horse had finally noticed I was handicapped.

Not that she felt sorry for me. She merely realized we were different in ways that give her certain advantages in life, and she was sizing up how I had adapted to the challenge. My nose, which by human standards is generous enough, looked completely insignificant to the black horse.

It seemed to be the root of all my problems. The fact that my neck was little more than a pedestal for my head only made matters worse — as did the placement of my ears, which were small and completely immobile, and my eyes, which paid attention only to whatever was directly ahead.

The curious mare stepped away from the grass to lick my hand, touch her nose to my own, and brush her soft muzzle against my cheek. Once again, I was flooded with a barrage of sense images. I had never before noticed how much pleasure and satisfaction horses derive from touching, tasting, and smelling simultaneously. Whenever Rasa approached an interesting rock or an unusual tree, she would reach out with her swanlike neck and inhale a kaleidoscope of perfumed realizations as she rubbed her nostrils and sometimes even her tongue across the object. At the same time, her ears moved independently, like little radars scanning her surroundings for any signs of intrigue or danger.

From the perspective we shared at that pivotal moment, it seemed my front hooves had mutated into flexible appendages designed to pick things up off the ground and hold them to my nose. To Rasa, this was my most outstanding feature, though I got the impression it would be even better if my fingers had some sort of olfactory capabilities, for my sense of smell obviously wasn't nearly as refined as hers, no matter how close I got to what I was investigating. With my front legs constantly moving through the air, bringing things to my face and carrying them around, I had essentially relinquished another sense she found useful. Tabula Rasa knew something was up long before she could see or smell the specifics. Those pockets of air in the hollows of all horses' hooves accentuate vibrations traveling along the ground. Unexpected visitors have a harder time sneaking up on creatures who have amplifiers in their feet.

As in other herbivore species, equine eyes are truly amazing. Placed on the sides of the head, they are larger than those of an elephant or whale and twice as big as my own. In certain positions, Rasa could see 340 of the 360 degrees around her, with two thin blind spots, one immediately ahead and one directly behind. Of course, this meant that things looked rather flat to her, and occasionally she would even bump her nose on something right in front of her face, but if she really concentrated, she could muster a narrow band of three-dimensional vision by positioning her nose perpendicular to the ground and directing both eyes forward.

For the remainder of the afternoon, I hovered between Rasa's point of view and my own. I must have stared at my hands for ten minutes, marveling at their strange construction. When we hit the trail again, I couldn't help wondering if our unusually dexterous appendages are an innovation or merely a magnificent compensation awarded to an entire species of idiots savants. I was limited to getting around on two legs as a result, which made it necessary for Rasa to either carry me on her back or leave me in the dust whenever a quick getaway was in order. I obviously couldn't hear or smell as well as she could, but it was difficult to imagine just what I was missing. Consequently, it was Rasa's ability to see two wholly different ways that continued to impress me the most.

Human vision is great for focusing on a specific object and useful for analyzing all those things we like to make with our hands, including microscopes, pens, typewriters, and computers, which allow us to translate our observations into words to share with people we may never meet. But there is a trade-off. I can only see straight ahead, and while I can do that more clearly than my equine friends, it would help to switch to that magnificent wide view of theirs when I'm out in the world. Walking through the pasture with three or four feisty horses on the first cool day of autumn, I have to keep turning my head from side to side, making sure no one is about to run over me, hoping all the while that during those quick backward glances I'm not about to step into a hole or run into a fence. And what woman hasn't experienced the creeping sensation of traversing a lonely city street, wishing she could see who belongs to those vague footsteps trailing behind her?

By equine standards, human beings wander through life virtually oblivious to their surroundings, their brains sweating in a panic as they try to dissect little bits and pieces of information in a constant struggle to fill the colossal gaps of their perception. Yet this process only distracts them further, for as they deconstruct, classify, and mull over the details of one observation, they miss everything else going on around them. The senses become that much duller in city dwellers who insulate themselves from the natural world, relying on gadgets, habits, and secondhand information to tell them how to respond to every situation — as long as it remains in an urban context. Steve and I once took a musician and his wife out to see a sacred petroglyph site so far off the beaten path there were no signs to distinguish one dirt road from another. When we arrived, the man's wife, who was born, raised, and lived in New York City, literally short-circuited among those wide-open spaces. She refused to venture outside her hotel for the rest of their trip.

The day I became a horse for a few hours, I understood in a flash why two-legged creatures need so many statistics and experts to tell them what to do. The human herd actually encourages its members to dissociate from the body, the instincts, and the senses. Children are taught to narrow their attention, cling to the past, and focus on the future, thus losing their ability to fully function in the present. They become dependent on authority figures who themselves excel only in highly specialized environments and situations.

Tabula Rasa, of course, never encouraged me to change my ways. The world was too vast and intriguing at every moment for my apparent lack of interest to disturb her. She merely noticed my dilemma one day as if she were sizing up an old cow skull lying next to the trail. Yet once I saw myself in her eyes, I became disturbed by this uniquely human tendency to experience life as a series of overprocessed sound bites. The idea of constantly editing snippets of sensation and tapes of secondhand observation into extended works of thought lost its appeal for me that afternoon, and it took me months to reconcile my identity as a writer with the lessons I learned from my horse.

Secret Springs

There is a pool in the heart of the desert. The surface is as quiet as glass, though its waters are nourished by a mountain stream rushing endlessly underground. When the sun speaks in tongues and chases the clouds away for months, rivers turn to dust, dry grasses hiss tributes to the wind, eagles perch wings outstretched on columns of rising air, and the pond reflects it all in a luminous reverie that has never known stagnation. This is the spring that lives behind the black horse's eyes.

I am content to sit at the edge and toss thoughts like pebbles into its depths, watching the ripples expand in all directions. To the black horse, the human mind looks jagged, as if the roundness of experience has been cut up by ruthless lasers and most of it discarded in a great heap underground. Still, she embraces my saw-toothed ways, for in the mirror of her lake, they are no less beautiful than flowers blooming or vultures preening after a good meal.

— from "The Black Horse Speaks"

What does it take to imagine the mind of a horse, let alone describe it to others? For me, it began with that unsettling exchange in the desert and the subsequent desire to immerse myself in the day-to-day activities of the herd. I didn't merely observe behavior. I stepped over the line and allowed Rasa, Noche, and their pasture mates to influence me outside of human agendas and thought patterns. I didn't merely interpret what I saw. That would have given me a most limited view of the vast multisensory insights horses exchange through empathic, shared awareness. My four-legged guides led me into a realm beyond words, and for months I could not articulate my discoveries. I had followed my horses so far into the place of silent knowledge that I was quite literally speechless when it came to describing why I was spending so much "idle time" with them. Still, the pressure of not being able to communicate these visceral realizations to others of my kind was almost unbearable. I felt like I was trying to carry water back to the tribe with nothing more than my own two hands. What I could grasp would never be enough, and most of it would slip through my fingers before I reached the campfire.

Then one day this deep well of awareness reached a boiling point on its own, its currents rising up from the base of my spine, surging through my gut, and flooding my heart, where they were finally pumped up into my brain with such force that a series of strangely related poetic notions spilled out for days with no effort at all. These metaphorical images, which I later collected in the unpublished book "The Black Horse Speaks," evoked a complex nonverbal reality few of us two-legged creatures ever even notice, let alone master, mostly because we've become mesmerized by words. I understood at the most intimate level why Lao-tzu opened his famous Tao Te Ching with the caution "The Tao that can be talked about is not the true Tao." Yet like the elusive Chinese sage, I also felt compelled to give it my best try, no matter how futile it seemed. The phrases that initially poured into my computer were just as vague, paradoxical, and open to interpretation as the ones that dripped from Lao-tzu's pen more than twenty-five hundred years ago.

It was, then, not quite so simply a matter of finding other philosophical, psychological, and scientific theories that resonated with those metaphors. The final step was setting down the words you see here, the act of compressing nonlinear intuitive and somatic experience into the linear thoughts we have come to value so highly, the style of processing and communicating information most people consider the most advanced form of intelligence on earth. It is in many ways similar to translating a multileveled, nuance-infused language like Chinese or Aramaic into English — only worse. Like the proverbial finger pointing to the moon, my only hope is that the following discussion will give those who work and play with horses a sense of direction in experiencing this unique perspective for themselves.

Researchers are trained to value objectivity. Scientists are not supposed to get involved with their subjects or be moved by them. Some people will undoubtedly dismiss anything new I have to say about horses when I admit that my theories are based on actually feeling something, anything, in their presence. Our culture denies the wisdom of the body and the senses, deifying the mind in a vacuum, training us to stand in production lines or sit in cubicles at computers and sublimate our physical and emotional needs in service to the cold, objective logic of consumerism and competition.

No wonder increasing numbers of people get their thrills vicariously, through films, romance novels, and social media, where their words and fantasies act as safe, sterile surrogates for the risks and rewards of actual human contact. We are afraid to feel as adults because we were repeatedly discouraged from feeling as children and thus never learned how to manage our emotions. Our notions of human authority usually involve repressing authentic emotions in favor of those deemed socially acceptable — until the pressure builds, and true feelings explode all over the place. We commonly use food, alcohol, drugs, and electronic devices to medicate those unruly sensations into submission. In this way, people manage to put off the day of reckoning — and then blame the inevitable breakdown on addiction rather than on the deeply buried emotional messages underlying it.

One of our culture's most powerful and damaging myths is that the universe and every creature in it work according to predictable mechanical laws. The resulting overemphasis on scientific validation leads to a certain ineptitude in the ephemeral realms of emotion, imagination, and intuition. If a phenomenon can't be consistently and predictably measured or re-created in experiments, its existence is often denied. Anthropomorphism has become a deadly sin, not only in science but in society at large. We can hardly even anthropomorphize ourselves without threatening the system, for acknowledging the mercurial moods of body and soul challenges the very idea of clocking in from nine to five and churning out strategies, slogans, contracts, cogs, and widgets like robots programmed for one single purpose. Since the dawn of the industrial revolution, our society has promoted *mechanomorphism*, the inclination to see all living beings as machines. From the time of Descartes, much scientific inquiry has promoted describing everything from the body to the consciousness seemingly generated within it as mechanical phenomena.

In some circles, I've been accused of anthropomorphism, sentimentality, or just plain ignorance the moment I propose that riders and trainers cannot be truly effective without understanding how horses experience fear and anger, let alone sadness, depression, joy, and love. The head trainer at Wolverton's breeding farm, where I apprenticed, was a woman well versed in the classical arts of dressage and jumping, yet she and I once got into a heated argument over whether or not horses have emotions. "It's all instinct," she insisted, "purely a survival mechanism." She isn't the only experienced equestrian who holds fast to the notion that horses are biological machines incapable of genuine thought or feeling. This is socially conditioned pseudo-science talking, myths that feed the human ego and justify all manner of neglect and abuse. A mechanism, after all, has no soul and hence no say in how it's used.

"The Cambridge Declaration on Consciousness" set the record straight in 2012, proving that other species do in fact experience emotions and intentional behaviors. Yet change in the equestrian field and in animal husbandry is slow. Accepting that animals can think, feel, and make decisions is difficult for people who benefit from treating living beings as possessions, commodities, and vehicles for ego gratification. Still, it's important to remember that even close domesticated companions like dogs and cats do not always share our perspectives or priorities. I'm grateful that they often don't, especially in the case of highly social, nonpredatory animals like horses who offer alternative approaches to power, collaboration, and freedom through relationship, lessons that lead receptive human beings to greater connection, compassion, and well-being.

In this respect, the term *anthropomorphism* is still useful as a cautionary concept. It's important that we avoid indiscriminately ascribing human motivations to other species. We don't assume that people in different cultures handle and interpret life's challenges in the same way or even that all residents of a small town share the same values.

Life is far more nuanced than we'd like to believe. My trainer's assertion that emotionally motivated behaviors in horses are "just instinct," and therefore evidence of lack of deep feeling and intelligence, was flawed in its conclusions, for sure, but not completely inaccurate. As Webster's defines it, *instinct* is not necessarily the opposite of feeling at all:

1: a natural or inherent aptitude, impulse, or capacity

2 a: a largely inheritable and unalterable tendency by an organism to make a complex and specific response to environmental stimuli without involving reason and for the purpose of removing somatic tension

2 b: behavior that is mediated by reactions below the conscious level

It's obvious that emotion has remained a primarily instinctual phenomenon in humans as well. Most people deny and sublimate their feelings, keeping them well below the conscious level until the somatic tension becomes so overpowering that the emotion overrides reason and finally expresses itself, often in violent and self-destructive ways.

In his book *The Archetypes and the Collective Unconscious*, Carl Jung cites water as the most common symbol for the unconscious. That water is also frequently associated with emotion in countless mythologies worldwide points to the fact that feeling has been recognized as a less-than-conscious phenomenon in human beings for eons. To the conscious mind, which Jung characterizes as "an affair of the cerebrum, which sees everything separately and in isolation," feelings drag us down into an instinctual realm that, in our hubris, we believe is beneath us. The conscious mind knows spirit "only as something to be found in the heights. 'Spirit' always seems to come from above, while from below comes everything that is sordid and worthless." Yet the clinical experiences described by Jung, Freud, and just about every other significant analyst of the twentieth century have shown this obsession with all that is light and airy to be a form of escapism, "a refuge for all those timorous souls who do not want to become anything different." The field of psychotherapy as a whole recognizes that a descent into the depths of emotion, as well as into the personal and the collective unconscious, always precedes the ascent into greater consciousness, transcendence, and lasting change. My experiences roaming through the mindscapes of silent knowledge taught me that water is a metaphor for psychological processes that are capable of reflecting the vast nonlinear perceptions of all those things good and bad, creative and destructive, that have not yet become conscious.

Jung aptly describes the implications of this aquatic wisdom as it relates to the soul's journey:

> Whoever looks into the mirror of the water will see first of all his own face. The mirror does not flatter, it faithfully shows whatever looks into it; namely the face we never show to the world because we cover it with the persona, the mask of the actor. But the mirror lies behind the mask and shows the true face. This confrontation is the first test of courage on the inner way, a test sufficient to frighten off most people, for the meeting with ourselves belongs to the more unpleasant things that can be avoided so long as we can project everything negative into the environment. But if we are able to see our own shadow and can bear knowing about it, then a small part of the problem has already been solved.

Every horse I have ever known acted as a reflecting pool for me. From the moment I laid eyes on Nakia, I felt intimately connected to her, as if we were resonating with the same unspoken truth, though I wasn't prepared for the message behind our affinity. Somehow, this regal thoroughbred mare was able to mirror a host of unresolved issues, suppressed emotions, and unconscious attitudes I had not fully exorcised.

Though Nakia and I both refused to submit completely to the soul-demoralizing repression we had experienced, we were still influenced by the hidden scars of abuse, psychological wounds that revealed themselves in behavioral quirks and self-destructive outbursts challenging a system we felt powerless to change. She was held captive by a species that saw her as a possession, a beast of burden, a biological machine that loses its value if broken. Raised in a culture that emphasized predatory behavior and forceful, coercive methods for maintaining power over others, I was held captive by my inability to imagine a more effective way of being. I had been the victim of a man's efforts to control me through intimidation and criticism. Yet when sweet talk and bribery failed with Nakia, I had no idea how to gain her cooperation without force and restraint.

Nakia and I both wanted things to be different, but our best intentions were stifled by the tyrannies of old habits. Tabula Rasa was to be my fresh start, my clean slate, an innocent filly with no baggage or past trauma to muddy our relationship. It didn't take her long, however, to illustrate how profoundly handicapped I was in the world, not only in my sensory awareness but in how I remained blind to her true nature long after I thought I had evolved. Even with the painful insights Nakia provided, I continued to see Rasa through the haze of human conditioning that told me horses were lower life-forms, intellectual and emotional children in relation to their two-legged benefactors. In the beginning, I was able to understand her only superficially.

Still, Rasa's response to my human mindset carried no judgment. In its supreme equanimity, the lake behind the black horse's eyes contained the healing waters of transformation, its fluid vision embracing flowers blooming, vultures preening, and my own jagged, self-indulgent thought processes. The spring-fed pond simply reflected what *was*, providing me with an oasis of clarity and peace in which to expand my awareness. The millisecond my behavior began to change, the reflection portrayed the more sensitive, empathic, creative person I was becoming, with no attachment to the past or projection into the future on her part. Entering the rarefied reality my horse shared with me was like finding a watering hole in the desert.

Sympathetic Vibrations

Summer in Tucson is stressful. When the sun speaks in tongues and chases the clouds away for months, ocotillos shed their leaves, dry grasses become a fire hazard, and even the cacti have been known to shrivel. Two-legged and four-legged creatures alike rejoice when the sun sets. In such an extreme environment, light as a metaphor for consciousness takes on a whole new meaning. Desert dwellers survive by following the constant instinctual mantra to "head toward the dark," and they spend a good six months out of the year leaping from shadow to shadow, limiting their daily feeding migrations and social activities to shaded paths.

Long before I moved to Tucson, I was vaguely uncomfortable with across-the-board references to light as good and dark as evil. Such metaphors seemed not only simplistic but deceptive. After I spent a summer in the desert, I knew exactly why these clichés distressed me. Light without shadow, day without night, sun without rain — according to the laws of nature, these one-sided conditions are all deadly. In the inner life of human beings, the metaphors behind these images also apply. Western civilization's preference for reason over emotion, mind over heart, consciousness over unconscious insights have all led to some of the worst atrocities in human history, not to mention much unnecessary daily suffering. As psychologist and philosopher Thomas Moore eloquently observed, "Logos without Eros becomes sadistic."

We have created a culture in which the nourishing, life-giving waters of emotion, empathy, sensory awareness, gut feelings, and other forms of nonverbal awareness have dried up in the heat of our obsessive reliance on all that is light and logical and conscious enough to be mapped, explained, and controlled. I was a desert dweller in more ways than one before I gazed into the lake behind the black horse's eyes.

When I wrote the metaphorical passage I quoted earlier in this chapter, it was by no means an intellectual exercise. Those two paragraphs, and others like them, were spontaneous eruptions from my own subconscious, trying to express what I was learning in the realm of silent knowledge. Such insights could not pass directly from the nonverbal to the logical. The bridge between the two was made of metaphor, myth, and symbol — as it has always been, long before storytellers were able to record their tales in writing.

Rasa and I merged and exchanged information at the level of water in a multitude of ways. Across species lines, it could be no other way. As Jung observed, "Water is the fluid of the instinct-driven body, blood and the flowing of blood, the odour of the beast, carnality heavy with passion. The unconscious is the psyche that reaches down from the daylight of the mentally and morally lucid consciousness into the nervous system that for ages has been known as 'sympathetic.'" Here, Jung's choice of the multifaceted word *sympathetic* perfectly portrays my nonverbal experiences with Rasa and the other horses.

Webster's first definition of the word describes something that operates "through an affinity, interdependence, or mutual association." When the black horse and I were traveling through the desert, she carrying food, water, and sometimes my body for me, and by my tacking her up and later opening the packages that contained her lunch, we strengthened the feelings of affinity and interdependence we already shared through a long-standing association. That we were engaged in this activity for our mutual enjoyment reinforces Webster's second use of the word:

> a: not discordant or antagonistic
> b: appropriate to one's mood, inclinations, or disposition
> c: marked by kindly or pleased appreciation

The third and fourth senses of this word characterize the understanding created between us through "compassion, friendliness, and sensitivity to another's emotions" as well as through the innate sense of "approval" we expressed for each other at the most basic level. I now consider the once-tragic appearance of Rasa's lameness as a blessing because it allowed me to see her in a whole new way. Sentenced to walk beside her, I amused myself by getting to know this mare outside the context of conventional equestrian pursuits; I couldn't possibly seduce or abuse her into fulfilling my goals or accepting my point of view.

Interestingly enough, the three remaining definitions of *sympathetic* help explain the more mysterious aspects of our exchange. Number 5, "showing empathy," which Webster's describes as "the capacity for participation in another's feelings or ideas," was certainly at work the day I shared her perspective. Had I not been participating in Rasa's decidedly nonhuman point of view, I never would have seen my hands as hooves that evolved to compensate for my short neck and even shorter nose. But how do I explain this phenomenon without referring to an overactive imagination or the vague and mysterious concept of telepathy? Well, Webster's provides us with the clincher:

6 a: of or relating to the sympathetic nervous system
6 b: mediated by or acting on the sympathetic nerves
7: relating to musical tones produced by sympathetic vibration
or to strings so tuned as to sound by sympathetic vibration

As a viola major in college, I was fascinated by an obscure seventeenth-century instrument known as the viola d'amore, the "viola of love." More complex than its orchestral relative, the viola d'amore not only had strings on top of the fingerboard that players stroked with a bow or plucked with the fingers, it also possessed more delicate strings stretched underneath the fingerboard where the bow and fingers couldn't reach. In this way, the viola d'amore produced a most haunting celestial sound through the phenomenon of resonance.

Every time the performer played a tone coinciding with the tuning of one of the sympathetic strings underneath, that string would also vibrate, producing its own ghostly sound in response. In other words, if the violist put his or her finger and bow in the right position to play middle C, the sympathetic string tuned to C below the fingerboard would resonate as well. Back in the 1600s, when the instrument was invented, this creative use of resonance was seen as a metaphor for love: one system set in motion by the vibrations of another; two things, people, or strings, trembling alike in response to each other.

As I extended myself beyond human thought and behavior to attune with Rasa and the other horses, I began to recognize a parallel to this phenomenon in myself, and I almost always first experienced it at the level of the sympathetic nervous system and its related enteric and parasympathetic nervous systems. Conventional science holds that the sympathetic nervous system activates functions related to movement and alertness. In emergencies, it initiates the flight-or-fight response by conveying nerve impulses from the deep brain outward to body organs and tissues, causing the skin to sweat or develop gooseflesh, the eyes to dilate, the heart to beat faster, blood pressure to rise, the stomach to stop working, and the glands to pump hormones like adrenaline into the bloodstream, resulting in all the familiar symptoms of stress: shaking, sweating, pale skin, dizziness, nausea, light-headedness, shallow breathing, et cetera.

Working in close association with the sympathetic nervous system is the enteric nervous system, the network of nerves surrounding the esophagus, stomach, and intestines. In response to a perceived threat, the enteric nervous system engages a number of emergency measures, including releasing histamines and other chemicals to trigger inflammation in the small intestine. This attracts immune cells from the bloodstream to prepare for physical trauma. With the digestive tract full of bacteria, a knife to the gut is serious business. If the small intestine can arm itself with immune cells before the cutting blow is struck, the body has a better chance of surviving. This is certainly important for prey animals. One ancestral function of the enteric nervous system was to protect eohippus, the primordial horse, against infection resulting from the bite of a hungry saber-toothed tiger.

The parasympathetic nervous system, on the other hand, cues the body's rest and digest function after the threat has passed, decreasing heart rate and blood pressure, secreting gastric juices, constricting the pupils, and returning the small intestine to a state of equilibrium. The sympathetic, enteric, and parasympathetic nervous systems make up what's known as the autonomic nervous system (named for its ability to work automatically, or seemingly without conscious intervention), as opposed to the central nervous system, which includes the brain and the spinal cord and is thought to be more under the control of conscious intention. All these systems are of course interconnected, exchanging information back and forth, but the brain has traditionally been given credit for overseeing the entire process.

I find at least two problems with this standard description. First of all, it depicts the brain as the king of the body, or the master computer that controls all so-called lower functions. Second, it portrays the sympathetic nervous system purely as a self-preserving mechanism activated during times of crisis. In my experience, this perspective is too limited; it ignores all kinds of possibilities that arise when someone moves into the much more creative and expansive mode of thriving rather than simply surviving.

Let's face it, if a person is always scrounging around for food, fighting off packs of rabid wolves, or toiling away at two dead-end jobs just to make ends meet, he or she is much less likely to write a novel or compose a symphony. No scientist has ever been able to explain away the artistic impulse as a survival instinct, although it has been fashionable for much of the last century to describe every other biological and psychological process as something that helps an organism live long enough to propagate the species. The human imagination has helped people get out of some sticky situations and improve their lot in life, but it's only when creativity is released from worrying about survival that it reaches the level of art.

If Steve and I had chosen to have children, I wouldn't have had the money or the motivation to support a growing herd of horses, let alone spend so much time in their silent world and write a book about it. As an introspective, low-energy person, I recognized early on that I didn't have the constitution to be a Supermom, so I decided to override my motherly instincts and focus on writing. In Darwinian terms, I'm pretty worthless. In equestrian terms, Rasa is equally worthless. Our relationship is completely irrational; it makes sense only when you move out of the brain and into the heart.

By virtue of her injury and my desire to be with her regardless of what we could or could not accomplish, we were propelled into the realm of pure experience. I was no longer using my body, my brain, and my senses to survive or achieve; rather, I was using them to connect with and enjoy another being. In this context, my body, my brain, and my senses began to switch gears and show me what else they were capable of: namely, resonating with instead of reacting to stimuli. Here's where the sympathetic nervous system truly lives up to its name.

Gut Feelings

I'm milling around with my herd on a large pasture. Rasa wanders over and touches her nose to her belly, a signal that she wants me to scratch this hard-to-reach area. As I reach underneath her, she returns the favor by simultaneously rubbing my back with her lips. Rasa has just initiated the mutual grooming act, one of the most powerful bonding rituals in equine society. If I scratch her as fast and aggressively as her thick hide can handle, however, she will match my rhythm and pressure, leaving bruises on my fragile skin. So I ease the pace and refrain from using my nails, thus cueing her to give me a nice, hearty, toothless massage. After a few minutes of this vigorous interaction, we stand together and bask in each other's company. A hot desert wind blows softly through her mane and my own. My breathing slows down naturally to a rate that I've had trouble reaching through meditation. My heart expands with an indescribable warmth, as if a large and exquisite flower were blooming inside my chest. I've felt this before with human beings, and I've always called it love, only with Rasa it's mixed with a profound sense of tranquility rather than the fluttering of excitement or danger I've experienced with romance.

Noche is grazing in the distance. Suddenly, his head shoots up, and his ears prick forward. A split second before Rasa responds in the same manner, I feel like I've been kicked in the stomach. The hair on the back of my neck stands on end; I'm gulping quick, shallow breaths, and I'm poised to take off in any direction. Neither Rasa nor I can see what made Noche sound this silent alarm, but the waves of fear coming from his body affect our nervous systems well before he can actually turn and run toward us.

By this time, my skeptical higher brain has decided to take over. After all, what could possibly go wrong on such a beautiful October afternoon in this quiet rural neighborhood? I walk confidently toward the place where Noche initially spooked, both horses now snorting and trotting around in circles at a safe distance behind me. It turns out all this upheaval was caused by a man on a mountain bike. He does look sinister with his black spandex shorts, fluorescent blue riding shirt, mirrored sunglasses, and helmet shaped like the skull of the creature from *Alien*. He's also moving very fast, stirring up a cloud of dust, yet there are no footsteps to match his speed, just a constant, low whirring that would seem grossly unnatural to a horse. I can't help but laugh as I wave at the two-legged devil. Yet before I can turn around and reassure my horses that everything's fine, they're already standing just slightly behind me, considering his strange habits with a newfound sense of confidence they've obviously borrowed from me. As the man passes by, however, they dance in place a bit, and I know they're ready to make a beeline for the opposite end of the pasture if the creature suddenly leaves the trail and heads our way.

A few minutes later, I hear someone call my name and see the vague shape of a fellow boarder waving and walking toward us. She's smiling, shouting praises for this beautiful fall weather we're enjoying. Before she gets close enough to speak to me in a normal tone of voice, my stomach begins to constrict, my heart feels like it's made of cement, and I sense chaos all around her. Noche is already trotting away from this woman, despite the fact that he has been known to let her catch him and saddle him up for a ride.

"How are you?" I ask.

"Just fine," she says.

"No," I reply gently, "how are you really?"

"Well, my husband didn't come home last night," she admits as she bursts into tears.

Many of the sensations I just described would be characterized as *clairsentience*, the ability of entity A to feel what entity B is experiencing as if it were happening in A's own body. Like clairvoyance and clairaudience, this is widely considered a supernatural gift unavailable to the average person — if we're even willing to admit the possibility of its existence in the first place. My experiences with the horses, however, suggest it occurs naturally in all organic beings, an ancient yet highly refined sense the human race has suppressed through social controls that downplay somatic experience. Clairsentience is not a psychic phenomenon, not an example of mind over matter. It is more accurately achieved by fully accessing the mind *under* matter, those aspects of awareness directly connected to the body that are normally kept subconscious or unconscious.

My brain didn't initiate the flight-or-fight pose I suddenly took when Noche became startled, sending the directive down my spinal cord and into the sympathetic nervous system. In fact, if I had just stepped out of the car, there's very little chance I would have been affected by his fear, at least not viscerally. The hour I spent wandering around the pasture, bonding with all the horses, grooming Rasa, and being drawn into the expansive, meditative state that comes naturally to these animals essentially tuned my system to the equus frequency. When Noche spooked, I literally felt a shock wave in the abdomen, which set off a chain reaction of physical responses. I was aware of this sensation the moment it hit. The sudden constriction of the stomach, the quickening of the heartbeat, the urge to flee were already in motion as I felt the information move up my body and ignite a thought process that finally questioned the severity of the situation, allowing me to walk over to the disturbance rather than run from it. The calm amusement I inadvertently broadcasted to the horses when I waved at the biker was transmitted to them with equal efficiency, causing them to modify their behavior before I had time to turn around and consciously convey that everything was all right.

Interestingly enough, science has recently recognized the enteric nervous system as a complex, integrative brain in its own right. Within the yards of tubing that make up the large and small intestine lies a complex web of microcircuitry driven by more neurotransmitters and neuromodulators than can be found anywhere else in the peripheral nervous system. These allow the bowels to perform many tasks without central nervous system control. Cut the spinal cord in the right place, and a person is paralyzed from the neck down — except for the enteric nervous system, which continues not only to function but to learn and make decisions on its own, modifying its behavior in response to its environment. The sympathetic and parasympathetic nervous systems must also be able to operate independently to a certain extent; otherwise a quadriplegic's heart wouldn't continue to pump blood through the body. The heart actually has its own minibrain of about forty thousand neural cells. Evidence that this organ stores memories has been growing, especially in light of transplant patients who suddenly find they have the same food cravings as their donors, not to mention dreams that reveal the deceased person's name and physical appearance even when his or her identity was kept from the recipient.

Still, as amazing as our own individual bodies prove to be, my encounters with horses revealed that emotions and sensations are contagious — for good reason, as I later found out. I'm pleased to be able to share some of this newer research throughout this revised edition of *The Tao of Equus*. For a long time, though, incidents like the shot of fear I received from Noche were very mysterious to me. The horse silently jump-started my flight-or-fight response at a distance, seconds before I saw him turn and run. Over time, I realized that this invisible somatic form of communication is the birthright of all sentient beings. But how is it even possible?

Wireless Communication

Several recently discovered biological processes offer a deeper understanding of the technology of connection, you might say. Like other forms of technology, you don't have to know how it all works to use it in daily life. Take wireless communication. I can't begin to explain how my cell phone works, but I've come to rely on this mini–handheld computer for all kinds of daily interactions with people from around the world.

Wireless communication is an ancient concept, as it turns out. All living beings have the capacity to send visible and invisible messages to each other. What's more, horses, humans, dogs, cats, and other mammals are literally designed to nonverbally influence the nervous systems of others. So, yes, fear is contagious, as I learned from Noche, but so are feelings of peace and safety. And positive feelings are even more important because they actually regulate the nervous systems of self and others to achieve greater psychological and *physiological* health.

We are designed to help one another, not just to survive, but to feel safe, welcomed, and good. According to the psychologist and neuroscientist Stephen Porges, an innovation in the nervous systems of mammals allows them to modulate feelings of safety and danger through social connection. Starting in 1994, he wrote a number of books and papers on what he calls the *polyvagal theory*. Porges contends that in all mammals, "the neural pathways of social support and social behavior are shared with the neural pathways that support health, growth, and restoration."

His research suggests that our nervous systems are designed to *connect with others* in order to work at an optimal level. Let me emphasize this again. This is not just psychological. Physiologically, when we feel disconnected, the health of our hearts, our brains, and other systems are seriously compromised. Our capacity to heal, let alone attain higher levels of wellness, depends on forging safe and meaningful connections with others.

Porges contends that while reptiles have a *dorsal vagus nerve* that activates the parasympathetic rest and digest function, mammals also possess an innovation known as the *ventral vagus nerve complex*, which, according to author, mind-body researcher, and physiologist Ann Baldwin "rapidly regulates cardiac output to foster engagement, and recruits cranial nerves to facilitate facial expressions and vocalizations required for social behaviors." Her book *The Vagus Nerve in Therapeutic Practice: Working with Clients to Manage Stress and Enhance Mind-Body Function* offers extensive, reasonably easy-to-understand information on how the vagus nerve functions. She also outlines specific techniques for helping people access this powerful aspect of the parasympathetic nervous system in times of stress. Baldwin, who is herself an experienced rider, explains her original peer-reviewed research on equine-assisted therapy, including a number of compelling case studies on how horses help people heal, in part through activating the ventral vagus nerve complex. She and I have done some compelling studies on how certain horse activities help leaders become more effective by teaching them to consciously train their own nervous systems to positively affect others. The results of this research were published for the first time in her book. (See pages 195 to 202 in her book for an in-depth description of the multileveled research project we undertook over several years.)

Because all mammals have the same polyvagal nervous system, those of us who feel unsafe around humans can reap many of the same benefits from interacting with other mammals, because they're also designed to seek safety, regulate stress, heal, and thrive through social connection. This is why animal-assisted therapy can be so effective, especially for people who've been traumatized by aggressive members of our own species. If you don't trust humans, you can get these psychological and physiological health benefits from interacting with other species who are willing, and *able*, to connect. Horses take it one step further. Because they are not predators, they have a way of supporting us and empowering us to relate to the world from a strong, centered, supportive *nonpredatory* perspective.

Though there are some skeptics still out there, the polyvagal theory has been gaining respect in recent years, and not just among scientists. This theory is widely embraced among counselors, healers, and teachers who realized, through their own experience and observations over the years, that people truly need to feel connected and supported in life to excel.

Porges's work was introduced to me in 2016 by one of my close colleagues, Dr. Rebecca Bailey. She's a nationally recognized psychologist known for working effectively with trauma survivors, most notably Jaycee Dugard, who was rescued eighteen years after a high-profile kidnapping. Since equine-facilitated therapy was an important part of her healing, I highly recommend Jaycee's books on recovering from this ordeal. I also recommend Rebecca's book *Equine Connections: Polyvagal Principles* for a deeper understanding of how the polyvagal theory explains the effectiveness of this work. I quickly realized that this same theory also offers insight into the dynamics of horse intelligence and the powerful ways these animals interact with people. In later chapters, I'll show how Porges's work sheds light on the talents of gifted horse trainers.

But first, let's look at some earlier research. I'll start with what's visible, and then we'll get into some fascinating studies that show us how humans and animals can affect each other physiologically, even when there is no visible change in behavior or expression. All of these studies have one thing in common: they underline the fact that we are hardwired to share experience. And that's a good part of the reason why emotions are contagious. We even have special neural cells that make sensations and emotions more contagious than the common cold.

The Physiology of Empathy

In the 1980s, Italian neuroscientists were studying the effects of movement on the brain when they stumbled upon a strange and unexpected feature of the mammalian nervous system, one that quickly led to all kinds of research into the physiology of empathy. Researchers at the University of Parma placed electrodes in the brain of a macaque, a species of monkey. They were hoping to figure out which neurons were activated by hand and mouth actions. At one point, they isolated a particular cell that fired only when the monkey lifted his arm. Apparently they did this over and over again just to make sure, as scientists are prone to do, but I would have loved to have seen the looks on their faces when one of their lab assistants lifted an ice cream cone to his own mouth during one of those sessions, and that triggered a reaction in the monkey's cell associated with hand and mouth movement.

Subsequent studies suggested that our brains are peppered with tiny *mirror neurons*. These mimic what another being does in our brains, helping us to detect someone else's emotions and intentions through his or her actions. In a 2008 *Harvard Business Review* article, Daniel Goleman and Richard Boyatzis summarized the implications of mirror neurons for people: "Mirror neurons have particular importance in organizations because leaders' emotions and actions prompt followers to mirror those feelings and deeds. The effects of activating neural circuitry in followers' brains can be very powerful." Then they cite an intriguing study. Researcher Marie Dasborough observed the effects of two management approaches. The first group of employees received negative performance feedback, but these critical comments were supported by positive emotional signals — lots of smiles and nods. The other group experienced positive feedback, but the compliments were couched in negative body language — frowns and narrowed eyes.

Interestingly, those who emerged from the good-natured *negative* feedback sessions felt more optimistic than those who received praise from cranky supervisors. "In effect, the delivery was more important than the message itself. And everybody knows that when people feel better, they perform better. So if leaders hope to get the best out of their people, they should continue to be demanding, but in ways that foster a positive mood in their teams. The old carrot and stick approach alone doesn't make neural sense."

Turns out that, like horses, who are keenly aware of nonverbal cues, people respond to the emotional atmosphere behind our words more profoundly than they do to the actual content and meaning. But vocal tone, body language, and mirror neurons are just the tip of the iceberg. Research into the human-horse relationship continues to uncover even more subtle interpersonal dynamics. Nobody really understands the mechanism yet, but it seems that horses and riders don't have to see any evidence of movement in gesture to affect each other physiologically. This might seem obvious when you're riding a horse. You can feel what's going on in his body, and he can feel what's going on in yours, but emotions and sensations are contagious, even when you appear to be walking calmly beside each other. This is where we head into the invisible aspects of communication.

A 2009 article published in the *Veterinary Journal* reported on the phenomenon of emotional contagion. Researchers from the Swedish University of Agricultural Sciences performed a simple experiment designed to study the effect of nervous handlers on the heart rates of their horses. Twenty-seven horses of various breeds and ages were led or ridden at a walk by thirty-seven amateur equestrians. Both species were wearing heart rate monitors. Each team traveled a thirty-meter distance between two cones a total of four times. Just before the final pass, each person was told that an assistant who had been standing next to the path the whole time would open an umbrella as the horse went by. Now, as someone who's worked with a number of flighty horses over the years, my own heart skipped a beat just reading about this minor institutionalized threat. Right now, I actually cringe imagining the sound an umbrella makes when it flies open, especially when I visualize this happening five feet away from some of the feisty stallions I've encountered. And the effect of imagination, interestingly enough, is what the researchers were ultimately measuring.

Those scientific pranksters didn't even open the umbrella, as I'm sure any equine liability insurance company would be relieved to know. Even so, the heart rates of both humans and horses rose significantly as they passed the

now suspect lab assistant. If mirror neurons were involved in these physiological responses, they were bouncing off a projection screen in the heads of
the handlers. Even more remarkably, the researchers observed no behavioral
differences in either the horse or the handler when the animal was being led.
Riders tended to shorten their reins after the dreaded news was conveyed,
but especially in the case of people leading their horses, the mere human
thought of the umbrella's spooking power was enough to raise the arousal of
the horse, who I'm pretty sure would not have understood the experimenter's
warning in Swedish — or any other language, for that matter.

Let's not mince words here. What we're talking about is something that
many people would describe as telepathy. I like to use the term *wireless communication*, because we now have technology that allows computers to communicate through invisible connections. There's the internet, of course, and
cellular technology, but I think that AirDrop helps our logical minds to embrace the possibility that two beings in the same room can easily send information back and forth beyond the realm of spoken words, sound, and visible
body language. I use AirDrop every time I send videos and photos from my
phone to my computer. I don't need cables; I don't need the internet — just
a direct, invisible, silent transfer of information that's very fast and efficient.
I don't know how AirDrop works, but I use it constantly.

So I also recognize that I have the ability to use my body as a tuner, receiver, and amplifier for sensing feelings and intentions coming from others,
a kind of organic AirDrop effect. Because humans are taught to dissociate
from the environment and their own bodies, we tend to downplay rather
than develop this ability, but the information still manages to leak through
in the form of gut feelings and other kinds of intuition. Culturally conditioned minds seem to work overtime to discount insights that bypass rational thought, but neuroscience tells us that logic is slow. The brain itself has
the ability to gather and process somatic impressions (information coming
from the body) with the split-second accuracy of a computer calculating a
complex spreadsheet.

Logic is very useful at times, but it moves like a snail on quaaludes compared with the warp speed conclusions that are coordinated by *spindle cells*.
Four times larger than most brain cells, this special class of neuron has an
extra-long branch allowing it to attach to other cells more easily. Spindle
cells transmit environmental impressions, memories, thoughts, and feelings
at hyperspeed. Goleman and Boyatzis emphasize that

this ultra rapid connection of emotions, beliefs, and judgements creates what behavioral scientists call our social guidance system. Spindle cells trigger neural networks that come into play whenever we have to choose the best response among many, even for a task as routine as prioritizing a to-do list. These cells also help us gauge whether someone is trustworthy and right or wrong for a job. Within one 20th of a second, our spindle cells fire with information about how we feel about that person. Such thin sliced judgements can be very accurate as follow up metrics reveal. Therefore, leaders should not fear to act on those judgements, provided that they are also attuned to other moods.

And, I must emphasize here, provided that these leaders are also aware of their own projections and prejudices.

It works both ways, of course. Spindle cells, mirror neurons, and horse heart rate responses to threats imagined by humans add to growing scientific evidence that everyone, from your employees to your kids, your spouse, your mother-in-law, and your dog, is designed to read your mind to a certain extent. Kind of levels the playing field, doesn't it?

Here's an even more intriguing — or disturbing — bit of news, depending on whether or not you like to hide your emotions and intentions from others. In *Social Intelligence: The New Science of Human Relationships*, Goleman cites studies showing that not only does a person's blood pressure rise when he tries to suppress feeling, but the blood pressure of those interacting with him also rises. Lie detectors measure arousal fluctuations, but it turns out you don't have to be hooked up to a machine to reveal a hidden state of mind or to sense suppressed emotions in someone else. Living beings are actually hardwired to transmit and receive this information at a distance.

Of course, our human emphasis on verbal communication lessens awareness of this kind of valuable information over time. But anyone who retains or reclaims use of this natural ability can appear downright psychic compared to the rest of the population. As animals who are preyed upon in nature, horses have the volume of this little understood sixth sense turned way up. They become noticeably agitated in the presence of people who are *incongruent*, who try to cover anger, fear, or sadness with an appearance of well-being. This is not an equine judgment of our tendency to lie about what we're really feeling. It's just a reflection of emotion's physiology and of its contagious nature. Over the years, I saw that horses often mirrored the precise emotion being suppressed in the person they were interacting with. Then they would calm down the moment this person openly acknowledged that feeling — even if the emotion was still there. Let me say it again. The emotion doesn't have to change in order for the horse to show some signs of relaxation. Why is that? By making the fear or anger conscious, by becoming congruent, the person effectively lowers his own blood pressure. Even if only slightly, it's enough to drop the horse's blood pressure in response, which the animal will demonstrate by sighing, licking, and chewing, sometimes lowering his head as well.

One of the most dramatic examples I ever witnessed of this occurred during a 2002 session I facilitated with a woman who had been raped. Her therapist had recommended that she do some equine-facilitated learning sessions to gain a sense of empowerment in moving forward with her life. "Carrie" entered the corral with a very kind and peaceful horse named Sam. Reaching out to him, she began to cry. Sam stood there for a moment. Then he tossed his head defiantly and walked away with a bit of an attitude.

You can imagine how Carrie felt. "Everyone in my life is tired of my tears," she told me, "like it's time for me to just get over this terrible fear and sadness and get on with my life. But I just can't."

I was surprised by Sam's behavior myself. Then I remembered how often my horses would act out the hidden emotions of people they were interacting with, including me. "You know," I said, "I don't think Sam is rejecting you for feeling sad or afraid. Experience tells me there must be another, stronger emotion underneath those tears, an emotion that you aren't acknowledging. From the way Sam acted, what emotion do you think he might have been conveying?"

"Well," she said, "he seemed kind of mad at me."

"Yes, it did seem that way. But what if he wasn't mad at you? What if he was sensing something in you?"

I asked Carrie a series of questions that would help her connect with an emotion underneath the tears, an emotion other than sadness or fear or feeling the victim. She began pounding her fist on the nearest fence post and talking about how angry she was. This man had not only violated her but had turned her entire life upside down. He had taken away her trust in other people, in herself, and in life. Since anger most often signals a boundary violation, this emotion was a part of her body's legitimate reaction to being raped. But Carrie, like so many of us, had grown up being told that nice girls don't feel anger.

It might have been very upsetting for her to access this emotion in any other context, I realized afterward, but Sam did something that made it all OK. As Carrie was pounding the fence post, Sam suddenly turned around, walked over to her, and wrapped his head and neck around her, like he was giving her a big, supportive hug. Sam wasn't afraid of her anger because it wasn't being directed at him. He stood with her as she accessed this feeling. Sam was essentially telling Carrie that he felt closer to her when she became congruent, when she acknowledged an emotion she had been hiding even from herself. It was a stunning moment of healing that I don't think any human could have provided in quite the same way. Carrie left the corral feeling elated, deeply touched, and *heard*.

Unless you're a sociopath, your blood pressure, heart rate, and breathing intensify when you're frightened or angry, even when you're wearing your best poker face. It actually takes extra energy to hide these feelings. This adds to the anxiety radiating from your body through whatever complex process scientists are only now beginning to discover. Horses seem extra sensitive to this phenomenon. As Sam showed so dramatically, these animals can detect and act out, or simply walk away from, hidden emotions. Something operating beyond the scope of mirror neurons is at work in humans as well, or the blood pressure of someone who's suppressing emotion would not raise the blood pressure of those with whom he's interacting.

Again, it's important to remember that positive feelings are contagious too, but they have to be authentic and congruent, not a mask of a socially acceptable emotion. A person who truly feels peaceful in situations that unnerve others can have a calming effect on everyone around her. This is a key to becoming a great rider or a truly great leader. And it's very helpful at home. Parents and partners benefit from learning how to turn a tense situation around in connected, loving ways. Unfortunately, modern humans often create a highly unproductive sense of disconnection through a strange, destructive trick of the mind that affects everyone who reaches the age of reason.

Predatory Logic

I believe that one of the ways the autonomic nervous system interacts with the outside world is through *resonance*. Horses, who have much larger and more sensitive guts than humans, arguably have much larger brains in their bowels — and more resonant surfaces with which to detect nuances of information.

Consciousness as experienced by the cerebral cortex, the seat of so-called higher thought, is antiresonant. It tends to separate things and arrange them into neat categories like "good" or "bad," "right" or "wrong," "real" or "imaginary," "art" or "science," "spiritual" or "material." Once the individual or group mind forms an opinion about something, it becomes very hard to change, even if experience suggests one should. It's both discouraging and fascinating to me that musicians can specialize in the creative use of resonance and sympathetic vibration while the rest of society ignores the fact that our bodies are designed with many of the same materials and processes in place.

Before the widespread use of finely wound steel, the strings of the viola d'amore were made of catgut and stroked with a horsehair bow. Though synthetic materials are cheaper, serious students and performers still prefer horsehair. Many modern violin and viola players also prefer gut strings, which produce a richer, rounder tone, especially for the higher registers, which can sound too harsh and metallic with steel strings. Here we have a messy organic substance that resonates loudly enough to fill an entire concert hall with sound when it has been dried and cut into strings, causing the seats to vibrate and the patrons to weep in ecstasy. Meanwhile, mainstream science still thinks it's far-fetched that these same guts might function in a similar manner in the body that originally generated them — in a nervous system that was named "sympathetic" hundreds of years before people had the tools to truly analyze it.

The fact that I had to use an entire horse and not just a horsehair bow to reconnect with this vibratory wisdom shows just how difficult it is to override the influence of the intellect as it tries to claim credit for every significant process and insight the mind-body is capable of. It's almost as if human beings who reach the age of reason have to weather a hostile takeover waged by the cerebral cortex as it tries to subdue and discredit all other forms of sensual and emotional awareness.

Is logic inherently predatory? Stanford University anthropologist E. Richard Sorenson thinks so. I discovered his theories in a *Noetic Sciences Review* article by Christian de Quincey. Through decades of research and careful observation, Sorenson has developed a theory that distinguishes between two distinctly different human mindsets: "preconquest consciousness," characteristic of the minds of indigenous peoples, and "postconquest consciousness," typified by modern rationalism. Preconquest consciousness is rooted in feeling. Sorenson holds that tribal cultures are shaped by a lush sensuality where members grow up with a great deal of body-to-body contact. He observes that these people are highly sensitive to changes in breathing and muscle tension to indicate shifts in mood. Of course, I would also argue that these changes are often transmitted through resonance by the enteric, sympathetic, and parasympathetic nervous systems.

In any case, the effect is that when other tribe members feel good, the individual feels good; when others feel fear or anxiety, the individual takes on a similar affect. Sorenson calls this "sociosensual awareness," also an apt description of equine awareness. What is right or true or real is based, not on abstract concepts disconnected from the flow of life, but on what feels good in a given situation. This form of consciousness thrives on its ability to optimize feelings of well-being in the community, emphasizing "heartfelt rapprochement based on integrated trust" and an "intuitive rapport" among all the individuals in a group. Sorenson's insight coincides with Stephen Porges's descriptions of how the polyvagal nervous system operates as an innovation shared by all mammals. As I mentioned earlier in this chapter, Porges emphasizes that "the neural pathways of social support and social behavior are shared with the neural pathways that support health, growth, and restoration." In particular, the ventral vagus nerve complex, which lizards do not have, allows mammals to use their nervous systems to calm other mammals through feelings of connection and mutual support.

Postconquest consciousness, on the other hand, is confrontational, emotionally incongruent, and most certainly *disconnected*; a thesis is confronted and "conquered" by its antithesis, which is held to be right and true until it is overcome with great difficulty by a new synthesis. By its very nature, modern rationalism thrives on static ideals that promote a selective view of information removed from the flow of life. This mindset is actually threatened by authentic emotion, thus leading to the peer pressure–induced deception of self and others. Only feelings, experiences, and ideas that support the dominant thesis are considered worth expressing. Most disturbing, however, is Sorenson's observation that when postconquest reason meets preconquest feeling, the result is outright suppression of the latter — with dire consequences that have gone unchecked in our society for centuries.

Sorenson holds that postconquest consciousness automatically overshadows preconquest feeling, even if the rationalist's intent is honorable. He backs his theory with a firsthand account of how a group of Western tourists inadvertently obliterated a New Guinea tribe's entire way of life shortly after World War II. Within a week of contact, a form of consciousness based on trust, openness, empathy, and interactive rapport collapsed. Sorenson describes a "grand cultural amnesia" where a whole population forgot recent past events, customs, even what style of garment they had worn a few years earlier: "The selfless unity that seemed so firm and self-repairing in their isolated enclaves vanished like a summer breeze as a truth-based type of consciousness gave way to one that lied to live." He goes on to describe outbreaks of

> epidemic sleeplessness, frenzied dance throughout the night, reddening burned-out eyes getting narrower and more vacant as the days and nights wore on, dysphasias of various sorts, sudden mini-epidemics of spontaneous estrangement, lacunae in perceptions, hyperkinesis, loss of sensuality, collapse of love, impotence, bewildered, frantic looks.... Such was the general scene of the beach that week, a week that no imagination could have forewarned, the week in which the subtle, sociosensual glue of the island's traditional way of life became unglued.

The difficulties experienced by this tribe mirror many of the so-called evils of society with which we currently contend, gross maladaptations to modern life that no social program seems able to cure no matter how much money is thrown at the problem. According to Sorenson's theory, external changes in environment, education, and opportunity will have little effect as long as the postconquest mindset remains dominant and disconnected from feeling. Christian de Quincey, who was managing editor of *Noetic Sciences Review* when his Sorenson article was first published in that journal in 2000, contends that to heal the damage, reason and feeling must be reunited through "a transmodern spiritual or mystical intuition — a way of knowing that includes and integrates all the others."

"Reason doesn't have to decimate feeling," he writes. "It does so only when unplugged from its roots in the deep wisdom of the body. Reason is optimally effective when it retains or regains contact with its preverbal, somatic roots. Reason works very differently when we *feel* our thinking."

Many who have become disillusioned with the current state of affairs are instinctively attracted to horses. Over the years, I have found that these animals are indeed remarkably effective in helping us reach a new way of knowing, a state that integrates feeling, intuition, relationship, and preverbal body wisdom with the focus, will, inventiveness, and problem-solving abilities that are among the best qualities born from the postconquest rational mind. Because of their size and nonpredatory nature, because so much of our work with horses involves body-to-body contact, because they operate from the preconquest state of consciousness, these animals can reactivate the sociosensual mind in their human handlers and bring this long-forgotten knowledge back to the surface, where it can temper the destructive by-products of the rational mind.

Secure, well-cared-for horses can also activate the ventral vagus nerve complex in humans experiencing anxiety, helping them to feel connected and, consequently, safe. All mammals have this ability, but the horse's status as a large, powerful, *nonpredatory* being amplifies the effect. In Porges's terms, the equine nervous system can "coregulate" a "dysregulated" human. Equine-facilitated therapy practitioners can use this very natural process to help trauma survivors take advantage of the nervous system's ability to jump-start healing, restoration, and growth through the magic of connection.

Many equestrians have trouble reaching this state on their own. They get bogged down in conflicts that result from the postconquest rational mindset encountering a species that thrives on sociosensual forms of interaction. Remember, Sorenson's theory asserts that reason automatically dominates and suppresses the preconquest feeling-oriented perspective. Even so, a dedicated and emotionally present rider will sometimes stumble onto this state and find that his or her interactions with horses suddenly flow with effortless grace, but few can then describe the experience to others without sounding vague and mystical. This, in fact, is the mystery behind the seemingly supernatural abilities of the "horse whisperer."

In a mid-1990s article on Ray Hunt, one of a handful of nationally recognized horse trainers similar in style and philosophy to Monty Roberts, the interviewer describes what it was like to attend a Hunt workshop, outlines the basic concepts these guys use, and then quotes Hunt as saying that there is an indescribable "one other thing that makes it all work. And I don't know what that is." The writer says she was "glad" this "one thing couldn't be packaged and put on a menu and ordered up like some brand of beer. It was real though; and it could be known, but only in the moment."

I believe Hunt and his interviewer were referring to a complex of nonrational wisdom that the Taoists call "real knowledge" and de Quincey characterized as "a transmodern spiritual or mystical intuition." I also believe these exceptional trainers have stumbled onto the ability to activate the ventral vagal nerve complex in horses — that feature of the polyvagal system that creates feelings of safety, healing, and well-being in all mammals through social connection. But these trainers are not yet able to make this seemingly mystical, ventral vagus–based process fully conscious themselves, let alone describe it to others. One professional rider and clinician told me she feels she might jinx the magic by speaking of it or overanalyzing it. Yet in my experience, Hunt's ethereal "one thing" would like very much to be brought to widespread awareness, and to do that it must be translated into words that can at least point to what it is. It has taken me years of research into psychology, mythology, neuroscience, scientific treatises on the mechanisms of consciousness and creativity, Judeo-Christian images of humanity's fall, Taoist concepts of reality (the best vocabulary for describing the feminine forms of leadership and intuition that horses teach), and a continuous influx of strange experiences that motivated me to undertake the project in the first place. Ultimately, this is what *The Tao of Equus* is about, and the implications of my findings are relevant to all people, whether or not they've ever considered stepping into a ring with a wild horse or sitting on a tame one.

I've found that horses are supremely talented in helping us reach this integrative mindset, but it takes a respectful, partnership-oriented approach to access the wisdom they hold. World-renowned trainer and writer Dietrich von Hopffgarten tried to characterize his perception of it in *Dressage & CT* magazine when he wrote: "Only if we listen to our partner the horse...only if we try to achieve with *feel* and not force will we discover a certain degree of the secret. For me, this secret is the 'magical connection.'"

From the moment this magical connection hit me, I not only became obsessed with describing what it was, I began looking for ways to take the guesswork out of how others might achieve this life-changing state of being. The Voice of Remembering and the Horse Ancestors helped me immeasurably. During the time I sought to forge a stronger connection with their vast morphogenetic fields of influence, however, I was compelled to engage in actions that pushed the boundaries of what I considered sane, and I didn't have the theories of Sheldrake, Sorenson, de Quincey, Porges, and others like them to tell me what to expect.

As de Quincey observed in his *Noetic Sciences Review* article, "Interconnected feelings and altered states of consciousness appear to reason as magic — the undefinable domain of the shaman. Beyond reason, unities and communions of experiences and higher states of consciousness appear to reason as ineffable and noetic — the infinite domain of the mystic."

My purpose in sharing this personal journey is to communicate how frightening, perplexing, and ecstatic the reawakening of preconquest sociosensual awareness feels to someone like me who was raised in the postconquest cult of reason and how, over time, my work with the horses allowed me to integrate these two perspectives into that "magical connection," that "one other thing that makes it all work."

I'll admit I had to muster up quite a bit of courage to tell my story. I engaged in activities and thoughts that seem delusional when viewed from a logical perspective. But perhaps these strange events will also provide comfort and encouragement to those already striving to access their own powerful, yet decidedly nonrational, sources of wisdom.

As Deepak Chopra emphasized in a September 2000 *Rolling Stone* interview, "There's a thin line between psychotics and geniuses. They all tread the same razor's edge." Many times along the way, I wasn't at all sure which side of the line I was on.

Part Two

HEALING WATERS

If you have come here to help me,
you are wasting your time....
But if you have come because your liberation
is bound with mine,
then let us work together.
— Anonymous Aboriginal woman

CHAPTER FIVE

WISDOM OF THE PREY

There was a sofa in the tack room, but Rasa had little patience for clients who preferred to sit around and talk about their problems. She wanted people to feel their problems, to listen to the messages behind their feelings, and to stop thinking their true feelings were the problem. She was amenable to standing tied at the hitching post if that's what made a new student feel safe the first time he groomed her. She loved to be brushed and fussed over. Even so, she would dance sideways and begin to untie her own lead rope if the person holding the curry comb pretended to be brave, happy, relaxed, or in control when he was actually afraid, sad, angry, or unsure of the situation. The moment this person acknowledged the authentic feelings behind the façade, however, she'd sigh, lick her lips, lower her head, and stop fidgeting — even if the client was still afraid.

Rasa knew how to walk, trot, and canter around a single person standing in the center of the arena. At a moment's notice, she adapted to verbal cues, subtle nonverbal signals, even slight changes in body position and breathing. But no amount of shouting, begging, pleading, waving, stomping, crying, or snapping the whip would make her move unless the person asking was focused and making a sincere attempt to connect with her. If this person became particularly belligerent and accused the black horse of being stupid, she'd often move to the center and herd the human around in circles. Rasa was a master equine teacher and therapist.

People ask me how I trained her to be so confident and perceptive. Actually, it was more a matter of her training — and transforming — me. I simply learned how to trust Rasa's instincts and give her plenty of room to do her job. I discovered efficient ways of interpreting her insights into the constantly changing physical, mental, and emotional states of our clients. My primary responsibility involved translating this information into a language humans understood and suggesting more effective ways for them to form a true partnership with the horse. Finally, I helped people relate what they experienced in the training arena to the challenges they faced in life. To accomplish this, my mind was tuned to a frequency that rested dead center between human and equine modes of being — or, perhaps more accurately, represented a merging of them both. To this day, my effectiveness as an equine-facilitated therapy and experiential learning practitioner depends upon my ability to become a horsewoman in the most mythical sense, and the healing process accelerates when my clients become centaurs too.

While the practice of therapeutic riding for persons with disabilities emerged in the 1950s in Europe and the '60s in the US, the field of equine-facilitated psychotherapy didn't gain official recognition until the Equine Facilitated Mental Health Association (EFMHA) formed in the mid-1990s as a special section of the North American Riding for the Handicapped Association (NARHA), now known as PATH International. Therapeutic riding facilities around the country were quick to embrace the potential of horses as cofacilitators in the treatment of psychological issues, yet counselors and horse handlers still have difficulty characterizing why this modality works so well. The myriad variables and principles involved combine to create a powerful catalyst for change that's easier to experience than to describe in words.

When I tell people I specialize in equine-facilitated therapy and experiential learning, many of them assume that I correct behavior problems in horses. When I explain that it's the other way around, that I employ horses to help people explore their own emotional and behavioral issues and learn new skills to become more balanced and successful, even experienced equestrians sometimes have trouble imagining how the process works.

Like many forms of psychotherapy, with Freudians, Jungians, behaviorists, and Gestalt practitioners offering wildly different approaches to mental health, equine-based therapeutic methods can vary in significant ways, depending upon the orientation, training, creativity, and life experience of the facilitator. Adapting to the constantly changing needs and insights of the horses and humans involved requires a knowledgeable yet highly improvisatory tactic, where standard equestrian activities, educational practices, and therapeutic techniques mutually enhance and modify one another during an intricate interspecies collaboration. Before I share more theories to help explain this process, however, it's important to see how all the elements work together. This chapter provides an extended case study of how several horses in my herd helped a woman I'll call "Joy."

Since she was already seeing her own counselor, Joy enrolled in a series of private equine-facilitated learning sessions with me. In this respect, our goal was not to analyze her childhood, dwell on the past, or diagnose her in some way. We focused instead on practicing life skills, including leadership, mindfulness, self-awareness, and emotional and social intelligence. Still, certain issues did come up as the horses brought insight to Joy's preconceived notions and patterns of relating to others. As you follow a description of these lessons, watch for the following key elements:

1. The benefits of employing horses of various ages and backgrounds, including some who were abused themselves

2. Joy's overwhelming attraction to a horse who mirrored the traits of aggressive men in her life and her initial inability to recognize the danger this horse represented

3. How Joy learned to adopt an equine point of view to gain information from strong emotions, assess the intentions of others, and empower herself

4. How even the simplest equestrian activities — from observing herd behavior to choosing, grooming, and longeing a horse — provided insights into Joy's coping strategies and family history

5. Joy's exposure to assertiveness techniques through the act of longeing Rasa

6. Joy's difficulty in accessing her own authentic emotions and determining her true motivations

7. The myriad ways she initially succeeded in ignoring or suppressing her feelings and how Noche was finally able to break through her subterfuge

8. Moments of clairsentience exhibited by Noche and me in which we were able to feel emotions coming from Joy that she wasn't conscious of

9. Instances in which Joy could not think or talk herself out of falling back into destructive behavior patterns, despite years of traditional psychotherapy

10. How work with the horses helped her recognize and change those patterns

Reflecting Pools

Joy initially came to me hoping to overcome her fear of horses. Growing up in a wealthy, equestrian-oriented family, she'd been afforded the finest training money could buy. It was enough to make her body tremble, her legs weaken, and her head spin every time she even thought of stepping into the saddle. Her first instructor, a successful competitive rider based at a prestigious hunter-jumper stable, emphasized that horses should be managed with an iron will, a sturdy crop, and a good pair of spurs. The only emotions allowed in her riding arena were courage, pride, and determination. When twelve-year-old Joy fell off the finely schooled show horse her parents had bought her, the trainer ordered her to "get back on and make that idiot behave." In the coming months, Joy rode over many jumps, struggling to see each upcoming obstacle through a haze of tears that no one ever acknowledged. She didn't learn how to groom or tack up her own horse at the stable; relating to these animals on the ground was considered a lowly job for the hired help. To make matters much worse, one of the grooms managed to sexually abuse Joy while she was still in the saddle. The man had been charged with the task of leading the young girl's feisty mount as she cooled the gelding down during a long walk around the property. She never told her parents or her instructor what had transpired in the woods behind the barn.

Joy reached the point where she felt her life was in danger every time she took a riding lesson, and her supposedly push-button-trained thoroughbred was the only one who noticed. Zip would shy, bolt, buck, and spook in response to her anxiety. Joy found it increasingly difficult to control an impulse to run off in a blind panic whenever she approached the arena, and often Zip carried out her unspoken wishes. When her family finally conceded that the girl "just didn't have what it takes" to become a good rider, they sold Zip to a more ambitious young lady and assumed that would be the end of Joy's equestrian career.

The problem was that Joy loved horses. Even though she was afraid of them after her unfortunate experiences at the stable, she still yearned to be with them. When she heard of my program, she hoped she'd found the right place in which to conquer her fears. She was therefore completely mystified when I told her I had no intention of helping her get rid of her emotions, especially the ones she thought were negative.

"The only way you'll ever be safe around horses is if you learn to experience and process emotion as they do," I advised her that first day. This was a strange concept for a woman who'd been taught that horses were beautiful and powerful, yet stupid and impulsive animals possessing only the basest level of feeling. However, the idea that they might sense emotion in a way she could learn to relate to gave her a mild surge of confidence.

"My first instructor kept trying to teach me how to control my horse, but Zip always seemed to do exactly the opposite of what I asked," Joy remembered. "He was so unpredictable it made me even more nervous than I already was. After a while, I was just plain scared."

"What if Zip was simply acting out what you were feeling?" I asked.

"Then everything he did would make perfect sense," she replied, amazed and relieved.

During our work together, Joy learned that to horses, emotion is neither good nor bad; it's simply information. As animals that are preyed upon in nature, it behooves them to know when another herd member is feeling afraid or playful, angry or in pain, depressed or content. Though they ultimately strive for well-being in their relationships, horses don't consider so-called positive emotions any more important than the negative ones humans routinely try to suppress. To these animals, the ability to intuit fear in a distant herd member and act on this feeling without hesitation is a lifesaving skill, and their innate aptitude for resonating with another being's trust, joy, or confidence is a life-enhancing skill. These mindful creatures have developed a magnificent capacity for responding to subtle changes in the arousal of other horses as well as predators, a species-wide talent they easily transfer to interactions with people.

In their dealings with the human race over the past six thousand years, horses have become even more sophisticated in the nonverbal language of feeling. Through countless experiences that have no doubt been tagged with a big red flag in the equine morphogenetic field, even the most secure horse knows that any two-legged creature conveying the gestures of one emotion in order to hide another is either up to no good or delusional enough to be dangerous to herself and others. Joy, like so many people, fell into the latter category.

In his book *Body: Recovering Our Sensual Wisdom*, somatic psychotherapist Don Hanlon Johnson observes that people who've been convinced to mistrust the simplest of feelings and perceptions can be counted upon to obey family, peer group, and government policies about more complicated matters, even if these policies are obviously destructive or immoral. This is an ongoing problem for women with a history of abuse. As little girls, they learned to appear happy, helpful, brave, and polite when they really felt sad, frightened, rebellious, and angry. No one ever taught them how to manage or learn from those "bad feelings." As a result, they later found they could not rely on their own internal warning system to avoid the confident, well-groomed, expensively dressed man with a history of wife beating. When these women finally seek therapy in the face of extreme adversity, the culturally conditioned split between mind and body actually keeps them from changing the pattern. It's simply not possible for a battered wife to talk herself out of nonverbal postures of submission and conformity ingrained in her since early childhood. With her mind firmly focused on the ideals of freedom and a better life, she remains oblivious to the ways her body and personality were molded to support chauvinistic and authoritarian agendas, molds set in place without her conscious knowledge or consent. Women are ceaselessly preyed on in civilized society because, in order to conform, they relinquish the same somatic and emotional wisdom that allows horses, deer, and zebras to elude an attack in nature.

To please everyone else, Joy ignored her fear and kept plowing over those jumps, even though every fiber of her being objected. Suppressing her feelings and submitting completely to her riding instructor, she was set up to be sexually assaulted by the groom, who also took charge. Joy's parents were of no help. Embarrassed by strong emotion, they didn't want to hear about her anxiety; they wanted her to "tough it out" and "get over it." As I got to know Joy better, I also realized that her family relied upon her to feel *for* them, and so she began to consider other people's emotions and vulnerabilities as more important than her own.

In the ensuing years, Joy managed to fall into one destructive relationship after another. She was attracted to charismatic, outgoing, opinionated men who wooed her with promises to protect and take care of her. Hiding their emotions under a tough-guy façade, they were happy to let Joy intuit and respond to the feelings they refused to acknowledge — just as long as she didn't talk about it. This ability to empathize with others was her "talent," her contribution to the relationship. In Joy's estimation, the ex-boyfriends and husbands who proceeded to abuse her were basically good men who craved the right kind of nurturing and understanding. She hadn't been able to figure out exactly what they needed, but she was working on it. Despite several failed marriages and damaging relationships, Joy was confident that love would find a way. The problem was that Joy really did not grasp the nature of true healing and empowerment. Ignoring her own feelings, she had disempowered herself and fallen into the most insidious habits of co-dependence. By expressing, processing, and constantly making excuses for the feelings others never owned, she kept them from developing their own most valuable source of authentic power.

Intellectually Joy could discuss at length the current psychological theories about abuse and codependency, yet she never managed to change her behavior in response. Years of therapy, in fact, did not help her resist the attentions of a man who promised to be more lethal than all the rest. A month or two before I met Joy, she had fallen under the spell of a closet sex offender she had met on a business trip in Chicago. This attractive, dark-haired executive had a taste for both men and women and an occasional irresistible urge to seduce teenage girls. According to Joy, he was exciting, romantic, sad, and vulnerable in an endearing sort of way. She thought she could support his best qualities and solve his "problems" through love, sympathy, and understanding.

I knew nothing about the affair that first day, of course. After an hour spent discussing Joy's background, goals, and history with horses, I explained that our lessons would be designed to help her reestablish a connection to her feelings and use them to gather information in unfamiliar situations. I emphasized that as nonpredatory beings, horses had perfected a way of relating to the world that kept them from being victimized by carnivores. As women, we needed to resurrect this "wisdom of the prey" for our own protection. I related my image of the lake behind the black horse's eyes to a mindset she would learn to access through this work.

"Think of the region just behind your eyes as a crystal-clear pool capable of reflecting everything around you," I said as we headed toward a corral containing four of my horses. "This spring is fed by an underground river that allows all your subconscious emotions, intuitions, and bodily sensations to bubble up and rise to the surface of your mind. Don't reject anything that comes up. Try not to judge anything as good or bad; just let it tell you why it's there, what it means. And don't worry about being 'wrong' about anything. The wrong interpretation will still give you useful information — it will reveal a thought pattern or preconceived notion you hold that distorts reality. In order to change those patterns, you first have to be aware they exist."

Remaining safely outside the fence, Joy set out on her first task: assessing the different temperaments of the animals in the paddock. She was to use feelings, observations, and impressions to sense each horse's background and place in the herd from the ways in which they approached her and related to one another. She was to notice any emotions, thoughts, or memories the process brought up in her. Based on her findings, she was to choose the horse she wanted to groom. As Joy approached the corral, Noche moved away and adopted the blank look of dissociation. Rasa stepped forward to sniff Joy's hand, while Comet, a three-year-old filly, paced beside the black horse, waiting impatiently for a chance to check out the newcomer. The older mare suddenly turned around and walked away as Hawk, a new addition to the herd, trotted up from the other side of the pen, strained his neck as far as possible over the fence, and nibbled at Joy's coat.

"This one is so cute," she said, giggling with delight.

Joy was enchanted by Hawk, a seven-year-old gelding I was rehabilitating for a client. The previously abused horse had been rescued by an amateur equestrian who felt terribly sorry for him. In an effort to protect Hawk and make up for all he had suffered, the man and his family completely indulged the horse's fears and idiosyncrasies, causing him to become so stubborn and aggressive that the owner could barely ride him or even lead him around the backyard. Hawk was one step away from the killer's when one of my students took him on. Sensing that Rasa and Noche could help resocialize the gelding, I had put him with my herd temporarily. I also wanted to observe how he formed relationships with peers. At this early stage, he proved to be little more than a bully. In such a state of dysfunction, he was way too explosive for Joy to work with, but after hearing her descriptions of the men in her life, I wanted to see if she could recognize the danger he represented.

As it turned out, she was so attracted to Hawk that it took some effort to convince her to spend more time checking out the other horses. Joy recognized that Comet was a youngster. She described Rasa as a "strong and kind of aloof horse who had never been mistreated." She correctly guessed that Noche had been abused and didn't trust her. She thought that Hawk was "very sweet, highly affectionate, and outgoing."

"We had an instant connection," she said excitedly, "like I already know him. I feel the safest with Hawk."

"Before you make your final decision," I cautioned, "let's see how the horses react when there's something important at stake."

I tossed a flake of alfalfa into the center of the paddock, and all the horses headed toward it. Rasa managed to grab a mouthful before Hawk reared up, swooped down, and tried to bite her on the flank. He viciously kicked at Noche and chased Comet halfway around the corral. With dust flying and hay scattered about, the herd was in an uproar.

"Oh my God," Joy gasped. "I do know that guy. He's like most of the people in my life."

As we discussed the results of this exercise, Joy recognized a number of thought and behavior patterns that repeatedly got her into trouble. She had mistakenly associated the feeling of familiarity with safety. She had misread Hawk's disrespect of boundaries as affection. When he nibbled her coat, he was trying to see how much Joy would let him get away with, how easily she could be dominated. Joy's tendency to be captivated by superficially outgoing personalities also caused her to misinterpret Rasa's behavior. The black mare wasn't aloof; she'd just barely had a chance to touch her nose to the newcomer's hand as a sign of friendship and respect before she felt it necessary to move away from the fast-approaching bully.

After reassessing the situation in these terms, Joy decided that Rasa was the best horse for someone with fear issues to groom, and she was right. Because Joy acknowledged her own anxiety and inexperience, the mare was unusually gentle with her, so solid and accommodating that the woman's shaky, hesitant brushstrokes soon began to flow. Her face relaxed, and a radiant smile emerged.

Rasa was a master at coregulating anxious people. She proved crucial to stabilizing Joy's nervous system, breaking through her mistrust of horses during our first few lessons. The young woman's work with other members of the herd further eased her fears and raised her self-awareness considerably. I noticed that when she truly felt safe and supported, Joy was able to tune into some extremely subtle emotional states in herself and in the animals. Like many people with an early history of emotional, sexual, or physical abuse, Joy was a powerful empath, but her gift was in a state of arrested development. She couldn't use this ability to protect and empower herself. Her sensitivity seemed to actually draw her into abusive situations, where she used the same worn-out coping strategies despite the fact they consistently made things worse.

When Joy felt threatened, her awareness would recoil from her body and her emotions. She would adopt a submissive, childlike posture, try to endear herself with the challenger, latch onto some hidden vulnerability she had discovered in him, and attempt to nurture him at that level even as he took his frustrations out on her. This had been a temporarily effective way for a little girl to survive. Possessing neither the skills nor the resources to make it on her own, young Joy found ways to avoid neglect or abandonment, an especially important consideration since her father was an alcoholic and her mother was a raging narcissist with untreated bipolar tendencies. Joy's grandmother, the powerful matriarch of the family, fortified her own regal position by controlling the wealth and social standing everyone else stood to benefit from, doling out fleeting approval to those who indulged her whims while enduring her cruel insults and erratic, manipulative behavior. Joy's sympathetic demeanor and high tolerance for abuse raised her to the status of favored grandchild. She tried to please at all costs, making sure the people in power needed her in some way or at the very least found her cute, humble, and ingratiating enough to want her around.

Joy's coping skills reminded me of young Comet's way with the older horses. Joining the herd as a weanling, the filly quickly determined that Noche was in charge. I saw her forge an alliance with him that first day by lowering her head, diverting her eyes, and making the sucking gestures of a newborn, essentially saying, "I'm little and weak and oh so cute. Won't you take care of me?" It worked. Under the protection of "Grandpa Noche," Comet got away with things that the other horses would never dream of trying. When Hawk temporarily took over the herd, ousting Noche from his long-standing position in the most aggressive and flamboyant way I'd ever seen (the two later became best friends, interestingly enough), Comet immediately singled the bully out as her new best friend. Though he kicked out and bit and chased her without mercy that first afternoon, she always came back for more, managing to prance around like a little princess with her head poised low and to the side, shooting delicate glances in his direction, and, at the most appropriate moment, licking, chewing, and occasionally even making sucking noises like a foal. Within twenty-four hours, Comet could inch up to Hawk and eat out of his pile of hay. He still nipped her and kicked out at times, but it began to look more like a game that even Comet enjoyed playing.

When the opportunity arose for Joy to observe this behavior, she laughed and said, "I know exactly what Comet's doing. She swallows her pride and strokes Hawk's ego, but she gets exactly what she wants."

"And what's that?" I asked.

"Protection and privileges from the leader."

"But look what she has to put up with. Rasa doesn't play that game. She walks away and ignores Hawk when he's being aggressive. When he's calm and content, he lets her eat with him too."

"I admire her for it," Joy admitted. "But Comet is in the position to get the best food and more of it, no matter what mood Hawk is in."

"What if Comet could just leave the paddock and choose the members of her own herd, maybe become a leader herself?"

"Well, that's not really possible, is it?"

"Maybe not for Comet at this moment, but it certainly is for you."

Joy just stared at me in silence for a moment. She lowered her eyes, kicked at a clump of dirt, and looked off into the distance. "I guess I never considered that option," she said softly.

Running in Circles

Rasa took Joy under her wing, and for a while this was exactly what she needed. Just being in the presence of a calm, intelligent, emotionally responsive horse worked wonders for the young woman. To truly be safe with the horses, however, Joy needed to move beyond brushing the mare, cleaning her hooves, leading her around, and petting her while she was eating grass. It was time for the two of them to enter the round pen. While Rasa's strong, accepting temperament made the grooming process pleasant and rejuvenating for Joy, a new dynamic emerged when the halter and lead rope were removed. Rasa began to herd this successful businesswoman around like a foal.

"Look, she's nuzzling me and following me," Joy shouted, absolutely delighted. "I love you, Rasa," she said as she turned around and kissed the black horse on the nose. The two stood in the center of the arena for a moment, gently grooming each other. Tears welled up in Joy's eyes, but her body seemed poised for action. "I can't believe I can actually feel safe and protected with a horse who isn't tied to a post or being held by someone else," she marveled. "Come on, Rasa, let's go!"

Joy began to jog, and Rasa followed in perfect rhythm. "Just make sure you stay to the inside of the circle," I cautioned. "Don't get between Rasa and the fence. Keep in touch with your body and where it is in relation to hers at all times." The two trotted around the arena together. The woman laughed and leaped into the air. The horse bucked in response and took off at a full gallop. Joy stopped dead in her tracks, all the color running out of her face.

"Wow," she said, catching her breath. "I could have been kicked." Joy walked toward me, brow creased, shoulders tense and drawn. "I'm such an idiot," she declared with the startled, thankful, humbled look of someone who had just missed being hit by a truck.

"Don't negate everything else you accomplished because of one lapse," I said. "Learn from it. Reflect on the entire experience. Some very beautiful things were happening for a while. Just think back on what felt good and what felt threatening. When did this association become unsafe?"

The black horse ambled over and stood next to Joy as she analyzed her feelings: "We were in harmony, and it was magical. Rasa seemed to be following my every move, which was fine when we were walking. But as we picked up the pace, I couldn't keep my eye on her without losing my ability to look where I was going. Everything was moving too fast for that. I was having fun, but it also began to feel dangerous. Things felt like they were really about to get out of hand just before she bucked."

"So you actually perceived that shift before it happened, and yet you upped the ante by jumping in the air."

"Yeah, I guess I was swept away by the same building excitement that made Rasa take off."

"Think about how you could use these same feelings differently in the future," I said. "You knew things were about to get out of control." Joy nodded her head with a wide-eyed look of amazement. "Remember that feeling. Next time, step back, slow down, chill out, whatever it takes, just change your behavior in response to the warning."

"Maybe I just overreacted though," Joy replied. "I mean, that's what horses do. I should just get used to it."

"The point isn't what horses do, or what feels right to me, or what feels right to a bronc rider. You need to know what feels right to you. You may get to the point where you're perfectly comfortable standing in the middle of a herd of bucking horses, but the split second you feel the slightest tinge of fear or uncertainty, you better pay attention. This is the so-called special instinct that keeps the most experienced trainers in the world from getting hurt."

"Still, there was this feeling of ecstasy, of being in perfect sync with her, of being completely alive. I didn't want to lose it. I wanted it to get stronger."

"That's one good reason to ride her," I said. "I could saddle her up right now, and you could begin to explore that same sense of freedom and connection on her back, where she can't accidentally kick you."

Joy considered my proposition silently for a moment. I noticed her hand was shaking ever so slightly as she brushed her hair out of her face. She stepped away from Rasa. "I, I don't think I'm ready for that yet. I'm sorry. I'm getting dizzy and weak just thinking about it."

"Congratulations," I said. "You felt your fear, understood its message, and used it to stand up for yourself. Don't apologize for it ever again."

Joy did apologize for her feelings many times that day, but at least she was finally listening to them. Recognizing that she felt safer on the ground with Rasa, Joy decided that it might be better to learn how to longe the horse. As I expected, she cringed when I handed her the whip.

"Oh no, I don't want to hurt her," she said, pushing it away. "I don't want her to lose her trust in me."

"You can murder someone with the same knife you cut vegetables with," I explained. "The whip is only a torture device in the hands of someone who uses it that way. You can certainly longe a horse without it, but I've found it easier for people who are just learning this process to use the whip as a way to focus their intent and convey the variations in energy that let a horse know how fast to go. Think of it as an extension of your arm or a wand of communication that allows you to make your directions clear to the horse at a safe distance. Remember what happened when you ran too close to Rasa?"

Joy reluctantly took the whip from my hand, waved it unconvincingly in Rasa's general direction, and weakly said, "Let's go." The black horse barely acknowledged her existence.

"You see!" she declared triumphantly. "She's mad at me already."

"Oh really?" I replied. "Do you think you would have gotten her to trot beside you with such a lack of enthusiasm? Now take that same fun and energy, project it through the wand, and send her around the arena."

Rasa paid more attention this time. She started to trot off, then changed directions, walked directly toward Joy, and began to back her up, flailing whip and all, until the horse was longeing the woman in a small arc near the center of the arena. "Rasa just wants to follow me," Joy shouted, obviously agitated. "It's insulting to send her around in circles for our own amusement."

"Are you insulted?" I hollered back. "Look at what's happening. Rasa is longeing you. Actually, she's been in charge for days. She's been treating you like her child, protecting you, making you feel safe, playing with you, grooming you, and herding you around! She may have a lot of affection for you; she may even be amused by you, but she certainly doesn't consider you an equal at this moment. She has been saying, 'No' to the little things you've asked her to do all morning. On the way over to the arena, she easily convinced you to stop and let her eat grass four times. When you asked her to trot around the pen at a distance — and believe me, she knows what it means when a person stands in the center and picks up the whip — she decided to longe you instead. Rasa's ready to move. I can tell she wants to release some pent-up energy. She's just not going to do anything to give you the impression that you have authority. What does that tell you about your relationship with her?"

"I can't do it," Joy mumbled on the verge of tears. Her voice suddenly became shrill and defiant. "I won't do it! I don't want to be a part of any world where you have to crack whips and rule other people's lives just to keep from being victimized by them. The last thing I want to do is become like Granny and Bob and Michael and all the others. They think they're tough, but they're really much more afraid of life than I am. I won't stoop to their level." She dropped the whip on the ground and headed for the gate.

"Let me show you something before you leave," I said quietly, urging her back to the center of the round pen. Picking up the whip, I clicked my tongue, then engaged a long out breath as I moved the device toward the black horse's hip. Rasa walked out to the fence line and then began to trot. Feeling her oats, she broke into a full gallop, bucking and leaping into the air. Waves of power and exhilaration reverberated through the arena.

"I would never be able to keep up with her on the ground, and I certainly wouldn't want to be on her back right now," I said, "but I love being a part of this somehow. I love the connection that allows me to share her joy, resonate with her vitality, revel in the beauty of her movement. I love the connection that allows me to do this..."

I put the whip in a neutral position and began to breathe deeply. Rasa moved more and more slowly in response, downshifting from a furious run to an animated trot and finally to an energetic walk. I took a step back and motioned her into the center with another long out breath and a small movement from my hand. Ears forward and eyes bright, she stood panting beside me and pointed to her girth area with her nose. I immediately obliged. "She scratches my back; I scratch hers," I said. "With Rasa, though, it's usually her belly." Joy managed a pensive smile and began to rub the horse's withers.

"Rasa was ready to run," I continued. "She just wanted to put you in your place first."

"Why does somebody always have to be the boss?" Joy asked, shaking her head.

"It's not quite that simple," I said. "With Rasa and me, there are no more significant power plays. When I ask her to do something, it's not about dominance; it's about communication. But she has to respect me to be in the right frame of mind to listen. Sometimes, she convinces me to do things her way, and I learn something new in the process. Sometimes, I have to be especially assertive to convince her to do it my way, and she learns something new. This is the give-and-take of an adult relationship, a relationship of equals. Horses may be preyed upon in nature, but they aren't stupid, and they aren't weak. They're beautiful and powerful and proud of it, but they know they must remain sensitive, responsive, adaptable, and observant to avoid being eaten. They also know, as the old saying goes, that true strength is gentle, and true gentleness is strength. Whenever I reach this state of being in myself, Rasa will do anything for me, effortlessly. She acts as a barometer for me in this way all the time.

"It's not necessary to become a tyrant to avoid being victimized," I continued as Joy looked down at the whip, considering it anew. "If those were your only two options, then, of course, playing the martyr would be the noblest path. Most people in our culture, including you, obviously, have been raised to believe that we can only choose between those extremes. What I'm talking about here is a third option, an option that does not involve being aggressive or victimized."

"And what's that?" Joy asked.

"Let me just say that Rasa's one of the greatest assertiveness teachers I've ever known."

Joy took a deep breath and picked up the whip once more. She twirled it between her thumb and forefinger. I could see that she still had no idea how to gain Rasa's cooperation without the intimidating tactics that others had used on her. I myself had felt the same way just a few years earlier.

"Assertiveness is mostly a matter of focus," I told her. "But it's also a matter of engaging and projecting your will, what some people call intent."

To explain what I meant by those terms, I stared at my left arm and flatly told Joy I was going to raise it. Nothing happened. "Please, do it for me," I whined. Still, it dangled limply at my side. I tried to bribe it, shame it, scare it into submitting. I got angry with it, even slapped it, and still I couldn't get my own arm to move an inch. Finally, I looked at Joy, clenched my fist, and bent my elbow as if I were doing weightlifting curls.

"The invisible force that allows me to raise my arm is the same force that motivates Rasa to move when I'm standing twenty feet away from her," I said. "Without engaging and projecting my will, all the fancy tack, all the torturous or enlightened training techniques in the world are worthless." To further illustrate my point, I took the whip from Joy and pointed it toward Rasa's hind end, making the exact same sounds as I had the first time I longed her. She simply stood there, waiting, as if something were missing. I shouted. I cracked the whip. I swore. I jumped up and down. I threw the freakin' wand on the ground and stomped on it. Rasa didn't move. Finally, I waved my hand and took a step forward in an undramatic yet supremely focused manner. Rasa took off and trotted along the fence line.

"There are a couple of other things you need to remember as you practice this yourself," I emphasized. "Rasa has a strong will of her own. She also knows how to throw your focus off and confuse you in a bunch of seemingly trivial ways. This is actually one of the best techniques prey animals use to evade predators. In the training arena, horses use it to confound their owners, to put these people in their place. If your will and focus are stronger than Rasa's, she'll do what you ask, but she's going to test you at every moment. If she succeeds in distracting you, you'll eventually find yourself doing what she wants."

During the process of directing Rasa to move around the arena at a specific speed, change direction, and stop on cue, my now-enthusiastic client explored the finer points of will and focus: visualizing the desired outcome before making the request, breaking the task down into its basic elements, setting priorities, and noticing where Rasa was most likely to break Joy's concentration and take over. In the process, Joy also learned to become more assertive and focus more intently at the moment before Rasa made her move to control the situation.

For example, the initial goal was to have Rasa trot around the arena and, at Joy's request, slow down to a walk. At the outset the mare refused to move at all; then she proceeded to herd Joy around again. Shy and unsure of herself at first, the woman finally stood her ground, physically pushing Rasa out of her space at one point. This created an opening of respect in the mare's attitude that made it much easier to get her moving with a light flick of the longe whip. Once Rasa began to trot, however, she changed direction constantly, effectively challenging Joy's request for her to move around the entire arena.

"Notice where Rasa is most likely to change direction," I shouted over the fence. "There's a pattern to it, a method to her madness." The black horse was switching gears consistently at the gate and at a quarter of the arena to the left of the gate. "Now use the whip to signal Rasa to move forward just before she changes direction."

When Joy finally did muster up the needed will and timing, she did it so strongly she compelled the mare to gallop around the arena. Joy tried numerous words and signals to get the mare to slow down to a medium trot, but Rasa would only speed up. As the woman's frustration grew, she began to shout in a louder, more commanding way, sometimes rushing toward the black horse and making larger, more animated gestures. She was completely unaware that her body language was actually encouraging Rasa to speed up. Through a series of leading questions, I helped her realize she had another option: to move away from the horse, slow her breathing down, take on a more relaxed body stance, and visualize Rasa moving at the speed Joy wanted. Soon after, the mare was trotting around the arena.

By learning to recognize how her body language didn't match her message — by trusting in her powers of focus, intent, and visualization more than in shouting, pleading, and trying to intimidate the mare into cooperating — Joy was surprised to find that she could get the desired result almost effortlessly. She also learned that assertiveness was in fact an art form that required a sophisticated understanding of timing, concentration, visualization, anticipation of difficulties, constant reevaluation, the ability to regain focus quickly when thrown off course, and knowing when to press forward and when to back off.

We discussed Joy's occasional tendency to think she wasn't doing it right, that she wasn't "quite good enough." I assured her that this was in fact part of the process, that what she interpreted as making mistakes included the following important practices: assessing the situation, locating resistance, observing the resistance to understand its parameters, looking for alternatives, trying each alternative and assessing its success, matching intent with body language, getting thrown off-balance, and regaining balance. I emphasized that all these skills had to be rehearsed and refined. Unfortunately, the paradigm of force and intimidation that Joy grew up with didn't offer much practice in these procedures. If a person was loud enough, ruthless enough, and strong enough, he or she would prevail; all others would become submissive and repeatedly victimized.

Joy worked through several more exercises with Rasa and, by employing these techniques, was successful in directing the horse to move at a trot, change direction by request only, slow down to a walk, and finally stop. She marveled at how confident and empowered she felt.

"If you can do this with a highly aware 1,000-pound being," I said, "just think how effective you can learn to be with a 170-pound man who's not the least bit conscious of his own feelings and motivations."

The Eye in the Sky

In the coming weeks, Joy's life would change for the better in direct proportion to her reflective, nonjudgmental awareness of her emotions and the focused projection of her will. Of the two, the former proved the most troublesome. For all her empathic talents, Joy continued to vary in her ability to assess her true feelings, especially in tense situations.

After carefully comparing her initial experience with Hawk to her indulgences of a number of friends, family members, and ex-lovers, she realized she wasn't equipped to deal with the dangerous, dark-haired man in Chicago. She threw away his letters, refused to pick up the receiver when his number showed on her caller ID, and immediately erased his messages. Three weeks later, however, she hastily answered her cell phone while driving across town and heard his dusky voice.

"Jason really wants to change," she told me when she arrived for her lesson later that day. "He's in a great deal of pain. I mean, he was sexually abused as a child, and it really screwed him up. He's seeing a counselor now, and when I told him about the work I'd been doing with the horses, he was really excited. He wants to come down to Tucson during his vacation next month and do a few sessions."

"Isn't that the perfect excuse to see you?" I asked.

The left side of Joy's mouth slowly curved into a facetious half smile. "Well, I'm sure that has something to do with it. He said I was the one person he just couldn't seem to get out of his mind, that he would try to change for me or he'd never forgive himself. I think this might be the motivation he needs to finally conquer his self-destructive habits."

"You realize you're entertaining a relationship with a man who could be thrown in jail for the kinds of things he's admitted to you," I said flatly. "And those are just the escapades he's been willing to tell you about."

"I just feel so bad for him," Joy replied softly, staring down at her hands. "He's so alone. He never really learned how to connect with people except through sex, and it's not his fault. He was a victim too. Hawk's gotten so much better since you and the horses started working with him. Maybe we can do the same thing for Jason."

"That's a possibility," I conceded. "But it would take a lot longer than a two-week vacation with you and the horses. You can't save him, Joy, especially not in the context of a romantic relationship. He keeps searching for the perfect lover to cure all his ills, and that's a major part of the problem. Jason needs to learn how to love and rely on himself. He needs to take responsibility for his own actions and stop victimizing people in the same way he was victimized. He needs to change for himself, not anyone else. This is a tall order. Even if he is serious about changing, chances are he's going to stumble again and again, and people are going to get hurt, most definitely you. Besides, you already know how difficult it is to maintain proper boundaries with a sex addict, especially if you feel a physical attraction to him."

"We can take things more slowly this time?" she replied, not noticing her comments were beginning to sound more like questions than declarations. "I can set the pace?"

As Joy continued describing her master plan to help Jason, I noticed my blood pressure rising. The muscles in my neck began to constrict. I felt muddled and nauseated, like I was strapped to a merry-go-round spinning at fifty miles an hour. I wanted to leap out of my chair and take off running. A few moments later, I fought the urge to snatch her cell phone, dial Jason's number, and find out what it was about this man that could disarm a woman so effectively with a single long-distance conversation.

Then I heard one of the horses nickering over the fence and felt the warm spring wind blowing across my face. Something inside of me emerged from the seething cacophony of emotion without trying to change it, suppress it, or escape from it. I found myself staring into the lake behind my eyes, the same horse-inspired mental state I'd been urging Joy to adopt in assessing the messages behind disruptive feelings. Scanning the emotional landscape reflected in this now quiet pool, I realized that most of these sensations belonged to Joy in some way. My own feelings consisted primarily of frustration over my inability to control the situation, to protect this beautiful, gentle woman from her own self-destructive habits. It was becoming increasingly obvious that I wouldn't be able to talk her out of offering herself as another sacrificial lamb to the Jason cause. I couldn't reason with her, no matter how well I might help her analyze the situation.

"Joy, I'm not the one who can give you permission to see this guy," I said after a long silence. "I can't stop you from doing what you feel compelled to do, no matter how dangerous I think it is. It's not like I can lock you up in that corral over there to keep you from eating too much hay or running out into the middle of five o'clock traffic on Tanque Verde Road. The only thing I might be able to do is help you figure out why you're so attracted to this guy — expand your awareness of the situation. What does he have to offer you? What need does he fill? Exactly how does he make you feel? It must be something pretty significant if you're willing to ignore all his other serious faults."

"I don't know," she said. "When I try to think about it, I get so confused."

"Let's start with your body. What do you feel in your body?"

"Well...my head is spinning, and it's getting hard for me to speak, like something's stuck in my throat. Some part of me wants to run away, but my legs feel weak."

"Stay with these sensations," I urged, though I could see Joy beginning to disconnect. The look on her face reminded me of Noche trying desperately to get away from a crowd of new people without actually moving an inch, his eyes going blank, his mind retreating to some secret haven in an alternate universe. "What are these feelings telling you?" I persisted. "What is the message behind them?"

"I don't know," Joy replied tentatively. "Everything is getting cloudy, clouds everywhere." She sat silently for a moment. "I, I'm...feeling...much better...now."

Joy began to intellectualize the situation with a nervous, chatty rumination about her troubled childhood, her relationship with her father, and relevant details from her previous marriages. Ten minutes later, she came to the accurate yet oddly soulless conclusion that her relationship with Jason was an attempt to make up for all the people she couldn't help before by successfully healing one supremely damaged man.

"I just feel like I'm his last hope," she concluded. "There's something about him that's just so gentle, so sensitive, so unwilling to forgive himself for things he had no control over. It's like he's caught in some terrible nightmare he can't wake up from. He's doing the same terrible things over and over, things that seem to make him feel better for a few moments, but ultimately make him feel worse. He just can't stop himself."

"How do you really know all this about a guy you've only seen a few times?" I asked.

"I guess I mostly just feel it."

"Why do you feel it?"

"Because...I guess...I've felt these things...myself."

Joy looked like she wanted to run away, but she just sat there, still as a statue, the light behind her eyes slowly dissolving into the vacuous stare of dissociation. She was drawing back from her body to avoid her feelings. "Stay with me now," I said. "Just focus on one sensation, one message. What are you feeling?"

"I don't know," she said. "I'm probably way out of my league here. Maybe I can't help him."

"Do you see what you're doing?" I asked. "When you really begin to access your feelings, you deflect your attention to someone else. You're always more concerned with how someone else feels, how you can help someone else. Yet you just admitted to me that on some level you're just as much stuck in your own lonely circle of victimization. You're resonating with Jason through feelings the two of you share, but what about the sides of him you have nothing in common with, like his ability to manipulate men, women, and children for his own sexual gratification and then cruelly abandon them? You're shining a small spotlight on the part of him that's just like you and making up an idealistic story about it that will have a happy ending. In this way, he seems like a kindred spirit, but remember your brief experience with Hawk. Familiarity has nothing to do with safety. You have absolutely no chance of helping someone like Jason step out of the victim-perpetrator-rescuer triangle when you're bouncing back and forth between victim and rescuer yourself. The only way you'll be able to wake up from your own nightmare is if you start paying attention to your own feelings, in the present. In fact, I'm going to step off my soapbox now and ask Noche to help you work on it."

Because Joy was in such a dissociative state, I decided to let her simply groom the bay horse, hoping he might help her gain a better understanding of how she lost contact with herself whenever she felt threatened. I led him out of the paddock and tied him loosely so he would have some room to move if Joy's emotions proved too much for him. I set the grooming box about three feet in front of the steel hitching post so that he wouldn't accidentally step into it and spook. Joy picked up a brush and slowly walked toward him, speaking softly in her most sympathetic, reassuring tone of voice. Her body language was placid and completely nonthreatening, yet the gelding immediately pinned his ears back and lurched sideways to the limits of the lead line. Noche, the king of dissociation around human beings, was unusually alert.

"He's very nervous," she said, "very scared."

"What are you feeling?" I asked.

"I'm, you know, a little nervous about approaching him because I know he's afraid. I mean, I know he was beaten and that he doesn't trust new people, and I just want to help him feel more secure around me." Then, to the horse, she said in the tone of voice one would use with a baby, "Poor Noche, I know, I know. Everything will be OK."

I walked over to Noche and silently reassured him, bringing him back to the center of the hitching post. He stood calmly until Joy began to step forward. Once again, the bay horse shied away from this mild-mannered woman as if she were about to hit him with a tent pole.

"There's something going on with you, Joy," I reiterated firmly. "There must be, or Noche wouldn't be acting this way. If you're going to work with an abused horse, you have to recognize exactly what you're feeling at all times. Like a traumatized person, Noche is hypersensitive to the blood pressure, muscle tension, breathing rate, and emotions of anyone approaching him." I noticed that Joy seemed distracted. I tried to draw her attention back to the task at hand with a simple question. "Why is that, do you think?"

"Because he's always scared," she quickly replied.

"No, there's a purpose to it," I said emphatically. "Whether they have two or four legs, abused animals tend to become hypervigilant. That means they turn the volume up on all their senses to gauge the arousal level of others. In this way, a distrustful horse like Noche can tell what state someone's in long before that person can get close enough to cause him harm. This is part of the reason you're so good at empathizing with others. It's a powerful defense mechanism. As a prey animal, Noche's hardwired in that direction to begin with, but his early experiences with abusive riders have heightened this ability and, to a certain extent, have blown it all out of proportion."

Joy nodded thoughtfully. "You're right," she said after a moment of re-flection. "I could always tell when my mother was heading toward a rage and get out of the way before she actually exploded. I remember watching her legs darting back and forth as she paced around the house. I'd be crouched underneath a small, out-of-the-way end table in the living room, staying as quiet as possible so she wouldn't notice me."

"How did you control your fear?"

"I can't remember. I just knew I had to stay perfectly still or I might set her off."

"So you learned to tune into your mother's emotions before she ex-pressed them while suppressing your own anxiety and insecurity."

Again Joy nodded, her eyes now luminous with the power of this potent realization.

"That was a big accomplishment for a little girl," I said. "It was a very effective survival strategy — at the time. But in order to have any hope of brushing Noche today, you're going to have to process emotion in a different way."

The light in Joy's eyes suddenly subsided. She pursed her lips, and her brow began to crinkle. "Don't worry," I said. "You're not going to lose any-thing in the process. Remember, Rasa has never been abused, but she can tell what people are feeling at a distance too; she just doesn't respond to strong emotion in the same way as Noche. Rasa will object if you're emotionally incongruent, as you've seen, but all you have to do is become congruent. In other words, you only have to show her that you know what you're really feeling to calm her down. You can still be afraid or angry around her, and she'll actually make you feel better. That's what makes her a great therapy horse. If you can become more like Rasa, you might actually have a chance of helping some of these wounded people you seem to attract."

I could tell I finally hit the jackpot with that last comment. My previ-ously distracted client was listening intently. In all kinds of verbal and non-verbal ways, Joy was always insisting that her need to help others was more than a defense mechanism. It was a calling. I recognized early on that she had the intelligence, empathy, intuition, and tolerance for strong emotion that could eventually make her a great therapist. I suspected the horses might help her develop these abilities further, while mirroring the destructive be-havior patterns that held her back.

"There's a big difference between working with Rasa and working with

Noche," I continued. "Rasa has the capacity to calm and stabilize *you* when you feel nervous or unsure, partly because she has never been abused. But she also has an unusual ability to connect with and comfort others. She actually prefers to be around people more than horses. Interacting with Noche is an advanced move. He cannot take care of you. You have to *be* calm to reassure him. He doesn't want you around if you're afraid or angry. These emotions plug him into his own issues and probably activate memories of past abuse. Usually he dissociates, which is simply a way of running away mentally when he can't get away physically. For some reason, he's actively trying to increase the distance between the two of you despite the fact that he's tied. This tells me Noche is really worried about something. What do you think it could be?"

"Maybe I'm scared of him?" Joy asked feebly.

"Are you?"

"Maybe I'm afraid of hurting him," she replied flippantly. Then, turning to Noche, she told him she was sorry in her highest, sweetest baby-talk voice.

"In order to work with Noche, you have to own your feelings," I said, openly agitated with her demeanor. "If you don't, he'll continue to react to the anxiety you're carrying around. Whether you're dealing with an abused horse or an abused human, you have no hope of helping someone heal his own trauma if you're inadvertently setting him off with your unconscious emotions, then freaking out yourself and falling into a state of dissociation."

"I know," Joy said, a little too quickly. "But what can I do?"

"You can start by scanning yourself to figure out what you're feeling. Then you can take it one step further. You can learn to release those emotions without suppressing them. Don't decide you're not going to act afraid or angry anymore. That won't work with Noche, and it won't work with a human abuse victim who has survived by also sensing the hostility of others under all those smiling faces. You actually have to *not be* afraid or angry."

"Wow," Joy said. She rolled her eyes and let out a huge sigh, completely overwhelmed at the prospect. "How do I do that?"

"You listen to the message behind the emotion and respond to it. If you're afraid, for instance, you need to locate the threat and move to safety. Anger usually arises when someone has violated your personal boundaries in some way. You need to determine who stepped over the line and reinstate a boundary that makes you feel comfortable. The ability to know what you're feeling, grasp the message behind it, and respond to it quickly and efficiently is called emotional agility. To work with Noche, you'll have to develop a certain level of emotional agility, and you won't be able to do that if you're always running away from your feelings, which in your case means deflecting your attention to the emotions of others. So don't give me that 'Poor Noche, he's been beaten' routine. He's a twenty-five-year-old horse; that's at least seventy-five years in human terms. He has a great deal of life experience and wisdom. He's not a baby, and you can't mother him out of his fear, especially when he's responding to feelings you won't own."

"But I'm not feeling anything!" Joy hissed as if she were trying to shout and whisper at the same time.

"That's because whenever you feel threatened, you lose all contact with your body and your emotions. You dissociate."

"I'm still not really sure what that means."

"Dissociation is like plucking out one of your eyes, tossing it into the sky, and investing all your awareness in that single, disconnected, dreamy, idealistic point of view so that you can ignore all the uncomfortable, nasty, earthy things that are going on down below. From that vantage, your mind can make up all sorts of little stories about the way things should be or will be some time in the distant future when you win the lottery, get your first acting role in a major film, find the perfect man to take you away from all this, or fix the man you've got and turn him into the perfect mate."

Joy smiled sheepishly and looked at the ground.

"We all dissociate to a certain extent," I said reassuringly, "like when we're driving across town in heavy traffic and suddenly find ourselves at the office with no memory of how we got there. In the meantime, we've fantasized about ways to get that egotistical, good-for-nothing marketing director fired and take over his position. In extreme situations like torture and sexual violation, dissociation is a survival instinct that kicks into gear when the person being victimized is restrained. If you can't fight or run away from a particularly horrifying situation, some part of your awareness will withdraw from your body, like when you were able to sit perfectly still as your mother raged. I also watched you dissociate a few minutes ago when you started to access your feelings about Jason. You said everything was getting cloudy, that there were clouds everywhere. Remember how you suddenly felt better? You immediately fell into analyzing your troubled past with a total lack of passion. Then you came up with a whole bunch of idealistic notions about how your love would save a chronic sex offender who, in reality, could be caught and thrown in jail any day now. What helped you as a child is perpetually getting you into trouble as an adult because dissociation is not an appropriate long-term coping strategy. If you habitually check out the moment you feel threatened, you'll always be in the position to be victimized one way or another because you'll have lost contact with the internal warning system that tells you to get out of harm's way."

"Do you really think I'm in danger?" Joy asked, as if the thought had never occurred to her.

"You're the one who has actually spent some time with Jason," I finally said. "Call your awareness back down from the sky and listen to what your gut is telling you."

I coached Joy in a body awareness technique I had used with a variety of people in workshops and private sessions.

"Don't try to change anything," I cautioned. "Just scan your body and tell me what sensations you're feeling."

"I'm dizzy," she said tentatively, closing her eyes and then squinting as if she were in pain. "My legs feel weak. My stomach is churning, and my throat feels blocked."

"Breathe into the place where you feel the most tension or discomfort. Allow that feeling to expand. Ask it why it's there, what it means. If you can't get a specific message, just tell me the first thought or memory that pops into your mind."

"I'm thinking of Jason coming to see me," she said. "It's really making me nervous. I feel like I want to run."

"Stay with the feeling. Let it expand as you breathe in and then smile at it as you breathe out — not because you're trying to put on a happy face, but because you are acknowledging that your feeling is valid. It is your friend. It has important information for you. What's it saying?"

"Oh my God," Joy said as she opened her eyes. "I'm terrified. I'm terrified of Jason!"

"What could you change about this situation that would make you feel better?"

"I don't know. I don't know. I'm so dizzy. Let me sit down for a minute."

"Just stay with the feeling for a few more seconds. You can handle it; I know you can. What if you told Jason not to come to Tucson next month? Imagine actually saying that to him right now. How does that make your body feel?"

"The constricting feeling is going away," Joy replied. Her features soft-ened for a moment, then her face took on a conflicted, mangled expression of regret and worry. "I hate to tell him not to come. I think now more than ever that this work could help him."

"We're not concerned with Jason right now," I emphasized. "Just know that he doesn't have to come here until you feel safe with the idea. Don't make any plans beyond that."

Joy said she could live with this option as long as it was temporary, and after a few more minutes of deep breathing, the dizziness lifted. I handed her the brush, and she walked toward Noche. This time, the old sage mustang stood perfectly still as she rigorously groomed him. Joy talked about how light she felt, how wise and intuitive Noche was. Slowly but surely the conversation drifted back to how Jason could benefit from this work. The bay horse sud-denly jerked back to the end of the lead rope and stepped to the side.

"What happened?" she gasped.

"Something shifted," I said. "Do you see anything around that might have spooked him?"

A soft breeze rustled through the pine tree beside the hitching post as the horses nearby continued to doze in the sun. Neither Joy nor I could see anything that would have created such a strong reaction in Noche.

"Then check in with your body," I urged.

Joy scanned down her body.

"Wow, I'm dizzy again; my stomach is all tied up in knots, and my legs feel weak," she assessed, much more quickly this time.

"What emotion do you associate with those sensations now?"

"Fear. Terror."

"What were you talking about the moment Noche pulled away from you?"

Joy was agitated, almost angry for a moment. Then the air seemed to go out of her sails. Her shoulders collapsed, and she looked embarrassed, defeated.

"Jason," she said weakly as she backed away from the horse and me both. I thought she was going to cry, but she held back the tears. She looked at me slyly out of the corner of her eye. "Did you know this would happen?" she whispered, trying to make sense of the situation. "Did you know Noche would do this?"

"To tell you the truth," I replied, shaking my own head in disbelief, "I had absolutely no idea."

The Horse Inside

Joy spent another half hour working with her four-legged counselor. During that time, she became remarkably fluent in the technique of assessing her bodily sensations, allowing them to expand and reveal their messages, changing a thought or goal or boundary in response, releasing the emotion effortlessly as a result, and finally returning to a state of calm. Noche acted as a finely tuned barometer, allowing her to approach only when the slightest traces of fear or anger had left her system. Occasionally, I drew Joy's attention back to Jason, and each time, without fail, Noche would balk, indicating that the simple mention of his name was enough to raise her anxiety. In her efforts to release the tension, Joy thought of all kinds of ways she might be able to safely interact with the man, but Noche always maintained his distance. Telling Jason not to come to Tucson, cutting off all contact with him: these were the only thoughts that reduced Joy's arousal enough to allow her to enter the horse's comfort zone.

We turned Noche loose to roam the property and nibble some grass as Joy and I sat under a mesquite, processing the results of this very powerful impromptu lesson. While finally acknowledging that she needed to stay away from Jason to maintain her own sense of well-being, Joy began to grieve for him once more.

"This morning, I happened upon the most extreme case of abuse and neglect I've seen in a long time," I said, interrupting yet another soliloquy on the "poor man."

"Where? Here at The Ranch?" Joy asked.

"Yeah, unfortunately, right here. Can you believe it? The poor creature was in an absolute panic as her owner continued to drag her into a situation she objected to with every fiber of her being, a situation I know she barely escaped once before. Her whole body was shaking with fear and with the anger of having her basic needs so grossly neglected and ignored that I was tempted to call the humane society. But then the humane society has no jurisdiction over the human soul."

My student didn't catch the allusion to her own situation. "Oh my God, what did you do?"

"I'm talking about you, Joy. Your conscious identity's treatment of the graceful, sensitive, and gifted being inside is absolutely no different than the way Noche's abusive former owner treated him. Imagine someone bullying that wonderful, intelligent creature who just taught you more about yourself than any counselor could. Imagine someone bashing him over the head with a two-by-four and calling him stupid."

Joy flinched in response. "You beat yourself up in the same way all the time," I continued, "and you let others join in. Do you really think I should tolerate this kind of violence and neglect from you when I would never stand by and watch someone torturing a horse? The anger and panic coming from your body were so powerful I felt like I was being suffocated and beaten from the inside out. Emotions this strong can't be resolved through suppression or expression. The behavior that generates them must change.

"You have the capacity to become an empathic healer, whether or not you choose to use it in any formal way. But you can't help other people by feeling sorry for them and indulging them at your own expense. You will only kill the gifted part of yourself through the neglect and abuse you constantly inflict on yourself. Please, listen to your body, your emotions, and your soul — and not the twisted conditioning that's become your conscious mind. Your very survival depends on you actually making an effort to change, not just talking about it while you ignore or wallow in strong emotions you aren't truly listening to."

Joy looked shocked for a moment, yet rather than dissociate, her eyes momentarily reflected the most sublime feeling of compassion. She shifted in her seat uncomfortably, obviously disturbed by some of the things I had said. Still, she remained present and attentive.

"I am like one of those horses," she admitted. "And when it comes to myself, I'm a mean old trainer, it's true. I never thought of it that way before."

"Like most aggressive people, you were taught to be that way," I conceded. "You just deflected it onto yourself to avoid hurting others. Your heart is already in the right place. A shift in perception is what you need. When you find yourself in a volatile situation, become the horse. Stare into the lake behind your eyes. Scan the landscape around you without judging or idealizing others. Feel the rivers of physical, emotional, and intuitive knowledge rise up to the surface. Let the wild, sensitive, strong, yet gentle force of your own soul lead the way now and then. The woman who forms a partnership with the horse inside, who respects and listens to the wisdom of the prey, cannot possibly abuse herself or anyone else, and it will become a lot more difficult for others to victimize her as well."

CHAPTER SIX

THE POLITICS OF INTELLIGENCE

Not all cowboys use the cowboy method of "breaking" a horse. Buck Light is one who rejected the premise of necessary roughness in favor of respectful collaboration. Yet unlike Monty Roberts, John Lyons, Ray Hunt, Pat Parelli, and a host of other Western-style horsemen who make their living writing books and leading clinics, Buck was content to ride the range and tend to his horses in relative obscurity. In his own quiet, unassuming way, he taught me a series of lessons that proved to be significant keys in unlocking the mysteries of human-equine interactions.

Buck managed a working cattle ranch in southern Arizona. I met him through his wife, Dana, a formidable trainer in her own right who was also one of the founding members of Epona Equestrian Services. One night over dinner, my colleague casually mentioned that her husband's horses acted as if they were quite a bit smarter than horses ridden by the other cowboys. When Buck first arrived at the Arizona operation in the early 1990s, many of the cowboys ruled their horses with a philosophy of dominant intimidation — the bigger bit and bigger spur approach. Their horses were alternately sluggish and expressionless, then nervous and distracted. They were also prone to sudden outbursts of sheer panic in novel situations when the rider needed most to rely on his mount. These horses seemed to function at a purely instinctual level. They literally acted stupid, which in turn made their riders feel justified in treating them as "dumb animals."

Through a series of pivotal experiences as a horse trainer and cowboy in Wyoming, Buck had come to acknowledge the intellectual and emotional intelligence of his equine partners — the bigger brain and bigger heart approach. His horses were alert and gregarious, yet relaxed and thoughtful in their work. What's more, they would fight over which of their ranks got to leave the corral with Buck in the morning, even though this usually meant eight to ten hours under saddle.

The sometimes grueling job of trotting along miles of fence, making repairs and chasing stray cattle, requires each cowboy to keep a string of several horses who are ridden just a few times a week. On their days off, the horses of several cowboys graze together in one pasture, giving them plenty of time to engage in classic herd behavior. Strangely enough, whenever a horse previously ridden by another man was transferred to Buck's string, that horse would immediately move up in social standing among his equine peers. These horses seemed to have decided that carrying Buck around on their backs all day was a prestigious distinction in the herd. Or perhaps it had more to do with a previously sluggish, instinctually driven horse waking up and actually caring about his place in the world after experiencing the respect conveyed through Buck's flexible, supportive reins.

Either way, you'd think the other cowboys would acknowledge the difference they saw and adopt something closer to Buck's way of relating to horses. Over time, many of them did. During Buck's first year at the ranch, however, most of the men resisted the new boss's insights. They had invested too much ego in playing rodeo with a frightened young gelding as they tried to turn a thousand-pound creature into a push-button zombie. Some seemed to take sadistic pleasure in beating the horse over the head and calling him stupid when he panicked, throwing his "master" and leaving him in the dust after supposedly being "broke."

This is the politics of intelligence in the equine field, and it's not limited to the macho code of certain cowboys. The head trainer at Wolverton's breeding farm certainly wasn't the only experienced equestrian I met who held fast to the notion that these animals were biological machines incapable of genuine thought or feeling. It was my utter frustration in dealing with this human vanity that motivated me to explore the intricacies of equine intelligence and brain function. Over time, I collected scientific and anecdotal evidence suggesting that horses have incredible memories, that emotion plays a significant role in their learning process, and that they demonstrate forms of neurological activity essential to creative genius in human beings.

While working at a group home for persons with physical and mental disabilities, I also realized that people suffer under the same politics of intelligence. These highly sensitive human beings had been prevented from expressing themselves by physical and sensory difficulties, ignorance, and prejudice. Until the late twentieth century, they were routinely dehuman-ized and abused by the system, corralled and held captive in institutions as emotionally and spiritually debilitating as the most dismal stables. After volunteering at a therapeutic riding facility for people with cerebral palsy, autism, and various forms of developmental challenges, I was intrigued by the prospect of interacting more directly with these folks.

When an opportunity arose to work as a group home facilitator for an agency in Tucson, I found that the ways I related to my most challenging four-legged clients directly applied to my new two-legged clients. The adults I assisted at the group home behaved very much like abused horses, and I believe the roots of their frustration were the same. These people had no voice in mainstream society. It was nearly impossible for them to thrive in a competitive, logic-oriented atmosphere, and they certainly didn't do well on intelligence tests exhibiting such a bias. Like the horses Buck Light en-countered at the ranch, these people acted stupid sometimes because they were treated as if they were stupid. When afforded the respect, flexibility, and open-minded support that allow them to develop their own unique perspectives, persons with mental disabilities often prove themselves to be much more insightful and talented than previously suspected — and they have much to teach the rest of us in the process.

As I moved into equine-facilitated therapy, I wanted to experience the challenges these people face every day, so I pursued a part-time job at a group home for developmentally disabled adults who were also hearing-impaired. I didn't know sign language, but I got the position based on a rec-ommendation from Julia Standish, an Epona colleague who had worked as a group home manager for over a decade. The corporation I worked for, which owned a number of group homes around the city, had an excellent training program that covered client intervention techniques, profiles of their various disabilities, drug administration, sign language, basic behavior modification, and teaching and counseling methods, as well as procedures for creating and implementing treatment plans and evaluating client progress.

Since Arizona regulates services for people with special needs, group home facilitators are drilled in handling difficult clients without force or intimidation. Suddenly I was learning the clinical terms for many of the training methods I had instinctively developed with the help of my horses. One area that wasn't covered significantly, however, was nonverbal commu-nication. Though we discussed how to read a client's body language, little was said about how the emotional state of the facilitator could affect, or even lead to, a crisis. During my employment, I realized that the emotional congruency and arousal levels of staff members were particularly crucial at the group home, yet none of the corporation's trainers and administrators grasped how important these factors were in maintaining a safe therapeutic relationship with the residents.

I had a great deal of success with the group home's most difficult client precisely because I was sensitive to the nonverbal cues I was receiving — and giving. During my first month on the job, I was repeatedly warned to be careful with Charles, a stoic forty-five-year-old client considered the most unpredictable and violent member of the household. Like Noche, he was especially stiff and guarded in the presence of strangers, yet, like Hawk, the man was also known to fly off the handle at the slightest provocation. Charles had punched most of my coworkers in the face during their first month at the home, a pattern that had become a fearsome initiation for new employees. In the feeble hope of sparing me a similar fate, senior staff members warned me to keep my distance and maintain an unbending authority with Charles. The ones who had suffered the most serious injuries were therefore completely horrified when I quickly formed an alliance with him.

Charles was deaf and developmentally disabled with some autistic tendencies, but his eyes held a cynical, almost playful intelligence that told me he knew a lot more about what was going on around him than most people could fathom. Like other members of the household, he tested low on standard IQ tests, though he had learned to read and write at an elementary school level. Most of the residents worked in plant nurseries or factories during the day, but Charles's lack of patience with other people made it difficult for him to hold a job. He hated his day program. He refused to participate in most activities. He disliked being touched. He didn't even show any interest in television. Most evenings, he sat in a big easy chair staring into space, waiting to eat and go to bed. Dinner was the highlight of his day, at which time he would shovel food into his mouth as quickly as possible, a habit he perfected during years spent in an institution where aggressive clients stole food from their more passive neighbors.

For all these reasons, I could understand why most people treated Charles like a naughty child. To me, however, he seemed a reserved yet gracious gentleman who didn't suffer fools. Over time, I realized he possessed a clairsentient talent so sophisticated that the average person's chaotic and incongruent feelings sent him into a tailspin. Like Noche and his insightful interactions with Joy, Charles could pick up on someone else's hidden emotions at a distance. Once I realized this, I began to make sense of his outbursts by asking all the facilitators a simple question: "What was going on in your life the day Charles punched you?"

Most of my coworkers couldn't recall how they felt before their unfortunate encounter, but one young woman, a nursing student who had started six months before I arrived, clearly remembered the events leading up to the moment Charles broke her nose.

"It was one of the worst days of my life," Jenna said. "I had this big fight with my boyfriend. I got to the group home late and realized that no one had bought groceries over the weekend. I had to go shopping before I could fix dinner for everyone, so I was even more stressed. To make matters worse, Charles was having an especially bad day. He was agitated and uncooperative. When I asked him what was wrong and tried to calm him down, he hauled off and hit me."

"Were you by any chance putting on a happy face for him when you were really just fed up with the whole situation?" I asked.

"Well, yeah," she answered thoughtfully. "I was mad, but it wasn't the clients' fault. I didn't want to take my frustration out on them. That's what bothered me most about the whole thing. I was really making an effort to be nice to Charles when I wasn't feeling so great myself. I was trying to be supportive and understanding, and he broke my nose."

I suggested Jenna consider the possibility that, despite her best intentions, she received the blow because she was incongruent. I asked her to consider that this man, who was diagnosed as deaf and mentally disabled, a man seemingly caught up in his own hopeless dream world, had been acting out the stress, anger, and anxiety that Jenna thought she was hiding.

"Now that you mention it, no one warned me Charles was having a bad day when I started my shift," she conceded. "I thought it was strange that he could be in such a terrible mood and the person who took care of afternoon transport didn't notice it."

"I don't think Charles was in a bad mood," I clarified. "I think you were in a bad mood, and he picked up on it. When you tried to help him release emotions you refused to own, Charles gave you an emphatic nonverbal correction. The translation: 'You have a lot of nerve disrupting my world with your chaos and then trying to calm me down with your lying smile.'"

"But what would be the alternative?" Jenna asked.

"When I'm stressed or agitated, I tell Charles how I'm feeling," I replied. "This in itself ensures that my body language and my conscious awareness of the situation are congruent with my emotions. With the simplest signs, I tell him why I'm feeling that way and that it has nothing to do with him. I'm not sure how much he understands, but he will echo my movements. Last week, I was really agitated when the group home van broke down. I had to spend the afternoon making arrangements to get it fixed when we were supposed to go to the movies. Charles seemed very tense and confused, yet as he mimicked my signs for 'angry,' 'van broke,' 'need to fix,' 'no movie,' 'no popcorn,' and 'sad,' he began to calm down. I gave him a wide berth until I felt better, and I let Charles act as a mirror to tell me if I'd actually calmed down enough to enter his comfort zone. At one point, he began to take short, shallow breaths, rock back and forth slightly, and crinkle his brow, and I knew I was still too keyed up to interact with him."

Because of his limited ability to communicate, even in sign language, the staff never knew exactly what was going on in Charles's mind. My efforts to stay congruent in his presence, however, kept me from receiving his "initiation," and some of my coworkers took notice, with equally successful results. During the brief time I worked with Charles, we shared many beautiful moments. Rather than leave him to sit in his chair all evening, I invited him to help me cook dinner. When it came to food, this normally passive, stoic resident demonstrated real enthusiasm, an extensive vocabulary, and very strong opinions about what he wanted. He was a sloppy cook, but he knew how to fix his favorite meals and was quick to pick up new recipes. He was also extremely considerate, opening doors for me, handing me the utensils I needed before I asked, and cheerfully doing the dishes.

In the process of entering Charles's world and letting his interests lead the way, I gained some wholly unexpected insights from this sensitive man. One afternoon, when my coworker took the other residents to the park, I stayed home with Charles, who had refused to join the outing. Rather than flip through the cable channels, I decided to try a little wu wei with my quiet friend sitting in the corner. After all I had discovered simply hanging out with members of the equine tribe, the idea of doing nothing with Charles actually seemed an exciting prospect.

Normally, the group home was a whirlwind of activity with staff coming and going, cooking, doing chores, organizing events, and helping the clients with their ongoing studies of basic life skills, including both written and sign language vocabulary. But that afternoon the home was completely still; the chores were done, and Charles had already completed his signing exercises. He sat in his favorite chair, seemingly very pleased. Hoping to experience things from his point of view, I turned the sound down on the television and realized that without the spoken words and the feelings conveyed by the music, the movie on the screen was flat and uninteresting. I turned the TV off, sat across from Charles, and stared into space. As my breathing slowed, the rising and falling of Charles's chest became deeper and more relaxed in response. A few minutes later, I began to notice tiny multicolored lights dancing through the room, as if I were seeing the air, which seemed to be the case when the heater kicked on and these same tiny lights began to swirl and flow in the vicinity of the vent. I smiled at Charles, delighted. He smiled back. An incredible wave of ecstasy filled my body. This was the same feeling I had often shared with Rasa in the heat of those lazy summer afternoons we spent milling around the pasture. Was I resonating with Charles on a similar frequency? The thick, blooming sensation in my chest had nothing to do with a great ride, an intriguing conversation, an uplifting movie, a beautiful walk through the country, a good meal, or a nice bottle of wine. I was sitting in a dimly lit, functionally furnished, middle-class living room staring into space with a man who had no qualms about punching me if the spirit moved him. Yet it was a very different spirit moving us both at that moment.

I looked at Charles. Tears were streaming down the cheeks of his luminous face. My eyes too began to sting as my heart swelled with the most rarefied sense of compassion and love. I stood up and motioned Charles to meet me halfway. We hugged briefly in the center of the room. "Thank you for showing me your secret world," I signed.

"Secret world," he echoed with the subtlest of movements.

Not So Bright

Some of the most creative and innovative people I've known had to break through the stigma of "low intelligence" to reveal perspectives every bit as astounding as the one Charles shared with me. Kathleen Barry Ingram, the counselor with whom I cofacilitated some of my earliest successful equine therapy sessions, runs her own highly regarded private practice in Tucson. It wasn't until we had been working steadily together for eighteen months that she told me about her troubled high school years. Over dinner one night, I watched her fight back the tears as she remembered the humiliating private conference she and her mother endured at the Catholic all-girls school she attended.

"I'm sorry to say that Kathy didn't do so well on her entrance exams," Sister Mary Grace reported at the beginning of freshman year. "The scores suggest she's mildly retarded. I think preparing for college would be an unrealistic goal, so we're placing Kathy in our L program."

Kathleen's classmates included a girl with Down syndrome and a number of students who had difficulty with the special ed curriculum's remedial reading and math courses. Still, Kathleen insisted that no matter what it took, she would pursue a degree in psychology after graduation. No one seemed surprised when she flunked out of her first semester at a small Alabama college. Without the standard college preparatory courses her high school offered to most students, Kathleen was simply too far behind, the skeptical voices of her parents and teachers too fresh in her mind. A troubled marriage and two children later, she took up the challenge once again at the University of Colorado, this time graduating with a 3.9 grade point average. When she took the entrance exams for graduate school, however, she scored a twelve on a standard scale of one hundred.

"I was in the retarded range again," she said, managing a cynical smile. "I had a lot of anxiety about taking standardized tests, and I just couldn't see in the black-and-white terms those exams required. But this time I actually had a nun stand up for me, so in some way I had come full circle. Marie Ego, a PhD adviser at Lesley University in Cambridge, Massachusetts, told the admissions board to throw out my test scores and consider my academic record exclusively. She said that I was talented in ways those tests couldn't measure, and I'll always be grateful for that."

Kathleen received a master's degree in counseling psychology, again with an almost perfect 3.9 average, proving that Dr. Ego's faith in her was warranted. As a counselor, Kathleen used the knowledge and confidence she gained from her tempestuous academic experiences to empower other people who felt betrayed by the system. Her belief in the multifaceted nature of intelligence and its relationship to the emotional health of the individual coincided with my own observations of "problem" horses and their human counterparts. I had noticed a pattern in those suffering from a seeming lack of intelligence — in both species — including the tendency to dissociate in tense situations; a history of physical, emotional, or sexual abuse; above-average nonverbal awareness; an intolerance for emotional incongruity; and a lack of support from authority figures. As Kathleen and I continued our discussion, we realized she had all five of these elements working against her.

"Coming from an alcoholic family," she says, "my home life was so incongruent that nothing any of the adults did seemed to make sense. There was some physical abuse, but I can't remember much about it. I was in such a dissociative state that I still have no recall of anything that happened between the ages of eight and twelve."

In processing what she could remember, Kathleen saw that the difference between what people said versus what they felt and did caused her the most pain. As she became aware of how deeply this affected her, she noticed her clients were suffering from debilitating feelings of instability and betrayal resulting from the same pain. "It's a good part of what attracted me to equine therapy," she told me. "Most of my clients unconsciously pick up that people in their lives are not congruent, and this translates to a feeling of not being able to trust anyone, of not being safe in the world. At the same time, the men and women I counsel have a terrible time admitting their true feelings to themselves, let alone to others, because they've been taught to disregard their emotions by the authority figures in their lives. They're caught in this vicious circle of feeling confused and threatened around incongruent people, yet not being able to act congruently themselves. The horses are able to break this cycle by showing people what they're really feeling without sugarcoating it, yet somehow it's not so threatening when these animals see through you. I think it's because horses don't have any ulterior motives. They're just responding honestly in the moment."

The ability to lie, to oneself and to others, is prominent in postconquest consciousness. While animals will occasionally fake injury to draw a predator away from their young, their ability to deceive is limited by one important factor: they can't speak. Lies are almost exclusively based in language. People indoctrinated into the postconquest mindset are even more susceptible to deceit because they're conditioned to downplay sensory, emotional, behavioral, and intuitive input in order to focus on what someone is saying. They become mesmerized by intellectual arguments and verbal justifications for all kinds of selfish, destructive actions and unspoken animosity. I endured a barrage of insults and disrespect from my first husband for one simple reason: he consistently told me he loved me, assuring me that his criticisms were designed to help me become a better writer, a better person, a more beautiful woman. Never mind that I felt increasingly worthless.

For seven years, I was able to focus on the idea of love while ignoring reality. My mind actually colluded with my husband. It was my body and my emotions that finally convinced me I was unable to survive any further under those conditions. The month before I left him, I vomited every morning as I was getting ready for work. After ruling out pregnancy, I had to face the fact that I literally couldn't stomach his treatment any longer.

Similarly, Joy's mind remained under Jason's spell until Noche mirrored what she was actually feeling in her body. Once she reconnected with her senses, her emotions, and her intuition through work with the horses — and began changing her life in response — she became much less easily victimized by friends and family. A series of persistent physical symptoms began to lift as well. During the first few months of our association, Joy had been plagued by debilitating abdominal cramps for which doctors could find no cause. These difficulties were finally written off as "psychosomatic," a term Joy mistakenly interpreted as "imaginary."

"Psychosomatic illnesses can be painful and even life-threatening," I replied when she told me of the diagnosis. "It's just that conventional doctors have trouble treating these conditions because the source of the problem lies outside their jurisdiction, so to speak. Psychosomatic symptoms arise in response to stressful situations — relationship problems, unfulfilling jobs, unresolved trauma, and abuse. Just because your cramps don't seem to have a physical origin doesn't mean they're imaginary. In this case, you're lucky you're human. Horses literally die from the same symptoms you've been experiencing."

I told her about the enteric nervous system, how the small intestine, as a protective response, automatically becomes inflamed when the body feels threatened — even if the socially conditioned conscious mind refuses to acknowledge the threat. The equine digestive system, which is much more delicate than those of cows, goats, dogs, and humans, cannot withstand this inflammation for long. In nature, horses who escape danger without injury recover quickly. In captivity, however, these animals can't run away from unstable riders or high-pressure training methods. As a result, the small intestines of horses experiencing long-term stress remain inflamed, making them more susceptible to bouts of abdominal discomfort, or colic. One of the leading killers of domesticated horses, colic is attributed to everything from bad hay to impacted colons, parasites, and the ingestion of sand. Yet horses on the show circuit who benefit from the best food, the finest care, and the most innovative veterinary practices also experience a high incidence of colic, due to their stressful lives.

Over the years, I've seen numerous incidents of colic arise during seemingly minor increases in stress. A group of five Arabian mares living on pasture at The Ranch enjoyed perfect health for several years, despite the fact that the herd's out-of-state owner rarely came to see them, never groomed them, provided them with a simple diet of alfalfa twice a day, and paid for inoculations only once a year. Other animals at The Ranch who were blanketed on cold winter nights, fed all manner of vitamins, wormed quarterly, exercised daily, and given special supplements to expel sand from the digestive system suffered serious and even fatal bouts of colic while those five scraggly mares went about their business without a care.

It's important to note that this particular group of Arabians had a history of abuse. All of them possessed fine bloodlines and were slated for the show circuit but returned traumatized from extended professional training. Their owner tried to rehabilitate them, with little success; the mares were flighty, uncooperative, and prone to panic in situations that wouldn't faze the average horse. When it seemed they would never be safe to ride, the woman decided to turn them out and let them live in peace as a herd. Several years later, however, financial considerations motivated her to find the horses good homes. "Kaitlin," a quiet, compassionate physical therapist, took one of the mares on as a project, moved the horse to a large stall next to her friends, and began a long, slow process of gentling her. Within the first month of her training, this mare, who hadn't been sick for years, colicked, even though she was merely being haltered and led around the property.

She remained able to see and even touch noses with the other mares over the fence, but the fact was she had been separated from her herd. And though her new owner was a considerate, gentle person, the mare was suddenly learning to interact with a human again after relating exclusively to horses for years. These two factors were enough to send her gut into turmoil. Thanks to Kaitlin's patience and confidence in her, however, the horse eventually worked through her fear and its symptoms as she progressed toward longeing, saddling, and riding. (Despite Kaitlin's relative inexperience with horses, she managed to heal the effects of trauma in the mare by employing therapeutic techniques used on humans who've survived extreme experiences, a concept I'll discuss in detail in chapter 8.)

Another Tucson boarding stable hired "Scott," a former Vietnam War vet, to manage the barn and care for the horses. It soon became apparent, however, that he suffered from posttraumatic stress disorder. He was in a state of constant hyperarousal, overreacting to anyone who challenged his authority, including horses he perceived as difficult. Several borders mentioned that their animals were more flighty in his presence, even when Scott was having a good day. During the six months he worked there, four horses suffered serious bouts of colic. After the man was eventually fired for an unrelated reason, the owner of the operation couldn't help but notice that there were no incidents of colic for the entire next year.

In the weeks after I first watched Noche react so dramatically to Joy's unconscious fear of Jason, I began to notice other horses around town colicking during particularly stressful periods in the lives of their owners. One experienced rider who came to me for advice on relationship problems complained that two of her horses had recently colicked. "Jean" assumed they had eaten some bad hay, though she didn't know this for sure. As I questioned her further, I discovered that in the month leading up to the colic, her husband had asked for a divorce, and her daughter had been in a serious auto accident. I could see — and feel — that Jean was a nervous wreck. It was actually difficult for me to think straight in her presence, and I was agitated for two hours after she left. Another man who felt angered and betrayed after being passed over for a much-needed promotion proceeded to lose his beloved horse to colic. Both people were in states of emotional distress strong enough to affect me physically. I wondered how their horses must have felt associating with them every day.

Another woman at The Ranch adopted a formerly abused Arabian gelding who everyone insisted was hopeless. The sixteen-year-old horse was distrustful of people, head shy, extremely difficult to catch, halter, and lead. He was commonly described as "stupid," "psychotic," and, more colorfully, "loco." Nancy, however, felt a strong connection to Rocky, whose large, soulful eyes held so much promise one minute and so much fear the next.

One evening, Nancy's twenty-year-old daughter, Becky, asked me to take a look at the horse as I was about to get in my car and head off to dinner. "The vet thinks we should put Rocky down," she said. "He went ballistic yesterday during his checkup. My mom and the vet were just trying to get the halter on him, and he freaked out. He actually tried to jump the fence and cut his leg real bad in the process. He was so keyed up that the vet shot him full of tranquilizers and still had trouble wrapping the wound. Everyone says Rocky is dangerous. My mom feels terrible, but I don't want her to get hurt."

Walking toward Rocky's stall, I knew I had the final say as to whether this horse lived or died. The little bay gelding stood in the corner, obviously wary of my presence. I took a deep breath, asked for assistance from the Horse Ancestors, and slowly approached him as Nancy stood just inside the gate. A number of conflicting sense images filled my body.

"Has something particularly disturbing happened to you?" I asked Nancy. "Other than what happened with Rocky, are you upset about something in your life?"

"Well...," she said, "I lost my job last week."

"Have you been trying to act happy around Rocky when you're actually feeling sad, angry, trapped?"

"Yeah," she replied tentatively, not quite understanding why I was asking such personal questions about her when Rocky was the one whose life was on the line.

Rocky lowered his head and licked his lips, a sign I had come to read in my own horses as indicating the release of some previously unacknowledged emotion. In this case, Rocky's comfort level seemed directly tied to Nancy's hidden feelings. I walked toward him. He backed away. More images, more sensations seemed to arise from his wounded leg and his aching heart. I silently conveyed to Rocky that Nancy was his last chance, that I would try to explain his perspective to her, but if he couldn't bring himself to trust this woman, his worst fears would indeed come true. I told him I would convince her to give him one more month, one more cycle of the moon. The rest was up to him. After a good fifteen minutes of subtle interactions with the horse, he allowed me to briefly touch his shoulder.

"Imagine this," I finally said to Nancy, who now stood quietly, hopefully, next to the feeder about five feet away from Rocky and me. "Imagine that you were raped as a teenager. A few years later, you marry a man who seems very gentle and understanding. Yet once you have that wedding ring on your finger, he thinks you should just get over your conflicting feelings about sex. He suddenly treats you like he owns you. You know he loves you, but he's impatient with you. It doesn't make any sense, but you feel trapped, like you want to run away from this person, who you also realize is your only real hope for connection. Rocky feels like that. He knows you care for him, but just because you officially own him now, just because you pay his feed and board, doesn't mean he can automatically let go of all those years of abuse and mistrust. He can't become intimate so easily. Do you know what I mean?"

Nancy stared at me in silence for a moment.

"I do," she finally said, diverting her eyes as if suddenly embarrassed. She slowly looked up at me, shaking her head in disbelief. "Basically, you just told my life's story."

I was taken aback by this admission. The example I used had popped into my mind while interacting with Rocky. I had no idea it related to Nancy's life. Unprepared for a full-blown equine-facilitated psychotherapy session, especially one based on a sudden intuition, I nonetheless gathered my wits and proceeded to explain the concept of emotional congruency. I told Nancy she wasn't doing Rocky any favors by trying to suppress her negative feelings in his presence. This was not the way to calm him down and gain his trust. As I discussed Rocky's situation from a therapeutic perspective, it became obvious that Nancy's attraction to the horse stemmed from what I've come to call *emotional resonance*. People and horses who've experienced similar difficulties, betrayals, and abuses are like two strings tuned to the same note. Whenever Nancy was in a heightened state of turmoil, I explained, Rocky couldn't help but resonate with her. And the intensity would increase if she tried to hide those feelings. In such a state of incongruity, her emotions were fighting her intellect, begging to be expressed. This actually turned the volume up on the sympathetic vibrations exciting Rocky's own unresolved fears and frustrations, causing him to act these feelings out for the both of them. I asked her to consider the possibility that even though Rocky was afraid of the vet, his reactions were accentuated in the presence of Nancy, who it turned out was experiencing feelings related not only to the loss of her job but to a series of frustrations with her husband, who was having an affair with another woman in part because of his inability to deal with Nancy's childhood sexual trauma.

"Tell Rocky what you're feeling," I said. "Get it out in the open so he doesn't have to mirror it for you. He won't necessarily understand what you're saying, but by expressing your true feelings, you'll become congruent, and you'll release the extra tension behind those emotions."

For the next ten minutes, Nancy spoke candidly about the violence, shame, and betrayal she had experienced. She promised Rocky that she wouldn't push him, that she would treat him as she would have wanted to be treated by the men in her life. My eyes began to sting in response to her story. The moment I let go of my professional distance and allowed the tears to flow down my cheeks, Rocky stepped toward me and rested his face in the center of my chest. Just a few minutes earlier I had told Nancy that, unlike human beings, horses don't judge or reject us for what we're feeling; it's the act of trying to suppress our emotions that drives them insane. Rocky took that notion one step further. He showed us that even a horse written off as "loco," a horse considered too crazy to live, could feel safe enough to approach us the moment we let down our guard and began to speak from the heart.

Rocky did indeed take us up on our offer. The first month came and went without incident as the horse accepted the halter and began to lead and longe without objection. Six months later, he was a gregarious, even joyful member of Nancy and Becky's herd, and they made arrangements to start him under saddle in the spring.

Brain Acid

Intestinal turmoil and behavioral difficulties aren't the only symptoms associated with unresolved trauma. Particularly dramatic single incidents or long periods of low-grade stress have actually been shown to cause brain damage. And human and equine brains share the same basic structures. Both species have a limbic system and a hypothalamus, sites responsible for organizing emotion and memory; bodily functions like heart rate, blood pressure, and respiration; and the constant interaction between these elements — hence the literal connection between emotional upheaval and the quickened beating of the heart. Horses also have a polyvagal nervous system and a neocortex responsible for learning, reasoning, and correlating multiple sensory inputs. Even so, the human predilection for downplaying the intelligence of other mammals has led even dedicated equine researchers to question the purpose of the cerebral cortex in horses. In his book *The Nature of Horses*, Stephen Budiansky concedes that equines have "a relatively large brain for an animal of their size. The bad news is that they use most of it just to keep their feet in the right place." He argues that the huge range of movement horses display demands a large number of "hardwired controls" that don't leave much room for higher thought. This is an odd statement considering that the cerebellum, which sits at the back of the brain, is considered the seat of coordination, balance, and fine motor control. According to Leslie Skipper, author of the book *Inside Your Horse's Mind*, the equine cerebellum is, as expected, "exceptionally large and well developed, and it is this, rather than the cerebral cortex, which controls and fine-tunes those wonderfully graceful and athletic movements." Skipper uses color-coded illustrations of the equine brain to show that "areas of the cortex associated with voluntary movement in the horse are in proportion to the areas which govern sight, smell, hearing, etc.; this leaves a considerable portion of the cerebral cortex free for nonessential thought processes."

Many trainers argue that horses lack intelligence by pointing to the well-known fact that it doesn't work to punish these animals for a transgression unless the correction can be administered immediately, suggesting that the horse's memory of an experience dissipates after a mere two or three seconds. Skipper challenges this assumption by putting the rider in the horse's position: "Suppose you are a process worker, performing a specific task, and orders are being shouted at you in a foreign language which you may or may not properly understand. Let us further suppose that you make some error of which you are blissfully unaware. The supervisor starts shouting, 'You idiot! You've got it wrong!' But what have you done wrong? The supervisor does not explain, but simply keeps on shouting that you're an idiot, you've got it wrong. Do you think you would have the remotest idea what you had done wrong unless the reproof were directly connected to the error?"

The myth that horses lack intelligence is bolstered by four other misinterpreted factors: their gift for one-trial learning, their talent for evasion, the limbic system's connection between emotion and memory, and the destructive influence of stress hormones on the cerebral cortex. Because they're preyed on in nature, horses' survival depends upon their ability to process, recall, and elaborate on the lessons gleaned from a single experience. In the wild, they may only have one chance to get it right, so horses consequently became skilled in one-trial learning. Predators, on the other hand, show less facility in this area; they can make mistakes and live to hunt another day. Trainers who understand this feature of the equine mind can actually get better results with less time in the saddle. Eponaquest cofounder Dana Light, for instance, conducted a three-month colt starting class at a Phoenix community college. The students met only once a week with the horses they were assigned to train. Even so, the wild, completely inexperienced two-year-olds donated to the class made leaps and bounds within this schedule of six days off and one day on. They not only retained memory of what was taught the previous week, they often showed improvement at the beginning of the following session. The spirited colts acted as if they'd been thinking about what they had learned all week. Such a loose training schedule ultimately isn't rigorous enough for show circuit preparation because disciplines like jumping, dressage, and eventing demand athletic endurance and careful muscle development. This, however, is a physical, not a mental, consideration.

The problem with one-trial learning is that less experienced riders can accidentally create all kinds of unintended responses in their horses. For example, in less than a minute, you can teach a horse to lower his head by touching his nose. The trick is to hold your hand in place until he drops his head, then immediately let go and praise him. If, however, you startle the horse during your initial attempt, he will automatically jerk his head up and away from your hand, and you've effectively taught him the opposite of what you originally intended. Unfortunately, in one-trial learning, repetition isn't necessary to create a nasty habit. Of course the presence of incongruent people further exacerbates the situation. Since horses exhibit a particularly strong tendency to mirror the feelings behind the façade, people unconscious of their own emotions and motivations literally have no idea what they're communicating to and teaching these highly responsive creatures.

This leads to the second major factor, the equine talent for evasion, which wreaks havoc on people who prefer to train through fear and intimidation. A horse simply isn't giving his full attention to the lesson when he feels threatened; he's figuring out how to escape. These animals are masters of avoidance. I've seen them easily outwit doctors with fancy new cowboy boots, physicists with advanced degrees, and trainers who've been in the business for thirty years. Anyone who relies on fear and intimidation will spend a great deal of time blocking the increasingly inventive evasions his or her horse will devise. This dynamic creates the adversarial relationships many riders consider normal.

The limbic system's connection between emotion and memory storage adds to the dilemma: whenever a horse is afraid while being introduced to a new concept, he's thereafter inclined to experience fear every time he's asked to perform that particular move. If, on the other hand, a confident and well-cared-for horse is spooked by a novel situation, a trusted rider can calm him down by initiating movements that were originally learned in a safe and peaceful environment. One particularly powerful troubleshooting strategy combines instinct and positive emotional associations; a trainer gently teaches the horse to drop his head and round his back on cues that can be given from the ground or the saddle. This is a posture a prey animal will only adopt in nature when he feels secure. By instructing him to perform this action on request in a relaxed setting and making an extra effort to praise him for doing so, the trainer can later depend on him to respond to this same signal in an emergency, thus keeping him from panicking. Conversely, people who ride their horses in a head-high, hollow-backed position are always one step away from losing control, as horses take this posture when in flight-or-fight mode. I've helped many people cure their horses of running off simply by teaching them how to ride with the horse's back rounded and his head in a lower, more relaxed position.

Human memory is also stored via the limbic system. Thoughts with a similar nuance of feeling are filed together, even if they have no logical or chronological connection. Research shows it's much more difficult for people to recall facts if they're not in the same mood as when they learned them. For this reason, standardized intelligence tests may actually measure little more than how well a person can think, reason, and remember under pressure — or how much they learned under pressure to begin with.

I didn't truly understand the physiology of stress until I began collaborating with Dianna Hine, MA, a counselor with significant experience treating behavioral and learning difficulties associated with childhood trauma. In her book *The Baby Bond: How to Raise an Emotionally Healthy Child*, Dianna discusses the latest research on brain development, offering some startling realizations about the effects of stress. A study by Dr. Linda Mayes of the Yale Child Study Center concludes that particularly traumatic or repetitive stressful experiences in childhood actually shape the brain's structure. The brain develops by creating neurological circuitry patterns in response to experience. These responses not only dictate how the brain becomes organized but can interfere with the kind of development important to learning. When Dianna and I were creating an equine-facilitated psychotherapy program for troubled teens, she explained that many of these children were neurologically disabled, if only temporarily. Severely abused children, to use the most extreme example, consistently associate the feeling of stress with negative, even life-threatening outcomes. Unless this pattern is counteracted and other brain pathways are created, such people continue to respond to the slightest sense of pressure or uncertainty as an emergency, immediately falling into the flight, fight, or freeze mode. Dianna was interested in equine-facilitated therapy specifically because it creates new brain circuits through new experiences. Conventional cognitive psychotherapy falls short in this respect.

"When someone is in the flight-or-fight mode, the cerebral cortex becomes less active to prepare the body for instinctual troubleshooting responses," she explained. "Reasoning and other higher thought processes are a much lower priority at that moment. If you're trying to change the behavior of a child who becomes combative at the slightest sign of stress by trying to appeal to his sense of logic, you're working at a serious disadvantage, because the reasoning part of the brain isn't working properly at that moment."

Dianna and I developed techniques that use a person's sense of uncertainty in the presence of the horse to orchestrate a positive outcome, one resulting in feelings of strength, competence, and self-satisfaction. In this way, a new circuit is created. Rather than *uncertainty = danger = flight or fight*, another pathway emerges that essentially says, *Uncertainty can sometimes lead to pleasure and satisfaction*, something the child wants to hang around for. Thus the tendency to slip immediately into the flight-or-fight mode is weakened. I subsequently put this same strategy to work with an abused stallion named Midnight Merlin, and, as I describe in chapter 9, the results were impressive.

The problem for human beings and animals who've survived extremely traumatic situations, however, is that research suggests this level of stress can damage the brain. The higher thought functions useful in regulating and modifying behavior are not encouraged to develop, and the flight, fight, and freeze responses become dominant.

"Powerful hormones like cortisol are released in the brain in response to stress," Dianna explains. "Some researchers have actually referred to cortisol as brain acid because it destroys these cells with frightening efficiency. In brain imaging scans you can see dark holes of inactivity in the brains of children who have experienced significant trauma or long-term stress. The centers that tend to be targeted by this assault correspond with functions related to thinking, memory, impulse control, and the emotions."

"Sadly," she writes in The Baby Bond, "children emerging from these uncertain beginnings usually have a number of social problems and they are often blamed for behaving badly. They tend to be children who are overreactive, impulsive, anxious, angry, and hypersensitive and their behaviors and reactions are usually inappropriate. But they are just following what comes naturally to them — reacting as they have been programmed to behave. For [children] to be encouraged to develop traits such as thoughtfulness, cooperation, respect, and intellectual curiosity, they require a secure and consistently responsive environment."

Dianna goes on to cite a study directed by Megan Gunnar, a developmental psychologist from the University of Minnesota. Gunnar's work suggests that resilience to stress is affected by how secure and safe the child feels with his or her caretaker. Children under two show elevated levels of stress when put in seemingly minor situations, like being vaccinated or being separated from their mothers. After two, however, children who developed a secure bond with their caretakers no longer register this stress as they move into the world and deal with increasingly complex challenges. The insecure child, on the other hand, will continue to suffer from elevated levels of stress hormones, like cortisol, in contexts that simply don't faze the well-adjusted child. Dianna also notes other situations young children find distressing, "such as when they are around repeated screaming and fighting, even if it's not being directed at them, or when they are cared for by a parent who is depressed and disengaged."

People who've grown up facing these challenges are more prone to score lower on intelligence tests and do poorly in school, not because they're "stupid," but because their heightened responses make it difficult for them to function in situations others consider only mildly stressful. Short-tempered, intimidating teachers who habitually put students on the spot plunge the emotionally unstable student into the flight, fight, or freeze mode, a process that literally shuts down higher thought processes. The low self-esteem resulting from failing test scores and embarrassing classroom encounters further impairs learning as peers and role models categorize these people in increasingly negative terms.

Two studies cited in *Recovering the Soul*, a fascinating book on the mind-body connection by physician and author Larry Dossey, bring to light the effect a teacher's perception of students can have upon academic success. The Oak School experiment conducted by Harvard psychologist Robert Rosenthal involved 650 students and 18 female teachers. At the beginning of the year, the faculty was told a particular intelligence test indicated that 20 percent of the children enrolled would make superior academic progress. Teachers were provided a list of these supposedly promising students after the test was given, names that were in reality chosen at random. "At the end of the school year," writes Dossey, "the same test was given to the student body [again]. The result? The 'gifted' group of students demonstrated real above-average increases in their IQ's. In addition, the subjective reports of the teachers rated those students to be more outgoing, friendly, and intellectually curious than their peers." Rosenthal documented this same effect in an experiment measuring rat intelligence. Twelve students in an experimental psychology course were told that testing skills could be handed down genetically in rats through selective breeding. Six students were then given thirty rats supposedly bred from exceptional learners. The other six were given thirty rats from a gene pool selected for low intelligence. In reality, the rats all came from the same genetically homogeneous group. When all sixty were trained in the same learning experiment, however, the animals "whose trainers believed them to be superior actually did better from the outset, and raised their achievement scores far above those of the 'unintelligent' animals."

Based on an IQ test Kathleen Barry Ingram took during a particularly tempestuous period in her childhood, she was considered mildly retarded and discouraged from attending college. So how does one explain her ability to graduate with honors from the University of Colorado? Kathleen feels that the confidence and peace of mind she gained once she broke away from her family's dysfunctional environment — and recovered from their low expectations of her — provided the opening in which she could let her true talents rise to the surface. Joy's tempestuous family life also led to an inability to perform in school. Like Kathleen, she scored poorly on exams, no matter how hard she studied. "The only time I seemed to do well," she remembers, "is when I was able to complete a project without some sort of rigid time constraint. Under any kind of pressure, I would go blank." Her mother's constant contemptuous reminders that Joy and her brothers were "learning impaired" further aggravated the situation. One of her siblings, in fact, was transferred to a school for the mentally disabled after scoring particularly low on an IQ test taken shortly after Joy's alcoholic father died, leading to further insults from their now grief-stricken, emotionally unstable mother. Similarly, the aggressive cowboys Buck Light initially encountered at the working cattle ranch considered their mounts stupid and unreliable. The animals acted accordingly — until they were transferred to Buck's string and treated with respect.

These studies and anecdotes show that people in positions of authority have a significant effect on those entrusted to their care. If stressful learning environments and the negative perceptions of parents, teachers, and other role models aren't turned around early enough in the life of a troubled child or animal, the results can be devastating. The constant assault of hormones like cortisol on the brains of those under the stress of these misguided practices could arguably lead to a state of environmentally induced mental retardation. "Too many stress hormones flooding our system every day over years can cause numerous diseases and disorders," Dianna emphasizes in *The Baby Bond*, "as many people have discovered. High blood pressure and damaged organs tell us the flight or fight response has been forced to go too far. There is just so much stress a human being is equipped to endure."

In our work with troubled teens and horses, Dianna and I found that retraining both species to move beyond these debilitating patterns depended upon creating a low-stress learning environment. We introduced some instances of minor uncertainty in such a way as to foster positive, confidence-building outcomes that created more versatile brain circuitry. In talking with Buck Light and observing his interactions with working cow horses, I realized that the reason his mounts acted smarter than the horses of the rougher, more intimidating cowboys was that he was instinctively able to achieve this complex therapeutic goal whenever he stepped into the saddle. The good news was that the frightened, instinctually driven geldings transferred to his string became more confident, more thoughtful, more cooperative, and more gregarious relatively quickly under Buck's tutelage, suggesting they had plenty of gray matter left to compensate for previous damage.

Neurologists have shown that human beings use a relatively small percentage of their brain capacity. Perhaps we have so much extra gray matter in part to compensate for the debilitating effects of war, abuse, disinterested family members, role models' negativity, and the increasingly unforgiving pace of modern life — factors that literally eat away at our brains as they also destroy our souls. Yet for what purpose might we use all those extra cells if we weren't constantly recovering from assaults on the mind and body? Would creative genius become commonplace?

The Nuances of Superior Intelligence

Candace Pert, PhD, a research professor in the Department of Physiology and Biophysics at Georgetown University Medical Center in Washington, DC, has written a fascinating book on the biomolecular basis of emotion. *Molecules of Emotion* provides a theoretical framework in which the body functions as an important part of the mind, challenging the Cartesian notion that everything below the neck acts as a fleshy machine that simply carries the brain around. The title of her engaging audio program *Your Body Is Your Subconscious Mind* sums up her intricate research in a nutshell. Pert's theories are widely cited in the fast-developing field of mind-body medicine. The significance of her work in relation to equine-facilitated therapy could take up an entire chapter, but I'd rather encourage people interested in this topic to read her book directly, not only for better insight into this complex subject, but to understand the dilemmas innovative thinkers face in our culture. Part theoretical treatise, part autobiography, *Molecules of Emotion* candidly discusses the prejudices and difficulties women face in the almost pathologically competitive, highly incongruent field of scientific research, a subculture that absolutely demands people separate mind from emotion in order to succeed. Through her own rigorous experiments, Pert, ironically enough, provided evidence that the postconquest tendency to compartmentalize mind, body, and emotion constitutes a misinterpretation of reality, one that has little bearing on how living organisms function.

Pert's experiments were responsible in part for the now widespread depiction of the enteric nervous system as a complex brain in its own right. In the mid-1970s, she codiscovered the opiate receptor, along with Solomon Snyder, who was awarded the Nobel Prize for his work. (Her exclusion from the award, due to the male-dominated politics of the scientific community, makes for a particularly disturbing chapter in her book.) In any case, her research illuminates the form and function of neuropeptides, information-carrying chemicals affecting emotion and the physical and psychological responses to emotion. Pert found that receptor sites for these substances are located not only in the brain but throughout the body. The heart, for instance, which was historically considered the seat of the emotions, turns out to contain every single neuropeptide receptor associated with emotion that researchers have ever looked for. Free-ranging white blood cells called monocytes, which play a pivotal role in immune response, also have these receptors. Further studies indicated that neuropeptides are not only received at sites throughout the body, they are actually made outside the brain. In biomolecular terms, this means that emotion can be created by any organ or cell with the capacity to produce these information-carrying substances. Pert's work suggests that people experiencing so-called gut feelings are literally keying into the fact that their intestines, not their brains, are the source of particular emotions. She emphasizes that emotions are what link the body and the brain in a single dynamic system of mind extending beyond the wrinkled matter between the ears. "Think of the body-mind as a field of information and energy as opposed to a hunk of meat," she says, "then you realize that emotions are everywhere in the body.... They don't trickle down from the head. They're occurring simultaneously in the head and in the body."

Pert's research also demonstrates that many of the molecules of emotion found in the human brain and throughout the body are found in less sophisticated living organisms. When she studied the opiate receptor in a microscopic organism called the tetrahymena, she found this tiny protozoa creates and processes endorphins the same way the human system does. The term *endorphin*, which translates as "the morphine within," describes a series of substances created in response to pain. These same chemicals induce a sense of intense well-being, providing the euphoric feelings associated with the runner's high, the glow experienced after making love, and the sensation of deep peace during meditation. The idea that protozoa experience an ecstasy-producing chemical reaction is a paradigm-busting scientific realization. Since the time of René Descartes, many researchers were trained to believe that animals didn't truly feel pain, let alone happiness or euphoria. Yet why else would even the simplest organisms have opiate receptors no different in form and function than those found in the human body?

It was, interestingly enough, a serious horseback riding accident that gave Pert the direct experience of the opiate response she later explored through her scientific research. Lying flat on her back in the hospital, she was "doped to the gills on Talwin, a morphine derivative" given to ease the pain of a compressed lumbar vertebra. Pert would later prove that morphine and similar drugs work by binding to the receptors designed to receive the body's own opiate-like substances, the endorphins. At the time of her injury, however, she was weeks away from entering graduate medical school at Johns Hopkins University to train in neuropharmacology, the study of the action of drugs in the brain. After coming off an extended morphine-induced altered state, she passed her remaining time in the hospital by reading a book on the theory of the opiate receptors. "I remember marveling at how there were tiny molecules on my cells that allowed for that wonderful feeling I'd experienced every time the nurse had injected me with an intramuscular dose of morphine," she writes in *Molecules of Emotion*. "There was no doubt that the drug's action in my body produced a distinctly euphoric effect, one that filled me with a bliss bordering on ecstasy."

Pert contends that all biological organisms are "wired for pleasure," since species from the tiny tetrahymena to rats, tigers, horses, and human beings share the same receptors and neuropeptides capable of creating that response. Because endorphins are especially plentiful in the brain, she has also concluded that this particular organ is designed to maximize pleasure, an insight that further challenges the validity of forceful, fear-producing, punishment-oriented modes of training, teaching, and modifying behavior.

When the body recovers from stress, chemicals such as adrenaline and cortisol are replaced in the system by endorphins, which not only elevate mood but also improve higher brain functions, such as memory and learning. Some of Pert's most intriguing insights concern the frontal cortex, a part of the brain significantly larger and more finely developed in humans than in other animals. The seat of planning, will, and focus, the frontal cortex doesn't actually mature until people reach their twenties. (In terms of cerebral development, therefore, expecting a recent high school graduate to come up with a detailed life plan and remain focused enough to carry it out is like pressuring a child to run when he's still learning to walk.)

Pert noticed that opiate receptors tend to be especially plentiful in this part of the brain, and yet the count can also vary dramatically from one person to another. The frontal cortex is like a muscle; it must be exercised to develop properly. Experienced meditators and highly creative people show heightened activity in this area, suggesting that the frontal cortex is crucial to these functions. The euphoria of meditation and creativity undoubtedly result from huge numbers of endorphins binding with receptors concentrated in this part of the cortex when it's activated.

Over the years, I've noticed that riders who reject the stress-producing intimidation tactics of horse training actually do themselves a favor. They not only see a difference in their horses, they tend to leave the arena in a much calmer, and quite often elated, state themselves. When Joy succeeded in longeing Rasa through will and focus, my previously agitated student experienced a feeling of well-being bordering on ecstasy that stayed with her for several hours. It didn't take her long to realize she felt better after interacting with the horses than she did in practically every other facet of her life. By constantly tuning into her own mind-body system in order to remain congruent in the presence of these animals, she relieved the pressure of pent-up emotions. By riding and training the horses through frontal cortex mind-over-muscle techniques, she gained the cooperation of a thousand-pound creature in a seemingly effortless, stress-reducing way. Rasa wasn't forced into listening to Joy through fear or intimidation; the mare was deferring to the woman's more sophisticated powers of planning and intent. It actually appeared as if Rasa was borrowing Joy's focus. Whenever Joy lost her focus, Rasa immediately took over and began to make her own decisions again. In this way, the mare acted as a biofeedback agent for exercising Joy's frontal cortex.

Through intuition and experience, I've come to realize that horses have an especially well-developed talent for reading intent at a distance, essentially a survival strategy. In nature, a high aptitude for planning and focus is not particularly useful to prey animals. It's more important for them to remain in the reflective state of mind I've come to call "the wide view" or "all things equal." During my period of immersion in the equine perspective at Timothy Graham's Oasis ranch, I once asked the Horse Ancestors to explain the benefits of this perspective.

"In the wide view," they communicated, "nothing is given attention. Things call attention to themselves. All things are equal; attention flows across the landscape. In this way, it is immediately apparent when something moves out of balance. The most elusive prey does not seek. She carries no ambition. In this way, her mind is free to sense what is seeking.

"If the tiger walks the open field relaxed and wide of view, no horse stops grazing. Yet this same tiger hiding in the grass scatters the herd when things are no longer equal in his gaze. Concentrated attention gives rise to predatory action. One does not have to wait for the tiger's pounce to begin running. The narrow focus of his intent calls attention back his way."

The awakening of the wide view in Joy, a woman who was repeatedly victimized, was essential to breaking the cycle of abuse in her life. Through images like the lake behind the black horse's eyes and a number of activities designed to induce an expanded state of multisensory consciousness, she connected with her own internal sources of awareness, authority, and empowerment. The horses also helped her better understand her uniquely human powers of will and focus as a way to become more assertive, not aggressive, in her interactions with others. As I watched this process unfold in Joy's life, I was once again reminded of the appearance of predator and prey characteristics in the human psyche. The strengths of both ways of relating to the world are enhanced in therapeutic situations that bring this particular pair of opposites into balance.

A misuse of or overemphasis on frontal cortex function, for instance, actually seems to decrease creativity and awareness. Joy's childhood trauma taught her to engage her frontal cortex in order to ignore reality and focus on the future as she made up happy stories about how she would save her abusers, literally willing herself to endure highly toxic situations. Her work with the horses reoriented that focus back toward reality, toward the present, expanding her view to include emotional, sensory, and intuitive information while teaching her to use her will to become more assertive in getting the treatment she deserved — rather than making her more tolerant of abuse.

Our unique talent for language is associated with the temporal lobes, which are larger in humans than in any other mammals. This feature, combined with our increased ability to focus through the frontal cortex, creates the double-edged sword of concentrated attention. The frontal cortex's ability to filter out everything else allows us to pay attention to something through force of will. Yet sensations and feelings are constantly pouring into our body-minds. When we form a thought and narrow the focus of that thought enough to fit it into the context of spoken or written language, we are abstracting from that complexity. As we pass these simplified snapshots of reality on to other people, they eventually solidify into a cultural perspective that literally shapes the way we perceive the world. When we look at a horse, for example, we're filtering a stream of sense data through a stereotyped thought pattern, the pattern to which we've grown accustomed through parental and cultural reinforcement. As a result, a lot of data never comes to our attention. Because our culture overemphasizes the kind of abstraction needed to translate experience into language, we've reached the point where the emotions and memories we are most conscious of are set in motion primarily by thoughts and words.

In horses, it appears that memories are stimulated by emotion and the physiological sensations that give rise to those emotions. However, these animals do not seem to separate thought and memory from feeling and sensation. The four are always connected. (This is why an action like lowering the head will calm a frightened horse.) A horse's mind is literally swimming in a sea of nuance that also exists in the human brain before it filters experience through language. Most people identify themselves with what rises to the surface of that ocean and is captured by the frontal cortex–temporal lobe net. This net is woven by the habits of thought our language imposes on perception and the small amount of sense data that makes it through.

When a society functions primarily through its frontal cortex, its members increasingly engage in secondhand thought — thought based less on direct sensory experience and more on assumptions passed down by others. Too much secondhand thought leads to a kind of voluntary sensory deprivation, to the point where modern city dwellers find it advantageous to attend sensory awareness classes. In extreme cases, the modern human habit of emphasizing neural pathways between the temporal lobes and the frontal cortex while ignoring input from the sensory-rich limbic system leads to a loss of creativity and emotional responsiveness; the personality becomes flat. The effect is similar to that of a lobotomy, when the connections between the frontal lobes of the cortex and the limbic system are severed surgically. It is indeed disturbing that our cultural and educational systems can have a similar effect on healthy brains over time.

Interestingly enough, creative geniuses seem to think a lot more like horses do. These people also spend a rather large amount of time engaging in that favorite equine pastime: doing nothing. In his book *Fire in the Crucible: The Alchemy of Creative Genius*, John Briggs gathers numerous studies illustrating how artists and inventors keep their thoughts pulsating in a field of nuance associated with the limbic system. In order to accomplish this feat against the influence of cultural conditioning, they tend to be outsiders who have trouble fitting into polite society. Many creative geniuses don't do well in school and don't speak until they're older, thus increasing their awareness of nonverbal feelings, sensations, and body language cues. Albert Einstein is a classic example. Like Kathleen Barry Ingram, he also failed his college entrance exams.

As expected, these sensitive, often highly empathic people feel extremely uncomfortable around incongruent members of their own species and tend to distance themselves from the cultural mainstream. Through their refusal to fit into a system focusing on outside authority, suppressed emotion, and secondhand thought, creative geniuses retain and enhance their ability to activate the entire brain. Information flows freely, strengthening pathways between the various brain functions. The tendency to separate thought from emotion, memory, and sensation is lessened. This gives birth to a powerful nonlinear process, a flood of sensations and images interacting with high-level thought functions and aspects of memory too complex and multifaceted to distill into words. These elements continue to influence and build on one another with increasing ferocity. Researchers emphasize that the entire process is so rapid the conscious mind barely registers *that* it is happening, let alone *what* is happening.

Now, a person — or a horse, for that matter — can theoretically operate at this level her entire life and never receive recognition for the rich and innovative insights resulting from this process. Those called creative geniuses continuously struggle with the task of communicating their revelations to the world through the most amenable forms of expression — music, visual art, poetry, mathematics. Their talent for innovation, however, stems from an ability to continually engage and process a complex, interconnected, nonlinear series of insights. Briggs also found that creative geniuses spend a large amount of time doing nothing, alternating episodes of intense concentration on a project with periods of what he calls "creative indolence." Einstein once remarked that some of his greatest ideas came to him so suddenly while shaving that he was prone to cutting himself with surprise.

Other scientists have come to acknowledge the three Bs — the bus, the bath, and the bed — as where the most influential discoveries are made. I can add another B: the barn. As a journalist prone to writer's block, I quickly realized that a trip to the stable could provide the perfect lead for an article. Complete sentences would come to me when I was cinching up the saddle or hosing down a sweaty horse after a furious gallop through the desert. When I took an extended leave of absence from magazine writing to research a book on horses, this burst of creativity flowed in some unexpected directions.

My most profound breakthroughs in understanding the behavior patterns of horse-human interactions did not always come during formal training sessions. More often than not, new insights would hit me over the head when I was relaxing with my horses. After all the work was done, I'd set Rasa and Noche free to run around the property, and I would wander among the mesquite trees as my horses grazed beside me. Unsolicited ideas and pictures would take hold of me so consistently that I found it necessary to keep a notebook in the tack room. As I studied Briggs's insights into the creative process, I realized I was engaging in a predictable pattern of innovative thought. First, there's the stage of consciously working over the problem and asking the right questions. Then there's a period of incubation without any conscious consideration of the problem. Suddenly and unpredictably, the illumination seems to come out of nowhere — as if the problem almost had to be forgotten to be solved. Incubation and illumination are both part of the nonlinear feedback loop between the limbic system's field of nuance and the cortex's intermittent sparks of higher thought. Many of my clients have reported an increased sense of creativity and intuition during and immediately after their time with horses. Whether they worked in advertising, nursing, counseling, or science, these people sometimes found themselves solving significant job-related problems on the backs of their horses, problems for which they could previously find no solution while racking their brains in the much more serious and stressful atmosphere of the office.

Briggs observes that

> the creative state of mind seems indolent compared to the aggressive concentration of purposeful thought. [Yet] when a specific creative problem is being wrestled with, the solution or truth of vision must lie partly in the spaces between thoughts — the spaces of nuance and omnivalence. Looking back on it, creators may have the sense of not doing much of anything because their minds have been in those "great spaces filled with vague forms."

On the basis of my own experience, as well as my observation of a number of talented trainers and riders, I've come to realize that it is this openness to nuance, sensory awareness, and nonverbal communication — not any particular method or form of tack — that creates the level of interspecies rapport associated with the most efficient and successful trainers. A man or woman who truly deserves the distinction of horse whisperer is activating this process internally, recognizing it in the horse, and forging an even more complex feedback loop between the two of them. The sudden jolts of inspiration that artists and inventors use to create are firing off so rapidly between horse and rider that it's difficult for the most talented and eloquent trainer to even remember what took place, let alone describe it to others. Not only is she listening to the subtle whispers of the horse's body language, but she is listening to the whispers of nuance surging through her own body-mind and acting directly on illuminations arising from moment to moment that the horse, in turn, is listening to and adding to his own internal feedback loop.

When you've truly made the connection, riding a horse feels like a series of small revelations rewarded by surges of endorphins. Most of these insights, however, are put to use long before the conscious mind can fathom what is taking place. Flashes of clarity mixed with waves of elation flow as a stream of visceral responses. This is the so-called rider's high that keeps people coming back for more. It is the feeling of music in motion, of a sublime and silent improvisation between two souls that can never be accurately described.

A human mind tuned to embrace the entire body while connecting sociosensually with the body-mind of the horse is the key to equine success. I like to call this process the *bigger brain loop*, and my own experience of the phenomenon helped me understand why the methods and techniques devised by the world's finest trainers are empty, sometimes even dangerous gimmicks in the hands of riders who rely exclusively on the secondhand thoughts these men and women teach at their workshops. Any new, improved training method is simply a place to start, a chance to shift from a dead-end perspective and tune the body-mind of the rider directly to her mount. A student sensitive enough to develop this kind of relationship with her mount will eventually activate the bigger brain loop, and her horse will quite naturally help her make that leap. She not only has the potential to become a great rider or trainer, she will find the creativity arising from this feedback process seeping into other aspects of her life, and she will feel a forgotten part of herself resurfacing, like Persephone emerging from the underworld to mark the arrival of spring.

Horses have long been known to activate this process, as numerous cross-cultural myths attest. Pegasus spirited the heroes of ancient Greece to the stars of immortality, and the magical waters that nourished poets sprang up where his hoof struck the ground on Helicon, the mountain of the Muses. Mohammed received his sacred visions astride Alborak, the white winged mare who not only took him to heaven but also brought him safely back to earth again. These myths associate equestrian pursuits with images of divine inspiration, but they point to a truth all earthly riders have the potential to experience for themselves: even mortal horses can lead people to secret springs of lost knowledge, and they're fully capable of carrying the living dead, those lobotomized by the current societal paradigm, to a hidden realm of emotional and creative vitality, a kingdom that is indeed within us all.

CHAPTER SEVEN

HORSE WHISPERINGS

Buck Light rode broncs like nobody's business. As a young cowboy in Wyoming, he was one of the wranglers they'd send into a corral filled with bucking, kicking, striking, snorting horses. Sometimes the only way to break these ornery colts to ride, at least as quickly as the boss required, was to saddle them up, wrestle them to the ground, jump on their backs, and hang on as they leapt up and took off running across the arena.

"The hardest part wasn't getting on, or even staying on," Buck remembers. "It was jumping off without getting kicked at the end of that first ride. After a few days, a good number of the guys would be sitting around with broken legs, ribs, and arms. But those of us still standing didn't necessarily consider ourselves lucky. The worst was yet to come. The colts easiest to catch and saddle were the ones we all rode first. The ones left in the corral as we whittled down the herd were probably psychotic. They sure acted that way." ·

The "method" twenty-year-old Buck learned at the ranch involved more nerve, muscle, and testosterone than brains. As he matured, outlasting and in some cases literally surviving many of his cowboy friends, Buck began to develop a quieter, more thoughtful way of training horses. "Part of it had to do with the fact that I was getting older, and I realized my back and bones just couldn't take it any more," he says. "I had a reason to get smarter, and it was called pain. But I think the real turning point came when I was living out on the range without seeing another human being for months. My horse was my best friend, and over time, I came to treat him that way. I started really listening to him and learning from him."

Listening to his horse involved keying into the animal's moods and body language in a wholly nonverbal, sociosensual way, while considering the fact that his mount had his own likes and dislikes, thoughts and insights. By the time I met them in the mid-1990s, Buck and his wife, Dana, treated their ranch horses as colleagues and friends, allowing them to make decisions about the best routes to take and who got saddled up to begin with.

"Anytime we're riding in pasture looking for cattle, it's a working partnership," Dana told me, "and we don't consider ourselves the experts. The horses know where all the pastures are. Anytime we're gathering, they always tell us where the cattle are and the best route to get to them. I'd say that 90 percent of the time we think we've got a better plan and override the horses, we realize they were right when we hit a dead end or a deep wash. Occasionally they'll make a mistake, but it's usually because a route they used before was washed out during the last storm. I mean they'll actually look down at the place where the crossing used to be, then look right and left, momentarily confused.

"The first time Buck let me move cattle by myself, I had to bring three cows down a fence line and through a gate. I'd been training hunter-jumpers for years, and I was used to directing my horse every step of the way. Well, the cows didn't make it through the gate. They ran off in three different directions. While I was trying to go through the thought process of figuring out how to get them back together, the horse had already gathered those cows and pushed them through the gate. I almost fell off, it happened so fast. I learned to get out of the way and let the horses do their job. It's amazing how that kind of consideration will boost their attitude. We've gotten to the point where we decide who we're going to ride on a volunteer basis because horses who have a say in what they do enjoy this work, and they're practically begging to go out. With Buck, though, we sometimes have to make the final decision in disputes between several horses who want to spend the day with him."

Finding humility in the presence of these animals is the first step in a series of life-changing experiences that turn an average trainer into an innovator worthy of national attention. As Sam Powell wrote in his book *Almost a Whisper: A Holistic Approach to Working with Your Horse*:

> The seemingly simple change in my perception of the horse from a dumb animal that needs to be defeated to an animal with a well-structured culture with wants, needs, and a desire to be comfortable led to many other physical, mental, and spiritual transformations. I came to realize that many of the difficulties I had encountered during my younger years were the result of my ego-oriented perception of

the world. Understanding this led me to a way of permanently correcting the problem by eliminating the cause.

Widely recognized North American equestrian authors like Powell, Ray Hunt, Tom Dorrance, Pat Parelli, John Lyons, and Monty Roberts all speak of giving their horses choices, of listening to the animals and expecting them to be responsible for their actions. Though some "horse whisperers" originally learned their craft from the best trainers in the business, these modern Western-style clinicians consider the horses their greatest teachers. The biggest mistake novice equestrians make in idolizing a nationally recognized cowboy-style horseman involves trying to follow his methods without appreciating the awareness, self-knowledge, and horse sense he perfected while creating those methods. Some clinicians, however, unknowingly perpetuate the problem by focusing on particular activities and the special tack they've designed to go along with them, ignoring the almost entirely nonverbal physical, psychological, and spiritual nuances that bring the techniques to life. At larger workshops where people are coming and going, it's also difficult to make sure audience members hear the entire presentation, especially the all-important safety tips. People certainly can't pick up the intricacies of focus, will, confidence, emotional congruency, and other aspects of nonverbal communication watching from the bleachers.

Shawnee Allen, one experienced horse owner and breeder I spoke with, complained that after studying books by Dorrance, Lyons, and Parelli, she was "frustrated because they talk about a special relationship with the horse, but never explain how to achieve it, or they give you the mechanics of their training methods, and after trying them you realize that something is missing because you usually don't get the same results they do. I have always felt that essential information was left out either because these trainers didn't know exactly what it was they were doing different or they didn't know how to explain it."

The most popular clinicians inspire people. They demonstrate the potential of human-equine interactions based on trust and communication. They know how to create the consensual relationships many riders crave with their own horses. As gifted trainers with tremendous experience addressing all kinds of equine-related challenges and emergencies, nothing really surprises them anymore. The ability to keep their cool in the presence of a rearing, bucking, striking horse impresses audiences, as does their ability to calm these animals and get them focused enough to start cooperating very quickly. They are experts at reading body language and responding to subtle changes in the animal's arousal, making split-second adjustments that release the pressure of physical, mental, or emotional discomfort in the horse before it escalates into panic.

Over the years, these trainers have developed a highly sophisticated, yet for the most part unconscious, level of sociosensual awareness. They easily engage mind, body, and intuition to activate the bigger brain loop I spoke of in the previous chapter, an innovative state of awareness that detects, processes, and elaborates on extremely subtle nuances. They know exactly what they want the horse to do, and they're focused enough to project their intent at a distance, yet they're also responsive to the horse's continually changing physical and emotional cues, and they're willing to make adjustments based on an individual's temperament, physical conformation, talents, and special needs. They have developed a series of activities — and, in some cases, special tack — that help less experienced riders become more focused, more coordinated, and more conscious of the horse's perspective. In performing those moves, many of their students do indeed begin to develop a rapport with their horses. Problems arise, however, when people assume the magic is in the mechanics of a clinician's method, that if they just perform the right series of gestures, they too will become horse whisperers.

One worst-case scenario in Tucson involved a middle-aged man who went out and bought a mustang filly after attending a two-day workshop with a well-known trainer. "Raymond" decided to follow the clinician's advice to free longe the horse at a canter until the animal cooperated in changing direction, slowing down, walking to the person, and standing still. The method stipulates that if the horse refuses to listen or becomes aggressive in any way, the trainer should simply send her back out to run around the pen until she gets tired and feels like paying attention.

Lacking the finesse that comes from experience, the man proceeded to scare the horse into a frenzy. He became increasingly frustrated when the young mare refused to respond to his requests for her to slow down and come to him. Like Joy's initial attempts to get Rasa to slow down while free longeing her, he ran toward the mustang, shouting for her to stop in an increasingly loud and commanding way, causing the filly to run faster and faster in response. He was probably afraid of the animal to begin with, having never owned a horse before. Though I didn't witness this fiasco (it took place at a boarding facility across town), the scenario exemplified the typical difficulties faced by novice riders, challenges easily surmounted under a trainer's direction. Raymond, however, didn't want to hire anyone to help him. He had just spent a couple hundred bucks on a clinic and another eight hundred on the mustang. He thought this qualified him to start an untamed horse. But as Buck Light likes to say, "Buying a hat and a horse doesn't make you a cowboy." Raymond had no idea how to make the horse comfortable or read her subtle signals. He undoubtedly broadcast his own fear and uncertainty to the filly at a sociosensual level, even as he was trying to cover it up with a tough-guy image.

The tragedy is that rather than asking for help, trying a different approach, or calling it a day when the horse refused to listen to him, he literally ran her to death trying to make her conform to a method he had watched from a distance. The clinician had made it look so easy and sound so logical. Raymond probably figured that if he tried harder to attain his goal, the innocent young mare would have to comply. The horse did listen to Raymond, but he wasn't experienced enough to realize it. She responded to his aggressive movements with the panic she would normally experience with a predator. When he ran toward her hollering and waving his arms, she sped up, as she should have done regardless of what he was shouting.

Ignorance is not bliss in working with horses. Had the man bothered to study the clinician's book before experimenting on his new filly, he would have come across a long list of important considerations for round pen work emphasizing the horse's safety and well-being above all else. Raymond was subsequently arrested on animal cruelty charges. After paying a stiff fine and suffering a period of public embarrassment, he was free to buy another horse if he chose. The filly, however, didn't get a second chance.

Reading books, watching videos, or attending clinics offered by gifted trainers can lead to breakthroughs in horse-human relationships — if riders remain sensitive, responsive, realistic, and, most importantly, *present*. In a culture that conditions people to downplay experiential, somatic, sensory, emotional, and intuitive knowledge and to focus on the secondhand knowledge learned from authority figures, many people truly believe that if they buy the right equipment, analyze the clinician's every move, and follow the method to the letter, they will succeed. I've even seen dedicated followers of a particular trainer actually dress like their idol. In the process of mimicking the expert, however, many of these students can't truly connect with their horses, because they're too busy trying to remember what the clinician said or did, effectively ignoring the nuances of what those real, live beings in the arena are communicating to them.

The situation is further exacerbated when a nationally recognized equestrian certifies people in his techniques and allows them to lead workshops devoted entirely to his methods. One especially successful clinician, a talented, highly personable horseman I'll call "Terry," truly seems dedicated to improving the lives of horses by educating their owners. I've gained valuable perspectives and pointers from his workshops, books, and videos, yet I've found that some horses respond better to other methods. Terry himself readily adapts his techniques to fit the situation, creating new approaches that he subsequently passes on to others through his vast multimedia network. One local horse owner, however, returned confused and demoralized from a clinic led by "Jon," one of Terry's certified trainers.

"Jon spent half the morning doing a sales pitch for all the tack Terry created," "Karen" told me. "It was a stretch for me financially just to pay the fee for the all-day workshop, so I couldn't afford to buy the special halter, lead rope, and modified whip we were supposed to use. When I had trouble getting my horse to respond to the cues we were learning, Jon told me it was because I hadn't invested in the proper tack. He pretty much ignored me for the rest of the day."

When I watched Karen try to perform one of the techniques demonstrated at the clinic, I realized she simply wasn't assertive and focused enough to get the desired reaction from the horse. To make a point, I picked up a three-foot-long mesquite branch lying outside the arena. Using this crooked old stick, I directed the horse to perform the move. "It's not the tack," I emphasized. "It's the intent that counts. Over time, people who work with horses choose the tools that feel most comfortable to them, sometimes modifying them to meet their specifications, but these same tools may feel cumbersome to other, equally talented trainers." This is why many innovators create their own specialized tack. Linda Tellington-Jones uses a modified dressage whip colored white, which makes it easier for the horse to see her various cues. Pat Parelli uses a stick about the same length with a rope attached to the end, creating a shorter, more stable version of the longe whip. But these aren't magic wands that automatically transfer the secret wisdom of the trainer to anyone who buys them. It's what the handler projects and communicates through these tools that makes the difference.

Jon learned Terry's methods, but he didn't quite grasp the message behind them. As he moved up through the ranks, passing each of Terry's proficiency tests along the way, Jon mastered the mechanics of someone else's style, though he was probably physically and mentally well suited to the approach to begin with. Through this process, he learned the value of assertiveness, intent, congruent message sending, sociosensual awareness, nonverbal communication, and how to respond to a variety of horses in different situations. He was developing these skills unconsciously while he focused on the proper use of the tack in carrying out an increasingly complex list of activities perfected by his mentor. When he became certified to teach others, however, Jon still had no idea it was the *qualities* people develop through the method, and not the method itself, that lead to success.

Despite his best intentions, Terry hit the classic pitfall of creating an empire based on standardizing what was originally innovative. He began marketing his technique as if it were the only approach capable of teaching riders to truly connect with their horses. The certification process he established became an increasingly rigid hierarchy. Only people interested in learning his techniques exactly the way he performed them would rise through the beginner, intermediate, advanced, and instructor levels. These people were teaching a method that carried his name, and he understandably felt uncomfortable endorsing trainers who might not transmit his ideas verbatim. Yet in making sure the people he certified focused on his methods exclusively, the system he created gave birth to an instructor like Jon, a man without the necessary insight and flexibility to help Karen. The woman, in fact, felt betrayed and ripped off after attending his workshop. She was ready to tell everyone she knew that Terry's method was a pyramid scheme designed primarily to market his equipment until I explained the situation to her through my own understanding.

One of Terry's first certified instructors was banished from the fold when she challenged the effectiveness of some of his methods and dared to suggest her own alternatives. Like a spiritual community centered on a guru, a hierarchy focused on the codified techniques of a single authority figure cannot accommodate a student who becomes empowered and begins to think for herself. Then again, why would someone capable of creating her own style and innovations want to teach under someone else's name? Terry, for instance, was inspired by Tom Dorrance, a trainer who influenced a host of now-famous Western-style clinicians. None of these men went on to teach the "Dorrance Method." They developed their own techniques and ways of relating to horses, while respectfully crediting Dorrance as a mentor.

When a trainer begins to attract international attention, however, the temptation to establish standards for certification becomes overwhelming. Publishers and marketing directors see the potential for increasing sales as the clinician tours in support of his books. People who've made significant breakthroughs with his method pass the word, and the demand for workshops and lectures rises. Eventually, the clinician realizes he can't possibly accept all the personal appearance offers he's receiving. So he sends some especially talented and loyal apprentice to disseminate the information in his name. There's absolutely nothing wrong with this — at least in the beginning. Problems arise, however, when the process of training trainers to represent the method becomes more of an assembly line than an apprenticeship responsive to the talents and challenges of each individual student.

Once the original innovator becomes too busy to personally oversee the development of his assistants, he has to create more standardized tests for determining proficiency. But a person who performs the techniques perfectly may not understand the method well enough to teach it. He or she also may not be able to handle the responsibility and notoriety of becoming a leader in the field. I've seen certified trainers of a particular method, and in some cases the original trainers themselves, take out their personal issues and frustrations on people who've invested a large amount of faith and money in attending a clinic. Often this breach of trust takes the form of the same tactics I watched Wolverton use on his employees at the breeding farm where I apprenticed. One particularly talented clinician, "Gina," taught me a tremendous amount about a certain aspect of riding. When her methods didn't automatically work on Rasa during a demonstration, however, she used a lot of technical jargon to explain that the mare was worthless in such a way that even made me feel grateful for her insights — despite the fact that I was reduced to tears. Gina also managed to so thoroughly confuse one of the most experienced and innovative riding instructors in town that this woman left the business for five years. Somehow Gina was able to praise "Jenny" for her expertise as a trainer while undermining her on a nonverbal level. When Jenny and I met up several years later and talked about our experiences with Gina, we realized that even though the woman's methods were sound and useful, she exhibited a tendency to covertly degrade anyone who made her feel insecure. She would actually become competitive with certain people who attended her clinics, especially those who exuded a sense of autonomy and personal empowerment. Gina could therefore be profoundly incongruent at times, and I'm quite sure she wasn't consciously aware of it. In all likelihood Rasa refused to cooperate with her for this reason alone — and, in fact, when I used some of Gina's techniques on Rasa at home, the mare had no trouble following my cues.

Many people are aware of the problems arising from proliferating clinician empires, and there's a lot of complaining behind the scenes. But business associates and certified instructors have invested too much faith in their leader; they tend to see the problems as resting with other clinicians, not the one they follow. Many private riding instructors become skeptical of all clinicians as they watch what happens to horses after some of these nationally recognized trainers leave town.

Completely inexperienced riders will spend several hundred dollars to attend a two-day workshop with a famous equestrian. They'll buy all the special tack, books, and videos; then they rush out to buy a green horse because such an animal is significantly cheaper than a carefully trained one. But when these people try to follow the methods demonstrated at the clinic, they haven't developed the coordination, balance, understanding of equine conformation and body language, intuition, or level of sociosensual awareness they need to put the techniques effectively to use.

I also realized, through the polyvagal theory, that exceptional trainers use their own nervous systems to *coregulate* the nervous systems of flighty or aggressive horses. This crucial ability is not something you can learn from a book, video, or weekend workshop. Like weight lifting, you must practice over time, experientially, to build up your ability to *self-regulate* under increasingly stressful situations before you can calm and center a dysregulated horse. People new to the equestrian arts can't control how their nervous systems respond to an unruly thousand-pound animal. Fearful horses escalate when they sense a rise in blood pressure from a handler tensing up and holding his breath. Just as dangerously, animals with a more dominant streak respond to dysregulated humans by taking advantage, becoming increasingly aggressive. Even a secure, relatively well-behaved horse can sense when his owner is nervous and confused, and such a horse might assume he should run the show.

People and horses get hurt under these conditions. After being tossed or trampled, the more serious novice will seek out a good local trainer and progress under this person's direction. But many people bedazzled by the clinics refuse to get the help they need. Their prospective mounts become spoiled backyard horses or, if they're lucky, are sold to someone willing to invest time and money in properly training them.

The solution as I see it involves a more sophisticated partnership between clinicians and riding instructors. This will happen only when nationally recognized trainers accept responsibility for the hoopla they create. For every person capable of learning a method by watching videos and attending workshops twice a year, many more are injured or simply lose interest.

Clinicians truly interested in the welfare of horses should advise people attending their presentations that regular lessons with an experienced instructor will help them develop the nonverbal qualities it takes to truly connect with and coregulate their horses. In order to encourage people to study with someone locally in between workshops, however, these innovators must be willing to admit that their way isn't the only way and to coach students in the qualities to look for in a humane trainer. The notion of "The Method" capable of automatically giving anyone who follows it the powers of an innovative trainer must give way to dedicated equestrians willing to support one another in exploring the ethical, experiential, emotional, sociosensual, and intuitive qualities that bring the best methods to life.

Polyvagal Considerations

When Dr. Rebecca Bailey introduced me to the polyvagal theory almost twenty years after I wrote the original version of *The Tao of Equus*, it was like blasting a spotlight into a dingy, darkened barn. All kinds of training challenges suddenly made sense. Most importantly, specific solutions became apparent, many of which were counterintuitive to the ways that people commonly relate to horses. As it turns out, the very structure of the mammalian nervous system *demands* that equestrians avoid any teaching method relying on fear, pain, and intimidation, as well as the kind of disconnected behavior that results from treating animals as objects.

To recap, neuroscientist Stephen Porges contends that in mammals, "the neural pathways of social support and social behavior are shared with the neural pathways that support health, growth, and restoration." His research suggests that our nervous systems are designed to connect with others to work at an optimal level. This is not just psychological. Physiologically, when we feel disconnected, the health of our hearts, our brains, and other systems in our bodies becomes seriously compromised. Our capacity to heal, let alone attain higher levels of wellness, depends on forging safe and meaningful connections with others.

In *A Pocket Guide to the Polyvagal Theory: The Transformative Power of Feeling Safe*, Porges emphasizes that all mammals need other mammals to "interact with, to survive." Even more importantly, they need to develop "the ability to reciprocally regulate each other's physiological state, and create relationships to enable individuals to feel safe."

As mentioned in chapter 4, the polyvagal theory contends that mammals evolved a sophisticated nervous system with an innovation called the *ventral vagus complex*. Lizards have a *dorsal vagus nerve complex*, part of the parasympathetic nervous system responsible for activating the rest and digest function. In emergencies, animals shift into the sympathetic nervous system to engage the flight-or-fight response. In extreme life-threatening situations, when it's not possible to flee or fight, the dorsal vagus comes back online with its own emergency function: an immobility response, where the animal freezes.

Mammals have a dorsal vagus that can perform these functions. But they also have the ventral vagus innovation that promotes mutually supportive social behavior. This is why Porges calls his work on this subject the polyvagal theory: because mammals have the dorsal vagus complex we share with lizards *and* the ventral vagus that creates new possibilities.

The ventral vagus influences muscle movements in the face, eyes, and ears. This allows all mammals to engage in sophisticated expressions that communicate the desire to connect with and coregulate each other to manage stress. So, truly, the lone wolf concept so many individualistic people relate to does not make biological sense. We are not designed to function as lone wolves. Even wolves are not designed to be lone wolves! (Wolf packs are complex social units.) Mammals are designed to care for and uplift one another, to reach out to others and invite connection, in part through vocal tone, eye movements, and facial expressions.

Lizards, who do not have a ventral vagus complex, cannot move their eyes and faces to convey welcoming or stressful emotional states. Think about it: it would be shocking to walk by a lizard resting on a fence post and see its eyes widen in surprise. It would be even stranger to see that same lizard frown — or smile, for that matter.

Interestingly, it's not just angry or fearful faces and loud, intimidating vocal tones that can cause nervous system dysregulation in others. Porges's research shows how people with bland facial expressions and monotone voices can increase feelings of anxiety and disconnection in humans and other mammals. Trauma survivors in particular can become unnerved by bland facial expressions and monotone voices.

Young children can also suffer developmental issues through neglect. Extremely depressed parents, for instance, may manage to take care of a child's basic physical needs. But lack of connection to the child through peaceful, engaged eye contact, smiles, expressive vocal tone, and warm embraces can be devastating for a child's developing nervous system, as the ventral vagus nervous system needs to be activated through connection.

If you had supportive parents, interacting with a stoic, disconnected person may feel more like a puzzling inconvenience. It's hard to tell what the person is thinking or feeling, right? But if you had abusive or neglectful caretakers, interacting with someone with a perpetually blank, disconnected look on his face can feel unnerving. Examples abound in the average high school or college classroom. For people who haven't experienced significant trauma, a perpetually serious, unexpressive professor comes across as boring. To a survivor of trauma or neglect, such a person can put the nervous system on alert, activating vague feelings that question the safety of the situation and the trustworthiness of the professor, whose lack of expression makes him look and feel more lizard-like than human.

So, according to this research, if you are a mental health professional working in the field of equine-facilitated therapy and you've been taught to adopt bland facial expressions to convey a sense of neutrality, you can cause both the horse and the human client to feel a vague sense of instability or lack of safety. Varied facial expressions and vocal tone are crucial to conveying the sense of connection that mammals depend upon to learn, heal, and grow.

The importance of facial expressions in working with horses has been ignored for the most part. Equestrians are often told to "go neutral" to relieve pressure and reward the horse. Yes, it's important to relieve pressure by going neutral with the whip, hand, or leg pressure. But neutrality in facial expression is truly counterproductive, causing the horse's nervous system to register a lack of safety through connection.

Many people are under the impression that horses are perpetually stoic themselves and certainly not capable of registering changes in human faces. But in recent years, studies have shown that horses *do* communicate with each other through a variety of facial expressions. As it turns out, they actually have one more facial expression than chimps and only ten fewer facial expressions than humans. Another study showed how a horse's blood pressure rises when she is looking at photographs of angry or fearful people. The horse's blood pressure lowers when she looks at photos of relaxed facial expressions.

In their natural state, equines are quite gregarious and expressive. Stoic horses are shut-down, dissociative animals who have been intimidated into perpetually submissive behavior. The fact that so many people do not think that horses have facial expressions is a sad commentary on how many of these animals have been trained into states of disconnection, depression, and learned helplessness. Certain techniques, such as laying the horse down, can activate the dorsal vagus emergency response, thrusting the animal into tonic immobility, a freeze state activated through extreme fear. Many people still talk about "breaking a horse to ride," and that turns out to be an accurate description of what some people do to a horse's spirit in order to use him like a tool. In response, many horses become machinelike in all their interactions with humans. This creates a vicious cycle: the bland, disconnected looks on a broken horse's face in turn cause people to feel even more justified in treating the animal like an object, which further perpetuates superficial interactions between the two species.

Even when a rider is praising a horse, the interaction is often clumsy and shallow. I see far too many riders "reward" their horses with an obligatory slap on the neck, maybe a formulaic "Good boy!" comment accompanied by a bland, disconnected look on their own faces. Lack of authentic connection is counterproductive on so many levels, yet it is encouraged in so many (largely unconscious) ways. No matter what riding discipline or training method you subscribe to, it's essential to remember that the nervous systems of mammals, including humans and horses, are designed to connect to feel safe, and feeling safe is necessary for promoting wellness, for supporting regulated development of the nervous system, and for encouraging psychological growth and creativity.

A Woman's Touch

Women are often credited with being more relational than men. This carries over into their natural inclination to connect with their horses. However, one of the most interesting, and frustrating, aspects of the horse whisperer phenomenon is its blatant disregard for the innovations of female trainers — and its ambiguous relationship with women in general. In Nicholas Evans's modern myth, an ambitious mother, her disabled daughter, and their traumatized gelding are all healed by the sensitive cowboy savior. In the film version, the whisperer is subsequently injured emotionally by his contact with these women; in the novel, he is killed.

When the film and novel both discuss the horse whisperer legacy, these innovative trainers are categorized exclusively as *men* who bucked convention — *men* who brought a new era of gentleness, respect, and cooperation to a grossly inhumane equestrian tradition. But if we compare the techniques of Monty Roberts, Ray Hunt, and Buck Brannaman (trainers Evans interviewed while researching his novel) with author-clinicians Linda Tellington-Jones, Mary Wanless, Sally Swift, and Peggy Cummings, it's apparent that the latter have developed gentler yet highly effective approaches to training that often prove safer for beginner riders. A person experimenting with the methods of these women would not run the risk of longeing a horse to death while practicing skills observed at one of their workshops. Still, even the more aggressively marketed female trainers remain in the background of public attention, and the horse whisperer phenomenon has done nothing to further awareness of their innovations.

Part of the reason Monty Roberts received so much media attention is because he could gentle, saddle, and ride a green horse in under thirty minutes, a feat that fits into the time constraints of television news programs like *60 Minutes* and *20/20*. Clinician John Lyons regularly performed similar transformations in workshops. Unlike novice equestrians, however, these men have decades of experience under their belts. They can use their own nervous systems to coregulate a dysregulated horse. They're aware of subtle nonverbal communication that's difficult to describe in words, and they can bypass steps that beginner riders ignore at their peril. Roberts is also very clear about the fact that he developed some of these techniques to save the lives of mustangs slated for slaughter.

At age thirteen, he and his brother accepted the challenge of starting a group of 130 wild horses under saddle in the ridiculously short period of two months. To make matters worse, these survivors of a local rodeo's wild horse race had already been traumatized by their initial contact with humans. As a group of cowboys lassoed, saddled, and ran the frantic horses before twenty thousand cheering spectators, twenty of the animals died or were injured enough to be put down — much to the excitement of the audience. Each time one of the horses fell to the ground, writhing in agony, Roberts would hear ecstatic voices exclaiming, "Crow's bait! Crow's bait!" The young man's task after the race was "to make the mustangs worth more alive than dead," he writes in *The Man Who Listens to Horses*. "A schooled mustang might fetch a buyer at the October auction; an unbroken one was destined for Crow's Landing. Their lives...were in our hands." Roberts perfected his craft as an emergency measure, trying to make the best of a cruel rodeo event he believes should be abolished. For the average equestrian, however, trying to replicate such an ambitious timetable is unnecessary, and it can actually distract people from issues that arise after the horse has been saddled and ridden for the first time.

In her book *For the Good of the Horse*, English trainer Mary Wanless attributed many of the physical and behavioral difficulties people experience with horses to ill-fitting tack and unbalanced, tension-producing riding techniques. As she wrote:

> A large number of the riders and horses I see are coping relatively well despite the shortcomings of the horses' saddles and their shoes, but I also see some extremely well-intentioned riders who have failed to notice that their horses are all but crippled by them. Over the last few years I have come to believe that at least 60 percent of the horses I see show signs of pain or discomfort which could be alleviated through attention to their saddles, feet, or teeth. Many more would benefit from a thorough check from a physiotherapist, chiropractor, or massage therapist who can trace patterns of tension throughout the horse's body.

Wanless noted that "other authorities have suggested that over 85 percent of competitive horses have their performance compromised by such physical problems."

The trainer's books and workshops addressed everything from enlightened riding practices, creative visualization, and how the handler's physical and mental state affects the horse to equine dentistry, farriery and gait analysis, nutrition, saddle fitting, bodywork, physiotherapy, herbalism, aromatherapy, energy medicine, homeopathy, acupuncture, horse behavior and language, and the intuitive skills of animal communicators. Wanless's holistic approach demonstrated openness and compassion grounded by years of serious research. She didn't promote a method so much as she helped people develop the knowledge of and sensitivity to nuance that are crucial to long-term success. There are no quick fixes in her books. Her techniques and suggestions were designed to help horses and riders enjoy and support one another as they share in a journey to optimum health and performance.

Linda Tellington-Jones also promotes a holistic approach to riding and training. Beginning with the formal presentation of the Tellington-Jones Equine Awareness Method (TEAM) in 1978, interest in her techniques has spread to six continents, with learning centers in Australia, Canada, Germany, Austria, Switzerland, Russia, and the United States. Throughout her adolescence in Canada, showing in hunter-jumper, English, and Western pleasure classes, she learned a variety of methods then standard in the horse industry. By age sixteen, she was training and teaching professionally. In 1961, with her then-husband, Wentworth Tellington, she started the Pacific Coast Equestrian Research Farm in Badger, California, which provided a rigorous and innovative course of study attracting equestrian students from nine countries and thirty-six states. In the early 1970s, she also collaborated with Ursula Bruns, publisher of an alternative German magazine for recreational riders. Their countless hours discussing riding and training techniques led Bruns to create, with Inge Behr, a unique eleven-day course for beginning adult riders known as the Bruns/Behr Method, which emphasized fun, relaxation, and stress-free learning. Thousands of people graduated from this revolutionary course.

In the mid-1970s, Tellington-Jones herself went on the road to teach a series of clinics to riders all over Europe. During this time, she became attracted to the work of Dr. Moshe Feldenkrais, an Israeli physicist who made significant breakthroughs in managing physical dysfunction and maximizing athletic performance in humans. She went on to complete professional training with Feldenkrais at the Humanistic Psychology Institute in San Francisco, an experience that profoundly affected her approach to working with horses. "He believed that the human nervous system was capable of learning through a single experience, without repetition, with the use of nonhabitual movements, as long as they were nonthreatening and did not cause pain," she wrote in *An Introduction to the Tellington-Jones Equine Awareness Method.* "I began to adapt this idea to work with problem horses. The concept that we could change the horse's behavior in a few lessons was totally revolutionary. I had believed, like most people, that a horse could learn only through repetition."

After working with hundreds of people and their problem horses, Tellington-Jones developed a series of ground exercises and riding techniques that, with minimal use, resulted in permanent personality and behavioral changes. Through these activities, handlers learned how to create a stress-free learning environment that made unusual demands on the animal's mind as well as his muscles, expanding awareness of the connections between physical and mental processes in both horse and rider. She later changed her acronym to TTEAM, for Tellington Touch Equine Awareness Method, to emphasize a series of circular touches she developed that, though similar to massage, are actually designed to influence the horse's nervous system by activating processes connected with cellular intelligence. Unrelated scientific studies carried out by Candace Pert and other mind-body researchers later supported observations that these touches release tension associated with trauma and memory held in the body. Tellington-Jones has since become interested in modifying her techniques for use on humans.

Clinician Peggy Cummings began exploring alternative equestrian strategies as she moved into her forties and realized that years of traditional riding had taken their toll on her body. Sally Swift's Centered Riding techniques introduced Cummings to the benefits of bodywork and taught her a number of principles useful for tension-free, pain-free riding. Linda Tellington-Jones added to Cummings's knowledge of the whole-horse-and-rider concept, while Major Anders Lindgren taught her techniques for more specifically addressing the horse's issues. Building on these innovators, Cummings came up with Connected Riding, a program emphasizing flowing natural movement in both species. In her work, she helps students understand the physical and mental habits that block freedom of movement. "As you explore Connected Riding," she writes in the introduction to her book, "you'll find that it will challenge some of the basic principles you've learned about riding — especially in terms of position and aids. It will ask you to become self-reliant and understanding. It will ask you to become a student of the horse — not just a student of riding. And, finally, it will ask you to take responsibility for leading the dance that connection creates."

While many traditional competitive riders remain skeptical, instructors specializing in therapeutic riding have been quick to embrace the innovations of these visionaries. The Eponaquest program uses a combination of techniques adapted from the methods of all the women mentioned above, in addition to some practices derived from Pat Parelli, John Lyons, and Monty Roberts. There are, however, two important areas that both male and female clinicians neglect to meaningfully address: the emotional and spiritual issues arising from human-equine interactions. Even seemingly open-minded, holistically oriented trainers tend to avoid discussing emotional difficulties in their books and workshops. It's as if they fear opening the Pandora's box of dysfunction that simmers just beneath the surface of so many of these interspecies relationships, in some cases with good reason.

While the majority of trainers shy away from hot emotional topics, however, the best clinicians recognize that a well-balanced, well-adjusted rider is more likely to produce a well-balanced, well-adjusted horse. As Pat Parelli wrote in his book *Natural Horse-Man-Ship*, "You've got to have your act together. You have to become collected in the human sense." And yet Parelli fails to elaborate on exactly what human collection looks like or how one might achieve this apparently essential state of being. He also contends that because the horse is "the best teacher of feel, timing, and balance," you should "play with your horse and work on yourself." Parelli succeeds in outlining methods for how owners can constructively play with their horses, but his book never suggests how they might work on their own issues. Over time, however, he did enlist the expertise of psychologists and other professionals who could help develop some insight into what he began to call "emotional fitness."

In the book *Of Women and Horses*, Native American horse trainer GaWaNi Pony Boy discussed the notion of balance in making a great equestrian. "To date," he wrote,

> I have never met a champion who was also a jerk. I have met a few fleeting stars who were far too egotistical to even talk to, but those men whom I consider champions are very nice people. As for trainers, I have never met a truly great male trainer who was egotistical or macho. Now I have met many macho male horse trainers and every one of them seems to have more problems with horses than is necessary; but the great male trainers I have met are also really great people.

GaWaNi Pony Boy described a trainer who is "probably among the top five in the United States. This man is sensitive, caring, soft-spoken, calm, has smiling eyes, and is generally a really nice guy. Sensitive, caring, soft-spoken, calm — we think of these qualities as feminine, don't we? Is it possible that horses respond better to men who are in touch with these feminine qualities as well?" He also characterized the great female trainers as "strong, aggressive, demanding of respect, and what I would consider powerful. Aren't these qualities generally labeled as masculine?" As he reflected upon this juxtaposition of male and female qualities, GaWaNi Pony Boy decided that "balance is the most fundamental factor affecting how well you ride. Balance is what determines your ability to teach the horse within his own ability. And balance, it seems, is what the horse searches for in a human companion."

To assist clients in developing this balance, however, trainers must begin to address the emotional issues horses bring up in their owners. These animals are already inclined to reflect the authentic feelings behind the socially acceptable masks people wear. The fields of equine-facilitated psychotherapy (EFP) and equine-facilitated experiential learning (EFEL) are based on this observation, and, as I discuss in workshops for horse trainers, some of the techniques used by EFP and EFEL professionals can be easily adapted to more conventional riding lessons. With a little coaching, trainers can learn how to deal with emotional issues that impede performance, in themselves and in their clients, without inadvertently opening the floodgates to discussing every last injustice students have experienced.

The Tao of Effective Leadership

In many ways, it's encouraging, even remarkable, that men like Tom Dorrance, Ray Hunt, and Monty Roberts emerged from the rough-and-tumble world of bucking broncos and branding irons to promote a more humane approach to horse training. Roberts, however, admits that he lost his faith in dominance techniques when he was beaten by his father, a wrangler from the old school whose violent methods of starting young horses had much in common with how he related to young Monty. In *The Man Who Listens to Horses*, Roberts candidly discusses how his childhood difficulties partially inspired his ability to work from the horse's perspective and follow equine body language cues. In negotiating the elder Roberts's aggressive, uncompromising attitudes, Monty and the colts that came to his father's ranch were in the same predicament. Roberts later observed that women more easily adapt to the methods presented at his clinics, a phenomenon he's not quite sure how to explain. Yet a pattern emerges in comparing his childhood oppression with the mixed messages and prejudices women throughout history have confronted: revelations and innovations come more readily to those who are betrayed or invalidated. Even women raised in idyllic circumstances tend to orient less toward wielding absolute control over others and more toward using skills associated with relationship. Some tough and dominant female trainers have, however, made names for themselves in competitive riding, mostly because that's what they thought it would take to gain the respect of people attracted to this sometimes cutthroat subculture.

In reality, the most humane methods espoused by both male and female trainers stem from rekindling a relationship with nature based on collaboration and sensitivity rather than fear and intimidation. Consciously or unconsciously, they develop qualities associated with what Taoist philosophers characterize as yin, or feminine, styles of leadership to balance the yang, or masculine, qualities emphasized in the human world. Like the ancient Taoists who embraced feminine wisdom and direct interactions with nature, these trainers look to the horses themselves as teachers and try to align with their natural abilities and behaviors.

Rather than dominating or disregarding nature, as most Western philosophies and religions attempt to do, Taoism recognizes that the primordial wellspring of existence expresses itself *through* nature. You don't have to be a practicing Taoist to appreciate these insights or put them to use in the riding arena. From a Judeo-Christian perspective, the Tao is not a synonym for God. It is more specifically a description of the way God works through nature, a term that describes the unfolding of creation. In this sense, Taoism is not an exclusive religion but a system of thought that emphasizes aligning oneself with the flow of nature's currents as the most effective path to a long, healthy, peaceful life.

Early Chinese sages discovered the Tao through introspective meditation and silent observation of nature. Lao-tzu, who may have been an actual historical figure or merely the pen name for a group of anonymous sages, wrote the most famous work on this subject approximately five hundred years before the birth of Christ. His Tao Te Ching advises people to "know the yang, but keep to the yin," a role that embodies gentleness, responsiveness, humility, flexibility, emptiness, stillness, and submission in relating to this universal force. At first glance, this value system seems insulting to women striving for equal rights. We don't get ahead in business by quietly yielding to the whims of our most self-assertive colleagues, but by showing ourselves to be more accomplished and ambitious than they are. Lao-tzu, however, was not encouraging people to passively submit to aggression. In fact, he didn't much care for human authority in general. Instead, the "Old Master" believed the entire planet would run a lot more smoothly if men and women would simply let go of their limited perspectives, follow the Tao, or "governing principle of nature," and, as a result, connect with the primordial force that set this process in motion long before people appeared and arrogantly assumed they needed to fix it. The only way to align with the Tao is to defer to its authority, and in order to do that, a person has to become quiet and receptive enough to feel its presence, sensitive and adaptable enough to follow its direction, spontaneous enough to move with its flow whenever it unexpectedly changes course, modest enough to realize that the individual mind can never fathom the vast workings of this universal principle, and trusting enough to know that wherever its currents lead, the Tao ultimately acts in everyone's best interest.

These are the same qualities the equestrian arts require in a well-trained horse. The intricate, dance-like movements of dressage are performed by animals responsive to the subtlest of aids. A minute change of balance, slight pressure from the leg, an almost imperceptible squeeze of the reins, even the position of the rider's tongue in her own mouth can affect the horse's course of action. At the grand prix level, a rider appears to do nothing at all as her powerful warmblood stallion artfully zigzags across the arena, twirls 360 degrees in the southwest corner, and gallops gracefully back toward the center, changing leads every two steps. The animal seems to have memorized some sophisticated routine, yet if the contestant were to suddenly dismount and offer her seat to an inexperienced member of the audience, that same horse would meander around the ring like a drunken sailor. It is the rider's own focus and balance, her sense of clarity and stillness in the midst of activity, and her capacity to harmonize with the horse's natural abilities that create the right conditions for such an impressive display of human-equine collaboration. And it most certainly is collaboration. Performing at this level is exhausting for both parties if the horse doesn't voluntarily accept his rider's direction and trust her judgment. Certain dressage movements cannot even be executed if the animal is tense and resistant.

Still, there are plenty of other equestrian pursuits where force seems to work faster than cooperation — at least for a while. A mediocre trainer can employ all kinds of fancy bits, spurs, and other gadgets to compel a horse to move forward, hold a certain head position, jump over obstacles, and stop on cue. He or she may even win a continuous succession of shows with those gimmicks, but there's always a price to pay. The horse's underlying resistance taxes his physical and mental reserves, leading to burnout, injury, and unpredictable explosions of frustration that can endanger the rider's life. People who regularly grapple with these difficulties continue to use such methods because they want to make the most money with the least expenditure of time and effort. As a result, the show world is filled with owners and trainers who start horses too young, push them too hard, and hide a growing list of problems with painkillers and medical procedures. As long as a certain percentage of these animals do well on the show circuit, they can still pull in a profit for their owners after the inevitable breakdown. In the quarter-horse world, it's common to pay large stud fees for the services of champion seven-year-old stallions permanently lamed by the demands of futurities, competitions that put increasingly unfair demands on colts whose young bones have not fully formed. In the race world, a disabled broodmare can always throw foals that will bring a good price, especially if she managed to win a few rounds as a two-year-old. A hunter-jumper gelding with a chronic joint problem isn't much use to anyone, but a savvy trainer can sell him for top dollar if he or she can make it to the national finals and find a gullible buyer before the horse gives out completely. Less successful horses become tax write-offs, though their subsequent fate isn't nearly as secure as those whose stalls are lined with ribbons.

This sad state of affairs is merely one symptom of a species-wide over-reliance on masculine values that spread throughout the world during the course of human history. Along the way, a handful of seers showed the ultimate impotency of this imbalance, but relatively few people took the message to heart. The notion that might makes right prevails in many contexts to this day, despite the fact that such crude methods of leadership have proved to be wasteful and inefficient. As Lao-tzu illustrated twenty-five hundred years ago, an overemphasis on force, rigidity, territorialism, logic, planning, and single-minded self-assertion only serves to alienate people from the ultimate source of power in the universe. In Taoism, as in Christianity, the weak inherit the earth because they are humble and responsive enough to follow God's plan. Yet unlike Judeo-Christian leaders, Taoist sages specified that the very qualities people needed to cultivate for achieving this state of union were virtues traditionally exemplified by women. Lao-tzu's predecessors realized that if they wanted to dance with the creative forces of the universe, they had to give up the lead and take the feminine role. They also respected the fact that their wives and daughters had a head start.

According to Taoist scholar Ken Cohen, early expressions of Taoism were free of patriarchal attitudes, offering men and women equal political power and opportunity for enlightenment. This vision of a classless, egalitarian society was eventually usurped in China by the Confucian ideal of order, social hierarchy, clear division of labor, and male dominance. Confucius's belief in the inferiority of women infiltrated all aspects of the culture as Chinese wives were tied to their homes with bound feet and forced to serve the male population without concern for their own development. Still, an effective minority continued to master Taoist principles in secret, and some women sages felt that their lowly position in life provided a shortcut to enlightenment. Male practitioners of Complete Reality Taoism, a sophisticated "science" of immortality developed around 1000 CE, noticed that it was easier for women and children to master the alchemical practices. They had less of a stake in, and consequently a less compulsive need to uphold and defend, the strict precepts of society. Traditionally minded husbands and fathers unknowingly helped many women lay the groundwork for their own spiritual liberation by subjecting them to oppressive, hypermasculine cultural practices that assured their lack of faith in the system. In addition, flexibility and responsiveness, both crucial to Taoist practice, were qualities girls perfected as they progressed through marriage and motherhood, while boys tended to become more rigid and self-assertive. Numerous Chinese folk tales describe ambitious men studying Taoist principles for decades with little result, only to find that their wives had effortlessly mastered the arts and were qualified to take their husbands on as apprentices. The majority of these stories end on a tragic note as male pride gets in the way, and the woman ascends to the heavenly realms alone, leaving a frustrated and angry man behind. (This is a common theme in the equestrian arts as well. In the United States, relatively few men attend clinics presented by Linda Tellington-Jones and Peggy Cummings, yet you'll find a steady base of both sexes at workshops led by clinicians like Pat Parelli and John Lyons. A lot of men don't feel comfortable taking direction from a female instructor, no matter how many books she's written or how many times she's proved her methods.)

Taoist leadership has nothing to do with alpha-style intimidation tactics, and in this respect, it has much to offer riders and trainers looking for new ways to approach their craft. Equine society works loosely on the basis of what could be called a pecking order *at times*, but it's not as strict or predictable as most people believe. A submissive mare may rise in status by forming an alliance with a respected matriarch, who in turn may defer to this seemingly low-ranking herd member's moods and desires. A bully may seem to be in charge, but the other horses will keep their distance. People who try to establish an alpha position through intimidation tend to get the same response. A horse coerced into performing may seem to execute the moves correctly, but the animal's heart and soul will not be in her work. She will avoid her rider at every opportunity, give him only what he requires through force or habit, and never show him the depth of her true potential. Lao-tzu's model of leadership, on the other hand, is an unobtrusive, nurturing, less-is-more philosophy that promotes forming alliances, not dictatorships. The person in charge must be as responsive and flexible as his followers. In fact, according to Lao-tzu, the leader is often most effective when he is the one who follows.

Horses readily respond to this perspective and provide consistent feedback in the process. They have no vested interest in upholding the coercion paradigm. They can't be bribed with material goods. They can't be distracted with sweet talk and promises. They immediately see through the slightest incongruities of emotion and intention. In activities moderated by humans, these animals are focused and collected only to the extent that the rider is focused and collected. As a result, horses are consummate trainers of human leaders. Skills learned in the riding arena directly apply to human situations, though it quickly becomes apparent that people are much more tenacious than horses in clinging to old habits, perceptions, and ways of relating. Still, men and women have a better chance of changing their response to the dominant paradigm if they first build their confidence outside it. Working with horses from a yin-over-yang mindset provides that opportunity.

At more advanced levels of this practice, however, students gain perspective on how to use the so-called masculine virtues to the greatest advantage — in horse training and in life. Yin and yang are often characterized as flexibility and firmness, stillness and movement, or softness and hardness, respectively. Taoist practices appear at first to emphasize the yin, but that's only because in Lao-tzu's time, as in our own, human beings rarely employed feminine forms of wisdom. People are conditioned to resort to the yang, to engage in aggressive action and adopt a firmness of mind and body fed by social structures that are resistant to change. To align with the natural response of the horse, riders learn to access other attributes, those yin elements facilitating a sociosensual partnership between the two species. However, succeeding here is only the first step. The real magic comes in reuniting the yin with the yang.

Liu I-Ming, in his treatise *Wu Tao Lu*, says that if we are always hard, we become impatient, impetuous, and aggressive. If we revert to the soft, we will become ineffective. As the balance of opposites in the universe, the Tao calls for "firmness of will with flexibility of action, neither rushing ahead, nor lagging behind." More advanced schools emphasize "stillness within movement" and "true intent." Here "stillness" doesn't refer to actual physical stillness but, rather, to inward tranquility in the midst of action. One of the finer points of Taoist practice is determining the source or quality of each action in order to gauge whether it is the movement of the primordial mind of Tao (sometimes called "real knowledge") or whether it is mixed with projections from the conditioned human mentality (often referred to as "conscious knowledge"). The I Ching characterizes this state as "tranquil and unperturbed, yet sensitive and effective." A common Taoist saying calls for human beings to be "always calm, yet always responsive, always responsive yet always calm."

This ability is most useful in work with horses, and the best trainers seem to develop it naturally by interacting with the animals. As Monty Roberts observes, "My pulse rate is always low, and I never allow myself to become tense, whatever situation might occur." Yet in order to achieve anything of consequence, the rider has to employ certain virtues associated with the yang: namely, planning, will, and focus. An agenda of some sort is required for the horse and rider to progress. The trick is understanding when to let go of that working strategy and tap a more expansive viewpoint. Horses respond best to what the Taoists call "true intent." When the conscious, discriminating mind is calm and responsive, the right solution or cue comes from a higher source of insight, seemingly without effort. Call it intuition. Call it the bigger brain loop. Call it divine guidance. It may very well be a combination of all three. In any case, realizations gained through true intent are always more innovative and effective than options suggested by the strict linear thought processes of a conditioned mentality. While the Taoists were among the first people to recognize and name this ability, it's the state of mind creative geniuses either possess from birth or stumble upon at the first major turning point in their careers.

Through the ages, many people developed skills like true intent and stillness within movement through studies of the martial arts, but these are ultimately combative postures. Riding a horse rests upon another principle the Taoists hold dear, that of "noncontention." In this capacity, equestrian pursuits have a leg up on the martial arts when it comes to forging a vital connection between two life-forms as they learn to move in harmony.

Laying the Horse Down

There's a shadow side to the rising interest in enlightened training techniques. Through Nicholas Evans's popular novel *The Horse Whisperer* and Robert Redford's subsequent film adaptation, public fascination with the horse whisperer mystique made it possible for some fringe trainers to use their knowledge for questionable purposes. Living in the Southwest, I saw several older men who never actually rode the range adopt the persona of the kind, wise, folksy cowboy who "helps horses with people problems." Some have legitimate experience in the equestrian arts, dabbling in rodeo or working at racing operations. Others are vague when it comes to how or where they learned their trade, yet like the snake oil salesmen of the Wild West, they have the moves down, and they're remarkably adept at telling people what they want to hear. The most dangerous shysters use the heightened level of nonverbal, sociosensual awareness they developed training horses to manipulate clients. They can spot a lonely, confused, codependent woman a mile away, especially one with a nice, private miniranch and a few horses needing the "right" kind of training. Pretty soon, the owner is following the whisperer around like any other member of the herd, offering food, money, a pleasant place to stay, and a little sex on the side. I've seen it happen more than once — with some devastating consequences for the women involved. These men use the latest training buzzwords to mesmerize novice riders, but their techniques with horses and people have more to do with distraction and disempowerment than with true partnership and connection. Some trainers have also learned a few dramatic practices that produce instant personality changes in horses by taking advantage of physiological responses to stress that arise in prey animals.

There's a difference between aligning with nature for the mutual benefit of horse and rider and manipulating nature for selfish ends. The former leads to greater balance for everyone involved. The latter results in the trainer quickly gaining control at the long-term expense of the horse. Sometimes, even the most well-meaning and experienced trainers have trouble distinguishing between the two. People who lack integrity and self-awareness repeatedly cross this line without a second thought.

The practice known as "laying the horse down" is a classic example. The fact that this technique was portrayed during a pivotal scene in both the novel and film versions of *The Horse Whisperer* sets a dangerous precedent for many amateur equestrians. Shortly after the movie came out, I had to talk several people out of duplicating this method with their own horses and actually had trouble convincing them to take the time to work through their problems with less intrusive techniques. To the casual observer, it appears an unruly horse can be "fixed" in record time by this impressive trick. However, the act of forcing a prey animal to lie down by tying up one of his front legs, dragging him to the ground, and sitting on him in this vulnerable position until he submits causes such an intense fear reaction that the dorsal vagal immobility response is activated. The result is a sudden change in personality. The horse acts like a zombie, which to people who prefer a machinelike mount appears to be a miraculous cure for chronic disobedience.

Laying the horse down in this way takes advantage of several biological processes that shield all mammals from feeling the impact of an attack. After all, when a large predator succeeds in pulling a horse down and immobilizing him, it usually marks the end of the battle. This reaction differs from common shock, because an animal can freeze before any physical damage occurs and, under certain circumstances, can remain in a lesser form of this dissociative state even after the danger has past. Some tribal hunting cultures believe that nature has shown the utmost compassion in providing a mechanism that allows a prey animal's soul to leave his body before the heart stops beating, thereby sparing him the pain and horror of being eaten. Traditional equestrian-based cultures in Siberia have been known to perform similar moves on horses about to be sacrificed with the express intent of releasing their spirits before striking the fatal blow. To look into the vacant eyes of a horse that has been subjected to this technique is to know there's some truth to these notions.

Dana Light saw the method used many times during her years working at ranches, training stables, and trail riding operations. Horses receiving this treatment immediately lost status in their herds and were sometimes completely ostracized. She believed that by laying the horse down and holding him down until he submits, the animal is frightened within an inch of his life. "He loses the will to live," she says, "and he simply doesn't care what you do to him anymore. The herd immediately senses this and adjusts to it, in some cases acting as if he doesn't even exist. I would never do this to a horse unless he was so dangerous the only alternative would be sending him to the killer's."

Some commercial trail riding stables have been known to perform the procedure on horses most riders would perceive as only mildly difficult. Owners of these operations can't afford to have a member of the string react to unbalanced, sometimes fearful beginner riders by bucking or running off with them. Their horses are obliged to walk the same trails day after day. They're expected to endure people who pull their mouths and kick their sides unmercifully. Some stables also require their mounts to stand around saddled for long stretches of time, waiting for prospective riders. Animals too spirited or willful to submit to these demands can be "corrected" in a single afternoon.

Long before I really understood what the method entailed, I had the opportunity to rehabilitate a horse who showed all the symptoms associated with this extreme technique. "Spike," a handsome palomino who worked on a dude string, managed to find a new owner when thirteen-year-old "Bonnie" fell in love with him during a trail ride. Her parents bought the older, more reliable gelding on the spot, thinking he would be a safe beginner's mount for their horse-crazy daughter. He seemed the perfect choice, at least at first. Problems arose, however, when Bonnie tried to bond with him and ride him around the arena at a local boarding stable. Spike, who had spent years following the horse in front of him down a well-weathered path, was dull and listless. He had the same glassy, distant look in his eyes that Noche adopted around strangers. While the horse seemed physically capable of doing what Bonnie asked, it took so much effort to direct his every move that she was becoming discouraged. She was also disappointed that Spike didn't seem to care about her one way or the other, no matter how often she rode him.

Over two months, I helped the young lady gain Spike's trust through a series of exercises on the ground and in the saddle. I also used some simple massage techniques and TTouches (those gentle, circular touches Linda Tellington-Jones developed to enhance cellular intelligence and mind-body awareness). The goal was to lure Spike out of his perpetual state of dissociation and back into contact with his body through pleasant, supportive, confidence-building activities. I also suggested Bonnie set aside time to hang out with Spike, petting and playing with him without any particular agenda.

The horse slowly came back to life. His eyes began to twinkle. Soon he was whinnying and running up to Bonnie when she approached his stall. Much to my own surprise, however, the formerly quiet, complacent gelding became difficult to manage for several weeks as a result of these efforts. Once he woke up from his dissociative trance, he wasn't automatically willing to defer to Bonnie's authority, and he didn't seem to remember some of the things he had learned in his previous mindset. Spike, in fact, acted like a completely different horse. He would run off with Bonnie in situations that had never fazed him before. Since the slim teenage girl didn't have the strength or experience to deal with her now-unpredictable companion, I decided to treat Spike like a three-year-old. I taught Bonnie how to train him from the ground up as if he had never been exposed to the bit and bridle. He was, of course, more stable and trustworthy than a young colt. We were simply revisiting activities he had learned in a cloudy, disempowered state, retraining him from his newly awakened perspective. He progressed quickly, becoming more enthusiastic and cooperative along the way. As I watched the process, I began to understand how severe a personality change his former occupation — and the training techniques designed to make him more compliant — had induced in him. If laying Spike down had separated his mind and spirit from his body, then correcting this injustice was akin to soul retrieval. Any skill he'd learned in his previous state of dissociation seemed now to be a vague, dreamlike memory at best.

It wasn't until I began working with human trauma survivors in the late 1990s that I found clinical explanations for this phenomenon. Pioneering somatic therapist Peter A. Levine made significant breakthroughs in treating people with posttraumatic stress disorder (PTSD) by studying the predator-prey relationship in nature. The first chapter in his book *Waking the Tiger: Healing Trauma* opens with a description of what happens to an impala attacked by a hungry cheetah:

> At the moment of contact (or just before), the young impala falls to the ground, surrendering to its impending death. Yet it may not be injured. The stone-still animal is not pretending to be dead. It has instinctively entered an altered state of consciousness shared by all

mammals when death appears imminent.... Physiologists call this altered state the "immobility" or "freezing" response. It is one of the three primary responses available to reptiles and mammals when faced with an overwhelming threat. The other two, flight and fight, are much more familiar to most of us. Less is known about the immobility response. However, my work over the last twenty-five years has led me to believe that it is the single most important factor in uncovering the mystery of human trauma.... The physiological evidence clearly shows that the ability to go into and come out of this natural response is the key to avoiding the debilitating effects of trauma. It is a gift to us from the wild.

Levine discovered that parts of the brain activated in life-threatening situations are the same parts of the nervous system people share with other mammals. Over time, he also noticed that the human ability for rational thought would sometimes interfere with instinctual impulses to flee or fight in an emergency, leading to an even more dramatic freeze response he calls the Medusa complex, referring to a term coined by Gaston Bachelard in 1948. "As in the Greek myth of Medusa, the human confusion that may ensue when we stare death in the face can turn us to stone. We may literally freeze in fear, which will result in the creation of traumatic symptoms.... Traumatic symptoms are not caused by the 'triggering' event itself. They stem from the frozen residue of energy that has not been resolved and discharged." Levine describes the energetic profile of the freeze response as being similar to what happens to a car when the driver floors the accelerator and stomps on the brake simultaneously. "The difference between the inner racing of the nervous system (engine) and the outer immobility (brake) of the body creates a forceful turbulence inside the body similar to a tornado."

Levine observed videos of wild animals released after the trauma of being captured and vaccinated or fitted with radio collars, an ordeal experienced as a predatory attack. Most interestingly, even predatory bears coming out of the freeze response would shake violently and then run off their excess energy the same way prey animals do. When Levine slowed down videos of the initial tremors, he realized that these strange movements were also related to running. Based on these findings, he believes that "the key to healing traumatic symptoms in humans lies in our being able to mirror the fluid adaptation of wild animals as they shake out and pass through the immobility response and become fully mobile and functional again."

The subtleties involved in various ways of laying down a horse coincide with Levine's theories. A horse methodically trained to lie down by a trusted trainer, for instance, is not the least bit traumatized. The geldings Buck Light laid down at the ranch in Wyoming also remained spirited and alert, despite the fact that they were forced to the ground and no doubt frightened by a group of cowboys who were complete strangers at the time. This rough-and-tumble training technique was designed to immobilize the horse just long enough for the rider to jump into the saddle. The fact that the animal was immediately allowed to jump up and take off running essentially gave him the opportunity to "pass through the immobility response and become fully mobile and functional again," as Levine wrote. Pulling a frightened horse to the ground and sitting on him until he stops struggling, however, is a way of inducing and solidifying the freeze response, creating a perpetually dazed mount who thereafter wanders around in a trance that was originally biologically designed to spare him the pain of being eaten.

Years after Spike was forced into the worker drone mindset of an obedient trail horse, he exhibited the same tendency to shake and run when he began to come out of his dissociative state. In reflecting on this response years later, I suspected the horse had been laid down at some point in his training. The only problem was that Bonnie happened to be in the saddle when Spike "woke up." Had I understood this, I never would have let my inexperienced student ride the horse during the transition. Luckily, Bonnie fell off only once, suffering little more than a few bruises and getting the air knocked out of her. My subsequent impulse to start Spike from the ground up allowed him to work off the effects of his internalized tornado of repressed energy as he galloped and bucked around on the longe line for the first few days.

Comedian Woody Allen once remarked that he wasn't afraid of dying — he just didn't want to be there when it happened. "In this characteristic one-liner," Levine observes, "Woody Allen quips a fairly accurate description of the role played by dissociation — it protects us from the impact of escalating arousal. If a life-threatening event continues, dissociation protects us from the pain of death." To give readers an idea of what this protective response feels like, he offers a quote from David Livingstone's diary. While traveling through Africa, the famous explorer, who was almost eaten by a lion, found himself in a strange and comforting altered state after the predator pulled him down by the shoulder and shook him violently. "The shock produced a stupor similar to that which seems to be felt by a mouse after the first shake of the cat," Livingstone reported.

> It caused a sort of dreaminess in which there was no sense of pain nor feeling of terror, though [I was] quite conscious of all that was happening. It was like what patients partially under the influence of chloroform describe, who see all the operation, but feel not the knife. This singular condition was not the result of any mental process. The shake annihilated fear, and allowed no sense of horror in looking round at the beast. This peculiar state is probably produced in all animals killed by the carnivore; and if so, is a merciful provision by our benevolent creator for lessening the pain of death.

"The best way to define dissociation is through the experience of it," Levine emphasizes.

> In its mildest forms, it manifests as a kind of spaciness. At the other end of the spectrum, it can develop into so-called multiple personality disorder. Because dissociation is a breakdown in the continuity of a person's felt sense, it almost always includes distortions of time and perception.... The woman being raped, the soldier facing enemy fire, or the victim of an accident may experience a fundamental disconnection from his or her body. From a corner of the ceiling, a child may watch him/herself being molested, and feel sorry for or neutral toward the defenseless child below.... In trauma, dissociation seems to be a favored means of enabling a person to endure experiences that are at the moment beyond endurance — like being attacked by a lion, a rapist, an oncoming car, or a surgeon's knife.

Or, in the case of a horse, pulled to the ground and forced to lie there until he submits, by a trainer who has absolutely no regard for the animal's emotional and spiritual well-being.

Related to this issue, however, is an intriguing interpretation of the climax to Evans's *The Horse Whisperer*: After all the progress the hero makes with the collaborative techniques depicted earlier in the book and film, the main character resorts to the ultimate quick-fix, force-oriented tactic of laying the horse down at the moment he himself becomes emotionally overloaded by the unexpected arrival of his love interest's husband. This "kinder, gentler" trainer loses all sense of judgment when his male rival appears. He dramatically illustrates his physical dominance over a thousand-pound animal whose trust he had been gaining with subtle, humane approaches. The horse whisperer's use of this old trick signals his weakness in dealing with his conflicting emotions; it's certainly not a strategy to emulate. (Monty Roberts, in fact, publicly objected to the inclusion of this scene when he heard Robert Redford was making a film of the novel.) In the book, the main character continues to work himself into such a state of confusion and remorse that he finally commits suicide by stepping into the striking hooves of an angry stallion — who, as it turns out, is simply trying to defend his mares from a perceived threat.

Ultimately, the sensitive cowboy who helps horses with people problems is incapable of dealing with his own people problems, a downfall I've witnessed in the savviest of trainers. It is perhaps the most potent paradox of the equestrian arts that people can learn to remain calm and collected in the presence of a rearing horse, yet crumble in the face of feelings too strong to be suppressed or ignored, feelings that quite naturally surface in horse-human interactions. Managing authentic emotion, it seems, is one of the last great frontiers in the riding arena...and in life.

CHAPTER EIGHT

FOUR-LEGGED THERAPISTS

When people began measuring horsepower in units of 746 watts and driving carriages fueled by gas instead of muscle, the dynamics of our six-thousand-year-old partnership with the horse changed practically overnight. Interest in the species seemed destined to fizzle as machines of all kinds replaced these magnificent yet outdated beasts of burden. As the twentieth century reached its halfway mark, most people living in the United States considered horses expensive diversions for the elite. Yet a quiet revolution was taking place behind the scenes. Women were emerging as the primary caretakers of these animals, and with this shift came an interest in the horse as companion and confidant.

"Men made all the decisions about horses in my early days in the 1930s," reveals veterinarian and writer Matthew Mackay-Smith:

The horse's preference was never contemplated. It was rare for a horse to be allowed much leisure during his working life or given a protracted "retirement" at the end of it. Palliative treatment was scorned as unprofessional: Veterinarians were expected to return a beast to usefulness. Horsemen were rarely intentionally cruel, but the horse's feelings — and any notions that he had an intrinsic individual value of his own — were of no practical interest and received no attention. Mine is the first generation to grow up with a nonutilitarian view of horses.

In his *Equus* article "A Change for the Better," Mackay-Smith reflected on the years when the horse's primary status as beast of burden and mode of transportation gave way to a new role as "the instrument and servant of personal athletic achievement." Interest in equestrian competition grew by leaps and bounds in the 1940s and 1950s. Though many people continued to see the horse as a means to an end, Mackay-Smith noticed that

> riders who partnered not only physically but emotionally with their horses rose to the top. The old methods based on coercion just didn't work as well and became the refuge of the incompetent and the impatient. Women succeeded well out of proportion to their numbers or opportunity. And as increasing numbers of men who worked in stables headed to the city in pursuit of "real" jobs, the care of horses fell more and more to women.

Horse lovers who weren't involved in competitive riding began to notice other valuable qualities in the species. In the 1930s, Bazy Tankersley experienced the therapeutic value of human-equine relationships as two of these remarkable creatures literally carried her through some difficult childhood years. "When I was ten, my widowed mother remarried and transplanted us from Illinois and Washington, DC, to New Mexico," she told me. "I was the only kid still at home, and we lived out on a ranch, so she bought me a really nice cow pony. Well, I spent so much time on that cow pony he was in a state of perpetual exhaustion, but I was finding a different dimension. I was involved with a horse as a companion, a horse that brought me solace for having lost everything in my previous life and starting a new life virtually by myself."

Bazy's enthusiasm eventually warranted the purchase of an Arabian mare, a spirited breed known for its endurance. "She was the first horse I ever had who wanted to go out riding as much as I did," remembered the woman who went on to establish Al-Marah Arabians, one of the largest farms in the US devoted to the breed. "It was no question of catching her; it was a question of getting away from her. I experienced not only the psychological lift of this big, gorgeous animal wanting my company, but I discovered that Arabians were almost an art form because I started reading about them and looking at pictures. Our relationship had a spiritual impact too, because of the devotion my two horses showed each other. After I went off to boarding school, my mare died of sleeping sickness. When they dragged her out of the corral that she shared with the cow pony, he broke the fence down to go with her. I didn't realize animals bonded that deeply."

Bazy's childhood equine friends gave her firsthand knowledge of the healing potential of the species. They helped her deal with grief, loneliness, and pivotal life changes. Without those animals by her side, the girl probably would not have adjusted so well to some of the most serious challenges a young person can face. It's no surprise, then, that she went on to support several therapeutic riding programs over the years. As the twentieth century came to a close, she also started the Animal Therapy Association (ATA), a national nonprofit organization designed to bring the field into the mainstream. The board's long-term goals included assisting in the establishment of degree programs at universities and supporting serious research documenting the effectiveness of animal therapy in various contexts. In this effort, the ATA board formed a working partnership with People, Animals, Nature, Inc. (PAN), an Illinois-based nonprofit with international influence. Established in 1997, PAN disseminated information about the vital linkages between healthy human growth, development, education, and contact with animals and natural environments, providing a mutually supportive network for emerging animal therapy programs worldwide.

The formalized practice of therapeutic riding emerged in Europe in the early 1950s as a tool for improving the lives of persons with disabilities. The North American Riding for the Handicapped Association, which I mentioned in chapter 5, was founded in 1969, officially bringing this treatment to the United States and Canada. The organization, now called the Professional Association of Therapeutic Horsemanship International (PATH International), sets safety standards, certifies instructors, and accredits therapeutic riding operations nationwide. What started out as a form of physical therapy eventually expanded to include clients with psychological issues, as horses were found to be unexpectedly talented in dealing with mental and emotional needs. Therapeutic riding instructors began exploring activities that capitalized on the highly perceptive nature of the species, leading to the creation of the Equine Facilitated Mental Health Association (EFMHA) in 1996, a section of NARHA committed to developing best practices and standards for this field.

Barbara Rector, MA, who founded EFMHA along with Isabella "Boo" McDaniel, MEd, also started the nationally recognized equine-facilitated psychotherapy program at Sierra Tucson, the residential treatment center used as the model for Sandra Bullock's horse-assisted therapy escapades in the film 28 Days. Barbara went on to establish her own Adventures in Awareness program, which expanded the equine therapy model to teach life skills and promote a holistic state of wellness in members of the general public.

Barbara was one of the first people to articulate and expand upon the horse's uncanny ability to detect incongruent emotions in human handlers. "Every riding teacher giving a lesson sees it," she told me. "When the person is unable to access what's going on in her own body and mind, the horse will express it behaviorally or actually even become locked up in his own body." Over time, she realized this equine talent, which caused so much trouble in conventional equestrian pursuits, could be used to help people who have trouble recognizing and managing their emotions. "I saw this time and time again with the kids at [Sierra Tucson's] adolescent unit," she continues. "They were up there because they put their fists through plate glass windows or beat up their parents. You put them in a round pen with a horse, and they can't hide what they're feeling, so they learn how to listen to their feelings before they become unmanageable. What's more, the horse doesn't judge what they're feeling and doesn't hold grudges. As soon as the person acknowledges his fear or anger, a horse with a talent for this work will walk over to him and lend him support."

Barbara found that instinct alone couldn't explain the sophisticated reactions horses exhibited in the presence of people dealing with all types of physical, mental, emotional, and spiritual challenges. Josh, a student attending one of her early workshops, happened to be blind from birth, and he did surprisingly well in getting an Arabian gelding named Dundee to cooperate with him in the round pen after some initial adjustments. When his session was over, however, Josh asked if he could have a few minutes to himself before the next person took her turn. He just wanted to wander around the ring alone because he'd never experienced the sensation of moving at liberty in a new environment without his cane. The horse, who had never encountered a person with a visual impairment, watched Josh's tentative steps for a moment before walking directly to the young man's side and putting his withers in the same position a sighted guide assistant would take. Each time Josh lost his footing, Dundee moved in close, providing his body for balance. Together, they walked, jogged, and ran. Even Barbara was amazed as they began to move in figure eights. No one has ever been able to explain how Dundee knew Josh was blind or why the horse was motivated to act as the boy's guide.

When Barbara first told me this story, I figured there was probably no way to reproduce the phenomenon on demand or to study it in the lab. Then I heard about the Guide Horse Foundation, a nonprofit organization established in 2000 by Janet and Don Burleson to train miniature horses for the blind. Based in Kittrell, North Carolina, the couple cites the compact breed's calm, thoughtful nature, phenomenal memory, and willingness to be of service as the qualities that make these animals natural guides. What's more, minihorses live an average of thirty to forty years and are less costly to maintain than a large dog, whose life expectancy is a mere ten to twelve years.

Still, innovators in equine-facilitated therapy have come to appreciate the far more unpredictable, even miraculous episodes of healing that occur between horses and humans when the animals are allowed to take the initiative. "At some point I realized it wasn't about training, and it wasn't about the therapeutic intervention," says Maureen Fredrickson, who was elected president of EFMHA in the late 1990s and founded her own multispecies therapy program and education center, Animal Systems, Ltd. "It's about recognizing that animals, especially those animals that are healers, have a sense of what people need. They're a lot more empathetic than we give them credit for, and they have a willingness to care for those who need help in ways that most people have to be medically trained to do."

As former vice president of programs at Delta Society, an organization that trains animal-assisted therapy practitioners and promotes the field in general, Maureen, a social worker, is one of a growing number of mental health clinicians who've witnessed episodes of significant emotional healing that simply can't be explained by any current theories of horse intelligence and perception. The most dramatic example took place during a workshop she held for adults dealing with midlife transition issues. One of the self-discovery and confidence-building activities Maureen regularly employs involves a free-form interaction with a group of gentle horses set loose in an arena. The only rule is that the participants can't use their hands.

"I wanted to level the playing field," she says. "When people use their hands, they always have some way to attack, to grab, or to control, and the horses don't have that ability. You put your hands behind your back, and suddenly you're not really in control."

While most of the people attending this particular workshop were amenable to the idea, one woman admitted an intense fear of horses. After exploring her options, including standing outside the fence and simply watching the others, "Jenny" agreed to walk into the pen if she could stand behind Maureen. Ten people stood evenly spaced around the arena when

Maureen's twenty-four-year-old standardbred, Murphy, walked into the center of the circle. It wasn't long before the stately gray gelding singled Jenny out and began to approach her with the utmost caution and sensitivity.

"He started playing with the person next to Jenny," Maureen remembers, "rustling her shirt, playing with her hair. Every once in a while he'd turn around and look toward us. At first I thought he was looking at me, trying to check in with me, to see if I was going to tell him to stop. He did this three or four times before I realized he wasn't looking at me. He was looking at Jenny standing behind me. I could actually hear her shaking. I asked her if she was all right, and she said she was and wanted to stay. Finally the horse turned around and looked right at her. She started to gasp. The horse took a step toward her, stopped, put his head down, picked up a little piece of wood, and was twirling it between his lips. It was the strangest thing I've ever seen. He'd drop that stick and then he'd waggle his ears and make these funny faces at her. Then he'd take another step and pick up another stick. I couldn't figure out what he was doing, but he finally worked himself right up to her and ran his nose over her face. Then he walked away, and she let out this big gasp. She said, 'That must be what it's like to be mothered.'"

Murphy circled around and stood next to another woman. He picked up a stick and dropped it on her shoulder, then made eye contact with Jenny again. "I mean he leaned his head forward and looked at this woman," Maureen emphasizes. "This went on for a couple of minutes, then I mentioned that I thought Murphy was just trying to be funny. She started to laugh. He started walking towards her again. He did the same routine with the sticks, got up to her, ran his lip all over her face, and then pushed her in the solar plexus with his nose and knocked her back a few steps."

Jenny started to cry, once again commenting that Murphy was showing her what it was like to be mothered, hinting at a background of childhood abuse and neglect. In the midst of her rising emotional turmoil, Murphy stepped behind her and lay down next to her, leaning his back against her. The tears spilled down her cheeks as Jenny talked more specifically about the betrayals she suffered at the hands of her parents. The other participants stared in silence. A few moments later, Murphy got up, walked away, and shook the dirt off.

"By then we'd lost control of the group," Maureen says. "People were going crazy, shouting that this couldn't be happening, that horses just don't lay down next to people. I decided we needed to get a little space. We went down to the other end of the arena as she continued to talk about the abuse she'd experienced. Murphy marched through the group, walked right up to her, and laid his chin on her shoulder. Again, she started telling him about what had happened to her.

"I thought, 'No one really should hear this.' I mean we were supposed to be talking about midlife transition issues. Then she started to sob. She put her hands out in front of her, and he laid his head in her hands. At that point, she threw her hands around his neck and really sobbed, and the horse curled his head and his neck around her, as if he were literally trying to hug her. This lasted maybe two or three minutes. She told him all kinds of things. Then she seemed to get control of herself again. Murphy kind of ruffled her hair a little bit. She let go of his neck, and he walked away, as if to say to me, 'OK, it's your turn now; you fix the rest.'

"When we debriefed her later, we asked her, 'Where did you go to?' She said, 'I don't know, but he took me somewhere.' The whole incident reminded me of the spirit horse and the ancient Celtic belief that the horse was the transition between the worlds. Whatever Murphy did for her, he took her to some place that was healing and nurturing and then brought her back to us."

The experience profoundly affected Maureen's perception of equine intelligence, providing her with an illustration of the unusual abilities individual horses exhibit when allowed to interact with people outside conventional equestrian contexts. "What really concerns me now is trainers who say that animals look to us for leadership," she says. "Frankly, I'm not sure what we could offer a horse as far as leadership. We can't tell the difference between the good grass and the bad grass in a field. We have lousy hearing. We can't see 340 degrees around us. Maybe horses can't figure out a maze, but where on the plains would you find a maze? We know that tests like SATs are biased toward a white population in the same way that animal intelligence tests are biased toward carnivores. Let's give these animals the space to show us what their talents really are, because I don't think we have a clue."

My own foray into equine-facilitated therapy stemmed from the research I initially conducted for an article on horse-human relationships in 1993, a subject that ultimately led to this book — and my full-time business. In testing my conclusions, as well as experimenting with the theories of other riders, trainers, and therapists, I found that the motivation to develop and continually modify my own methods came naturally. Yet it was the horses who set the agenda, more often than not during those unexpected moments when they blew all accepted notions about human superiority, equine intelligence, and the nature of true healing right out of the water. I can't remember how many times I watched some theory perfected through painstaking research bite the dust as the horses refused to fit into it. As time went on, my experience with these talented creatures inspired me to explore the most adventurous scientific and philosophical interpretations of reality. Even so, the more I learned, the less confidence I had in the ability of any single theory to embrace the potential of the horse-human connection. And so I became comfortable collaborating with mystery.

Ultimately, my willingness to relinquish accepted concepts and respond authentically in the moment led to an increasing ability to navigate through the unknown, to become more fluid and adaptable, to embrace all experiences and emotions as meaningful information. These were the most valuable skills I learned from my horses. They were the same skills most valuable to our students. Spontaneous transformations occurred when I stepped back and allowed things to happen naturally while drawing my clients' awareness to the little things, the things most easily ignored, the things over which I had no control, the things that were most difficult to capture in words.

"Achieve without trying to achieve anything," Lao-tzu advised in the Tao Te Ching. "Savor the taste of what you cannot taste. Make a small thing great, and the few into many." This little book of wisdom was filled with insights that seemed paradoxical in writing but made perfect sense in the riding arena. "There are too many laws, when all you have to do is hold on to the center," he wrote. "Desiring nothing for himself, [the sage] knows how to channel desires. And is it not because he wants nothing that he is able to achieve everything?"

Whenever I overrelied on specific goals and objectives for my horses or my clients, our interactions felt stilted, the outcomes mundane. When I threw out lesson plans and simply created a safe space for collaboration, breakthroughs became commonplace. Over time, I approached riding lessons, horse training, and equine-facilitated activities as a jazz artist enters a jam session. A musician may have the scales, melodies, and rhythms at his fingertips, but "it don't mean a thing if it ain't got that swing." In jazz, technique is subservient to the spirit of the moment. The art of the jam session encompasses a group of players who meet on common ground by stating the theme of a standard everyone knows, which serves as the basis for a series of improvisational interactions that may eventually sound nothing like the original tune. Sometimes a new song emerges in the process. In a horse-facilitated jam session, standard activities like grooming, riding, and round pen work provide the setting in which an interspecies improvisation occurs. The facilitator has myriad equestrian and therapeutic methods that she employs, not according to a rigid plan, but according to necessity, ready to be further modified if the situation calls for it, yet used only when the timing is right. This person is not the boss or even the lead player. She's more like the drummer who supports the other artists and keeps the rhythm going. Even so, no one member of the ensemble can take credit for what happens. The magic occurs in the interaction, in the space between the participants. As Lao-tzu observed: "Thirty spokes on a cart wheel go towards the hub that is the center — but look, there is nothing at the center and that is precisely why it works!"

In my search for ways to explain equine-facilitated activities for personal and professional growth, I once again found the Old Master's perspective beneficial. I began to see Taoism as a philosophy of experiential learning, one that downplays the intellectual tendency to predict and control. In Lao-tzu's words, the sage "leads by following" the continually changing needs of the people he claims to serve. He "comes from the virtue of not-striving, and from knowing how to link with other people's energy." He "tries to help us be true to who we are without ever standing in our way." As I stepped into the world of horse training and horse-facilitated human development, I began to live these ideas, not because they sounded good, but because they worked. In the process, I developed a deeper understanding of feminine styles of leadership and empowerment useful in coaching the increasing numbers of women attracted to Eponaquest's workshops and lessons.

The Difference between Sex and Connection

There's a long-standing perception in our culture about the attraction that women feel for horses: that the relationship between the two is inherently lascivious or, at the very least, a substitute for sex. After all, when girls suddenly become captivated by these magnificent creatures and are allowed to pursue their obsession through riding lessons or actually owning a horse, they tend to show less interest in boys than their nonequestrian peers. Going horse crazy is equally prominent among women in their prime who are experiencing major life changes, particularly relationship problems.

As a riding instructor and equine-facilitated therapy/experiential learning practitioner, I must admit that most of my female students fall into one of these two categories: adolescent girls or women in transition. Of the people who attend my lessons, workshops, and horse training classes, fewer than 20 percent of them are men. While this is surely related to the fact that I'm a woman instructor who does not teach jumping, roping, reining, cutting, and other equestrian pursuits more likely to attract male thrill seekers, the overwhelming presence of female clients in my business reflects a national trend. One study estimated that women represent over 80 percent of consumers who buy horse-related merchandise, revenues of which add up to a billion-dollar industry in this country. The gap between the sexes closes among those who show and train professionally. To the women I encounter in my practice, however, horses represent something much more profound than profit, sport, or hobby. The vast majority of amateur equestriennes are looking for a relationship that is simultaneously nurturing and challenging, one that strikes a potent balance between intelligence and instinct, strength and grace, beauty and power, spirituality and sensuality. When these people experience the slightest hint of the sheer, unbridled euphoria that comes from moving in perfect rhythm with a thousand pounds of heart and muscle, there is absolutely no turning back.

Over the years, I've come to realize that horses are not a substitute for sex. Rather, sex is often a substitute for the kind of multisensory connection that horses, unlike many people in our society, are able to provide without reservation. Sex as portrayed in the media — and as played out in many short- and long-term relationships — is a quick-fix high that briefly, and just barely, quenches our thirst for true intimacy. Yet the need for authentic connection cannot be met as long as the very qualities that support relationship continue to be washed out of the fabric of human existence. In his book *Body: Recovering Our Sensual Wisdom*, somatic psychotherapist Don Hanlon Johnson analyzes the intricate web of social conditioning leading to this widespread state of disconnection. A number of concepts developed in Western culture over the last two thousand years work together to disengage and isolate us from our own sources of power, sensuality, and creativity. These concepts include the body as "slave" or "machine" to the mind, the mind as "king," "boss," or "master computer" of the body, the invalidation of the senses, the denial of emotions, the subjugation of the feminine, and the overemphasis on stability, outside authority, and established methods.

"The mind-body fracture that prompts us to discredit our sensual wisdom is reflected in the ancient divisions between men and women," he writes.

> We have constructed a mythical world in which men in gray flannel suits who sit at computers or in board rooms planning mass slaughter are considered prototypes of reasonable behavior, capable of directing the destiny of our planet, while women who take care of their homes and children or who work as secretaries, or nurses, often alone in their old age, are thought to be irrational sources of error or even sin, unfit to make any major decisions about pubic affairs.

Our society often portrays children as masses of thoughtless instincts that must be programmed by a class of experts. As we grow to adulthood, these oppressive attitudes are reinforced by body-shaping methods designed to evoke suspicions about the reliability of our own perceptions and feelings. According to Johnson, people encounter these nonverbal messages in posture-training, dance, and gym classes, where they're taught the "right way" to stand, move, and express themselves and, more recently, the ways in which "ideal" manifestations of the human form move across the television screen or pose seductively in magazines. In many schools, boys and girls with supple bodies and minds still walk to class in straight lines and sit in stiff wooden chairs arranged in rows that focus their attention on a single adult expert. Anyone caught looking longingly out the window or refusing to sit still is sent to the principal's office, punished, intimidated, or, when all else fails, medicated into submission.

On an intellectual level, Johnson observes, our society appears to reject authoritarianism. We are children of the American Revolution dedicated to the promise of freedom and personal expression. But our institutions do not behave as if they are upholding this sacred trust. Rather, they purposefully condition us to conform and submit to a small population of authorities who routinely use and discard the majority of human beings as replaceable parts in a great industrial mechanism.

Johnson cites the writings of the Austrian analyst Wilhelm Reich, who characterized the nonverbal postures of conformity taught from childhood as "the physiological anchor of the social incapacity for freedom." Reich observed that "bringing up people to assume a rigid, unnatural attitude is one of the most essential means used by a dictatorial social system to produce will-less, automatically functioning organisms." The problem with this kind of conditioning, however, is that many of our personal and interpersonal conflicts come from confronting new situations with these same old stances. We keep up ingrained patterns of posture, behavior, and thought even when they're obviously not working.

In the face of such rigidity, interacting with a horse can be an unusually constructive act of rebellion, an opportunity to awaken from the mental and physical trances of conformity. Some of my most inspiring clients are successful businesswomen in their thirties, forties, and fifties who are finally in a position to pursue their childhood equestrian dreams. During their first few rides, these people are invariably astonished at how stiff their bodies feel as their mounts inch along at a stilted, wooden gait. Even avid runners, weight lifters, and cyclists discover they have unconsciously adopted restrictive habits that grossly inhibit freedom of movement — postures, imbalances, and areas of tension that visibly affect the movement of the horse. After all, no matter how good these ladies look or feel, most spend just as many hours sitting at a desk as their less active colleagues, and when they work out, a machine often mediates their actions.

The field of therapeutic riding has proved that no mechanical device can match the effectiveness of the horse in treating a variety of physical disabilities. The simultaneous front-to-back, side-to-side motion of a sound equine activates and strengthens muscular nuances in human stroke and accident victims that can actually help them regain the use of their legs. A study conducted by Dr. Bill Benda at the University of Arizona and Nancy McGibbon of Therapeutic Riding of Tucson (TROT) has shown measurable improvement in the mobility and flexibility of children with cerebral palsy from just a single therapeutic riding session.

A few of the more adventurous experiments exploring the therapeutic effects of equine encounters suggest that horses are so effective in this context because they act on multiple levels, relaxing and supporting the rider in such a way as to create a wider opening for healing to take place. Just brushing or petting one of these animals, for instance, has been shown to significantly lower blood pressure. A University of Arizona study led by Dr. Ann Linda Baldwin showed that grooming a horse for ten minutes also increases heart rate variability, a measure of heart health. Other research suggests that stroking a cat, dog, or horse releases the hormone oxytocin in both the human and the animal involved. Oxytocin buffers the flight-or-fight impulse in favor of a calm-and-connect response. It both inspires and rewards connection, increasing trust, learning capacity, and social recognition circuits, and causing mammals to reach out to strangers rather than instantly reject them. In her book *Made for Each Other: The Biology of the Human-Animal Bond,* Meg Daley Olmert lays out an intricate multicultural theory showing how oxytocin brought humans and animals together in mutually supportive partnerships thousands of years ago, leading to *mutual domestication* as humans and animals became more cooperative and trustworthy during this process.

Respectful, empathetic interactions with horses also activate the ventral vagus nerve complex in both species, jump-starting feelings of safety through connection. As Porges contends, this in turn promotes recovery from traumatic events. Add to this the fact that horses are not predators, and you begin to understand why someone who has been mistreated by predatory members of her own species can relax during simple activities with these powerful yet gentle creatures. Horses like my mare Rasa and Maureen Fredrickson's gelding Murphy also exhibit a natural therapeutic orientation and a marked interest in humans. These secure, insightful beings can co-regulate a dysregulated human, and they seem happy to do it. A person interacting with such a horse will feel safe and supported as her ventral vagus comes online, allowing her nervous system to redirect energy and resources away from a survival orientation to circuits designed for healing, restoration, and growth.

Such research legitimizes the powerful influence that horses can have on persons with physical, mental, and emotional disabilities — as well as on supposedly healthy, well-adjusted individuals. But there are other, more mysterious aspects of human-equine interactions that can't be measured, or even recreated, and thus continue to be ignored by statistic-happy counselors, agencies, and medical institutions whose clients could benefit from horse-facilitated therapies.

It never ceases to amaze me how profoundly even the most confident, well-heeled professional can be affected by riding around in a small circle on a horse attached to a lead line. Some of the most exciting moments in my practice happen when a first-time equestrian realizes that to liberate the horse's body from mirroring her own physical issues, she has to breathe into her abdomen, unclench her jaw, relax her shoulders, release her pelvis, and allow her upper torso to float quietly over hips that follow the naturally fluid pace of her mount. Tears of joy or wails of sorrow quite often accompany this seemingly minor breakthrough, for what is unlocked in the body tends to unlock the emotions. At this moment, a woman begins to realize how much of her innate grace and vitality she has consciously or unconsciously sublimated, restrained, or sacrificed to make her way in life.

Some realizations are more dramatic than others. Occasionally, a beginner riding lesson will trigger repressed memories of sexual abuse or feelings of anger for violations the woman thought she had already dealt with in therapy. However, the intensity of such an experience is tempered by the horse's strong and steady presence. With careful and sensitive coaching, the rider is able to work through her initial shock and grief on horseback while accessing a sense of empowerment that assists her in further processing the information with a psychotherapist. One of my students, "Ann," was an incest survivor who thought she had dissected all the related issues with a series of counselors. The first time she stepped into the saddle, however, she was outraged to discover how much the trauma had affected her sense of physical freedom. She was also surprised at how quickly she experienced profound liberation on the back of the horse. Years of therapy had not helped her regain ease of movement in the pelvic region or even notice it was an issue in the first place. She made it clear, however, that this somatic revelation was possible only because it had occurred in the nonsexual context of horseback riding. Over the years, intercourse with even the most caring men had caused her to lock up and shut down even more.

Like Joy, Ann also demonstrated a tendency to dissociate in stressful situations, a problem that made success in business and personal relationships all the more difficult. When a skillful troubleshooter is needed, even some of the most intelligent, hardworking survivors of sexual assault tend to freeze, making it possible for less talented colleagues to outshine them in the mildest emergencies. Women who can't think under pressure or handle heated interpersonal encounters are not considered management material. These people tend to be repeatedly passed over for promotions no matter how dedicated and talented they otherwise prove themselves to be. They also find they can't deal with family problems effectively. Either they shy away from promising romantic relationships at the slightest sign of disagreement or they let their husbands, and later their children, walk all over them when a difference of opinion leads to heightened emotions.

Once I understood the physiology of the immobility response through Stephen Porges and Peter Levine's writings, I was able to help women release these dissociative patterns in much the same way I had dealt with Spike, the former trail horse who had been trained into a similarly impotent altered state. The key was getting these people to move whenever they lapsed into freeze mode, using the energy of the horse to jump-start muscle groups associated with running. I eventually came across another equine-facilitated therapist whose intuitive response to an abuse survivor coincided with these insights. Leif Hallberg, founder of the Esperanza Center and author of several books on equine-facilitated therapy, worked with a woman who experienced flashbacks of sexual violation while taking a riding lesson. As her client slipped into a dissociative trance, Leif felt the instinctual urge to shake the woman out of it by compelling her student to trot the horse. The effect of this faster gait tossed the woman gently up and down while simultaneously moving the muscle groups associated with jogging. Like a prey animal trembling and running off after coming out of freeze mode, the movement released the pent-up energy in the student's pelvic area, and she ended the session in a state of relief and empowerment, despite the sudden emergence of her long-suppressed memory.

The parallels between the altered states experienced by a horse who has been laid down and a woman who has been raped became even more apparent, curiously enough, when I studied the equine symbolism used in Vodou trance cults. The Hausa Bori culture in Nigeria, an urban variation of a pre-Islamic religious system emphasizing interactions with the supernatural, refers to its mediums as "horses," as do a number of Vodou sects in Haiti and Jamaica. Through a series of initiation rites, those called to the profession of medium learn to yield to invisible forces that are said to "ride" their human mounts for a variety of purposes. At first I was intrigued to find that Vodou horse mediums are predominantly female. Then I read that these sects exist on the fringes of dominant cultures offering women little or no participation in religious and political affairs. Nigeria's conversion to Islam made respected matriarchs the property of their husbands and sons. Haiti's male-dominated society also considers its feminine population to be of a lower class. For women treated as slaves and outcasts in their own communities, it's not such a big leap of faith to become a willing servant to the gods. "Horse" is an optimistic metaphor for such a position, an animal that always manages to convey some semblance of beauty and dignity while carrying the master's weight.

"Authorities in every kind of society have worked to keep the role of women carefully defined and controlled," writes Don Hanlon Johnson in *Body*. "Fascists, Communists, Muslims, Hindus, Catholics, and conservatives in our own society have been united in the necessity of keeping the 'wife' confined to her solitary role in the home." Even "Freud argued that women actually retard the advances in civilization." Johnson also quotes Octavio Paz in summarizing the Latin view of the gender: "Whether as prostitute, goddess or grande dame or mistress, woman transmits or preserves but does not believe in the values and energies entrusted to her by nature or society. She is a domesticated wild animal, lecherous and sinful from birth, who must be subdued with a stick and guided by the reins of religion."

In some misogynistic cultures, women are quite obviously treated — or, more accurately, mistreated — like horses. The Bori and Vodou religions are both possession cults; mediums retain no memory of the actions they perform when the spirits "ride" them. Anthropologists studying the phenomenon have determined that people attracted to these sects have already been so demoralized and damaged by the dominant culture that they've lost the will to live their own lives. Wife beatings and sexual violations are commonly ignored or even considered socially acceptable. These acts of violence induce an immobility response in some people that can be co-opted for any number of purposes. Like wild mustangs forcibly pulled to the ground and frightened within an inch of their lives, these women have given up the ghost, even though their hearts still beat. It comes as no surprise that Bori "mares of the gods" spend the better part of their days working in houses of prostitution. A medium's ability to dissociate from reality while another entity takes control of her body is just as useful in the bedroom as it is in the trance possession ritual.

The immobility response not only explains why many victims *cannot* fight back during rape; it also offers insight into why women in violent marriages do not simply leave. Once these aggressive, degrading interactions reach a certain intensity level, the dorsal vagus overrides the sympathetic nervous system's flight-or-fight mode. By activating the immobility response in his wife, the abuser essentially trains her to submit like a broken horse, and her dissociative, machinelike demeanor becomes a *physiological* cage that she cannot escape.

As my staff, clients, and instructors learned more about the immobility response, it became apparent that people subjected to long-term domestic violence need others to intervene and support them in leaving abusive situations.

"When we were exploring the polyvagal theory in a workshop you and Dr. [Rebecca] Bailey led, I realized that my own daughter was in trouble," one colleague told me. "Emily" had been concerned about the way "Eileen's" husband treated her for quite some time. "Yet when I voiced my concerns to other family members, they said, 'Oh, she's a grown woman; she can leave any time she wants.' I started noticing that Eileen was increasingly dull, depressed. She had all the signs of dorsal vagal shutdown, that vacant look in the eyes, the expressionless face, the monotone voice." Emily reached out to Eileen and told her that she would need help to leave, that her current state of mind would prevent her from thinking clearly and making the proper arrangements. "Don't worry about the details," Emily told her daughter. "We are here for you." A few days later, Emily and her husband drove to Eileen's house and helped her gather some belongings. "She went through some treatment; the fog began to lift; and she was able to get through a somewhat contentious divorce. She has a great job now and even leads a support group for other people facing similar challenges. My daughter is back!"

In my work with rape survivors, I sometimes use the example of the Vodou trance phenomenon to articulate the effects of sexual violations. The personality profile of a Hausa Bori horse medium helps to clarify the difference between the intuition and responsiveness of an empowered woman and the obedience extracted from a disempowered woman. Soulless acquiescence has nothing in common with the kind of trust and surrender required to engage in a cocreative relationship with Spirit, follow God's plan, or align with the Tao, and it's certainly not the way of the horse. As demonstrated in previous chapters, these animals are much more likely to reveal their myriad virtues in conscious collaboration with their human caretakers. In the fine art of dressage, for instance, both the horse and the rider are empowered, and at times it's hard to tell who is following whom. Until an abuse survivor understands the difference and reconnects with her own sense of will and self-awareness, she will have trouble gaining the cooperation of a horse, leading a business meeting, or obtaining the respect of her children.

Toward this end, Ann, who had recently adopted a twelve-year-old survivor of sexual abuse, wanted to offer her new daughter riding lessons as a therapeutic agent and as a reward for good behavior. After several sessions, my client was enthusiastic about "Callie's" progress, but she felt she needed to cancel lessons for a while following several incidents of disrespect at home. Ann worried about protecting Callie as the girl approached adolescence. She wanted to nip any sign of rebellion in the bud and knew that riding was one of the privileges Callie valued the most.

"My daughter has already experienced inappropriate sex, and I'm afraid it will be too easy for her to fall in with the wrong crowd," Ann said with a sigh. "At the same time, I can see that the atmosphere at the barn and the influences of the horses are having a positive effect on her. I'm just not sure what to do."

"Think of it this way," I replied. "The horses are providing Callie with a feeling of excitement, that sense of elation we all get when moving in close contact with another being, but perhaps even more importantly, she's learning that she can experience this level of ecstasy and connection outside a sexual relationship. At the same time, she's gaining self-confidence, balance, and the ability to maintain self-control under pressure. She has really bonded with the horse she rides, and he's teaching her how to be assertive yet patient, focused yet responsive in her dealings with him. A one-hundred-pound, instinctually driven fourteen-year-old boy is going to have less influence over a young lady who knows how to contend with a thousand pounds of fast-moving muscle. Callie is learning the art of relationship in a safe setting where she also feels a great deal of joy, and she's willing to get up at six a.m. on the weekend to do it. Is this any less valuable than taking her to group therapy once a week?"

Callie was allowed to continue with her riding as mother and daughter explored ways of working out their differences in an atmosphere of cooperation, rather than fear and restraint.

CHAPTER NINE

THE STALLION FACTOR

While many women respond to the horse as a symbol of feminine empowerment, the stallion offers a potent metaphor for the challenges men face in learning to modulate their own physical and emotional needs. Mismanaged male energy is frightening to behold when it reaches critical mass, especially if you happen to be in its path. Survivors of the 1999 Columbine High School tragedy in Colorado and subsequent school shootings know this all too well, but any parent of an angry teenager has glimpsed the torrential force of testosterone surging out of control, and it's not pretty. Yet when you take a frustrated sixteen-year-old boy aside and ask him why he just slammed his fist through the wall, he's likely to shrug his shoulders and mumble, "I don't know." And the truth is, he really doesn't.

When I first met Midnight Merlin, no one was sure if he would ever be able to break the cycle of fear and aggression he exhibited seemingly without provocation. Hypersensitive to the slightest gesture or change in tone of voice, he had been known to take even the most benign request for cooperation as an affront, exploding without warning into a violent rage that left most people he encountered shaking in their boots. Rehabilitating a stallion with a chronic anger management problem is a dangerous task. Normally, I wouldn't consider investing the time, energy, and awareness it takes to bring such a horse back from the edge, but something in Merlin's soulful gaze beckoned me to accept the challenge. There seemed to be a quiet wisdom and a deep well of kindness lurking behind his tough-guy façade. Or was it simply the calm in the eye of the hurricane?

It didn't help that Midnight Merlin was a registered black Egyptian Arabian, a prime specimen of the hottest of breeds with bloodlines emphasizing flamboyance, agility, energy, intelligence, and emotional sensitivity. His was the kind of intelligence that can easily manipulate even the most savvy two-legged handlers, the kind of agility that can leap sideways, rear, and spin 180 degrees without warning, the kind of sensitivity that can turn into a time bomb if bullied into submission. These are the same character-istics that gave him the potential to become a truly impressive mount, but somewhere along the way, the fifteen-year-old stallion had come to associate his phenomenal vitality with anxiety, fear, and unbridled rage. He routinely experienced the very expression of his life force as a threat that plunged him inexorably into the flight-or-fight sequence: preparation for emergency, uncontrollable impulses to flee or fight, disorganized frenzy, and, finally, im-mobility in extreme situations.

Like many stallions who've been mishandled, Merlin couldn't be trusted to engage in the kinds of activities other horses take for granted. What's more, the trainer responsible for him skipped town without warning, leav-ing no forwarding address, no money for board, and no information about Merlin's legal owner, who, according to rumor, lived somewhere in New Mexico. The owners of The Ranch on Tucson's east side took care of the abandoned horse for six months, but Merlin's strength and volatile temper made turnout such an ordeal that he was relegated to an isolated, roomy corral and given plenty of food and clean water but little stimulation or interaction. Any good-natured soul who attempted to put a halter on him and lead him to the arena for a little exercise was subjected to fits of biting, rearing, bucking, and very obvious attempts to wrap the unsuspecting horse lover around a tree.

The first few times I reached out to touch him, Merlin jerked around and menaced me as if I had shocked him with a cattle prod. After trying approaches that had worked on unruly horses in the past and interview-ing some people at The Ranch who had observed Merlin's interactions with his previous trainer, I realized that his anxiety increased to dangerous levels around conventional equestrian activities and tack. With few options left, I proceeded to gain his trust through purely experimental techniques, some of which I developed from studying psychological treatment strategies used on human trauma victims. Like Merlin, these people are plagued by hyper-arousal and panic attacks. Those who don't lapse into freeze mode tend to explode at the drop of a hat because of the intensity of their emotions. The feeling of being out of control in itself becomes so frightening that they experience any sense of their own vitality as threatening. Separating anxiety, anger, and terror from feeling alive is an essential part of the treatment, as is creating a safe environment where the person is coached in regaining control over his own life force without lashing out at others or trying to run away. The key lies in a secure attachment to a therapist who can help the survivor regulate his emotional and physical arousal when renegotiating the kinds of experiences and actions that remind him of the original trauma.

According to Maryanna Eckberg, a California-based psychologist experienced in working with human torture and abuse victims, the therapist's office will not feel safe if a client finds himself constantly reliving past memories, flooding with intense emotion, and leaving the session feeling disorganized, fearful, and vulnerable. Indispensable in the treatment process is the strong, emphatic presence of a therapist who can contain the anger and suffering communicated by the survivor while maintaining clear boundaries. Trauma experts like Eckberg and Peter Levine emphasize the importance of releasing only a small amount of the intense energy, associated images, and emotions of extreme experiences at a time, allowing the nervous system to assimilate the stimulation step by step. This slow-motion approach opens up space for dissociated memory to reassociate, for the coupling of anxiety with life-force energy to come apart, and for thwarted defensive responses to feel a sense of completion.

These observations proved immensely helpful to me in working with Merlin. In reintroducing him to standard equestrian activities and tack, I had to constantly monitor his arousal level. If I didn't back off and stabilize him in time, he would explode in any number of ways, once dragging me to the ground with a sudden pull on the longe line, other times rearing over me with a horrific display of fear turned into rage. If I held my ground and was able to contain his frustration without becoming emotionally and physically dysregulated myself, I would invariably notice a shift toward greater trust in me and confidence in himself. If I exhibited the slightest gesture of panic or lapsed into fear-based anger, Merlin would escalate into a frenzy that would leave both of us feeling spent and vulnerable. The following day, I would see a decrease in the stallion's sense of trust and self-control that I would have to work even harder to regain. Overall, however, our associations were positive, even miraculous at times. The feeling of quiet wisdom and kindness I originally sensed in him would come forward and stay with him for longer periods. I would often leave our sessions in a state of calm heightened awareness.

I had been working with the stallion for two months when Linda Zimmerman of The Ranch finally tracked down his original owner, a New

Mexico–based horse breeder named Shawnee Allen. From her, I learned that Merlin had led an idyllic existence on her ranch for the first decade of his life. Shawnee appreciated his flamboyant beauty for its own sake, and the stallion was rarely ridden or exercised formally. He was simply turned out several times a week to run freely through grassy, tree-lined pastures where he was able to play with some other horses over the fence.

The problems began when Shawnee sold him at age ten to a well-respected local trainer, a deal that involved some cash and some trade in training for one of her colts. Yet when Shawnee stopped by this person's stable a few weeks later to see how the other horse was progressing, she found Merlin standing in the corner of a darkened box stall with his head tied between his legs. The stallion was spoiled and destructive, the trainer insisted; he needed to be taught a lesson. Shawnee decided then and there to buy Merlin back, removing him from what appeared to be a grossly inhumane situation. But the damage was already done. Merlin was fearful, aggressive, and filled with anger and mistrust of anyone who walked around on two legs. Shawnee didn't know how to coax the stallion out of a state that was becoming increasingly dangerous. Eventually, she came across a confident, smooth-talking trainer who seemed to have some rapport with Merlin. With promises to safely rehabilitate the horse and market him throughout the Southwest as a stud, the man loaded Merlin onto his trailer and drove off, only to abandon him in Tucson some time later.

Shawnee felt incredible remorse. More than once she had tried to do right by Merlin, only to have him return worse off than when he'd left. Though she loved the horse, she knew she couldn't handle him. After talking with The Ranch owners, who spoke highly of the inroads I had made with the stallion, Shawnee decided to give it one last try. If I could develop a consistent and constructive rapport with the horse in one year's time, she would turn Merlin's papers over to me. If not, she would trailer him back to New Mexico and let him live out the rest of his life on pasture.

Owning a stallion had never been one of my goals. As a trainer and instructor specializing in equine-facilitated therapy and experiential learning, I needed gentle, well-socialized horses for my program. Still, there was something about Merlin that would not be ignored, some intangible sense of promise that compelled me to accept Shawnee's offer, even though I could see no practical purpose in it. Other than the experience and insight I was gaining rehabilitating such an extreme case, I doubted Merlin would ever become stable enough to work in a therapeutic setting, even if I gelded him.

What I failed to realize, however, was how perfect he was for my program, even in his current state of distress. Up to that point, I had been concentrating on women's issues, working with horses as cofacilitators to boost self-esteem, teach boundaries and leadership skills, and deepen my clients' awareness of core feelings and bodily tension that were inhibiting their ability to reach their full potential. However, shortly after I made that year-long commitment to Merlin, I received several opportunities to work with adolescent boys. One family inquired about doing some intensive equine-facilitated psychotherapy with counselor Dianna Hine and me. The parents were experiencing the stresses inherent in raising three boys, one of whom had just turned twelve and was showing increasing signs of rebellion.

"Jesse" was not at all thrilled about coming to The Ranch. Sitting under the mesquite trees next to the corrals, he looked sullen and resentful as his mother expressed frustration with his angry outbursts, lack of cooperation, and intolerance for his younger brothers. She also voiced her skepticism of conventional talk-oriented counseling in Jesse's case because he had become increasingly nonverbal in his responses, especially to adults. Sure enough, when Dianna asked him some subtle questions to gauge his self-awareness, the young man responded with a series of shrugs and variations on the phrase "I don't know." He was equally reluctant to begin work with the horses.

Acting on impulse, I took Jesse and his father over to Merlin's corral and began to tell his story. The horse had been raised in a loving home, yet he experienced nothing but trouble when he was exposed to the pressures of the outside world. As a stallion, it was natural for him to challenge authority. Male horses in particular are prone to rearing, kicking, and biting as they prepare to battle for the privilege of running with a band of mares. In the wild, however, an adolescent quickly discovers that he must learn to control his tremendous energy, or he will be ostracized. An experienced alpha mare will never let a new stallion claim his rightful position if he acts like a bully and a tyrant all the time.

The dynamics of energy control are much more precarious in the civilized world, where stallions must learn to interact with human beings as well as other horses. Many studs, like Merlin, never reach their full potential because they're taught to despise and fear their own vitality, forced to suppress it through increasingly rigid outside rules and restraints. I told Jesse that Merlin had experienced much heartache and strife from some of the adults in his life and had developed a lot of violent coping strategies in the process. I also emphasized, however, that I didn't think anyone ever intended to abuse him. The sheer power of unbridled male energy is frightening to people. Some recoil and allow themselves to become victimized by it. Others try to shame it into submission. Still others turn that fear into anger, sometimes using inappropriate or extreme measures to regain control. As an apprentice trainer, I told Jesse, I was advised on the proper way to beat a stallion with the lead rope when he got a little rambunctious. All of these options, I stressed, teach male horses and their human counterparts to associate the expression of their life force with pain, frustration, and violence, rather than helping them learn how to channel that energy in more constructive ways.

Merlin's first trainer no doubt found that the techniques she used to start most colts weren't producing the same results for this highly charged horse. With his extreme sensitivity, endless energy, and indomitable spirit, Merlin tended to up the ante rather than submit to outside authority. The horse and his trainer probably engaged in a battle of wills that produced violence from both sides, weaving a tangled mass of traumas, resentments, and destructive habits into the stallion's impressionable nervous system. The process of releasing old memories and coping strategies while laying new, more effective behavior patterns was a fragile, time-consuming process for a seasoned adult like Merlin. Similarly, many men with chronic anger were never taught the proper way to channel and control their own innate power, and as such they have no means to help their sons deal with the overwhelming feelings and effects of approaching manhood.

In the months I had worked with Merlin, I realized that the energy unique to males is a neutral yet undeniably intense force that can easily overwhelm the emotions. It can surge beyond control with very little warning and will look for any excuse to express itself. As the creative drive of the species, it brings new life into the world, new works of art, new levels of physical and mental mastery in sports and business. But it can just as easily release itself in destruction.

Merlin taught me that the energy rush comes first and the unbridled expression of it is too often mistaken for anger or fear by the one experiencing this surge, as well as by any observers in the vicinity of such an outburst. If negative emotions become routinely associated with this innate power, there's very little chance that its owner will learn how to release it in slower, more controlled and constructive ways. The prevalence of male violence in our society, historically and in the present, is directly related to attempts to suppress what is essentially a natural gift. Negative associations and restraints do little to help people develop this raw and explosive power into a mature manifestation of life force.

Jesse quickly understood that what he and his family were increasingly interpreting as angry outbursts were the same volcanic eruptions of male energy that made Merlin such an awesome and fearful sight. These surges are directly related to natural hormonal changes in the body. Mares and geldings (male horses who have been castrated) are much less likely to experience sudden rushes of uncontrolled energy and tend not to be as flamboyant as stallions. Through his rehabilitation and training, Merlin was learning to appreciate his own vitality and channel it into physical movements of uncommon grace and agility. Jesse could learn to do the same.

We spent the afternoon doing simple exercises with a much more gentle horse that allowed Jesse to learn how to modulate his own arousal level, control his fear of new activities, and release his frustration before it joined forces with his burgeoning energy and turned into rage. The following week, Jesse's mother had tears in her eyes when she reported how deeply the experience had affected the entire family. She had seen her son in a new light, as a vital young man fully capable of controlling himself. An unspoken mutual innovation arose in their interaction: Jesse's parents refrained from nagging him about his chores, and Jesse suddenly seemed motivated to do them without being asked. He even made an effort to take care of his youngest brother when he noticed his mother was dealing with a particularly stressful day.

As for Merlin, he became a valuable asset to the Eponaquest program, teaching young men as well as their parents, teachers, therapists, and, in some cases, parole officers about the dynamics of masculine energy and the special challenges we all face in learning how to better manage this colossal force — even as he and I continued to work through multiple layers of trauma and self-control.

An Ambitious Invitation

In revisiting Merlin's story, I feel it's important to stress that I learned more from him than he learned from me. Through our interactions, I reached new levels of emotional agility, nonverbal sensitivity, self-awareness, and confidence in the face of adversity, personal qualities that subsequently allowed me to work more effectively with traumatized people. I also exercised the ability to regulate my nervous system in the midst of some very scary situations.

It's fascinating to revisit Merlin's story from a polyvagal perspective. The stallion had no connection with horses or humans to draw upon when I met him in 1999. Dangerous and unpredictable, he lived in an isolated corral, unable to activate his ventral vagus through interactions with calmer, more secure horses. He was so intimidating to humans that no connection was possible there either. Merlin habitually upped the ante so defiantly that even the seasoned clinician who promised to cure him with natural horsemanship techniques eventually got spooked and skipped town.

I had been studying off and on with an experienced stallion trainer, Shelley Rosenberg. I asked her to stop by one day to evaluate a few of Merlin's outlandish antics. Shaking her head incredulously, she looked at me and said, "Run. Don't just walk away from this one. Run!"

Unwilling to accept her initial assessment so easily, I invited her to help me explore innovative ideas for rehabilitating this supremely wounded horse, using principles I had learned from working with trauma specialists in my equine-facilitated therapy practice. Shelley silently considered my proposal for a moment, then began to nod, tentatively, as I outlined some of my ideas. She clearly had the experience and curiosity to take on this risky experiment. Working at a stallion station, where she was responsible for mating as well as sperm collection, Shelley had handled situations daily that would have caused me to keel over in a dead faint. She agreed to see what could be done, as long as we moved slowly and didn't take unnecessary chances.

Together, we unknowingly took advantage of polyvagal principles, transforming Merlin's aggression in ways that words could never touch. I learned, first of all, that I could borrow Shelley's confidence. Her ability to stay calm and think clearly in the face of extreme equine aggression was actually contagious, to Merlin *and* me. More specifically, Shelley could co-regulate us both as I was learning how to approximate the ways her nervous system would respond to Merlin. And I really had to be in her presence to learn this. I had to *feel* what it was like to do something different in response to Merlin's aggression.

In the midst of the stallion's rising panic, I could so easily catch his over-whelming tendency to go into fight-or-flight mode. Yet when I was ready to jump the fence and run screaming into the desert, Shelley could remain aware, empowered, and centered. She could do something I can only de-scribe as counterinstinctual: she could temper the fight-or-flight response, not just in her body, but in Merlin's body and in mine, if I was standing nearby. In this way, she could often turn a volatile situation around before Merlin exploded in fits of rage. At that time, like many accomplished horse trainers, Shelley wasn't totally conscious of what she was doing. She didn't know how to explain it to me. I just had to be around her. I had to study with her. I had to absorb it through osmosis. It wasn't about a method, and it certainly wasn't about anything she said at those moments. It was a high level of nonverbal communication in action. It was as if in over forty years of experience with horses, her nervous system had been tuned to respond to fearful, aggressive, or confused horses in increasingly productive ways.

Over time, I also gained some of the skills demonstrated by Shelley, and I began to use them with people as well. As an adult and as a writer, I was able to pay attention to the process of developing these techniques. As a musician, I was very sensitive to the nonverbal elements of what was being expressed and communicated. And, finally, I believe that as a music critic, I was experienced in finding ways to somehow describe in words what was essentially beyond words. Still, until Dr. Rebecca Bailey introduced me to the polyvagal theory almost twenty years after I met Merlin, I did not know how to explain our success with the stallion in a single sentence. Dr. Steven Porges gave me the vocabulary I needed to say this: "Shelley and I gained Merlin's trust and cooperation by maintaining connection with him when he was afraid or angry, using our nervous systems to coregulate his nervous system."

Over time, I discovered how to transfer those practices to working with humans who were afraid or aggressive. These days, I offer a sequence of progressive skills during horse-facilitated workshops and have even learned how to teach some of these tools in my online courses.

The latest research suggests that cognitive therapy is sorely deficient in resolving many of the issues related to posttraumatic stress disorder because emergency responses bypass the neocortex, activating the amygdala and the limbic system, areas of the brain people share with other mammals. This explains why some of the latest techniques used on human survivors of extreme experiences work equally well with horses. In his bestseller *Emotional Intelligence*, Daniel Goleman discusses how "emotions have a mind of their own, one which can hold views quite independently of our rational mind." The arousal of the amygdala can spur a person to action before the neocortex even registers what's happening. As a repository for emotional memories that may never become fully conscious, the amygdala continues to influence behavior, hijacking the mind when a relatively benign situation stirs up emotions similar to those experienced in the original crisis. The amygdala's "method of comparison is associative," Goleman writes; "when one key element of a present situation is similar to the past, it can call it a 'match' — which is why this circuit is sloppy: it acts before there is full confirmation. It frantically commands that we react to the present in ways that were imprinted long ago, with thoughts, emotions, reactions learned in response to events perhaps only dimly similar, but close enough to alarm the amygdala."

Equine-facilitated therapy takes the trauma survivor through a series of activities that explore and modify the client's reactions to emotions like anxiety, fear, and anger. Rather than fall into the flight, fight, or freeze mode at the slightest sign of uncertainty, a victim of childhood abuse, like Joy, learns to recognize her authentic feelings, use them as information, and experience positive, self-esteem-raising outcomes. The process works by creating alternate response patterns through new experiences. Activities are designed to keep the client's arousal at a more manageable level while also providing the counselor with an opportunity to intervene in the midst of intensifying emotional reactions.

Remember, Joy wasn't able to talk herself out of old coping strategies. Though she gained some awareness, years of traditional psychotherapy did not alter her reactions to strong emotion or even bring many of these feelings into conscious awareness. She had no idea she was afraid of the tall, dark sex offender in Chicago, though the suppressed emotion still plunged her into a disempowered, dissociative state in which he could more easily manipulate her. Joy actually had to witness the effect her unconscious fear produced in Noche to believe it existed. While she was experiencing this emotion, I coached her in techniques for recognizing the message behind the feeling, breathing into the tension it created in her body, and changing a thought or goal in response. As she practiced this over and over again, with Noche acting as her emotional barometer, Joy was able to create a more effective response pattern that offered her amygdala a different series of memories to associate with fear, memories in which she stayed present and began to breathe into the tension rather than recoil from it and dissociate. Similarly, Merlin, whose amygdala dictated that he become violent in response to uncertainty, learned to lower his head, round his back, and breathe in response to situations that previously threw him into unbridled aggression.

Logic, punishment, and praise, elements commonly used to change behavior, are ineffective in the early stages of trauma therapy because wounded people and animals have come to associate almost any increase in energy, including a sense of their own vitality, with anxiety, fear, or anger. Both Joy and Merlin would sometimes panic when they felt particularly good, a re-action that puzzled me at first. Joy also admitted that she found it difficult to experience pleasure (sexual or otherwise) unless it was associated with danger. This not only resulted in an attraction to unstable men, it also man-ifested as a tendency to shut down or flee when she felt positive emotions, regardless of the relative safety of the setting. Her emotional brain associated feelings of happiness, joy, and sensual excitement with grave consequences. For these reasons, Joy could suddenly become fearful or dissociative even if she was having a good day. Separating anxiety from the feeling of being alive was an essential part of the learning. As she progressed to riding Noche, for instance, I made sure Joy was able to maintain a consistent level of calm at a walk before she asked for the trot, and I encouraged her to breathe deeply, with even in breaths and out breaths, through any expression of strong emo-tion, whether it involved fear, anxiety, joy, pride, or ecstasy. Noche made my job easier. His ability to balance her and keep moving even as he responded to her mercurial moods kept Joy from falling into freeze mode. I could also tell the split second she would start to lose focus, because Noche's trajectory around the arena would become more erratic. The horse's talent for sensing subtle changes in Joy's physical and emotional states, as well as his ability to literally carry her through instances of fear and dissociation, were invaluable in helping the woman renegotiate a host of old memories and responses.

The therapist's goal in working with trauma survivors is to teach her clients to modulate their own emotional and physical arousal levels while she consciously contains the horror and suffering communicated by them, making sure they release only a small amount of the intense energy, associ-ated images, and emotions of extreme experiences at a time. In this effort, the professional has to be able to regulate her own nervous system without lapsing into incongruity. Many victims of abuse, human and horse, have learned to rely on nonverbal cues to assess the intentions of others, and they're extremely sensitive to incongruent emotions in anyone proposing to help them. Whenever I became fearful of Merlin, for instance, he would automatically escalate into a frenzy, even if I appeared calm to people watch-ing outside the arena. Noche could tell when Joy was afraid, no matter how skillful she was at hiding it from herself. Charles, at the group home, knew when the facilitators were nervous, anxious, or angry, and he would become violent if they tried to conceal their authentic emotions. Training in emotional intelligence, nervous system regulation, and nonverbal communication is equally essential for equestrians and for therapists who propose to work with anyone who has experienced trauma.

Horse Training for Therapists

Personal skills useful in treating traumatized people can't be absorbed by reading a book, listening to a lecture, taking a test, or engaging in role-playing exercises. Emotional congruency and calmness in the face of adversity are qualities developed through experience. Therapists, health care workers, and law enforcement officers usually get this experience by interacting with subjects who are actually panicking — and hopefully they get it under the direction of senior staff members experienced with trauma. The system is far from fail-safe, however. Sometimes young professionals get injured or otherwise emotionally traumatized themselves in the process, creating an amygdala-based memory in their own brains that may move them to overreact to less intense situations in the future. To save face in the presence of their peers, they may continue to put up a front of confidence and authority while internally recoiling in horror, creating an incongruent response that will unnerve a person in a heightened state of nonverbal awareness. I've treated a number of survivors of extreme experiences who were further traumatized by the very people who were called to help them, people who unconsciously escalated the situation.

To address these issues, Kathleen Barry Ingram and I designed a series of equine-facilitated workshops in the early 2000s especially for professionals who deal with trauma. In 2013, Dr. Rebecca Bailey and I created a modality called Connection Focused Therapy (CFT) with a more formalized sequence of activities we could use with clients and also teach to therapists, educators, first responders, and family members who support survivors of extreme experiences. The CFT model became even more effective when we added polyvagal-informed principles in 2018.

After teaching self-regulation and coregulation skills with gentle horses, we do a bit of nervous system "weight training" with progressively more challenging horses. Interacting with a flighty, aggressive, or dissociative horse brings personal issues to light in a supportive environment where health care workers can discuss their fears, frustrations, and insecurities, learn to manage their own conflicting emotions, and actually practice more effective ways of dealing with frightened, aggressive, or dissociative people. Through this work, professionals increase their sensitivity to nonverbal awareness and develop an appreciation for atypical forms of intelligence. They explore the connections among physical, mental, and emotional states. They increase awareness of personal beliefs and areas of bodily tension that inhibit optimal relations with patients, clients, and residents. They see the effects of their own incongruent emotions and learn strategies for calming panicking clients. As they develop the poise and self-control needed to deal with a sensitive thousand-pound being, their ability to monitor and modulate the arousal levels of their human clients becomes second nature.

Though I had witnessed the effects of incongruent emotional states in facilitators at the group home where Charles lived, I didn't truly understand the importance of this kind of training for counselors, nurses, orderlies, and even law enforcement personnel until I encountered a young woman who had been inadvertently brutalized by a succession of all these types of people during a crisis situation. Shortly after her release from a drug rehab center, "Liz" came to work with the horses. As a child, she had competed in local hunter-jumper shows, and her mother thought that an equine experiential learning program might draw her out of a debilitating depression. Though Liz had spent time in a hospital psychiatric ward and had completed an extended treatment program for crystal meth addiction, the twenty-year-old former college student still had difficulty socializing with others. She was distrustful and uncommunicative with the counselors her family tried to send her to. She had no appetite for food or life. At eighty-five pounds, she was wasting away, and her parents were legitimately concerned.

During her first visit to The Ranch, Liz looked unusually frail and vulnerable as she stepped out of the car and ambled over to the horses. After asking her a few questions, I could see she either couldn't or didn't want to talk, and she seemed embarrassed by the fuss everyone was making over her. When I suggested she might be able to get her strength back by riding Noche, however, her eyes lit up. For the first fifteen minutes, I followed the usual therapeutic routine for people dealing with an extended illness or a physical disability: taking her through a series of breathing, stretching, and balancing exercises on the horse, drawing her attention to areas of tension and discomfort in her own body, teaching her how to get messages from these sensations, and suggesting ways of moving beyond these blocks. I was amazed at how quickly she came to life. By the end of that first session, Liz was cantering Noche bareback around the arena with a confidence I rarely see in my more advanced students.

Over the next two months, Liz proved to be a skillful, fearless rider who blossomed in the presence of the horses. Though she remained reticent about sharing her experiences with me, she quickly grasped the need for emotional congruency in relating to the animals and was therefore all the more motivated to learn techniques for accessing her feelings, determining the messages behind them, and changing a thought or habit in response to them. As long as I kept the sessions focused on the horses, she was willing to address personal issues as they related to her ability to ride and train. For instance, when she had trouble longeing Rasa, Liz talked briefly about her difficulty being assertive with friends and family members. When young Comet refused to pick up her hooves to have them cleaned, we discussed the difference between bullying the filly into it and breaking the task down into smaller steps that she could understand, making her comfortable with the process rather than pushing her toward the ultimate goal. Liz admitted that she had often felt forced into accomplishing certain tasks before she was ready, though she refused to elaborate. Much more quickly than I expected, however, the nonverbal dimension of our sessions with the horses helped Liz regain the focus, will, self-esteem, and physical strength she had lost to her addiction.

Three months into her work at The Ranch, I decided to let Liz help me rehabilitate a little bay mare who was unable to control her fear of new situations. At the slightest provocation, "Calliope" would spin around, buck, and take off at a full run, sometimes leaving her owner in the dust. Under saddle, the mare would automatically adopt the head-high, hollow-backed posture associated with flight or fight. Calliope's retraining involved teaching her to lower her head and round her back, a difficult task to accomplish in a horse so jittery and flighty she made a normally confident rider like Liz nervous.

"The key with Calliope," I stressed, "is to make sure both the horse and the rider feel secure before moving on to the next step." Liz watched as I refrained from getting on the mare until she stood calmly, a state I encouraged in part by breathing in certain highly productive ways while visualizing the desired outcome.

With Merlin, I had learned that engaging an extended, relaxing sigh could instantly calm him. His frantic disconnected expression would seem to melt, and he would look at me with soft eyes, sometimes walking toward me with relaxed, inviting body language. I've since learned that a long out breath activates the ventral vagus, causing a shift from sympathetic escalation (flight or fight) into that part of the mammalian nervous system that communicates feelings of safety through connection.

At the time Liz and I were working with Calliope, I only knew that this long out breath worked like a charm. I didn't know why. I also learned from other horses that shifting into long, even in breaths and out breaths put me into a paradoxical state of calm yet heightened awareness that horses responded to with trust and attentiveness. It was especially helpful in teaching them something new. In working with Dr. Ann Baldwin on some studies related to horse-human interactions in 2017, I found out this breathing technique jump-starts *coherence*. Ann explained that the long, even in breaths and out breaths bring the parasympathetic (resting) and sympathetic (active) nervous systems into balance, creating a state of relaxed alertness that regulates your nervous system, helping you think and respond creatively in situations that might otherwise cause stress. Through several research projects, Ann and I confirmed that horses are attracted to people who shift into this state. At a distance of twenty feet or more, these sensitive animals can tell when a human *starts* to become coherent. At that moment, a horse milling around a pasture will often lift his head, look directly at the person, and walk right over to him or her.

With Liz and Calliope, I was unable to describe why this form of breathing worked because I didn't have the vocabulary to do so. But I could reliably demonstrate its effects. Upon mounting, I sat on Calliope's back and began massaging those parts of her neck where she tended to lock up, subsequently doing some TTouches to help release tension patterns and cellular memory in the area until she dropped her head and let out a huge sigh. Then I cued her to walk. The mare threw her head up once more and began to fidget. I resisted the urge to hold my breath, engaged the long sigh, then began to breathe evenly in a more coherent rhythm, creating a sense of support and acceptance that was transferred to the mare at a sociosensual level. Five minutes later, Calliope was beginning to lower her head as she ambled around the arena.

"Have you ever wandered into a room containing an agitated person and suddenly felt agitated yourself?" I asked Liz from the saddle. My student nodded. "That's an aspect of what's called sociosensual awareness, the ability of someone else's moods to affect you at a physical as well as an emotional level and vice versa. Often we aren't conscious of how someone else's breathing, blood pressure, and muscular tension are affecting us. This person doesn't actually have to touch us or even speak to us to transfer the general tone of the feeling. We suddenly feel agitated and start reacting to the emotion without realizing it belongs to the man standing three feet away. We take this anxiety with us when we leave the room, maybe even dig up some unresolved family issue associated with that emotion. By the time we get home, we're ready to infect others with it.

"Horses have a high level of sociosensual awareness for good reason. If one mare suddenly becomes alarmed, that fear sweeps through the rest of the herd, causing everyone to run before most have time to see what the trouble is. Yet if someone can infect you with his negative mood, you can infect him with a positive mood. You just have to be aware enough to understand what's happening to both of you at a nonverbal level. Take Calliope. She initially made me nervous in this simple riding exercise because she was nervous. But rather than give in to the feeling, I recognized it, determined that it was her issue, not mine, and proceeded to turn the dynamic around by adopting the postures and breathing associated with a calm yet still aware, centered state, encouraging her to do the same. As you can see, it didn't take her long to respond. What do you think would have happened if I had been unconsciously affected by her fear while adopting a strict, uncompromising attitude? What if I had tightened my shoulders and began taking short, quick breaths without even noticing I was tensing up?"

"She probably would have run off with you," Liz replied.

"What if I had then jerked the reins to make her stop, or even fallen off, then slapped her and shouted at her for being an idiot?" I asked.

"She would finally have a reason to be afraid of you."

"Well, it would still be her fault, wouldn't it? In that state, she's out of control, and she's endangering the rider's life."

"Yeah, but you're supposed to calm her down, not the other way around," Liz said in an unusually passionate tone of voice. "You're being paid because you're supposed to know how to help her."

"Exactly." I proceeded to direct the mare through a series of transitions from walking to stopping and stopping to walking, with episodes of TTouches and massage in between. When Calliope was relaxed enough to move into a walk without tossing her head, we worked on a similar series of transitions into the trot.

A week later, Liz stepped into the saddle and learned how to modulate her own arousal level to make Calliope feel comfortable. She also began to pick up on the mare's nervousness at a sociosensual level and differentiate it from her own feelings. This allowed Liz to engage various breathing signals and, if necessary, downshift into a walk the moment before Calliope would normally try to buck or run off, thus saving both horse and rider from possible danger. In the process of creating a safe, responsive, low-stress rehabilitation environment for the mare, my student was moved to tears. At the end of her ride, she finally shared the unfortunate series of events that had led her to lose trust in the very people who were called in to help her when she was escalating into a state of blind panic.

As a freshman at a West Coast university, Liz told me, she was caught between her desire to study art and her father's insistence that she pursue a more practical field, like accounting or computer science. The compromise involved taking a few art classes, ostensibly to fulfill her humanities requirements, while enrolling in the college of business to please her parents. While time seemed to fly when she worked on projects for her painting and sculpture classes, she couldn't seem to concentrate on her other homework. Liz barely passed her business courses that first semester, and her father threatened to pull her out of college if she didn't show significant improvement.

During her second semester, the young woman became so discouraged and depressed that she gained ten pounds and could barely stand to get out of bed in the morning. Finally, her roommate suggested she try some crystal meth, an illegal form of methamphetamine that would supposedly give her the energy to study, boosting her powers of concentration, elevating her mood, and helping her lose weight in the process. During those first few weeks, her grades improved. She lost twenty pounds and found she could study for hours, for days even, without feeling tired or hungry. The downside, however, was the dreaded crash that occurred when the drug wore off, a low feeling more intense and longer lasting than those produced by both speed and cocaine. Liz suffered from insomnia, restlessness, and severe cravings for the drug, motivating her to take even more of it. A few nights after midterm exams, she experienced a psychotic break, leading to a series of nightmarish encounters with a health care system that traumatized her as much as or more than the drug itself.

"I had no idea how nasty crystal meth could be," she says. "I just thought it was a form of speed, and I felt great at first. I felt like I could do anything. After a while, though, you start hallucinating, not directly because of the drug, but because it interrupts normal REM sleep patterns. You can't process experiences through dreams, so your mind starts to lose touch with reality while you're awake, and your responses to little things become much bigger than normal.

"One night, I had a fight with my roommate. I felt this overwhelming animosity coming from her, and I began to imagine she was part of a conspiracy of people who were trying to hurt me. The resident assistant came in to tell us to quiet down, and I got even more paranoid. I mean I actually started throwing books and glasses and screaming bloody murder. Well, pretty soon, the police were called in, and they confirmed my worst fears. They tackled me, handcuffed me, and dragged me out of the dorm. I really believed they were going to shoot me and dump my body in the woods somewhere."

Liz was taken to a local hospital. "Everyone there was shouting at me, shaking me, threatening to tie me up," she remembers. "I can't imagine why they thought this was supposed to calm me down. As I look back on the entire experience, there were numerous moments when a few supportive words or gestures from a calm person could have turned the entire situation around. If someone had been able to treat me like we've been treating Calliope, it would have made all the difference." Every person Liz came in contact with, from the police to the doctors to the orderlies at the hospital, succeeded in escalating the situation. "I understand now that they were probably scared and confused themselves," she says, "but all they did was convince me that I needed to fight for my life."

When Liz awoke from the sedative they finally injected her with, she was tied to a bed in a stark, foreboding hospital room. Again, she panicked, and again an intimidating orderly arrived, threatening her with continued sedation and restraint if she didn't calm down. Staff members subsequently grilled her about her drug use, acting alternately cold and disgusted with what she revealed. By the time she was assigned to a resident psychiatrist, Liz felt completely demoralized. Her misguided attempts to succeed in school had landed her in a mental ward where she was treated like a psychotic criminal. After surviving a notoriously difficult withdrawal from crystal meth, Liz managed to humor her therapists just long enough to gain her freedom. Back in the relative safety of her parents' house, she wanted nothing to do with the outside world.

Liz's story helped me understand the perils of emotional arrested development, a state of culturally induced insensitivity shared by everyone who tried to help Liz. The Western mind is trained to expect unconditional obe-dience from the body and the emotions, yet this perspective keeps people from learning to process feeling in its subtle, more manageable forms. Once the pressure of anger reaches the critical mass of rage, for instance, the emo-tional brain hijacks the neocortex, which is then left to deal with the dam-age — to oneself, one's family, or one's property — after the storm blows over. Imagining that people can control strong emotion by simply willing it into submission is as foolish as trying to control an unruly horse. In a crisis, a mount who hasn't learned how to trust and communicate with her rider suddenly leaps to the side and takes off, leaving the poor man in the dust to consider just what little power he has. You'd think that after a few close calls with errant emotion, most people would look for another approach, one that involved working *with* nature rather than against it. Many, however, choose the seemingly more convenient option of medicating their emotions into submission. Despite widespread press coverage of the problems associated with addiction, people with no training in managing their emotions, or even listening to them in the first place, find it as difficult to "just say no" to drugs as they do to controlling their emotions to begin with, especially men and women dealing with unresolved trauma and abuse. If someone feels anxious or troubled, it's easier to reach for a scotch or Valium than suddenly muster up the level of self-awareness it takes to get to the root of the problem. If this person is tired, she may drink an entire pot of coffee. If she's really depressed and unable to function, she might try a more powerful stimulant.

Self-medication seemed like a viable option to Liz, who grew up in an alcoholic family where no one discussed their feelings or, heaven forbid, ad-mitted they might need help managing them. Liz's father, a retired military man, ruled the family with an iron fist and expected his daughter to do what he said. This included herding the girl toward a career she had no interest in, rather than helping her find a practical application for her artistic lean-ings. Taught to suppress her true feelings and follow the advice of all those adults in life who "knew what was best for her," Liz had no idea how to gain information from her emotions, regulate her nervous system, assert her own will, and make her own decisions. When her entire body revolted against studying business by plunging her into a state of intense depression, she tried to force herself into complying with her father's wishes through chemical means, a choice that ultimately put her sanity and her life on the line.

Collaborating with Emotion

Around the time I was working with Liz, I came across an audiobook called *Becoming an Empath*. In her succinct, insightful definitions of emotions as information-carrying signals, author Karla McLaren describes depression as "the stop sign of the soul." She emphasizes that this debilitating yet "ingenious stagnation" follows a period in which a person refuses to listen to the messages behind sadness, fear, anger, or grief. "In a world where we're taught to ignore our emotions, dreams, and true passions, where we enter blindly into the wrong relationships and the wrong jobs, depression is our emergency break," McLaren writes. Depression takes over when "what we were doing and where we were going didn't match up with our inner desires."

Mind over matter simply doesn't work if the emotions refuse to cooperate. As Candace Pert has observed, emotions are what link the mind and the body, bringing sensual information, irrational yet legitimate worries, and authentic desires to consciousness. When these neural pathways are strengthened, a mindful person can use focus and intent to influence physical functions like blood pressure and even immune response, but only if suppressed emotions aren't creating neurological static and hijacking the frontal cortex. It's simply not enough for a woman to think happy thoughts about a new relationship when the amygdala keeps comparing minor disagreements with her boyfriend to instances of physical abuse she experienced in her first marriage. She needs to develop new coping strategies for dealing with fear and anger, in part by being honest with the man in her life and asking for his cooperation, while getting the professional help she needs to work through the unresolved trauma.

In their purest forms, fear, anger, sadness, and passion are instructive signals of the psyche, telling the individual when to press forward, back off, trust a business prospect, forgive a friend, or reconsider an entire relationship. Suppressed emotions don't go away; they putrefy into toxic thoughts and habits, eventually evolving into mutant forms that relieve the pressure in less conscious ways, undermining health, happiness, and usually a few innocent bystanders. According to McLaren, anger, which sometimes intensifies into rage and fury, can also mask itself as boredom. Someone afraid to stand up for her rights, set proper boundaries, and command the respect she deserves in her family will often cope with the resulting anger through apathy. In this way, she can be sullen and sarcastic without raising her voice, but the long-term emotional toll on significant others, especially children, can be almost as damaging as violent rage — and there are never any visible bruises that might alert teachers, doctors, and extended family members that the child is suffering from her mother's covert expression of unresolved anger.

Therapists and researchers like McLaren and *Emotional Intelligence* author Goleman are challenging centuries of overemphasis on rationality in our culture. "The connections between the amygdala (and related limbic structures) and the neocortex are the hub of the battles or cooperative treaties struck between head and heart, thought and feeling," Goleman writes. "This circuitry explains why emotion is so crucial to effective thought, both in making wise decisions and in simply allowing us to think clearly."

While strong emotion can hijack the neocortex, the absence of emotion can also hinder higher thought. Dr. Antonio Damasio, a neurologist who heads the Brain and Research Institute at the University of Southern California, has studied patients with damage to the prefrontal cortex–amygdala circuit. Though these people show no deterioration in IQ or cognitive ability, Goleman explains,

> they make disastrous choices in business and their personal lives and can even obsess endlessly over a decision so simple as when to make an appointment. Dr. Damasio argues that their decisions are so bad because they have lost access to their emotional learning.... Evidence like this leads Dr. Damasio to the counterintuitive position that feelings are typically indispensable for rational decisions; they point us in the proper direction, where dry logic can then be of best use.... Ordinarily the complementarity of limbic system and neocortex, amygdala and prefrontal lobes, means each is a full partner in mental life. When these partners interact well, emotional intelligence rises — as does intellectual ability. This turns the old understanding of the tension between reason and feeling on its head: It is not that we want to do away with emotion and put reason in its place, as Erasmus had it, but instead find the intelligent balance of the two. The old paradigm held an ideal of reason freed of the pull of emotion. The new paradigm urges us to harmonize head and heart. To do that well in our lives means we must first understand more exactly what it means to use emotion intelligently.

Toward this end, Goleman cites a definition of emotional intelligence developed by Yale psychologist Peter Salovey that divides the basic abilities involved into five domains. If there's a primary area in which horses excel as therapists and educators, it's in exercising and increasing awareness of emotional intelligence on all these levels.

1. Knowing One's Emotions

Goleman describes this as the "keystone of emotional intelligence." He stresses that an "inability to notice our true feelings leaves us at their mercy. People with greater certainty about their feelings are better pilots of their lives." In my work with trauma survivors, business executives, troubled teens, parents, and even experienced counselors, this has proved to be the greatest hurdle to leading a well-balanced professional and personal life. The postconquest mentality of suppressing authentic emotion in favor of modeling socially promoted thought and behavior actually trains emotional self-awareness right out of people. Those who manage to retain this ability in the midst of cultural conditioning are ahead of the game, but researchers like Salovey, Goleman, McLaren, and Harvard Graduate School of Education psychologist Howard Gardner are working to change the system. Gardner, in fact, has developed school programs designed to enhance emotional intelligence and expand education's definition of intelligence in general. "The time has come," he told Goleman, "to broaden our notion of the spectrum of talents. The single most important contribution education can make to a child's development is to help him toward a field where his talents best suit him, where he will be satisfied and competent. We've completely lost sight of that." As Liz illustrated, the consequences of this gross oversight can be grave. Depression, drug addiction, and psychiatric trauma all resulted from the fact that she received no support from her family in accessing her feelings and developing her talents. For this reason, national drug prevention programs must address the issue of emotional intelligence, not only in schools, but in society at large. Teens can't "just say no" to marijuana, ecstasy, crystal meth, and the ever-increasing popularity of prescription drugs if they're trying to self-medicate emotions parents and teachers aren't willing to acknowledge, let alone help their children process.

2. Managing Emotions

It's impossible for a person of any age to handle feelings appropriately if he doesn't know what he's feeling to begin with. Equine-facilitated therapy and experiential learning tools and activities work on both of these issues simultaneously. Joy's story provides a dramatic illustration of how horses respond to and draw out hidden emotions that even highly experienced human counselors aren't aware of. These animals make split-second adjustments to both positive and negative changes in the handler's behavior and state of arousal, offering people timely rewards or consequences not only for their actions but for their ability to access their true feelings and adjust to them. People are used to judging others as being either good or bad on the basis of a few isolated experiences, their own prejudices and projections, and the opinions of those close to them. Once this impression is formed, the human mind becomes increasingly blind to what's happening in the present. This accounts for a wife with two black eyes and a broken rib insisting her husband really does love her as she continues to weather his angry outbursts or a drug addict in her early twenties who ignores evidence of her own sensitivity and intelligence to uphold her parents' mythology that she's the black sheep of the family. When such a person changes her behavior for the better, she often receives resistance from her spouse, parents, and friends, who find it uncomfortable to alter their static beliefs about her and move beyond the well-worn ways they have related to her for years. When this same woman makes positive changes in the presence of a horse, however, the animal immediately responds positively — while continuing to call her on episodes of dissociation, the inappropriate expression of anger, and incongruent emotions, among a variety of other complex emotional coping strategies. In this way, equine-facilitated practices employ a form of biofeedback for practicing self-awareness, emotional management, and relationship skills that human role-playing exercises and discussion groups can't begin to access.

3. Motivating Oneself

"Marshaling emotions in the service of a goal is essential for paying attention, for self-motivation and mastery, and for creativity," Goleman observes. "Emotional self-control — delaying gratification and stifling impulsiveness — underlies accomplishment of every sort." When Joy learned to longe Rasa through will and focus, she was exercising these abilities to move a thousand-pound creature at a distance. She had to overcome feelings of fear and inadequacy. She had to muster a sense of assertiveness to gain the mare's respect and cooperation. She had to modulate the energy she was projecting to keep Rasa at a trot and tone it down when her enthusiasm inadvertently sent the mare into a canter. In the saddle, Joy realized how difficult it was to process all the sensual information she was receiving while focusing on the task at hand, even to perform a simple figure eight at the trot. Keeping Noche at a consistent speed required a sophisticated level of sociosensual awareness, poise, and self-control. If Noche sped up, she needed to squeeze the reins and adjust her seat just enough to slow him down without cueing him to stop. Whenever he tried to downshift to a walk, she would need to sense his intentions and give him a little kick to keep him going, without inadvertently encouraging him to canter. If this wasn't enough, she also had to keep her mind on where she was going. The second she lost her focus on the ultimate goal, Noche would take over and begin to trot toward the gate. In mastering this complex array of skills, Joy dealt with feelings of frustration, confusion, fear, and even anger as she discovered it really was possible to keep her mind responsive to minute changes in Noche's body and her own, while visualizing the desired outcome and exercising her will to move Noche toward that goal with each succeeding step.

4. Recognizing Emotions in Others

Goleman calls empathy "the fundamental 'people skill.'" Yet the ability to determine another person's feelings and intentions is often skewed by an overreliance on language. Wolverton, the owner of the breeding farm who was a master at the bait and switch tactics of logical idealism, could mesmerize his employees with artful discussions of his equestrian expertise and his benevolent intentions while undermining people nonverbally. When I focused on his unspoken emotional tone and body language, I was able to sidestep his efforts to take out frustrations and insecurities on me, relying on nonverbal sensitivity I had developed from working with horses.

While I've since learned how to teach this skill to others, I've also employed the horses in helping counselors evaluate clients who aren't expressive enough to even hint at what their issues might be. "Janice," a high school senior whose parents were worried about her lack of communication and motivation, sent her to "Clarissa," a therapist who had significant trouble drawing the young girl out of her shell. When Clarissa brought Janice to The Ranch, however, we were both amazed to find that the young lady possessed a particularly graceful and responsive leadership style as she longed Noche with more skill than my most experienced riding students. The problem was not a lack of assertiveness or motivation per se; it was instead related to her position as the youngest child in her family. Janice was used to letting other people function for her. All she had to do was wait around long enough, and her mother, father, or siblings would become impatient and take the lead. Janice's family was not consciously aware of this dynamic, and it might have taken the counselor months to figure out what the problem was — even if Janice had been able to discuss her feelings. The turning point came when Clarissa watched how Janice responded to a number of different activities in which the horses mirrored her unconscious emotional states and as yet undeveloped talents. Employing the horses as master empaths provided a shortcut to revealing hidden issues and feelings too subtle for even an accomplished counselor like Clarissa to ascertain on her own.

5. Handling Relationships

"The art of relationship," writes Goleman, "is, in large part, skill in managing emotions in others." The ability to read subtle social signals and reassure others in times of crisis can be crucial to success in business and family life, particularly for those in the caring professions. These are the same skills the horses teach with remarkable speed and agility in equine-facilitated programs. One of my students, an upper-level manager at a successful computer software company, came to our women's empowerment workshop with no previous horse experience and went on to study privately with me. Within two sessions, she had transferred the techniques she learned to calm unruly and frightened horses to stressful business meetings. After creating appropriate boundaries and controlling the arousal level of a horse, she found it much easier to deal constructively with the typical computer programmer, who may score off the charts on an IQ test but perform at abysmally low levels in the human relationship department.

"Some of the key players I work with can be quite aggressive and emotionally immature," she reported. "Instead of putting myself in the struggle, I have used these techniques to bring me back to a center of strength and calm. I've been surprised at how this has helped me and even more surprised that the calmness seems to be contagious."

As social animals, horses understand the intricacies of forming and sustaining relationships. They readily respond to the same nonverbal cues of dominance, submission, and cooperation used in human encounters. Through a series of modified equestrian activities, participants in Eponaquest programs gain practice in establishing appropriate boundaries and directing these powerful animals through mental focus, emotional congruency, creative visualization, and clarity of intent. Students explore assertiveness techniques and consensus-building relationship models that illustrate how to take the reins of any situation without lapsing into the pitfalls of dominance, alienation, intimidation, or victimization. They experience the process of establishing a vital, emotionally present connection that fosters an effortless sense of cooperation with the subtlest of cues. When the connection is weakened or broken, students also see how they must resort to force and restraint to get a crude approximation of those same results — with much more effort and risk.

All of these skills are especially crucial for people who work with trauma survivors, whether the situation is related to domestic violence, natural disaster, or, as in Liz's case, a drug-induced panic. Those who serve any function in crisis intervention need to know how to calm others while maintaining proper boundaries. If they can remain congruent at the very least and exude a sense of confidence mixed with equanimity and compassion at their very best, law enforcement officers, health care workers, and counselors can avoid inadvertently escalating crises and more efficiently and economically treat people exposed to extreme experiences.

This, of course, is easier said than done. The entire field of Western medicine is incongruent. Interns are expected to endure tremendous stress without complaint. Those more inclined to express their true feelings are perceived as not dedicated enough or not able to handle it. In this highly competitive field, any sign of weakness might motivate ambitious colleagues to come in for the kill. Many health care workers suffer from minor forms of posttraumatic stress disorder themselves as they deal with trauma survivors on a daily basis, yet these professionals feel they would endanger their jobs by acknowledging chaotic emotions and asking for help. The most common coping strategy is to become numb to strong emotion in the client while ignoring and suppressing their own needs and fears.

For the situation to change, the system must value emotional and social intelligence enough to make it a formal part of employee training and management. After all, if these professionals can learn how to administer potentially lethal drugs and assist in open-heart surgery, they can most certainly absorb stress-reduction, nonverbal communication, emotional awareness, self-regulation, and coregulation techniques, especially if such skills improve relations with clients, facilitate the healing process, and enhance cooperation in the working environment. In the meantime, people like Liz will continue to suffer the consequences as well-meaning but overworked and undertrained police officers, nurses, doctors, and orderlies descend upon the panicked like a group of cowboys lassoing a frightened mustang and dragging her to the ground, some of them invariably getting kicked in the process.

CHAPTER TEN

THE WOUNDED HEALER

·In Greek mythology, Chiron was a master musician, a wise philosopher, a powerful oracle, and a respected astronomer wielding an unusually eclectic body of knowledge, especially for a four-legged man. Jason and
Achilles studied with the centaur, who not only strengthened their bodies
and sharpened their minds but instructed them in the soulful art of discovering their destiny. Catching a glimpse of one student's upcoming trials,
Chiron taught the as-yet-unrealized hero to make the poison-tipped arrows
that guaranteed his triumph in battle, an impulse that ultimately changed
the centaur's own destiny. The two were practicing archery in the forest one
day when the young man accidentally shot his teacher in the right knee.
Delirious and limping in agony, Chiron retreated to an underground cavern
to repair what would have been a fatal wound for the average mortal. In the
process of trying different remedies, the centaur created the healing arts and
went on to teach these skills to Aesclepius, the Greek god of medicine.

In most mythical texts, Chiron is mentioned only in passing, but his
obscure story was resurrected in 1977 when astronomer Charles T. Kowal
discovered a small yet unusually bright object orbiting between Saturn and
Uranus, which he named after the legendary centaur. Newspapers had a field
day, announcing that a tenth planet had been found before researchers declared Chiron to be a "minor planet," grouping it with bodies like Ceres,
Eros, and Hidalgo. In the late 1980s, however, Chiron challenged its original
designation by exhibiting the characteristics of a comet while measuring over
fifty thousand times the typical comet volume, becoming one of those rare
bodies in the solar system to be classified as both comet and minor planet.
Its orbit also proved more eccentric than originally anticipated as it crossed
those of Saturn and Uranus, at times venturing closer to Earth than the
former and farther away than the latter. Astrologers subsequently combined

the myth of the centaur with the comet-planet's unusual characteristics to create a symbolic picture of Chiron's influence on earthly life. The placement of Chiron in a person's astrological chart is said to indicate a point where she was deeply wounded, a place that paradoxically holds the seeds of her greatest gifts.

Through a potent series of synchronicities, Chiron ushers in the era of the wounded healer. As a centaur, he symbolizes the multidisciplinary genius that arises from reuniting body and mind, instinct, intuition, and reason. His holistic approach to teaching and healing integrates the physical, emotional, mental, spiritual, and relational aspects of the individual. The symbol's combined human and animal form, dual status as comet and minor planet, and unusual orbit support the archetype's function as a bridge between multiple states of being. The astrologer Eric Francis describes Chiron as the connecting point "between the eccentric, unpredictable, futuristic, and inventive world of Uranus (pure energy), and the traditional, structured, predictable, and past-oriented world of Saturn (pure form). Chironic people often strive to ground new ideas into existing forms, and bring structure to innovative ideas."

The timing of Chiron's discovery, coinciding with the rise of alternative medicine in the late 1970s, captured the imagination of body-mind researchers and somatic psychotherapists, a number of whom embraced the centaur as a kind of patron saint. A quick search on the internet, for instance, produced a list of several counseling services using Chiron as a business name, designating a form of therapy that transmutes difficulties into gifts and traumas into sources of strength. In the 1980s, for example, the Chiron Centre for Body Psychotherapy in London actually taught therapists to stay connected to their own wounds and vulnerabilities "as the basis for understanding and meeting both the pain and the potential of those they work with." In its online brochure, the organization stated:

> The archetype of the "wounded healer" also has implications for the power dynamic in therapy and offers a position which complements the stereotype commonly held of the therapist as near-omniscient and all-powerful. The benign face of this image is the wise guide and good parent, but this is necessarily shadowed by the potential for manipulation, exploitation, and abuse. The therapist as "wounded healer" stays connected to [her] own pain and is not as

easily seduced by inflation or the client's need or conviction that the therapist be "sorted out," "together," or beyond pain and conflict.

The more I read about Chiron, the more intrigued I became, and the more I realized that my therapeutic philosophies and experiences were in sync with this image. The fact that Chiron's right knee was wounded in some versions of his story did not escape me, for my journey down this particular path of healing and transformation was facilitated by an injury to Rasa's right stifle, which functions as her knee in human terms. The black horse's subsequent lameness brought so much grief, pain, and confusion in the beginning and such profound insights, intuitions, and gifts in the end. Had she been able to follow a conventional equestrian agenda, Rasa herself might never have demonstrated her therapeutic talents. I didn't need to have our astrological charts done to recognize that this single Chironic moment of wounding changed the course of our collective destiny.

Beyond this personal epiphany, however, the image of the centaur as a holistic healer, philosopher, and teacher turning misfortune into medicine coincided with Eponaquest's therapeutic and educational missions. I had long been urging my students to become centaurs themselves as we explored those aspects of horse knowledge capable of balancing the postconquest, predatory side of human nature. I had also noticed that significant moments of healing occurred when counselors and instructors acknowledged their vulnerabilities and when clients began to access the gifts behind their suffering.

The late Moshe Feldenkrais, whose work so profoundly influenced Linda Tellington-Jones's equine-training innovations, embodied the Chiron archetype to the point of actually gaining his insights from a wounded knee. A soccer injury to this joint left him virtually disabled. When doctors gave him no hope for full recovery, he refused to accept the diagnosis. Like the centaur, he retreated into a period of intense isolation and self-discovery, somehow believing that if he could recreate the exploratory consciousness of the newborn, he might learn to walk again. After immersing himself in a state of complete inactivity, he slowly began to function. In the process, he explored multiple possibilities of movement, healing his knee and discovering ways of teaching others to recover their sensual learning abilities. Feldenkrais became one of the fathers of somatic psychotherapy, a field that acknowledges the connections between body and mind in facilitating recovery from both physical and psychological illness. Today, the Feldenkrais methods of Functional Integration and Awareness through Movement are taught worldwide.

Somatic psychotherapist Don Hanlon Johnson found, however, that — as in the horse whisperer phenomenon — people who teach the techniques of Feldenkrais, as well as other mavericks, tend to emphasize the method while failing to elucidate the meaning behind it. As he stresses:

> Practitioners are trained to imitate the "moves" developed by the founder without being prompted to explore the radical conversion he or she underwent. Clients are often encouraged to learn the techniques but not educated to recover their own sensual authority, [yet] before [these innovators] became publicly recognized experts with defined methods, they all experienced similar conversions from alienation to authenticity. During those events they learned valuable lessons about how we all might reconnect with our bodily wisdom.

The tendency to mimic the innovator while trying to avoid the some-times painful personal transformations he or she endured proves to be as widespread a problem in psychotherapy as it is in horse training. Many counselors are afraid to acknowledge their own vulnerabilities. A significant part of the Eponaquest training program for health care workers involves teaching these professionals how to create the personal boundaries needed to keep them from becoming enmeshed while remaining open enough to form an emotional alliance with the client, sometimes using their own wounds to gain insight into the patient's needs and dilemmas.

During a pivotal encounter with Noche, one experienced abuse and ad-diction counselor discovered how this process leads to significant moments of illumination for both client and therapist. At a half-day introductory workshop for health care workers cofacilitated by Kathleen Barry Ingram and me, "Joaquin" volunteered to enter the round pen with the bay mus-tang. By that time, all the participants were aware of Noche's past mistreat-ment, and they immediately picked up on his tendency to dissociate around new people. As expected, he stood at the far edge of the arena with his back turned to the audience, barely acknowledging Joaquin's presence. The man slowly approached the horse, commenting that he could see Noche didn't really want to engage, that he needed some space.

"I could tell Joaquin wasn't sure how to break through that barrier," Kathleen remembers. "He was professionally detached. Noche was aloof, and the result was two beings who would have been comfortable standing three feet away from each other all afternoon."

In this case, the concept of wu wei proved ineffective, because neither party was in the frame of mind to connect. Joaquin, who admitted to a childhood history of abuse himself, was essentially walking on eggshells around the horse. At that moment, I recognized the difference between a responsive, emotionally present approach to doing nothing with someone and a detached, intellectual, wait-and-see attitude more akin to observing a rat in a lab experiment. Joaquin emerged from this stalemate feeling terribly sorry for Noche. Yet, like Joy's inclination to coddle the horse while ignoring her own fears, the counselor subsequently revealed that he was more afraid of connecting with his own pain than he was of hurting Noche. Kathleen encouraged Joaquin to access the former victim inside, to remember how the protective patterns of shutting down, hiding his feelings, and alienating others led to intense periods of loneliness. Then she asked him to go back into the round pen and see if he could reach out to Noche.

Joaquin slowly walked over and placed his hand on Noche's shoulder, talking softly. No one could hear what the man was saying as the two stood next to each other, and when Joaquin stepped away, Noche followed him. The two walked around the arena shoulder to shoulder. Joaquin picked up the pace, eventually jogging in a serpentine pattern. Noche moved with him in perfect sync, as if the two were connected by an invisible halter and lead. Noche and Joaquin exhibited the characteristics of "join up," the ultimate goal of Monty Roberts's intricate free-longeing method designed to create a sense of trust and rapport between the horse and his human handler. Joaquin had achieved join up simply by standing next to Noche and admitting his true feelings.

"It was such an eloquent example of being gentle and respectful while also understanding how the survival skills people develop can keep them disconnected for the rest of their lives," Kathleen says. "Joaquin was euphoric when he walked out of that arena the second time. The horse gave him a marvelous gift, a felt sense of the magic that occurs when the healer can be present and vulnerable, when he can embrace his own dark night of the soul and use it to relate to others."

As the Jungian psychoanalyst Clarissa Pinkola Estés, author of *Women Who Run with the Wolves*, has so often emphasized, "All strong souls first go to hell before they do the healing of the world they came here for. If we are lucky, we return to help those still trapped below." As seasoned travelers between the world of the living and the realms beyond, horses are masters at facilitating these heroic journeys. Sometimes they carry us through the unknown. Sometimes they walk beside us. Sometimes they mirror the wounds we refuse to face. All the while, they remind us that in the peaks and valleys between fear and courage, agony and ecstasy, we are not alone.

"You can just sit with these animals and have an amazing feeling of peace and connection come over you," Joy once told me. "It's as if they've taken you back a thousand years, when people were able to feel a part of something much larger than being human. When I felt this opening, I was able to connect with a much larger, more courageous, more compassionate part of myself."

The Elements of Destiny

In his book *The Soul's Code: In Search of Character and Calling*, author and analyst James Hillman, who originated post-Jungian archetypal psychology, discusses the acorn theory. He proposes that each life is formed by a particular image, an image that calls the individual to a destiny, just as the mighty oak's destiny is embodied in the seemingly inconsequential acorn. His hypothesis is inspired and elucidated by Plato's myth of Er, from the ancient Greek philosopher's best-known work, *The Republic*. The story holds that before birth, each soul selects a particular image or pattern to be lived out on earth. Because the trauma of entering this world causes each of us to forget all that took place before we arrived, the blueprint of this calling is entrusted to a soul companion the Greeks called the daimon (pronounced "dye' moan"), a guardian angel of sorts that guides each person toward embodying and fulfilling his or her purpose. According to Hillman, "The daimon remembers what is in your image and belongs to your pattern, and therefore your daimon is the carrier of your destiny."

The Soul's Code speaks of childhood idiosyncrasies, accidents, and traumas as necessities that point us in the direction of our calling. The book encourages us to recover our "true biography," the narrative of our lives that is not chronological but instead orbits around the innate image or purpose we came here to express. Hillman dares to envision personal experience "in terms of very large ideas such as beauty, mystery, and myth." He asserts that we quite often go into therapy to recover the core image that will finally make sense of our lives. He also cautions that unless we can find a counselor who grants primary psychological reality to the call of fate, the daimon's urgings will continue to appear "as eccentricities, compacted with angry resentments and overwhelming longings."

Hillman offers an innovative view of repression, suggesting its negative effects result from ignoring the reality of the acorn and failing to learn from the mistakes we made in our relationship with it. Constantly revisiting past abuses from the mindset of a victim is counterproductive and misses the point. The daimon sees the seemingly unfair or tragic moments in our lives as openings for the innate image to reassert itself. Procrastinating or fighting this destiny is what causes pain. In this sense, Hillman was one of a growing number of analysts who were trying to put the soul back into psychology.

According to Hillman, the acorn, or soul's code, asserts itself in urges that seem to come out of nowhere, childhood fascinations and odd behaviors that stand out from familial or societal conditioning, peculiar turns of events that "strike like an annunciation: This is what I must do. This is what I've got to have. This is who I am." Looking back, the overriding theme of my early years, the sensation I couldn't shake that persisted into adulthood no matter how illogical or unnatural it seemed to other people, was this: I never felt comfortable being human. As a child, I behaved as if I was carting around the soul of a four-legged creature in a two-legged body, and I was not happy about it. I shunned dolls in favor of stuffed animals and begged to eat out of a bowl on the floor. Though I learned to walk at nine months, I still wore holes through my jeans from scrambling around the house on hands and knees, and I often refused to answer my parents unless they called me Bambi, Rudolf, Leo, or Black Beauty. My four favorite alter egos represented an uncanny balance of predator and prey: wolves and deer, lions and horses, any of which I could call up at a moment's notice.

As I got older, I spent more time outside than inside, catching snakes, raising frogs and praying mantises, even sitting in a large maple tree and hand-feeding some raccoons, much to my parents' horror. However, it wasn't until I discovered the horse trader's farm through the woods beside our house that I began to resonate with my true calling. After school, I'd sneak over to the old man's back pasture and spend the afternoon cavorting with his ever-changing collection of all breeds and colors, learning their language, bucking, snorting, and kicking up my heels with the feistiest members of the herd, sampling their favorite grasses, and convincing the amenable among them to take me for a ride. Without a bit and bridle or even a halter and lead rope, there was no way for me to force even the most complacent of geldings into carrying me around. These massive creatures had to be willing to follow me over to the fence and stand still long enough to let me climb onto their backs. They had to *want* to be with me. Figuring out ways of winning their friendship became an obsession and an art form over the four years I spent experimenting in secret with this transient herd. I knew better than to tell my parents I was actually riding the horses, or they never would have let me out of their sight. But since they refused to buy me a pony of my own, I settled for the next best thing — and arguably learned more in the process.

I would later discover, through Joy and others like her, that an expensive horse and the finest training money could buy did not always afford the recipient a deep understanding of equine behavior. In fact, it was the oldest, least valuable horse on the trader's property who proved to be my greatest teacher during those early years. I called him Nakia, and he responded to the name, despite the fact that I had no idea what made me choose that word to describe him, where I had heard it, or what it meant. With protruding ribs and a stilted, arthritic gait, the bone-colored gelding obviously had one foot in the otherworld. I knew the trader was planning to sell him at the next killer's auction, that this was Nakia's last stop on the way to the glue factory. Still, I felt no anger, fear, resentment, or resignation in his presence. His eyes reflected the most rarefied sense of gentleness. His entire demeanor seemed to say, "Everything is as it should be," and he was beautiful.

When I was with Nakia, it was impossible to feel sorry for him. Still, I racked my brains for a way to save his life, even considered stealing him and riding away one night with a backpack full of supplies before it hit me that two hastily made sandwiches and a box of granola bars wouldn't get us past the freeway. To no avail, I begged my parents to plunk down a hundred bucks for the horse and let me keep him in the backyard. At the very least, I managed to convince my father to sneak out there one day and meet the old fellow. Dad took a picture of Nakia and me standing side by side in the knee-high grass, a now crumpled, faded old photo — half eaten by the family dog — that I've carried with me through college, two marriages, and two moves across the country. It was the only picture ever taken of me with one of the trader's horses.

For twenty-one glorious spring days, Nakia and I roamed through the pasture as if time didn't exist. I fed him carrots and apples, trotted with him along the fence line, lay across his back in the sunshine, and massaged his tired muscles. Then one day, I jumped off the school bus, threw my books down, and ran to the trader's place, only to fall convulsing to the ground with breathless sobs. Nakia was gone.

The childish, hopeful, unconditional love I felt for the old horse, however, seemed to raise my status in the herd. I no longer felt tolerated but accepted. I also sensed that I had to avoid complacency at all costs if I was to be treated like another horse. Even the yearlings were ten times bigger than me, their thick hides and sturdy bones able to withstand a kick that would have killed me. Some of the ex–racing thoroughbreds were particularly dangerous. I learned to recognize their state of mind at a distance by analyzing their movements, postures, and the ways in which the other horses related to them. I also had to be on constant lookout for the trader himself, who came upon me riding bareback a couple of times and threatened to tan my hide if he ever caught me again. My fellow herd members proved to be of immeasurable assistance in helping me avoid a beating; the key was to remain alert enough to monitor what everyone else was feeling, seeing, and doing. Then, even the most subtle changes in the horses would warn me of the old man's approaching presence long before he got close enough to see me. Maintaining this level of awareness was never a chore. For me, it was much more difficult to deaden my senses in order to deal with the intensity of the human race.

Unlike many survivors of traumatic experiences, my empathic proclivities did not develop in reaction to childhood abuse, but in response to a group of animals who reinforced the preconquest state of consciousness at a pivotal point in my development. My continued association with the horse tribe from the ages of nine to thirteen allowed me to strengthen my sociosensual talents as I passed the age of reason. I practiced resonating with the emotions of others long after most people suppress this capacity and forget they ever had it. The persistent presence of the empathic mindset, however, proved to be more trouble than it was worth. I had no one to teach me how to protect myself or process all the information I was picking up. Most of my insights were trapped at a nonverbal level, though I was very much aware of what I was feeling and who it was coming from, aware enough to be tortured by it in the "civilized" world, where people acted like everything was fine while broadcasting completely different emotions. A whirlwind of emotional cacophony surrounded most humans I encountered. When someone in my general vicinity radiated despair, anger, or stress of any kind, it seemed to hover around his body like a poisonous mist. If he decided to direct such feelings at me, the reaction was even more dramatic. A cruel remark could cut into me like a dagger. The words themselves were of little consequence; it was the energy behind them that was so devastating.

It's not surprising that I preferred to play alone, in nature, with my animal companions. Horses, dogs, and cats could get angry or cranky, of course, but with them an outburst of distressing emotion provided useful information, and then it was gone. My four-legged companions didn't internalize their feelings, haul them around, and unleash them on innocent bystanders when the pressure got too dense. These creatures moved through life in a peaceful, balanced state accented by moments of pleasure and pain, fear and elation, playfulness and repose that came and went like clouds moving across a clear blue sky.

The Flashlight in the Human Brain

Even before I read Hillman's book and began to incorporate his theories into my equine programs, I instinctually realized it would be a gross betrayal of Joy's calling to see her purely as a victim. Though she had inherited a lucrative business from her family, Joy didn't have to work. In fact, she managed the company and its associated foundation part-time, showing little interest in this aspect of her life. She spent the majority of her days tending to a wide variety of relationships with extended family members and friends, many of whom had their own tragic stories to tell and were looking to Joy for support. The woman felt she was performing a service for people scattered across the country who refused to get the help they needed. With no financial motivation to get her degree and set up a counseling practice, Joy was nonetheless thrust into that position by people who "didn't believe" in psychotherapy. She felt this was her calling, her main reason for being born into such a dysfunctional family.

While I resisted this notion of hers at first, thinking she was simply engaging in a great deal of codependent behavior, I couldn't help but notice that Joy's entire face would light up whenever she shared a story of how she had successfully used something she learned with the horses to deal constructively with an agitated family member. Over time, the woman proved remarkably adept at adapting her equine knowledge to some highly disturbed people. I had also seen time and time again that Joy's most startling break-throughs hinged on convincing her that a certain personal or codependent behavior pattern was actually hurtful, not helpful, to others. The more I discovered about her family, the more I also had to admit that for many of these people, Joy probably was their only hope.

Joy's empathy, compassion, and desire to be with troubled people stood out in her family. Despite her tendency to dissociate, her ability to control her anger and anxiety while calming others was an impulse no one else seemed to share. Even her sensitive older brother, who had become a social activist, was prone to rebellious acts of rage that escalated family problems. Joy was the person staff called to handle Granny when she was in "one of those moods of hers." In fact, Joy was the one everyone seemed to look to in a crisis. I could see that to survive, this woman would either have to cut off all contact with her clan or learn the proper techniques for handling a mansion full of people with addictions, anger management problems, and a host of physical, emotional, and sexual abuse issues. She would need to develop proper boundaries and become emotionally agile to avoid becoming enmeshed and drained. In short, she would need the skills of a psychothera-pist without the potentially threatening title of psychotherapist.

As I grasped the intricacies of Joy's dilemma, our equine-facilitated sessions suddenly changed course, offering the woman her own Chironic experience with a wounded horse. Two months after she progressed to riding Noche, Joy bought a twelve-year-old gelding who initially seemed to have a stable, patient, giving personality. She found Whistler possessed a strong will, however, when he began to show signs of intermittent lameness. Rather than engaging and strengthening Whistler's hind end, his former owner had unknowingly ridden him on the forehand across miles of rocky trails at top speed, a practice that tends to break a horse down as he gets older. Joy purchased Whistler in time to reverse the damage before it resulted in permanent injury. Still, she had to contend with his blatant discomfort and graphic objections to altering the unbalanced, potentially destructive ways of moving that had marginally worked for him most of his life.

Joy, therefore, was suddenly thrust into my position. She knew Whistler's well-being depended upon the change, yet he was physically and mentally uncomfortable with a new style of riding. Through the frustrating transition, Joy learned to be responsive to the horse's continued resistance without in-dulging him. She practiced the subtle art of knowing when to insist, when to back off, when to reassess the progress, when to bring in expert opinions, and how to evaluate the sometimes conflicting advice of several different veterinarians, acupuncturists, trainers, and nosy, opinionated bystanders. At times, Joy looked to me to make the final decision, but I refused to take the bait. Instead I helped her face the stress and uncertainty of being the one in charge of Whistler's fate by engaging her analytical, empathic, and intuitive skills. I found myself motivating someone else to strengthen and balance a variety of different states of awareness that I had practiced during those early, more experimental days with the herd. In the process, I reflected on my own pivotal encounters with the horses in my life and began to understand more deeply the insights I had gained.

When I was bombarded with an overwhelming sense of mystery, myth, and calling in the presence of my herd, I was fortunate enough to find two counselors who treated my strange experiences and obsessions as soulful realities. Patricia Hursh, PhD, and Lewis Mehl-Madrona, MD, PhD, not only convinced me of my sanity, they gave me the tools to work with the visions and voices that wrestled me away from the mundane reality my upbringing provided. Though I saw Dr. Mehl-Madrona only once and Dr. Hursh a half-dozen times during the first year of what later became a close association, their influence was invaluable. The techniques I received allowed me to do exactly what was necessary for the acorn to emerge from its long-buried resting place and grow toward its full potential. In the process, I began to relate to the Voice of Remembering as my daimon, the soul companion who never forgot what my purpose was, how it had come into being, and how intimately it was connected to the calling of Tabula Rasa.

The metaphorical musings dictated by the Voice of Remembering didn't truly become useful to me, however, until I was able to connect my symbolic imagery with current theories on the workings of the mind. Finally I could explain, in ways that "reasonable" people would be more likely to understand, the observations I had captured through the unconventional format of "The Black Horse Speaks," and I realized that poetry, myth, and mysticism also function as travelogues through the realms of nonverbal experience. I wouldn't have remembered the details of what I had perceived if I hadn't found a way to record my observations while I was in, or just coming out of, altered states of consciousness. The metaphors that arose in "The Black Horse Speaks" reminded me not only of where I had been but of how I had gotten there and, consequently, of how I might return to a similar frame of mind. Over time, I was able to analyze the journeys I took with my horses, describe them more concretely, and, as a result, begin to teach others how to achieve a more fluid mental and emotional identity through equine-facilitated therapy and experiential learning. As the Voice of Remembering helped me understand the human mind from a mythical perspective, "she" also pointed me in the direction of some adventurous scientific theories as I looked for ways to interpret metaphors like the lake behind the black horse's eyes and the flashlight in the human brain:

The flashlight in the human brain is an extraordinary tool. On the handle is a dial. Turn it all the way to the left, and you generate the concentrated lasers of reason, with related positions for literal forms of communication. Where I come from, people emphasize these settings to the exclusion of all others, mostly because it takes years to master the art of carving up living experience into narrow rays of thought. It's like dissecting the inner workings of some alien creature. Generally you have to kill it first, but then you can preserve the carcass, study it from many different angles, and slice off a few choice cuts for others to consume and digest.

As you move the dial toward the right, the streams of light get wider and a lot less lethal. You can illuminate progressively larger sections of landscapes teaming with endless varieties of life, but without your laser, you have no means to immobilize specimens, and you certainly can't dice them into pieces small enough to fit into little packages made of logic. As a result, you have no souvenirs to send home, no jerky to give others a taste of where you've been. But that doesn't mean these regions don't exist or that they aren't worth visiting.

However, there is a tiny camera inside the flashlight. If you push the button underneath the dial, you can take pictures of anything you see, no matter how broad the beam. These Polaroids are crude and flat. The colors aren't nearly as vivid as the real thing, and dimensions are deceptive. But sometimes, they inspire others to play with their flashlights and shed light on places that left brain functions can't traverse. These snapshots are called "myths." They're best interpreted by story-tellers and poets who know how to paint with language. Large brushstrokes are preferred, allowing listeners to feel snatches of truth seeping through the spaces between words.

Psychologists have determined that between 7 and 10 percent of human communication is verbal. Considering that more than 90 percent of the messages we send back and forth to one another happen outside the influence of words, we sell ourselves short when artistic modes of expression are the first programs cut from schools. These seemingly impractical skills are highly specialized forms of communication that bring nonverbal experience into focused awareness. In my equine-facilitated practice, I teach clients how to solidify and interpret their own elusive nonverbal insights through poetry, storytelling, and mythmaking as the horses awaken intuitive and sociosensual forms of awareness. Students can then consult this record of their experiences after returning to a "normal" state of awareness. Clients experiencing strong emotion find it difficult to speak as the limbic system overrides the neocortex. Artistic expression exercises different pathways in the brain, allowing speech to function outside the narrow bandwidths of logic, helping people document feelings and awareness states that can't be accessed through reason. Learning to interpret these symbols builds a bridge between the thinking brain and the emotional brain. This last step may very well be the most important in altering behavior. Artists able to express ineffable feelings and experiences may still lead deeply dysfunctional lives because they haven't made the leap of consciousness to integrate their insights and change in relation to them. To transform destructive emotional patterns, clients must first bring unconscious processes into awareness, interpret that nonrational information, and then transfer the insights to the frontal cortex, where they can exert their will and focus to change their responses to formerly disruptive emotions.

The lake behind the black horse's eyes and the flashlight in the human brain were among those metaphors that allowed me to articulate the nuances of several very different thought processes. When I encountered E. Richard Sorenson's theory of preconquest and postconquest consciousness, I had already intimately explored both of these mindsets myself. I didn't have to travel to New Guinea and inadvertently ruin an entire tribe's way of life to recognize the predatory nature of logic (though I'm certainly glad Sorenson was there to record this unfortunate event). The laser behind my own eyes was an image of mental conquest, of having to capture, dominate, or dismember something in order to appreciate it, of judging the components of life outside their constantly evolving contexts. I realized that the resulting tendency to discard whatever slices of perception didn't fit into the current dominant "theory of everything" leads to a most disturbing yet predictable conclusion: as it reaches the age of reason, a mind tuned exclusively to left brain settings invariably cuts itself off from the vibrancy of its own life force and the sensual, intuitive ancestral wisdom flowing through it.

I was fortunate enough to associate with a group of horses who welcomed me into their tribe and tutored me in the finer points of sociosensual awareness. From this expansive view, I realized how tragic it was for the human race to habitually indoctrinate its children into a warlike state of consciousness to the exclusion of all other possibilities. *Homo sapiens* weren't the only ones to suffer under this system, however. Throughout history, horses were among those animals who had carried our burdens and often saved our hides as they were sacrificed on both sides of countless battles. Even so, we could still rely on their descendants to help us end the siege. If only we would step off our high horses and appreciate them as sentient beings, they might be willing to lead us to the lost keys of paradise.

All human children briefly drink from the rivers of life, which continue to flow outward in the four directions, far below the surface, though the gates of Eden are closed. Yet the source bubbling up inside the infant soul is a fragile opening. Once the lightning sword ignites, these quiet springs are buried under mounds of shredded thought. Four-legged creatures are spared this caustic fate. Their waters continue to rise, forming a pond behind the eyes that can never be disrupted by judgmental fault lines and fires of reason.

To the black horse, the landscape of man and woman rumbles like earthquakes ravaging ancient battlefields, and the conflict still continues in the throes of devastation. She wanders along the perimeter, grazing through her life, occasionally jumping out of the way of flying shrapnel. Yet like all beings possessing a secret pool, she's willing to offer a drink to those who thirst and an oasis to those weary of the fight.

Her gift to me was greater. Though she chose never to feel the rapture of words and lasers, the black horse had been sentenced to reflect their altus purpose or roam forever through a mist between two worlds. She had to find a way to turn her story into sound. I'm not sure if it was destiny or synchronicity that struck down my paltry goals and brought me to her aid. I only know the rivers of paradise still surge beneath the earth, and the flashlight in the human brain is waterproof.

I really had no idea what that last paragraph meant when I first wrote it, but I knew it documented a subconscious transformation. My ability to record and analyze the details of this awakening later proved useful to those attending Eponaquest's equine-facilitated workshops. As I created the conditions for sociosensual interactions to occur between humans and horses, I watched my herd initiate this same transformation in people from all walks of life, but Rasa stood out as the true therapeutic genius. In my mythical writings, I sensed this was not only her calling but her salvation. My human ego, however, didn't truly believe a horse could have a calling, let alone a need to carry it out for spiritual reasons. Consequently, I initially fell into the classic psychoanalytical habit of interpreting visions related to Rasa purely as elements of my own psychology. I doubted these insights were directly relevant to her or to a wider public, but over time, I would realize I was wrong.

The Latin word *altus* means both "high" and "deep." The idea that Rasa was compelled to "reflect [the] altus purpose" of the most human aspects of consciousness — namely, speech and logic — suggests that she possessed an innate talent for helping people see their own thought patterns from a new perspective, one that illustrated both the limitations and the unused potential of the postconquest mind. This she could accomplish with the ease of a prodigy. To truly be effective, however, she had to rely on someone who could translate the information she was providing. Otherwise, she would be sentenced to "roam forever through a mist between two worlds." Her reflections would remain trapped at a nonverbal level, where they would be of little use to the very people she was called to help.

With the wisdom of hindsight, I think it was both destiny and synchronicity that brought me to her aid — and she to mine — though at the time my paltry goals included training her for one-hundred-mile endurance races so that I could get as far away as possible from my own species. Through our interactions, I learned much more than I initially wanted to know about the workings of the postconquest mind, the reasons behind its violent tendencies, and the other states of awareness we suppressed or ignored at our peril. At first, this only made me feel more angry and alienated from the culture in which I was raised. For a good year and a half, I wanted nothing to do with people and could barely stand to be around them unless I had anesthetized myself with enough alcohol to subdue all the disturbing unspoken messages I was picking up. Over time, however, my work with the herd allowed me to appreciate the wisdom behind my own form. I learned to accept others as they were without compromising my values or losing the increased sensitivity I was gaining from the horses. I became adept at reflecting without judgment and interpreting Rasa's voluminous nonverbal commentary on the increasing numbers of people who came to our workshops and private lessons.

The frustrating, yet ultimately enlightening, circumstances of our association propelled us toward the fields of equine-facilitated therapy and experiential learning. The horses and I developed a symbiotic protocol for helping people reconnect with sociosensual, intuitive, and morphogenetic forms of consciousness. This did not involve suppressing the human gifts of speech and logic but simply putting them in their proper place. The part of the mind that reasons and analyzes experience is "waterproof." In other words, it can plunge into the realms of aquatic awareness and illuminate the normally subconscious aspects of the sympathetic and parasympathetic nervous systems. In order for me to develop the techniques and activities that allowed this transformation to take place in others, however, I had to spend years experimenting with multiple styles of awareness. In the process, I experienced the fears and pitfalls of thought that make it so difficult for civilized human beings to achieve a more fluid, expansive state of being.

Still, there are places where words can never go, states that cannot be translated into the most far-fetched myths. Pouring through an electric darkness that sparkles with promises of many colors, plunging into a great womb of emptiness that dreams the universe, my human ego would have been shattered if the black horse hadn't already helped me find a way to exist without it. These images dance around the edges of what I experienced when I finally had the courage to release my identity from the predictable patterns of "higher thought." In the process, the horses led me through a series of transformational mindscapes most often traveled by mystics.

In his bestselling book *The Power of Now*, spiritual teacher Eckhart Tolle describes his pivotal experience with the void. A relentless, often debilitating sense of anxiety had marked his early years, culminating in a life-changing struggle to maintain his sanity one night not long after his twenty-ninth birthday. In the stillness of his darkened room, he was gripped by feelings of such fear and existential loneliness that he realized he couldn't live with himself any longer:

This was the thought that kept repeating itself in my mind. Then suddenly I became aware of what a peculiar thought it was. "Am I one or two? If I cannot live with myself, there must be two of me: the 'I' and the 'self' that 'I' cannot live with. Maybe," I thought, "only one of them is real."

I was so stunned by this strange realization that my mind stopped. I was fully conscious, but there were no more thoughts. Then I felt drawn into what seemed like a vortex of energy. I was gripped by an intense fear, and my body started to shake. I heard the words "resist nothing," as if spoken inside my chest. I could feel myself being sucked into a void. It felt as if the void was inside myself rather than outside. Suddenly, there was no more fear, and I let myself fall into that void.

Tolle has no recollection of what happened next. However, he awoke the following morning in a state of deep peace and bliss that lasted for several months before it diminished in intensity. The world felt "fresh and pristine, as if it had just come into existence." The simple furnishings in his room took on the glow of the miraculous. "Without any thought," he wrote, "I felt, I knew, that there is infinitely more to light than we realize. That soft luminosity coming through the curtains was love itself."

This rarefied state of consciousness was similar to the one I often experienced with my herd after all the two-legged creatures left for the day. With Rasa and Noche by my side, the journey wasn't the least bit traumatic, and I began to understand firsthand why so many myths depict horses as seasoned travelers between the seen and unseen realms. I wasn't literally climbing on their backs, but I was riding them into the otherworld as I resonated with their expansive, meditative perspective. In the presence of these quiet, soulful creatures, my thoughts would gradually dissipate. My heart would swell. The mesquite trees would begin to radiate a soft white light in the darkness, and I would dissolve into the embrace of a colossal mystery. Trusting in the fluid reflections of sociosensual awareness, I also discovered that "I" was not the lake behind my eyes or even the river of collective wisdom that surged beneath it. Everywhere I looked for myself, I melted into the scenery. Was I everything all at once, or was I simply an illusion? Night after night, the horses stood over me as I lay in the grass and peered into the darkness.

There is a pool in the heart of the desert. The surface is as quiet as glass, though its waters are nourished by a mountain stream rushing endlessly underground. When the sun goes to sleep and the earth hides the moon, owls prowl the sky, bats toss alien melodies against obsidian walls, black horses chase coyotes through indigo fields, and the pond embraces it all in a luminous reverie that will never again know stagnation. This is the spring that lives and breathes behind my own eyes.

I am content to melt into the scenery and leave thoughts like pebbles resting soundlessly on the shore. To the woman I've become, the human mind looks like an open road emerging from thick, old growth forests. It meanders through new grasslands covering the scars of countless wars, past ancient volcanoes rumbling from the depths, up toward treacherous precipices with views beyond forever, and down into labyrinthine canyons of long forgotten dreams. The laser rests beside me. I need no artificial light, for in the mirror of my lake, even the faintest stars are magnified in the immensity of pure reflection.

For a time, I left the all-consuming habits of reason behind. In the process, I also gathered enough experience and courage to step off the paths of civilized mystical experience, some of them worn into ruts so deep the people who traveled them could not help but have tunnel vision. Concerned almost exclusively with human suffering and redemption, most religions offered no maps through the territory I was compelled to explore. As far as the rest of my species was concerned, I was on my own.

The desert stretched out before me, darkness giving way to a light so bright and loving I knew my flashlight would be useless. The black horse danced up ahead. I took a deep breath and followed her into the blazing unknown.

Part Three

MESSAGE AND MEANING

I will break down the gates of bronze
and cut through the bars of iron.
I will give you the treasures of darkness,
riches stored in secret places....
I form the light and create the darkness,
I bring prosperity and create disaster,
I, the Lord, do all these things.

— Isaiah 45:2–3, 7

CHAPTER ELEVEN

NEKYIA

There's a poster hanging, of all places, in the women's restroom at a Tucson hair salon. "Experience is the hardest teacher," it reads. "You get the test first and the lesson later." In my dealings with the Ancestors, I most often received the reason for the lesson long after the exam as well. This proved to be a disconcerting and at times even frightening way to study the wisdom of the horse. In the long run, however, it taught me how to trust my inner resources and navigate the darkest reaches of the human psyche. From these journeys, I became familiar with ancestral memories that still influence the collective unconscious of both species — and occasionally erupt into our civilized world with a vengeance.

Six months after I discovered the Horse Ancestors with Patricia Hursh, I was regularly using this force as an invisible, interactive troubleshooting service for the training dilemmas I encountered. Still, I had no idea how I had tapped into this collective wisdom or what it might want from me in exchange. The persistent feeling that the Ancestors had some other, more complex agenda than simply helping me to "fix" problem horses plagued my dreams and waking hours with a vague yet steadily increasing sense of anticipation. But whenever I asked this presence about its purpose, the images would diffuse into clouds of static agitation. I felt like I was trying to watch TV with a radio. Either the circuits were jammed with too much information or my primitive tuner couldn't pick up the frequency.

After weeks of frustrated attempts at clarification, it finally occurred to me that I should request specific information on how I might communicate more effectively with the Ancestors. I immediately saw two rivers flowing parallel to each other. The one on the right called itself the River Equus and the one on the left, the River Anthropos. The image ended with the two curving in toward each other. They lit up where they crossed, then continued to flow separately, with the River Anthropos on the right and the River Equus on the left. I saw these same rivers merge into each other further downstream, creating what looked like the lower half of a figure eight. There the currents mingled completely and began to surge back upstream, each side now carrying the collective waters of both.

The vision portrayed two streams of consciousness, one human and the other equine, running parallel to each other in space and time. In Rupert Sheldrake's terms, the River Equus and the River Anthropos represented the morphogenetic fields of the two species. Information would be exchanged wherever they crossed, yet the greatest potential for communication seemed to involve their convergence, an event that suggested a strange new possibility. Could the River Equus circulate back upstream to retrace the landscape traveled by the River Anthropos from a new perspective? How would the history and behavior of the human race look to one who took this journey?

A few nights later, the Ancestors elaborated on this waking vision through a particularly vivid, emotionally charged dream: Men and women with almond eyes and long black hair were escorting me along a precarious trail that just barely allowed us to navigate without plunging into the canyon below. Though I trusted them completely, their peaceful, knowing faces couldn't quite relieve the wrenching, constricted, tugging sensation in my solar plexus. Even so, I was thrilled to be a part of this procession. Suddenly, the narrow pass gave way to a stunning view of Death Valley, and I marveled at the sight of this stark, dramatic landscape filled with horses of every breed and color. They were running through the lowlands like a river as far as the eye could see. Two figures emerged from this endless herd: the vivacious dark bay thoroughbred mare I had bought in Tucson and the worn-out, bone-colored gelding I had played with as a child. "Nakia," I shouted, and the unlikely pair whinnied a nameless challenge in response.

Upon waking, I was left with an electrifying sensation that everything was unfolding according to plan. The night before, I had pleaded with the Horse Ancestors to explain how I might better communicate with them, and once again, I had seen the two rivers crossing as I drifted off to sleep. Out of this nexus came the vision of Death Valley and the two horses known to me by the same name, Nakia. The image pointed to that single word, but I still had no idea what it meant, where I had heard it, or why I had associated it with two completely different horses twenty-five years apart.

I spent the next two days in the library (this was in the days before the internet) searching through dictionaries, encyclopedias, collections of myths from around the world, and paperbacks designed to help parents choose the perfect names for their babies. I tried a variety of different spellings. Finally, I found an entry for the word *Nekyia* in a literary guide, and I almost dropped the book when I read its meaning. The Nekyia refers to a scene in Homer's *Odyssey* in which the hero attempts to find his way home from a foreign land by consulting the spirits of his ancestors.

Believed to have been written in the eighth century BCE, the *Odyssey*, along with Homer's *Iliad*, is one of the earliest works of Western literature. Having studied classical music rather than classical literature in college, I had never read it, but the epic poem obviously had thousands of years to assert itself in the human morphogenetic field. During my secret childhood excursions to the old horse trader's farm, I had named the first gelding I really felt close to Nekyia without knowing or caring how to spell it. Could my subconscious have been trying to express its desire to connect with the Horse Ancestors even at that early age? Would *The Odyssey* offer me hints on how to solidify my partnership with this same field of collective wisdom and, finally, discover its purpose?

As I read the ancient prose poem, armed with a book of interpretive essays, I realized that the goals and impulses behind my quest were in direct opposition to almost every facet of Odysseus's journey. Even so, the process by which he navigated through the fearsome landscapes he encountered created a map I was able to follow in reverse. Homer's hero strove to find his way home from a foreign realm filled with powerful, wholly irrational goddesses who could turn people into animals and mesmerize warriors with lotuses and siren songs. Along with the usual threats of being slain in battle, dismembered by monsters, and drowned in the sea, his soldiers faced the constant danger of being seduced into relinquishing their ambitions to wallow in fields of sociosensual pleasure, the very fate that most horrified their leader.

Odysseus was the thinking man's hero. Having sacked Troy with the ruse of the gigantic wooden horse, he won his battles through "cunning intelligence," and his loyalty rested with Athena, the Greek goddess of war, who was also the goddess of reason and the protector of city life. The favored daughter of Zeus, Athena sprang from her father's head already an adult and dressed in armor. She therefore could be seen as the goddess of postconquest consciousness, an archetype disconnected from feeling, ready to wage war on all who challenged the tenets of civilization and refused to deify the rational mind. As the greatest of Athena's success stories, Odysseus received ongoing praise for his "trickery" and "deceit." Characterizing him as the "far best of all men for planning and words, while I among all the gods have glory by reason and cunning of intelligence," Athena bestowed her favors upon him as a kindred spirit. *The Odyssey*'s hero trusted the only major feminine archetype in the Greek pantheon who was not born of woman or goddess. Divorced from the more threatening aspects of femininity — namely, emotion, sensuality, and an intuitive connection to nature — Athena provided a larger-than-life image of the reasonable man's ideal woman. Odysseus's mortal wife, Penelope, was a manageable complement to the virgin goddess, a paragon of domesticated virtues, a faithful woman content to spend her days weaving and her evenings fighting off the attentions of suitors — even years after her husband was seemingly lost at sea.

Blown off course and forced to roam through a series of fantastic worlds in books 9 through 12 of *The Odyssey*, the hero on his quest for a return to normalcy was under constant attack from the mythical and nonrational elements of existence, symbolized by a host of far less virginal, far more independent women. The threat of a loss or forgetfulness of self through sensuality was an ongoing theme as Odysseus repeatedly escaped the clutches of these goddesses by overcoming their temptations. At just the right moment, however, he could distract or befriend them long enough to wrestle some crucial information that would ultimately put him back on track.

Among his crew of warrior-sailors, Odysseus was the only one who could stay focused on his homeland in the face of supernatural seductions and overwhelming challenges to his rational mind. Tenacity, cunning, and an infallible ability to concentrate on his ultimate goal in the midst of cultural chaos were the qualities that brought him home in time to deceitfully kill his wife's suitors and reclaim his kingdom. Ultimately, Odysseus was not so much a soldier of the sword but a warrior of the laser. Written more than two thousand years ago, Homer's *Odyssey* defined the potential of mental heroism at the dawning of postconquest consciousness.

My story, on the other hand, was that of a woman who felt equally homesick but in the land of logic. The loss or forgetfulness of self I constantly fought was tied to living in a culture that wanted me to reject the deeply empathic, intuitive soul inside that yearned to fully connect with nature. Where Odysseus gained information on how to navigate through the irrational realms from the residents themselves, I read books by rational men filled with theoretical maps to the otherworld. The only trick, as Odysseus found, was to resist the spell of the alien culture and avoid assimilation. I had to deal with patriarchal archetypes and men of reason who weren't so much interested in seducing me to stay as they were in threatening, dominating, and shaming me into submission, but as one misplaced foreigner develops a soft spot for another, I had a certain respect for Odysseus, a mythical man who gave me the tools to find my own way home. Still, if Homer's epic was a tribute to the newly forming postconquest mindset of the ancient Greeks, what was the meaning behind my own journey?

Purely intuitive or purely rational insights never satisfied me. Like the Chiron archetype, my inclination was to "ground new ideas into existing forms, and bring structure to innovative ideas." The challenge was to integrate body, mind, and spirit not only in perceiving the world but in sharing my experiences with others. In this effort, I was drawn to the theories of reasonable men and women who weren't afraid to look at life's irrational elements.

The Liberation of Mind and Memory

"I have been and still am a seeker," wrote Hermann Hesse in the prologue to his novel *Demian*, "but I have ceased to question stars and books; I have begun to listen to the teachings my blood whispers to me."

Leaders in mind-body medicine have begun to take such sentiments seriously. "The mind is in the blood," asserts physician and author Larry Dossey, "just as Hesse implied. This is not a poetic statement; it is not a metaphor; it is a literal truth." In his influential books *Space, Time & Medicine*, *Beyond Illness*, *Recovering the Soul*, and *Reinventing Medicine*, Dossey, a former practitioner of internal medicine, has drawn together studies that anchor the holistic health movement in a model that's both scientifically respectable and spiritually invigorating.

Based in part on Candace Pert's research into the molecules of emotion, Dossey holds that "the new understanding of the role of the blood makes it appear as if the brain has broken loose from its moorings and is coursing throughout the body wherever the blood flows." Yet Dossey takes the body-mind theory one giant step further. His description of the "nonlocal" nature of mind places it not only outside the brain but outside the body altogether. The multidisciplinary evidence he uses to back his assertion fills several books, but the basic theory boils down to this: The mind is not fixed in space and time; it is not generated by the brain or even the neuropeptides and neurotransmitters synthesized throughout the body. Rather, the mortal brain and body act as receivers for mind, in much the same way a television translates waveforms into pictures and sound. In this sense, Western scholars and researchers attempting to locate the mind in the brain or the body are operating from the same faulty perspective as someone who takes a TV apart to find out how it makes all those programs. If you throw your fancy new digital set out the window and watch it smash into a million pieces, *Good Morning America*, *Dancing with the Stars*, and *60 Minutes* will still be floating invisibly through the air, despite the fact that you can't detect them with your senses. So it is with nonlocal mind, implying that the thoughts, memories, and perspectives you hold will continue after your physical "receiver" shuts down and is buried in the ground. The nonlocal theory also asserts that your mind existed in some fashion before you were born.

Dossey's nonlocal mind theory coincides to a certain extent with Rupert Sheldrake's theory of morphogenetic fields in that both create a case for memory existing outside the body of the individual. Sheldrake himself has used the television metaphor in describing his theory to general audiences. His work suggests that the developing organism tunes most easily into channels related to its own species, fields of collective knowledge that influence the growth of the individual physically, psychologically, and socially according to patterns developed by past members of the same species. The process by which these fields exert their influence is called *morphic resonance*, or "form" resonance. Sheldrake's theory argues that the embryo in a pregnant mare becomes a horse because the fetal cells are tuned to the horse frequency and resonate with the field that carries the collective blueprint of the species, just as a string tuned to C will only resonate with another string tuned to C through invisible sound waves flowing between them. Yet biological entities are much more complex than strings, gaining information and altering their behavior in response to the environment in myriad ways. As a result, Sheldrake specifies, ancestral thoughts and experiences not only affect existing members of the species; the thoughts and experiences of each new generation in turn add to and modify the morphogenetic field.

In his commentary on Sheldrake's work, Dossey asserts:

> The present does not come into being only to die, it is preserved in an invisible morphogenetic record that thereafter makes a contribution

to future events. In this way, thoughts are plowed back into the universe, into a kind of cosmic memory bank.... This view of the universe suggests that it is brimming with thought, alive with mind and consciousness. This is a view that sets the stage for nonlocal mind — mind unrestrained by space and time, mind not confined to the brains and bodies of single persons.

Sheldrake and Dossey both point out that many religious and philosophical doctrines support the notion of a cosmic mind, including Mahayana Buddhism's idea of *alaya-vijnana*, a Sanskrit term meaning "storehouse of consciousness," and Theosophy's description of the Akashic records, where every physical and mental event is encoded in subtle dimensions of time and space.

The Hindu and Buddhist principle of karma describes an invisible force generated by a person's actions resulting in ethical consequences, consequences that affect not only the individual's present existence but his character and fate in future incarnations. The implications of this ancient theory can be understood at a different level through the lens of Sheldrake's morphogenetic fields. Popular interpretations of karma hold that beings come into form to work out the transgressions of previous existences. Souls return to earth again and again until they finally resolve their karma and are released from the cycle of birth and death. However, karma could also be interpreted as a collection of memories, habits, and perspectives that come together in the morphogenetic field to create the physical and psychological profile of a person who is challenged to alter the field itself. Whether the soul reincarnates, goes to heaven, travels to the otherworld, or becomes one with the mind of creation is not the issue in this model. Successfully working out one's karma transforms dysfunctional elements in the overall human morphogenetic field, an act that ultimately benefits future generations. Past life memories accessed through hypnosis or sometimes accidentally in times of crisis would not necessarily confirm an individual actually lived in another era. A person formed to change a destructive behavior pattern in the human morphogenetic field could just as easily be accessing the stored experiences of others who suffered as a result of that pattern in the past. In this sense, karmic forces would allow the person to tune into his spiritual lineage and retrieve the memories of those whose unfinished business he has been called to complete.

Though Sheldrake has a PhD in biochemistry and cell biology from the University of Cambridge, his theories have outraged more conventional scientists who've invested their careers in discovering how DNA carries a "genetic code" that somehow governs everything that happens to a developing organism. Sheldrake argues that since the bone, liver, and brain cells of an individual all contain exactly the same DNA, these researchers are putting an inordinate amount of faith in genetics as they desperately search for some mysterious hidden factor, some all-powerful internal ordering device that supervises the different cells to develop for specialized purposes.

"DNA, by providing the code for the sequence of amino acids, enables the cell to make particular proteins. That's all DNA can do," Sheldrake asserts.

> DNA helps us to understand how you get the proteins which provide, as it were, the bricks and mortar with which the organism is built, but it doesn't explain how these bricks and mortar assemble into particular patterns and shapes. The idea of DNA shaping the organism or programming its behavior is a quite illegitimate extrapolation from anything we know about what DNA does.... So what starts as a rigorous and well-defined theory about the way DNA codes the RNA and how RNA codes the proteins, soon turns into a kind of mystical theory in which DNA has unexplained powers and properties which can't be specified in exact molecular terms in any way at all.

The genetic code these scientists are struggling to crack in essence performs the same functions as Sheldrake's morphogenetic fields. The only difference is that conventional biology insists on limiting its search to a "mechanism" embedded in physical matter isolated from influences "outside" the body, while Sheldrake entertains the idea that the development and destiny of the individual is shaped by a collective nonmaterial force.

Mainstream geneticists remain loyal to reductionist notions of reality even as nonmaterial forces are embraced in physics, where it's been found that electromagnetic and gravitational fields act on material entities, sometimes over incredible distances, as in the moon's gravitational pull on the earth's oceans. Yet orthodox biologists have held book-burning parties in Sheldrake's honor because he has the nerve to suggest an invisible field might provide the missing link in determining how a chicken egg stays focused enough in its multifaceted development to produce a chicken — and that these same fields might shape the thoughts, behaviors, and calling of the individual.

A number of innovative scientists have put forth the notion that DNA doesn't so much contain a genetic code as it operates as a receiver for non-material information. In their book *The Living Energy Universe*, Gary E. R. Schwartz, PhD, and Linda G. S. Russek, PhD, discuss their universal living memory theory. Using established scientific tools and studies, these University of Arizona researchers show that all dynamic systems have memory; this includes not only complex biological organisms but subatomic particles, water, cells, crystals, batteries, electronic equipment, rainbows, planets, and even the vast reaches of empty space between celestial bodies. Through a vigorous discussion of resonance, physics, homeopathy, genetics, electric currents, and a host of strange yet repeatable experiments that challenge conventional scientific precepts, Schwartz and Russek demonstrate that everything in the universe is alive, eternal, and evolving. In a strange twist of fate, they use conventional science, logic, and empirical evidence to argue that every idea ever thought, every awareness ever generated is retained in the universe as information or memory. They also suggest that material and nonmaterial forms of information interact and evolve in response to one another. The universal living memory theory makes a strong case for the long-held yet up to now scientifically suspect assumption that consciousness survives death and, furthermore, that God not only exists but evolves through the interactions, perceptions, and input of all of creation.

Schwartz and Russek's theory embraces the idea of a big bloom as opposed to a big bang origin to universal development. The term, which comes from a footnote in Ken Wilber's 1996 book *A Brief History of Everything*, coincides with the Schwartz and Russek model of a living, remembering, self-revising universe in which all things are "in an energetic state of creative 'becoming,' a universal revising process of dynamic perpetual bloom."

The "systemic memory process" at the heart of this theory rests on a revised picture of the physics of resonance. Using the sympathetic vibrations exchanged between two tuning forks as a pivotal example, Schwartz and Russek describe the "reductionistic" versus "systemic" view of how information is exchanged:

> The nonsystemic (reductionistic) story is that when we strike tuning fork A and it begins to vibrate, the air begins to vibrate, and this vibrational wave travels to tuning fork B. Since tuning fork B is like tuning fork A (same size, shape, and constitution), it responds to the vibrating energy coming from tuning fork A and begins to vibrate in synchrony with it.

Of course what my elementary physics class failed to tell us was that after tuning fork B began to vibrate and generate sound, those sound vibrations would begin to travel back to tuning fork A... and A would now have the possibility of resonating with B!

If tuning fork A is separated from B, A will carry a systemic memory of its interactions with B and vice versa. The implications of this mutually influential process are further elaborated in the work of Nikola Tesla, the inventor of alternating current (AC) motors and generators that brought electricity to people around the world. He actually envisioned collapsing buildings through the subtle yet extremely powerful mechanics of sympathetic vibration. To explain how Tesla proposed to swing a building beyond the capacity to hold its form, Schwartz and Russek describe two ways to push a child on a swing:

> One way is through brute force. If we are strong enough, we can pull the child way back or push the child way forward, and begin each swing with a bang. We could call this the big bang approach to swinging. The other way is through gentle force. Here what we do is apply a soft force, and as the child swings slightly back and forth, we add a gentle push with each cycle of the swing. We "sympathize" with the cycle (vibration) of the child, and little by little, the child swings out further and further. We could call this the big bloom approach to swinging.

Tesla proposed that if you measured the subtle, spontaneous swaying of the Empire State Building, began to shift your weight gently and consistently in synchrony with the skyscraper, and continued this interaction over a long enough period of time, the big bloom of your swing would eventually topple the building. "What Tesla realized was that everything — yes everything — was vibrating," Schwartz and Russek emphasize. This vibratory conception of reality explains how seemingly inconsequential forces can move much larger, more solid objects in surprisingly effective ways.

My awareness of the Horse Ancestors began with an almost imperceptible feeling of pressure. The sensation grew steadily over time, until the colossal edifice of cultural conditioning portraying spirits as figments of the human imagination finally toppled under the influence of a gentle yet ultimately overwhelming force. The big bloom of this ancestral effort culminated in an opening of consciousness, rewarded and reinforced by the gift of the lavender rose, a flower that in turn symbolized the blooming of my soul's own destiny as a natural process to be nurtured, not forced. My willingness to experiment with this more expansive mindset led me to explore ways of actually communicating with a field of thought and memory previously of no more consequence to me than a single person leaning against the world's tallest building.

The Living Energy Universe employs this resonance to outline a model for the storage, retrieval, and continued evolution of memory outside the human body. At one point, Schwartz and Russek discuss how radio transistors and other receivers pick up signals by resonating with incoming vibrations, leading to theoretical possibilities for how other types of more subtle information might be accessed in the future. As they write:

> If universal living memory is ultimately everywhere, spanning out into the vacuum of space, then the possibility exists for everything to potentially register everything. A metaphor most of us can grasp is the modern development of cell phones.... Phone calls from hundreds of thousands, if not millions of people, are streaming down from satellites, going here and there and everywhere, including to my desk. But I do not hear any of them. However, my phone is tuned so that it can register a certain pattern, start ringing, and initiate communication. It serves as an antenna, tuner, and amplifier.

Schwartz and Russek muse that if the "Grand Organizing Designer," or GOD, is everywhere, spreading universal memory through the farthest reaches of time and space, making it possible for us to have access to information beyond our personal experience, "then how," they ask, "can we tune into all this information?" Their answer: "We need a Dynamic Noetic Antenna (if not a Divine Noetic Antenna)." Schwartz and Russek are among a handful of scientists who suggest that DNA might fulfill this role, making a case for the idea that DNA doesn't have the information needed for an organism's existence but, rather, tunes into it. In setting up this conclusion, Schwartz and Russek cite the work of Stanford University anthropologist Jeremy Narby, author of the book *The Cosmic Serpent: DNA and the Origins of Knowledge*: "Narby suggests that DNA may function as a receiver for a class of photons called biophotons. Since all electromagnetic signals, including bioelectromagnetic signals, can be viewed as being 'photons' — visible and invisible — the hypothesis that DNA and other molecules may function as selective resonators for photonic information and energy is challenging."

Though the terminology is different, Sheldrake's theory of morphogenetic fields coincides with Narby's notion of biophotons. Sheldrake specifies that morphic fields operate less like gravitational or electromagnetic fields and more like quantum matter fields. In quantum theory, if two particles have been part of the same system and then move apart, they retain a mysterious connection at a distance, called *quantum nonlocality* or *nonseparability*. Sheldrake expands on this model to not only describe how members of a particular species can be affected by one another at a distance but how interspecies associations might create their own nonmaterial fields of influence. His extensive observations of human-animal relationships suggest that morphic fields are created when living creatures form an emotional bond. The greater the bond, the stronger the field. When members of the same social group are apart, these fields continue to connect them and act as a channel for communication, offering a theoretical framework for the concept of telepathy.

Over the years, people who've had unusual experiences with their companion animals have embraced Sheldrake's theories. The scientist became privy to so many of these tales that he actively began to research the phenomenon of telepathy between pets and their caretakers, resulting in his book *Dogs That Know When Their Owners Are Coming Home, and Other Unexplained Powers of Animals*, which offers extensive statistical, anecdotal, and experimental evidence to support his theories.

When I read Sheldrake's text and Schwartz and Russek's *The Living Energy Universe* four years after I felt the presence of the Horse Ancestors, I was relieved to find that their ideas and observations aligned with my highly irrational experience. According to the theories explored above, however, my own genetic lineage provided me with the Dynamic Noetic Antenna to feel the calling of a seemingly extinct form of interspecies knowledge. Tracing my heritage back to the prehistoric horse tribes of Ukraine, I experienced a profound and at that time primarily nonverbal resonance with a culture based on both human and equine patterns of thought and behavior. The way of life emerging from this partnership thrived for three thousand years before it was finally suppressed by early city dwellers, creating a field of collective memory as substantial as any subsequent cultural movement. Civilizations thereafter enslaved the horse, using the species as a beast of burden to subdue and conquer the natural world rather than live in harmony with it. Even so, the wisdom of this far more ancient association lived on, waiting for the right moment to whisper its perspective to people with the desire and capacity to listen. My experiences resonating with the horse tribe during those long summer afternoons at Timothy Graham's Oasis strengthened the intuitive skills I needed to tune into this field of influence. In the process, I discovered that the force which defined itself as "wisdom that gives rise to the form of the horse" was alive and continuing to evolve as it waited for the right moment to reassert itself in the world. The Horse Ancestors had memory. They had an agenda. And they had the will and creativity to assert their perspective whenever the opportunity arose.

As I trusted my senses and intuition enough to accept this possibility, I realized that the Horse Ancestors represented a systemic viewpoint. Schwartz and Russek characterize the reductionistic, or nonsystemic, approach to nature as relying on the following concepts: independence, separation, closed systems, linear forms of thought and action, mindsets concerned with parts of the whole. Systemic concepts, on the other hand, promote interdependence, relationship, nonlinear as well as linear thought forms, circular interaction as opposed to linear action, wholes rather than parts, and flexible, creative approaches to processing experience. Compared with the reductionistic viewpoint, the systemic approach is dynamic rather than static, open rather than closed, interactive rather than active, connected rather than disconnected. In *The Living Energy Universe*, this mindset is represented as a sophisticated, evolutionary innovation capable of redefining scientific inquiry, yet the horses I lived and worked with already operated systemically every day. It was their influence that brought me out of the rigid, reductionistic, postconquest mindset. These animals helped me reawaken the sociosensual mind-body perspective and experience the gut-level exchanges of information that take place through resonance. Ultimately, my interactions with the horses put me on a path I never could have imagined in my wildest dreams. As I rode and trained them, they transformed me.

The Borderlands

It wasn't until I fully embraced the wisdom of the horse that I finally felt comfortable being human, a seemingly paradoxical feeling shared by a number of men and women who've made great strides in the Eponaquest program, clients who have attitudes, difficulties, and gifts in common. Like me, these people admit to feeling alienated by the society in which they were raised. Though highly creative, intuitive, and perceptive, many have trouble functioning in the so-called real world. Most suffer from a strong yet unfocused sense of calling, a feeling they have something important to accomplish during their lifetimes. None of the available careers or degrees, however, hold their interest for long. Some of these people float aimlessly from one job to the next, perpetually starting some dazzling new career or course of study, only to abandon it six months later. Others endure years of drudgery in a single unfulfilling position because they can't think of anything they'd rather do more. As a result, they suffer bouts of severe depression; some even consider suicide. Two of these people, in fact, told me concern for a beloved pet was the only thing that kept them from pulling the trigger.

Which brings me to the most consistent feature of this group: they're more comfortable around animals than humans. Because they're empathic, if not telepathic, these people tend to feel uneasy, even paranoid, in public situations. Like Noche, they sense the negative, sometimes aggressive emotions under those smiling faces, and they develop a pronounced mistrust of the human race. The coping strategies arising from their marked discomfort with incongruent people can be debilitating. Some of my clients deal with the distress by withdrawing, becoming shy and reclusive. Others depend on alcohol and drugs to turn down the volume. Still others invest all their hope and energy in a single romantic relationship, depending on one individual to satiate their craving for human companionship and ultimately driving their lovers away through extreme neediness. Regardless of how they express and deal with their anxiety, however, these individuals wonder if they'll ever fit in. They feel out of time, out of place, trapped in a culture that makes no sense to them.

I've come to recognize these people as *Borderland personalities* (not to be confused with the psychological profile of the border*line* personality). The term was invented by Santa Fe–based Jungian analyst Jerome S. Bernstein, who first noticed the phenomenon in a female client with many of the characteristics mentioned above. Hannah was a highly sensitive artist who painted angst-filled portraits of animals in various stages of stress, mutilation, and torture. Like many of the people I work with, she had trouble distinguishing between her pain and the pain of other beings. She lived in an almost nightmarish world of perpetual distress; yet, according to Bernstein, her dismal paintings also expressed the possibility of transformation. At first, he interpreted her stories of empathic shared awareness with stray dogs and cattle being taken to slaughter as projection, a simple case of a woman with a history of abuse identifying with animals she perceived to be in a similar situation. However, much to Bernstein's credit, he began to see into Hannah's plight much more deeply. He experienced a sense of numinosity in the room during descriptions of her interactions with other creatures. "The feeling was attached to Hannah, yet it was separate from her," he wrote in his article "On the Borderland" in the *Noetic Sciences Review*. "It seemed of a different dimension." Bernstein began listening to her more closely, trying "diligently to shut off my mind and my training." At first, "it seemed she was groping for a vocabulary that was beyond her reach — a vocabulary that perhaps yet didn't exist," but as Hannah became more adept at expressing her feelings, Bernstein realized her worldview coincided with that of the Hopi elders with whom he had studied while completing his analytical training. Borderland personalities and tribal peoples have one significant feature in common: a psychic connection with nature inseparable from spiritual and physical health. Borderlands, however, are thrust into a role for which their own culture simply does not prepare them.

On the basis of his experiences with Hannah, Bernstein went on to develop a description of the Borderland personality: a person who inhabits the "psychic space where the overspecialized and overly rational Western ego is in the process of reconnecting with its split-off roots in Nature.... Such people are the front line recipients of new psychic forms that are entering and impacting the Western psyche. They experience the tension resulting from split-off psychic material reconnecting with an ego that resists and is threatened by it."

As I read these words, I couldn't help thinking of my genetic and psychological connection to Ukraine, a name that literally means "borderland." This powerful synchronicity suggested that the Horse Ancestors not only physically inhabited a geographical region known as the Borderland in the distant past, they were current residents of a psychic space also known as the Borderland, a nonmaterial region of influence with the intent to reform the human relationship with nature — in the Ancestors' case, through the wisdom of the horse.

Bernstein describes the Borderland as an evolutionary dynamic on which the very survival of the human race depends. The people he has dubbed

Borderland personalities "experience and incarnate these new psychic forms into their lives." As I thought about it, I realized that if, in fact, Bernstein's insights were right, the phenomenon wouldn't be limited to human partic-ipation. Rasa herself was a Borderland personality, a horse who performed the role of liaison between the equine and human realms, both in her own herd and in my equine-facilitated practice. The transformational, often nu-minous horse-human interactions taking place through our work seemed to actually conjure up the Borderland, to draw it out of theory and into the field of experience. In an Eponaquest session, the collective improvisational interplay of all the participants created new patterns of behavior and aware-ness. The fact that I — and many of the people I worked with — admitted to feeling more balanced, more comfortable being human after we connected to and finally embodied the wisdom of the horse made us ideal case studies for the Borderland concept as well. Many of the therapeutic and educa-tional techniques used in the Eponaquest program were developed through the cocreative participation of horses and humans. Ours was an interspecies effort to bring new psychic forms into existence. The initial emphasis on feeling over reason, however, was only an intermediary step in reuniting the two. The ultimate goal and result of this work induced what Christian de Quincey characterized as "a transmodern spiritual or mystical intuition — a way of knowing that includes and integrates" the preconquest and postcon-quest mind. Our interactions along the Borderlands of human and animal consciousness fostered a systemic perspective, giving people a profound experience of interdependence with nature. That experience marked an evolutionary step forward from the dependent and independent stages of human-nature development, stages we were supposed to pass through on our way to embracing a more expansive worldview.

As I integrated this theory into my practice, I realized much of the anx-iety my clients endured stemmed from the discomfort of remaining in a state of arrested psychospiritual development. Rather than moving toward the integration of reason and feeling, they were either fighting against the postconquest world or stuck in the reductionistic mindset, one designed to create a healthy sense of self-awareness, emotional autonomy, and intellec-tual facility in adolescents and young adults. The postconquest perspective, however, was not the goal or culmination of human evolution. Our culture's relentless promotion of reason disconnected from feeling, intuition, and na-ture suggested that civilization itself was in a state of arrested development.

Borderland personalities, the people most uncomfortable with this situation, were literally being challenged to change the pattern, to create the forms through which society itself could reunite with nature in a cocreative relationship. These people had the psychological disposition to serve as liaisons between the spirit and material worlds, the human and animal realms, the habits of the past and the possibilities of the future, the local mind and the nonlocal mind. They were the shamans of modern Western civilization. Like the wounded healers of tribal societies, their inability to fit into the mainstream was not a form of pathology but evidence of a calling to help move humanity out of its adversarial relationship with nature. The suffering experienced by these Borderland personalities grew steadily in direct proportion to their efforts to ignore this calling.

Those of us who spent the greater part of our lives trying to fit the round peg of our holistic leanings into the square hole of reductionism experienced a lack of fulfillment and increasing anxiety. By forming a multispecies support system, exploring and developing the very talents that caused us so much trouble in the postconquest world, we all began to blossom. Clients who confessed to a long-standing discomfort with being human felt validated, empowered, and, finally, just plain comfortable. Artists who previously led frustrated, incongruent existences on the fringes of society gained greater access to nonverbal forms of awareness and learned how to integrate and transform in relation to their own symbolic insights. Counselors frustrated with conventional forms of talk therapy developed their intuitive, sociosensual, and empathic abilities. Disillusioned riding instructors realized they didn't have to cater to the show world, that they could run successful businesses emphasizing a noncompetitive approach to the equestrian arts. Horses considered too old, too lame, too emotionally damaged, or too uncooperative to be of use competitively excelled in the consensual, cocreative environment of equine-facilitated therapy and experiential learning.

In this respect, Noche became one of the unexpected stars of my equine-facilitated practice. When I first began seeing clients at the barn, I tried to protect the mustang from people uncovering strong emotions, limiting his participation to beginner riding lessons with my most stable students. Joy's interactions with Noche, however, changed my opinion of his potential as a therapy horse. The experience motivated me to welcome other "problem horses" into the Eponaquest herd, including Hawk, who had initially dealt with his insecurities by becoming aggressive. In the process,

I found that equestrian activities carried out in a therapeutic rather than a competitive mindset created the conditions for troubled horses and troubled people to heal one another. As Noche and Hawk mirrored the complex emotional states and dysfunctional coping strategies of our most extreme cases, the horses began to transform at the same time as their clients became more stable and empowered. I watched victims of some of the most disturbing acts humankind could ever imagine inspire behavioral changes in these animals that professional trainers could accomplish only with great difficulty. The horses were able to do the same for traumatized people. Staring into the vast reflecting pools of the equine mind, I realized that healing was less about helping someone analyze her childhood or work toward some preconceived goal than it was about helping her reconnect with the world from a position of empowerment and compassion, expanding her awareness to see things as they were, moment to moment. Only from the vantage point of fully experiencing and participating in the present did the past make sense and the future show its potential.

Harvard professor Edward O. Wilson, author of a number of books, including *Biophilia: The Human Bond with Other Species*, argues that people are genetically predisposed to be close to animals, plants, and other aspects of nature. Throughout thousands of years of development, the human brain developed circuitry to communicate with and evaluate the behavior of other animals. Only in the last century has it become possible for large numbers of people to insulate themselves from nature in the concrete jungles of their own design. In *Kindred Spirits: How the Remarkable Bond between Humans and Animals Can Change the Way We Live*, veterinarian Allen M. Schoen proposes that the theory of biophilia may "help explain co-species healing." He writes:

> The classic definition of healing is to make whole. And if we acknowledge that we are part of nature, being whole means taking advantage of all the opportunities nature provides to calm our soul and spirit. Although science has no definite answers, why not assume that sharing a home with a dog, a cat, or a bird — or sharing our lives with a horse or any other large animal — has therapeutic benefits that are deeper than simple stimulation of the opiate receptors in the skin through touch? Perhaps, through our connection with animals, we are stimulating some deeply buried aspect of nature within us, rekindling a lost connection that allows us to be

more than solitary creatures, but part of something greater — and therefore more healthy, more whole.

The polyvagal theory provides physiological structure to Schoen's idea that sharing our lives with animals "has therapeutic benefits." Add to this the hormone oxytocin, which buffers the flight-or-fight impulse in favor of a calm-and-connect response, and it becomes clear that *evolution has a heart*. Mammals possess innovations designed to move living beings from a purely instinctual kill-or-be-killed orientation toward an empathetic, mutual aid orientation. Through the ventral vagus, Stephen Porges emphasizes, "the neural pathways of social support and social behavior are shared with the neural pathways that support health, growth, and restoration." This encourages mammals to coregulate each other, communicating safety through connection, making it clear that our four-legged friends have nervous systems that promote caring for others.

I often encounter animal lovers who live alone by human standards. And yet they seem fulfilled and content. Clearly, their daily interactions with the horses, cats, dogs, donkeys, goats, and other soulful beings in their lives activate the same neural circuitry that people *should* but often fail to activate in one another. The postconquest mindset of dominance, incongruity, and disconnection works against biological imperatives designed to bring us together. Add to this ambitious theories about nonlocal mind and morphogenetic fields, and we do indeed begin to peer into that "deeply buried aspect of nature within us."

Once I formed a consistent and reliable alliance with the Horse Ancestors, I realized the level of wholeness needed to bring many of my two-legged — and four-legged — clients back to health involved aspects of nature that couldn't be seen, heard, or felt in normal postconquest states of awareness. Together, the horses and I developed techniques appealing to soul and spirit as well as to mind, body, and emotion, though the animals themselves didn't recognize these categories as separate. They were already operating from a holistic perspective.

"If there is an aspect of the mind that is indeed nonlocal," Dossey writes in the introduction to *Recovering the Soul*, "then this entity comes to resemble the soul — something that is timeless, spaceless, and immortal.... Unraveling the nonlocal nature of the mind is not just an exercise in psychology or science; it is an exercise in spirituality as well, because of the soul-like nature of mind that is nonlocal."

Dossey devotes an entire chapter in that book to human-animal relationships, paying special attention to the role of the shaman in tribal societies. *Shaman* is of Russian origin, coming from *saman*, a word in the Evenki language of Siberia designating a person who becomes a specialist in bridging the visible and invisible worlds as well as the human and animal realms. Ethnologists have come to apply this title to tribal healers, medicine people, and religious leaders from many cultures.

Among the qualities that made the shaman a cross-cultural phenomenon was the belief "that a kind of collective consciousness bound them together with the animal kingdom. So intimate was the sharing of the mind with the animals that shamans believed it possible to actually *become* an animal." Dossey goes on to quote the insights of Mircea Eliade, the preeminent twentieth-century scholar of religion. One of these passages from Eliade's 1964 book *Shamanism: Archaic Techniques of Ecstasy* mirrored my own experiences with Rasa and the Horse Ancestors with such accuracy that I'm compelled to requote it here:

The animal with which the shaman identified himself was...a mythical animal, the Ancestor or the Demi-urge. By becoming the mythical animal, man became something far greater and stronger than himself. We are justified in supposing that this projection into a mythical being, the center at once of the existence and the renewal of the universe, induced the euphoric experience that, before ending in ecstasy, showed the shaman his power and brought him into communion with cosmic life.

Dossey goes on to observe that

in the nonlocal, collective consciousness that wrapped man and animal together, it was not always the man who took the initiative in actualizing it. Sometimes the first overture was made by the animal. This is most obvious in the *call* of the shaman...and in his initiation....In the tradition of the Buryat shamans the tutelary animal is called the *khubilgan*, a term that can be interpreted as "metamorphosis."...Thus the tutelary animal not only enables the shaman to transform himself; it is in a sense his "double," his alter ego. This alter ego is one of the "souls" of the shaman.

During my heightened interactions with the Horse Ancestors, I sometimes slipped into the perspective of the horse who had become human. The story the Ancestors proceeded to tell of Rasa was a mirror image: that of a human who had become a horse. Some people would interpret these experiences as evidence of a horse soul reincarnating in human form and vice versa. Others would simply figure I had fallen completely off the deep end. To me, however, it didn't much matter if I actually had been a horse in a previous life, if I was tapping into the equine morphogenetic field, or if I was engaged in a shamanic form of shared awareness with my khubilgan. The result was that I had to stay open yet focused enough to process all the verbal and nonverbal information I received in this state in order to fulfill my obligation to the Horse Ancestors. "Tell the story," they would chant over and over again, the pressure slowly building with each cycle of that three-word mantra. And so I began to conceive of a way to combine my strange experiences on the other side of reason with a book on horse-human relationships. In the process, I finally mustered up the courage to step out of my limited human perspective and witness some pivotal historical events from an equine point of view.

CHAPTER TWELVE

SACRIFICE AND COMMUNION

If, as Schwartz and Russek illustrate, everything has memory; if, as Candace Pert's research insists, even single-celled organisms relate to the world through the same molecules of emotion that affect human beings; if, as my experiences with the horses suggest, animals have opinions, insights, feelings, and even a sense of will and destiny, then what truly defines the human race in relation to all the other creatures with whom we share this planet? Philosopher and author Jean Houston once asked an Australian Aboriginal woman this very question. "Why, we are ones who could tell the stories about all the others!" she answered without hesitation.

"All stories are true," professed novelist and short story writer John Edgar Wideman. This blanket statement can, in fact, be taken literally, because myths, legends, parables, and modern fiction all point to the seen and unseen forces that affect our lives. Without the continually unfolding rhythms and revelations of story, these interconnected, constantly evolving processes would continue to influence us subconsciously, and we would live our lives at the mercy of impulses and reactions of which we had little or no awareness.

Long before I discovered the theories of Sheldrake, Dossey, and Schwartz and Russek, the collective mind known to me as the Horse Ancestors presented itself as "the wisdom that gives rise to the form of the horse." Through my interactions with this nonmaterial field of influence, I was exposed to the notion that everything in the universe emerges through the struggle of thought and meaning trying to express itself through form. I began to see paintings, mathematical equations, symphonies, books, stars, clouds, horses, people, and the life histories of those people as information-carrying processes and substances. This was the single most important concept in helping me to face the strange experiences I was having with increasing regularity.

Rather than try to explain them away in rational terms or disregard them as illusions, I decided not to worry about whether my visions, and the myths that arose from them, were real or not. Instead, I treated them as valuable sources of information that could be interpreted without always being taken literally, as one would gain valuable insights from Homer's *Odyssey* or Mark Twain's *Huckleberry Finn*. My ability to decipher the confounding elements of my own life motivated me to develop techniques and perspectives capable of helping others deal with truly horrific, psychologically paralyzing experiences. This transformational mindset relied on the systemic premise that everything is interconnected and everything has meaning, a notion contradicted by reductionist philosophy. Healing in this sense hinged on facilitating a change in perception so elemental, the person had to be willing to question the most basic premises of society. She had to be able to endure the dissolution of her culturally defined self-image and stare into the void that lies between her familiar persona and the newly emerging, fully empowered, authentic self. She had to be willing to die to be reborn.

No therapist, member of the clergy, medicine person, parent, teacher, or role model can do this for someone. People willing to assist in this process can only create a place of safety and support in which it may occur — when and if the person is ready. A therapist, coach, or educator can listen. She can help interpret the strange sights and sounds along the way. She can take responsibility for her own feelings so as not to further activate a person who is engulfed in a heightened, vulnerable state of awareness. At certain moments, she can even act as a catalyst for change. Mostly, however, she can help by being *present*.

Most people are literally afraid of nothing. They would much rather adapt to a faulty, dishonest system than give up the security of their perception of reality. They would much rather complacently survive in a rigid hierarchy than thrive in the ambiguities of freedom. Freedom demands inner, not outer, authority. It pulls the cultural rug out from underneath you and plunges you into the limbo of endless possibility, a void that can be traversed only through the most divine interpretation of creativity: the presence of mind, heart, and soul to literally conceive something from nothing, feel it bloom inside, and finally endure the pain and consequences of releasing it into the world. The ability to give birth to a child fertilized by spirit is a religious image at the heart of Christianity, Taoism, and many other religions. But it is also an inherently practical image in helping people navigate the mindscapes of transformation.

In part because it takes such courage to face the unformed, in part because our culture doesn't prepare us for it, in part because society as we know it would change dramatically in relation to our ability to embrace ambiguity, most people would rather stagnate in the security of the known than evolve in the creative uncertainty of the unknown. The ones who lead comfortable lives rarely make a move toward change. It's the ones who've been most profoundly betrayed by the system who are ready for something new. If we perceive the universe as an interconnected, continually evolving, intelligent system of thought, memory, and meaning, suffering looks more like calling. As Lao-tzu observed: "It is upon disaster that good fortune rests."

The call may come through poverty, the death of a loved one, personal illness, depression, chronic dissatisfaction, or a purely psychological prodding that something's not quite right. The Buddha was born into wealth and power, yet his search stemmed from a nameless sense of discomfort he couldn't ignore, a feeling that his life of ease was empty and meaningless. Whether the motivation to change grows out of physical, mental, or spiritual anxiety, those seeking to give up their pain, along with the worldview that goes with it, open their hearts, minds, and souls to unimaginable vistas of possibility. Those standing alongside the periphery of a person undergoing such a transformation cannot help but be inspired or frightened, for this process attracts the most potent forces of healing through metamorphosis. "Blessed are those who hunger and thirst, for they will be filled," said a man who resisted every possible earthly enticement to follow his destiny. According to the universal living memory theory, his words are still echoing throughout the cosmos, though it's difficult for the postconquest mind to resonate with the wisdom behind them. Schwartz and Russek present a strong case for the idea that "the great historical religious figure called Christ, and other monumental religious figures before him, such as Buddha, implicitly modeled what science now terms living systems theory. Moreover, with the aid of the logic of the systemic memory process, we find scientific support for the controversial spiritual hypothesis that Christ himself may not only be eternal and alive, but evolving as a living energy system as well."

Sheldrake's theory complements this notion by suggesting that marginally effective yet long-standing habits in the human morphogenetic field sometimes need a supernaturally charismatic figure to disrupt the flow and bring new psychological and behavioral forms into existence. The human predilection toward violence, disconnection, and control over others is such an incessant pattern that we still find it difficult to resist these urges, even though a number of enlightened beings throughout history have modeled a more effective and connected way to exist in this world. Once a person gets to the point where the words of Christ, the Buddha, and Lao-tzu truly make sense, however, the reductionist perspective begins to lose its power, and the lion cannot help but lie down beside the lamb.

Civilized Savages

In celebrating the opening of the Roman Colosseum in 79 CE, Emperor Titus sponsored a series of games lasting 100 days straight. Gladiators weren't the only attraction. Before the professional warriors fought in the afternoon, there were public executions around lunchtime and "beast hunts" in the morning. Many arrived early to enjoy the spectacle of exotic creatures from the most remote corners of the empire running around the enclosure, dodging arrows, spears, and sabers. It was reported that during the first day alone, five thousand animals were dispatched "with the right degree of cruelty." Among the many service buildings surrounding the arena was a huge disposal pit for all the corpses produced by this brutal form of entertainment. Subsequent emperors tried to outdo their predecessors and kept statistics for posterity. One of them bested Titus by holding games for 122 days in which eleven thousand people and ten thousand animals were reportedly slaughtered.

Cicero saw the carnage as much more valuable than mere entertainment. The Roman historian praised the games for their ability to desensitize people to bloodshed and prepare them for battle. The vast Roman Empire was managed by force and intimidation. During the four hundred years the games flourished throughout the empire, prisoners captured during conquests provided a convenient source of ongoing amusement for the citizenry. The persecution of the early Christians also offered ready-made sacrifices for the "spectacles." Since they refused to fight back, however, these people were usually ripped apart by bears, lions, and other large predators — just to keep things interesting.

Scholars have offered numerous explanations for blood sport, but basically they considered it a by-product of a value system emphasizing control over nature and control over your enemies. When Emperor Constantine the Great — a Christian convert — finally banned the games in 325 CE, experts credited the influence of Christianity and the prohibitive costs of continually importing exotic animals as the major factors leading to the demise of the Colosseum.

Many people I've met in environmental activism, animal rights, and equine-facilitated therapy exhibit a marked disdain for Christianity, citing it as the primary influence on modern society's use of nature as a commodity. Yet, very much to my own surprise, the Horse Ancestors emphasized a strong affinity for the original message of Jesus Christ. Here was a man who reinforced the nomadic, nonpredatory perspective at one of the most brutal times in history. He was born in a stable and laid in a manger. He encouraged people to give up their possessions and wander the earth, letting God through nature take care of their needs. He abhorred violence, even for self-preservation. Ultimately, his influence came, not through force, control, or even convincing intellectual arguments, but through communion — through a form of direct personal involvement so intimate that it became symbolized by the human consumption of his flesh and blood. These gestures so profoundly challenged the basis of Greco-Roman civilization that Christ was able to turn the tide of increasing violence within a mere thirty-three years of earthly existence, only three of which involved actually hitting the lecture circuit. For all the conflict we endure in modern times, at least we use our stadiums for football and not public executions, beast hunts, and gladiator games. If Christianity had only accomplished the eradication of Roman blood sport, that in itself would have been an admirable achievement.

At a time when the Greeks were combining logic with conquest and the Romans were engaging in the ultimate predatory power trip, Christ was emphasizing love, sacrifice, and heart-centered communication. He shared most of his insights as parables and allegories, forms of speech emerging directly from nonverbal experience. His own spiritual awakening was not so much an enlightenment as it was an immersion in the waters of emotion, intuitive knowledge, and the rivers of collective wisdom that flow just beneath the surface of conscious awareness. To this day, baptism remains a primary sacrament in the religion he inspired, second only to communion in importance.

As I revisited his story from the Horse Ancestors' perspective, I recognized the image of the lion lying down beside the lamb in paradise as a Judeo-Christian formula for a well-adjusted human psyche, in which the predator works in harmony with the prey. At a time when human civilization was identifying almost exclusively with predatory modes of behavior, Christ declared himself the Lamb of God to create a powerful model capable of righting the balance. At the Last Supper, he gave away his life as food for others in the symbolic sharing of his flesh and blood. In this act, he made it clear that he wasn't facing execution merely as a martyr for a belief system; he was in part taking on the role of a prey animal in a way that was public enough and dramatic enough to reawaken this impulse in the human psyche whenever and wherever his story would be told.

The idea of a human being consciously adopting and accepting this role is associated not only with self-mastery but with the ability to transform the very creatures who eat this flesh. The Buddha, in a previous incarnation as a prince named Mahasattva, threw himself into the lethal embrace of a starving tiger and her four cubs. As the legend goes, this not only allowed him to progress toward enlightenment in a subsequent life, the predators who thrived as a result of his sacrifice were reborn as the Buddha's first five disciples. The predator/prey symbol for human wholeness also made its way into pagan Europe, most notably through the Celts' association with the horse. When the early Celtic tribes came in contact with Eurasian steppe nomads, these ancient Europeans absorbed not only the equestrian arts into their society but a predator/prey concept of balance as well. Statues of the horse goddess Epona depict a woman surrounded by horses and dogs, often in conjunction with the snake, an emblem of healing for the Celts. At a symbolic level, this image suggests the cooperation of predator and prey aspects in the human psyche, with the snake underlining the transformational qualities of reuniting this particular pair of opposites in the presence of a feminine archetype.

Information about the peoples credited with domesticating the horse in Ukraine around 4000 BCE is sketchy. However, descriptions of later versions of the nomadic horse tribes show that they were as much influenced by horse behavior as by human behavior at times and were in fact able to outmaneuver significantly larger Greek and Persian armies, because Scythian and Sarmatian horse cultures emphasized flight over fight as an honorable battle strategy. Early city dwellers returned from campaigns in the steppes with stories of women warriors they called Amazons, which their fellow countrymen found as fantastic as legends of Harpies and one-eyed giants. Around the time of Christ, however, the descendants of the horse tribes had already evolved into an increasingly patriarchal, seminomadic society influenced by trade relations with the Greeks and the Romans, who considered it a form of madness to give power to women. As feminine forms of wisdom lost status in the steppes, later nomadic cultures, including the Cossacks and the Mongols under Genghis Khan, became more cruel and predatory. Even so, the creation mythology of the Mongols continued to emphasize the union of predator and prey characteristics in the human soul — the first man was believed to have arisen from the mating of a wolf and a deer. Both animal figures were of equal importance at a totemic level, despite the fact that warriors invoked the more aggressive power of the wolf to assist them in battle. Still, these people recognized that the horse, a domesticated animal sharing the feminine or prey qualities inherent in the deer, was the foundation upon which a war could be won. For mythological and practical reasons, Mongol women maintained a level of political, social, and legal leverage unusual in other Asian and Near Eastern societies at that brutal time.

The rise of Muslim fundamentalism in recent decades has been similarly tempered in modern horse-based tribes. Thomas J. Barfield, professor and former chairman of Boston University's Department of Anthropology, has done extensive research on pastoral nomadism in the Near East and Central Asia. In travels to Afghanistan, he observed that nomad women weren't bound by the same rules of seclusion and veiling ruthlessly enforced in sedentary villages and cities, already stringent laws that were further enhanced when the Taliban took power in 1996. Since then, city-based women have been stoned in public for accidentally exposing an arm or even for simply forgetting to put the mesh covering in front of their eyes while wearing a burqa. Women must wear silent shoes so they can't be heard, and the windows of their homes must be painted over so they can't be seen. Barfield's research took place before the Taliban rose to power, and as of my interview with him in the late 1990s, he had seen no direct reports of the status of pastoral cultures under that more recent regime. Still, the differences between the treatment of sedentary and nomadic women were so pronounced that he said that he would "be surprised if the Taliban were enforcing veiling of nomad women in the countryside, although they might in cities."

For centuries after women completely lost their power in settled communities throughout the Far East, the Mediterranean, and the Middle East, ancient and modern horse tribes maintained a more equal partnership between the sexes, taking cues from the prominent roles that mares often play in the herd. Among the skeletons of ancient Scythian and Sarmatian warriors unearthed from Ukraine to Mongolia's Altai Mountains in the mid-twentieth century, many were later determined to be those of young women. In addition, surviving historical records from the pre-Christian era, including the writings of Herodotus, illustrate that the Greeks considered the steppe nomads barbaric in part because women were active participants in traditional horse-based societies and often played significant leadership roles. These and other factors offer some important nuances to consider when entertaining theories espoused by historians like the late Marija Gimbutas, suppositions that portray these people as male-dominated, bloodthirsty barbarians determined to destroy a peaceful Eden of goddess-worshipping agricultural settlements.

Nomadic Consciousness

While they most certainly engaged in conquest, the Scythian and Sarmatian tribes were difficult to engage in battle at times precisely because they had no cities to defend. Like the horses they rode, the steppe nomads sometimes preferred flight over fight. Herodotus himself provides a number of colorful anecdotes illustrating their infuriating habit of disappearing into the endless grasslands at the slightest provocation. Despite such historical descriptions, however, some authors and lecturers continue to depict the nomadic horse peoples exclusively as patriarchal invaders responsible for eradicating a vast network of gentle matriarchal farming communities during a "Late Neolithic Crisis." Studies related to the migration of Indo-European languages provide evidence to this effect. However, anthropological studies of ancient and modern horse tribes suggest that it's much more difficult for nomadic cultures to oppress their women, pointing toward the ultimate decline of the matriarchal paradigm as an outgrowth of city-based lifestyles where horses could be corralled and women could be more easily restricted to sedentary pursuits.

Sarah V. Barnes has written a series of novels imagining how horses may have been domesticated, including her first, *She Who Rides Horses* (to which I contributed a foreword). As a historian, she based these books on extensive research into the earliest nomadic cultures, those who lived in the Eurasian steppes during the fifth millennium BCE (a good thirty-five hundred years before Herodotus wrote about the Scythians of his time). Barnes, who is also an innovative trainer, riding instructor, and equine-facilitated learning practitioner, brings her full knowledge of horses to the project, drawing some intriguing conclusions from the latest archaeological evidence.

"Scholars increasingly agree that the Yamnaya, nomadic pastoralists living in what is now southern Russia and Ukraine after 4000 BCE, were the first to domesticate and ride horses," she told me during several in-person, phone, and email conversations we've engaged in over the years. "Along with archaeological, anthropological, and linguistic evidence, studies of ancient DNA all point to the same conclusions. Strong evidence also suggests that climate change, beginning around the same period, contributed to competition for scarce resources, which in turn produced shifts in the human psyche and behavior."

In this regard, she finds insights by psychologist Steve Taylor particularly compelling. His 2018 book *The Fall: The Insanity of the Ego in Human History and the Dawning of a New Era* argues that, as Barnes wrote me in an email, "the difficult new environment encouraged separation: separation between the individual and the community, between the mind and the body, and between the individual and nature."

In Taylor's view, the impacted populations, including those of the Eurasian steppe, grew increasingly disconnected, hierarchical, oppressive, and conflict prone. The nomadic cultures that emerged during the fourth millennium BCE were able to exploit a region grown more arid because of climate change by domesticating the horse and adopting wheeled vehicles. Evidence suggests they grew more warlike and patriarchal over time.

"Gimbutas's theory, that mounted warriors from the east overran the peaceable agrarian societies of Old Europe, has gained considerable credence in recent years," Barnes says. "But we must be careful not to imagine that anyone riding a horse was a menace to civilized society or in some way blame horses as a species for their use as a technology of war, as some have tried to do. In fact, rather than heralding a clash of civilizations, the first wave of 'invaders' to impinge upon settlements on the eastern fringes of Old Europe may have arrived before horse domestication and may have consisted primarily of rogue bands of young males sent to annoy the neighbors rather than getting into trouble at home.

"In any case, whether discussing the Yamnaya of the fourth millennium BCE or the Scythians and Sarmatians of Herodotus's era, no human culture capable of convincing herds of unconfined equines to cooperate could do so without at least some of its members being able to connect with the animals on a deep bioenergetic level. The first riders had to have been empathic, congruent, and trustworthy rather than simply domineering and exploitative. Otherwise, the horses, most of whom still had a choice in the matter, would not have been interested in engaging in the relationship."

Barnes emphasizes that domestication was not an event, but a process that occurred over hundreds of years: "Individual horses, whose ecosystem was shrinking, and individual humans, roaming with their cattle, goats, and sheep over an increasingly inhospitable landscape, chose to form a partnership. By enabling unprecedented mobility, horses, along with the wheel, allowed the Yamnaya to survive amidst arid grasslands not amenable to agriculture or even earlier forms of pastoralism. Most likely that partnership first had to be established before horses could be turned to more warlike purposes. Ever since, horses have offered humans a reminder of the possibilities of connection, thereby mitigating the worst effects of the disconnected world that horses involuntarily helped humans to create."

Modern Western civilization, of course, is more heavily influenced by the Greco-Roman legacy, a sedentary cultural "innovation" that actively repressed both feminine and nomadic forms of wisdom, eventually assimilating a watered-down Christianity because the movement could not be fully subdued or ignored. Even so, the postconquest mentality of the Greeks, reinforced by the Roman talent for brute force, was just barely, and only occasionally, tempered by the influence of Christ's nonpredatory perspective. As civilization spread throughout Europe and then into what are now the Americas, politicians, warriors, and entrepreneurs craving the spoils of war joined forces with power-hungry church officials to use the bait and switch tactics of idealism, reciting Bible verses out of context to justify and distract people from all manner of destruction and carnage. This is the most profound incongruity at the heart of our society.

The Bible contains the collective wisdom amassed by a nomadic culture. Much of what seems paradoxical in the writings of Moses and Jesus — and the countless others who contributed to this multifaceted volume — makes perfect sense in the context of a nonsedentary lifestyle. In Genesis, when God accepted Abel's sacrifice of a lamb over Cain's offering of the fruits of his agricultural labors, the Grand Organizing Designer was stating a preference for the pastoral lifestyle, one subservient to the cycles of the seasons and the needs of the animals, one that represented the systemic interdependence of humans and nature. Though my intuitive interactions with the Horse Ancestors directed me toward this interpretation, I subsequently realized it wasn't an original idea, but one that often emerges from human-animal and human-nature collaborations.

Daniel Quinn's award-winning novel *Ishmael* and Jim Corbett's brilliant but lesser-known nonfiction work *Goatwalking* use the Cain and Abel story to make the same point. In this sense Cain's impulse to murder his brother and build the first city represents the lethal animosity nomadic peoples have experienced in the presence of sedentary cultures since the beginning of time.

Quinn's fictional narrator discovers this bit of wisdom while engaging in telepathic debates with a gorilla who discusses the Leavers, hunter-gatherers who live in harmony with nature, and the Takers, city dwellers who arose after the agricultural revolution and aimed to conquer all other life-forms, destroying many species in the process. Corbett describes the religious and philosophical realizations he gained from "goatwalking," wandering through the desert with herds of milk goats, engaging in the nomadic lifestyle for extended periods of time. In this practice, he reconnects with the original meaning of the sabbatical, the Judeo-Christian version of "doing nothing" designed to bring about spiritual insight and renewal.

As punishment for killing his brother, Corbett observes, Cain forgot the meaning of the Sabbath and lost connection to the redemptive powers of nature.

> For millennia Semitic peoples have called wilderness "God's land," distinguishing it from settled areas possessed and remade to fit human plans.... The sabbath day is a time to quit grabbing at the world, to rest, and to rejoice in the Creation's goodness. During the sabbath year all are to cease making their living agriculturally, supporting themselves instead from the land's spontaneous, uncultivated growth. Debts are to be canceled and slaves are to be freed. Land ownership also reverts on the jubilee year; no one shall permanently subjugate the earth or another person.

Our entire civilization suffers from Cain's forgetfulness. We've become a culture of obsessive overachievers, leading to a host of stress-related illnesses and greed-related acts of violence. Corbett emphasizes:

> Settled people work relentlessly to remake and possess the earth because they can live only in man-made habitats where they are subjugated and used by whoever controls the land. In contrast, nomads take life sabbatically, as a gift from "God's land." Rejecting Cain's way, the prophetic faith recalls its nomadic origins when making its offering of first fruits, beginning with the words, "My father was

a cimarron Aramean" (Dt 26:5). From Tibet to Morocco, Kazakhstan to Baja, nomads identify with the cimarron, the domesticated animal that goes feral, the escaped slave who knows how to be at home in God's land...opening nomadic consciousness to insights unknown to peoples who worship owner-masters because they can live only within the man-made world's make-believe boundaries.

Goatwalking also bemoans the postconquest gift for incongruent idealism: "In a society at war with man and nature, a religion of peace and love might be fantasized into creed, rituals, and otherworlds while its professed adherents continued to live by conquest." According to Corbett, "To choose freedom is to cease collaborating with organized violence....Learning to live by fitting into an ecological niche rather than by fitting into a dominance-submission hierarchy opens human awareness to another kind of society based on equal rights of creative agency for all."

In traditional pastoral cultures, the predatory side of humanity protects the herd. Animals aren't treated as commodities but as members of an interspecies society. When the herd is culled, it's a sacred act of necessity, one designed not only to modulate the population, to keep it in balance with the land, but, in some tribes, to consciously merge with the collective wisdom of that species. Much of the time, however, these people subsist on products made from the milk and in certain cultures the blood of living members of the herd.

In searching for accounts of modern pastoral cultures, I came across a fascinating book by Linda Schierse Leonard on the nomadic tribes of Siberia. *Creation's Heartbeat: Following the Reindeer Spirit* describes the time she spent with the Even people, a culture physically and spiritually interconnected with herds of migrating deer.

The souls of the people and the reindeer are interrelated and interdependent. Each Even person has a special relation to a particular live reindeer that is his or her spirit guide....Without a reindeer, a living Even person is not a human being, the elder told us, since the people's nature is half-human, half-reindeer. In a deep spiritual sense, the Even people feel that they are reindeer and that the reindeer communicate with them.

Traditional cultures living in close association with nature, especially those based on an intimate symbiotic relationship with a particular animal, have extensive taboos concerning the humane and respectful preparation of the nourishment an individual animal provides. The kosher code of the Jewish faith, in which a holy man actively blesses each creature before the slaughter, is the only remnant we have of this impulse in Western society. The Jewish tradition strictly forbids cruelty to animals, outlining the specific procedures, prayers, and spiritual mindset for mediating such a sacrifice. Interestingly enough, kosher laws forbid the ingestion of blood on the grounds that such an act would "commingle animal with human life streams." When Christ offered his blood as well as his flesh at the Last Supper, his powerful symbolic gesture would have been readily understood as the act of merging his life stream with those of his followers. The Even people of Siberia, who believe they are half human, half reindeer, do in fact ingest the blood of their animals. The close connection between the two-legged and four-legged members of such a society further shows why Christ easily moved back and forth between metaphors in which he was depicted as a shepherd and as a lamb. Holy Communion was, in part, an effort to balance the predation running amok in the Greco-Roman world, offering a potent transfusion of nonpredatory wisdom in the wake of increasing violence. According to modern theories presenting DNA as a tuner for nonlocal mind, Christ may also have given his flesh and his blood to people as a way of infusing their bodies with his essence at a cellular level, allowing them to resonate with his message and his living, evolving memory — long after he, and the way of life he represented, disappeared. Church doctrine insists the bread and wine are literally transformed into the flesh and blood of Jesus through the communion ceremony, suggesting Christ's universal living memory is activated and focused through the act of eating and drinking these soul-infused substances in remembrance of him.

It can be argued that the directive to spread the good news of Christ throughout the world was never intended to convert "savage tribes" to a sedentary lifestyle but to keep the nomadic perspective alive wherever city dwellers tried to subjugate humans and nature in support of a disconnected, materialistic cult of owner-masters. I use Greco-Roman culture as the primary example of this tendency because of its overwhelming influence on Western history as the carrier of the postconquest perspective. Writers like Homer and, as I later found, the Roman poet Virgil recorded evidence of a time going back to the Trojan Wars when these societies still pulsed with the intuitive insights of myth, mystery, and emotion to balance the newly emerging forces of reason. Even Aristotle, who laid down the tenets of formal logic, held an organic, as opposed to mechanistic, interpretation of the universe as a living process. Over time, however, reason conquered feeling and intuition, suppressing and eventually outlawing them as deftly as the Romans set out to physically subdue the whole of Europe.

Yet from Egypt to China, India, and beyond, all sedentary cultures engage in similar patterns of forceful assimilation, the hoarding of material goods, the subjugation of women and nature, as well as the evils associated with owner-masters who feel their authority should supersede that of the lowly serf or citizen. Even in twenty-first-century America, our supposed democracy continues to support this model in the form of business hierarchies. The CEOs of major companies, and all their knights and nobles, subject employees to increasingly longer hours for less pay and benefits than they deserve. If they bow down to the system — sacrificing the Sabbath, their inner sense of authority, and their family life — some of these people gain favor from their lords, but anyone who hopes to move up the ranks must embrace the doctrines of conquest, materialism, obsessive achievement, and incongruent idealism.

At the dawn of the Judeo-Christian heritage, Abel received a divine blessing for the newly emerging nomadic pastoral perspective. His brother Cain, on the other hand, represented a sedentary lifestyle in which nature was molded into subservience to human needs. When God rebuked his offering and the way of life it represented, Cain rebelled by murdering his nomadic counterpart and building the first city, a pattern that civilization repeated over and over again until the lifestyle Abel symbolized was effectively suppressed. The apocalyptic visions that rose in the wake of Christ's death emerged at the point when the pastoral perspective was being eradicated by Greco-Roman expansion. His resurrection, however, signified that the wisdom he represented survived as a nonmaterial field of influence actively trying to reassert itself in the world. From the nomadic point of view, many of the fearful predictions contained in the Book of Revelation have already come to pass: we live in a world ruled by the Anti-Christ, a sedentary, reductionist, power-hungry, sadistic, money-worshipping culture disconnected from nature and the creative life force behind it. The promised return of Christ could be interpreted as a divine assurance that the systemic, compassionate, cocreative partnership between humans and nature first embodied by the pastoral cultures of the world will reassert itself in time.

Many of us still hear the words of Christ in church and listen to politicians quote Bible verses, yet our culture doesn't come close to living the message of the nomadic savior. In contrast to Athena, the patron goddess of city
life, logic, and war, a female archetype springing fully formed from the head
of a god, Jesus was born of a virgin without the more aggressive influence of
mortal man to overpower his compassionate, emotional message. In so many
ways, the elements of his life and legacy can be interpreted as a collection of
feminine values asserting themselves in the extremely predatory, intensely
masculine Greco-Roman culture. Jesus came into form as a man because
no woman would have had a chance to be heard in such a context, but his
message was much more yin than yang.

In *Creation's Heartbeat*, Linda Schierse Leonard feels a redemptive message in the nomadic, pastoral lifestyle, one that's in alignment with the messages I received from the horses and then saw anew in the words of Christ
and Lao-tzu, two men who received their divine visions in water and wilderness and returned for a brief time to the city to recite the wisdom of the prey.
"In these dark times," she writes, "we need to acknowledge and draw on a
new feminine energy — one that is both gentle and caring, not controlling
or afraid. We need a feminine force that is wildly ecstatic yet resolute and
tenacious enough to move through the World's Dark Night. We need to
be conscious, courageous, and patient enough to descend into the psyche's
depths to wait for revelation there and accept it." For Leonard, that spirit of
transformation is embodied in the peoples who migrate with the reindeer:

> Today we search for sacred spaces in which we can move freely, ac-
> cording to our nature. Our search is spiritual and physical, and the
> regions that beckon to us are wilderness — the vast and empty areas
> where silence and solitude allow original vision. Instead of the ar-
> chetypal stories of possession of the land and of conquest of other
> peoples, by which our cultures have defined themselves and by
> which we have lived, we need to create a new, more compassionate
> and caring myth to live by, one of reverence for nature. We need
> to relearn the earth's cosmic melodies and follow its rhythms, as
> the Sami and the Even people follow the reindeer. Understanding
> the ways of the people who follow the reindeer may be part of a
> "new story" for the next century, a story of redemption that many
> of us just now are beginning to write. Perhaps if we can release the

reindeer spirit inside ourselves, we can learn to run freely across the land without possessing it.

Through the lamb, the horse, the reindeer, and many other species, the wisdom of the prey has been calling from every possible angle, challenging those who can speak to tell their stories — stories with different characters and settings overlaying essentially the same message: the salvation of the world depends upon the resurrection of a heart-centered, systemic, cocreative partnership among human beings, nature, and the Source of them both through the reawakening of a nomadic, sabbatical, nonpredatory, feminine perspective.

The visions I received in extended meditations with the Horse Ancestors provided insights into events I wasn't initially prepared to face: graphic illustrations of Roman blood sports, the persecution of the early Christians, the carnage of European expansion, and the manipulation of Christian images used to justify these conquests — religious and political concerns I never would have considered relevant to the wisdom of the horse. Yet members of the species had been present during these pivotal moments in human history. They had died in the Colosseum. They had carried knights through the Crusades and conquistadors through the New World. The Horse Ancestors insisted I find a way to communicate the significance of these events from an equine point of view. The disquieting and in many ways perplexing historical perspective I've presented above is a distillation of the visions and commentary I received from interacting directly with the equine morphogenetic field, grounded by historical research I conducted in response to the intuitive input I was receiving. I had no idea how or when I might put this information to use in any practical sense — until I began accessing ancestral memories in my work with traumatized horses.

CHAPTER THIRTEEN

MYSTICS WITH TAILS

When I stopped treating horses as lesser beings, my perspective on life changed, irrevocably. In the process, I glimpsed the history of our species through equine eyes and realized our colossal ability to manipulate the environment had been more of a curse than a blessing to these sensitive creatures. We had planted our fields, fought our wars, and built our cities with the sweat and blood of countless horses, who were profoundly traumatized in the process. As I engaged morphogenetic states of awareness in my work with "problem" horses, I noticed that abuses suffered by living members of the herd often triggered residual memories of these ancestral traumas. Many troubled animals also showed an uncanny affinity for human survivors of extreme experiences — and vice versa. Over time, I realized this attraction stemmed from a need to remember, grieve, and purge the injustices of the past through the process of emotional resonance.

I originally met "Tricia" when she attended a women's empowerment workshop I facilitated with Kathleen Barry Ingram. Tricia's interactions with horses and people were tentative at first. In group discussions, she would dissociate and look down at her feet much of the time, though she opened up after connecting with Rasa. By the end of the day, she was able to accept some support from the other women. The results were dramatic enough for Kathleen to suggest Tricia continue to work with the horses. For six months, Tricia alternated counseling sessions with Kathleen and equine-facilitated activities with me every other week.

Mindful of her history of physical, emotional, and sexual abuse, I decided to let Tricia interact with Noche during her first private visit to The Ranch. It took her twenty minutes and extensive coaching to catch Noche in the corral, even armed with plenty of carrots. At the hitching post, I tutored her in creating a calming, reassuring presence while grooming. Wary of her every move at first, Noche slowly began to relax, though he never appeared completely comfortable. With the halter and rope limiting his options, he was easy to lead in a way that suggested he had long ago learned not to fight these restraints. After Tricia removed the halter in the round pen, however, Noche quickly trotted to the opposite end of the arena. The forty-nine-year-old woman eventually succeeded in gaining his trust enough to stand next to him, but she was quick to comment that Noche's eyes became vacant when she got close, as if he had, in her words, "gone somewhere else."

I asked Tricia if she ever had this experience of "going somewhere else" in an uncomfortable situation. Warily, she described the time she was raped as a child by an older boy in the neighborhood, a pivotal event in her life that led to numerous instances of "checking out" when she felt even mildly intimidated. Though her assailant was convicted after Tricia testified in court, her parents refused psychiatric help for their daughter and told her to forget about the embarrassing incident. As she approached adulthood, no one seemed to notice or care that Tricia was dissociating with increasing regularity. In this state, she was shy, polite, and easy to manage.

At age twenty, Tricia put on a simple wedding dress and walked down the aisle in a trance. Her parents had been pressuring her to get married, and even though she felt she wasn't ready, she accepted the proposal of the first man who took an interest in her. As she raised two children, she endured a host of mean-spirited manipulations from her husband, eventually turning to alcohol to mask her grief and dissatisfaction. Sex made her "check out," as did her husband's constant criticisms and temper tantrums. In this dissociative state, she was powerless to defend herself, though she tried to shield her son and daughter from the man's perpetual angst.

As she analyzed these events, Tricia gained greater perspective on her coping strategies by drawing parallels between Noche's past and her own. I got the ball rolling by comparing her tortured complacency to the soulless cooperation Noche exhibited when Tricia led him to the arena.

"With the help of your parents," I told her, "it sounds like your husband managed to get you to stand still long enough to put a halter on you, and he's been leading you around in a fog ever since."

Tricia laughed and discussed the similarity in more detail. She also felt that the dominance tactics of breaking a horse were similar to being raped, and she proceeded to outline aspects of Noche's personality that mirrored her own, including mistrust, dissociation, a kind of resentful submission, a tendency to overreact to minor threats, and a desire to flee the moment she felt able. Much to my own surprise, Noche moved closer to Tricia as she spoke more candidly about the betrayals she had experienced. Rhythmically stroking his neck, Tricia found the courage to go deeper into the long-suppressed feelings behind the trauma with little prompting on my part. Even when she began to cry, the horse refused to leave her side. A look of profound concentration replaced his formerly blank stare.

Normally, Noche made quite an effort to move away from people in states of emotional distress, a tendency that had become helpful to me in assessing a client's unspoken feelings. The horse was off lead when Tricia burst into tears; he could easily have walked away. What made him choose to stay? Noche actually seemed attracted to her grief, as if he was resonating with, even trying to amplify, the feelings she expressed. Tricia's tears seemed to release something in them both. Over the next two months, the horse and the woman became increasingly outgoing, and Noche's fear of new people dissipated significantly.

The situation reminded me of an even more dramatic episode of emotional resonance told to me by a woman I had interviewed a year earlier. "Alicia," a forty-six-year-old computer programmer from New York City, was in awe of the strange circumstances surrounding her breakthrough with a horse. When she heard from a mutual friend about the book I was writing, she called to share her experience with me. Five years earlier, she had checked into an Arizona-based residential treatment center to deal with the multiple abuse issues that had destroyed her siblings and left her afraid to leave her own apartment. Alicia's brother had committed suicide. Her sister had turned to drugs. Alicia, on the other hand, had become a workaholic who built a successful computer software company before experiencing a severe nervous breakdown in her early forties. Throughout her most productive years, she managed to hide the horror of her childhood experiences from herself and others — except when it came to animals. Alicia suffered severe panic attacks whenever she saw a dog or cat. A simple jaunt to a neighborhood restaurant was a major ordeal as she found herself crossing the street back and forth, sometimes ten or fifteen times, to avoid contact with people walking their pets. Through several months of intense therapy, Alicia slowly came to terms with the shrouded elements of her past. Her parents were part of a secretive neo-Nazi subculture thriving in a small midwestern city where her grandfather had served as leader of the local Ku Klux Klan. The children were raised in a strict militaristic environment with zero tolerance for insubordination. Alicia had been beaten, starved, locked in small closets, and tied outside in the snow for minor infractions, yet even after she moved away from home, she never breathed a word of what she'd witnessed and endured.

Despite her ability to recollect and deal with these memories after the breakdown, however, she was unable to transcend her fear of animals. Finally, a counselor recommended that she attend a weeklong equine therapy session in Arizona. The treatment center had experienced considerable success with its riding program for troubled teens and was expanding the model to address the needs of adult trauma and eating disorder patients. Alicia was invited to attend the prototype. While everyone involved was optimistic, the staff had no idea how effective one of their horses would prove to be in resolving some of the most challenging issues a human being can face.

The first day, the participants were instructed to walk down the aisle of the barn and look at the various horses employed by the program. A group of counselors quietly discussed the animals' reactions as each person passed by. Many of the horses had experienced various forms of abuse and neglect before they came to the center. Over the years, the staff had learned to trust the uncanny ability of their four-legged assistants to show an immediate affinity for patients who either shared a particular horse's personality traits or had experienced similar forms of trauma. The counselors gained a deeper understanding of each person's unspoken issues simply by observing which mare or gelding seemed most attracted to the individual. That horse would also become a member of the person's therapeutic team.

As each participant was paired with his or her equine partner, the horses were led out of their stalls and crosstied in the center for a subsequent grooming session. A stately gray gelding named Moses had chosen Alicia. Some patients were more enthusiastic than others, but she was the only one who insisted on standing just outside the barn for the rest of the afternoon. Alicia watched her fellow participants brush, stroke, and talk to their horses. Even though an unexplainable fear kept her from approaching Moses, she did feel a strong connection to the horse. It was the first positive emotional response she had felt for any four-legged creature, at least as far as she could remember.

That night she awoke with a startling realization. She had in fact experienced a close relationship with an animal, the first and only puppy her parents ever gave her. But the dog was never intended as a conventional gift.

He was to be a sacrifice for the cause. The night before six-year-old Alicia attended her first day of school, her father killed this beloved pet in front of her. "If you share our secrets with anyone outside the family," he emphasized, "this is what will happen to you." The child survived by forgetting the terrors she witnessed so she would never even be tempted to confide in another human being.

The therapists on call at the hospital spent the wee hours of the morning helping her deal with the grief of this long-repressed memory. As the sun rose over the mountains, however, Alicia sensed that something else in her past was ready to surface. Still, she insisted on participating in the day's events. She was eager to see if she could work up the courage to touch Moses after discovering the source of her fear.

Back at the barn, the patients were encouraged to take part in an exercise designed to help them discover for themselves the affinities they shared with their horses. Alicia volunteered to go first. "As you approach Moses, ask him if he has something special he wants to tell you," her counselor suggested. "Try not to have any preconceived notions about what he might say, just go with the first thing that comes to your mind."

Moses was standing quietly in the crossties as Alicia took a deep breath, voiced the question, and walked toward him. The barn seemed to collapse around her. She suddenly found herself staring up at the ceiling and writhing on the ground two feet in front of the horse. Alicia cried out in agony, clutching both hands over her eyes. At first she couldn't tell if she was feeling the horse's pain or her own, then she saw her grandfather's face. It seemed that she was too young to speak. Her parents were there, but they didn't lift a finger to help her as the old man held up the needle and injected the dye. The color, of course, didn't take, but Alicia's eyes developed significant scar tissue as they turned from a cloudy shade of blue back to their original brown. She would never be a worthy specimen of her grandfather's precious Aryan race, and he made sure she was punished for it, over and over again.

The barn was silent as the staff gathered around and helped her to her feet. Through the entire ordeal, Moses just stood there, silently witnessing her convulsions of terror, grief, and anger as if he had expected them all along. Not once did he kick or rear or try to run away. How could Alicia possibly be afraid of him now? She took those last two steps toward Moses and gently touched his face. A single tear welled up in the horse's left eye. Alicia reached out and caught it in her hand.

By the end of the week, Alicia was grooming her friend, cleaning his hooves, leading him around the barn, and hugging him in his stall. At the wrap-up on Friday, each patient was given the chance to read a profile of his or her horse. Everything the staff knew about these animals was contained in a series of handsomely bound notebooks that were passed out during the final session. Alicia learned that Moses had been rescued from an unusually abusive situation in Colorado. When the animal control officer arrived at the scene one stormy winter morning, he found the horse emaciated, badly bruised, and suffering from exposure to the cold. As the officer went to put a halter on the horse, he also noticed that Moses had a needle protruding from the base of his left eye. No one ever discovered what terrible event had inspired that level of abuse, but the scar tissue was still there for any veterinarian to detect in a routine examination.

Though the therapists recognized early on that Alicia and Moses shared a similar history, the staff had no way of knowing that she was carrying around repressed memories involving a sadistic assault on her own eyes. The mere presence of a horse who had experienced a comparable trauma not only brought this information to the surface, it provided a sense of empathy and support that allowed her to process the horror of her discovery in an efficient and constructive way. Alicia was able to draw strength from the horse's quiet acceptance of his past. The generosity of spirit he embodied made her feel thankful and blessed, giving her the courage to finally move forward with her life. She continued her therapy as she returned to work and stopped by the local Humane Society one day to adopt an adult dog with few chances of finding a home.

Something in Tears

The human healing process relies, in part, on the ability to remember, grieve, and finally let go of the injustices of the past. But some traumas, like the assault on Alicia's eyes, take place before people are old enough to speak, making it much more difficult for clients to process early life experiences through talk-oriented counseling. Professionals who work with trauma survivors are always looking for better ways of accessing and releasing the nonrational, emotional imprints that subconsciously influence behavior. This, of course, is the primary concern in working with traumatized horses, simply because they can't speak.

In my initial efforts to rehabilitate Merlin, I certainly didn't expect him to discuss his original trauma and have a good cry. But I could see from his dangerous reactions to simple equestrian activities that something significant had been burned into his emotional memory, something that could easily turn violent with the slightest surge of testosterone or adrenaline. Though I made headway with TTouches, TTEAM groundwork exercises, and techniques used on human trauma survivors, Merlin's increasing cooperation and thoughtfulness would suddenly snap without warning. Some days, he'd act the perfect gentleman as he was saddled, bridled, and longed in full tack, performing every move with grace. Other days, he'd pull back, break the lead rope, and run off as I was reaching for the bit.

By that time, I knew the amygdala (a feature of both the human and the equine brain) was capable of hijacking the neocortex when one key element of a present situation felt similar to a past trauma, yet this didn't make it any easier to handle Merlin's unpredictable outbursts. The subconscious mind frantically responds to events only dimly similar to the original crisis with thoughts, emotions, and reactions imprinted long ago. Merlin's worst episodes seemed as dramatic as those I'd read in case studies of human torture victims and prisoners of war. Was his first trainer really that sadistic?

While I could create a safe, consistent training environment physically, I couldn't always project a calm emotional presence. With a horse who lived in a state of perpetual hypervigilance, it wasn't enough to be congruent. I actually had to *be* calm to calm him down. If I was stressed or frightened, Merlin would invariably resonate with those feelings. A tinge of anger or fear in me seemed to activate a memory in the horse that would quickly amplify into rage or terror. Before stepping into his stall, I learned to scan my body-mind for the slightest hint of tension or emotion, determine the message behind it, change a thought or goal or boundary in response, and breathe into the feeling until it lifted. If I couldn't release a particularly strong emotion, I avoided doing anything ambitious with the stallion. Instead I would spend time with a generous, stabilizing horse, one with a confident, healing presence like Rasa, who could coregulate my nervous system. Sometimes after spending an hour with the black mare, I would be calm enough to work with Merlin, but a devastating loss in May 1999 made me extra sensitive to emotion, in myself and others. This factor alone led to the most frightening encounter I ever had with the stallion, an experience that ironically inspired the most powerful moment of healing in our relationship, bringing to light intuitive talents and insights I never imagined existed.

My mother, Martha Kohanov, had recently died from a brutal form of cancer. My best friend and closest confidant, she had been the greatest supporter of my writing and my work with horses. Her loss was devastating to our entire extended family. When I was back home after the funeral, the horses offered support and a welcome respite from the grieving process at times, but I was in an intensely vulnerable state. My ability to use my own nervous system to coregulate Merlin's was severely compromised.

The coal black stallion also fit into the drama of my mother's passing in a synchronistic yet puzzling way: I had met him at the beginning of her three-month illness, and she'd died on May 23, 1999, Merlin's fifteenth birthday. It was her life insurance policy that allowed me to buy Merlin and embark on the strange, mind-expanding journey that subsequently unfolded over the next eight years, until his death at age twenty-three. To this day, I feel a sense of wonder when May 23 rolls around. Memories of the stallion and my mother converge on the bittersweet anniversary of his birth and her death. Sometimes encountering the number 23 in the most mundane circumstances inspires feelings of numinosity as my mind swirls with thoughts of them both.

That first summer together was particularly potent. We were both raw, yet he was there for me in ways I could never have predicted. Though most emotions would send Merlin into a violent outburst, he seemed completely unfazed, even comforted, by my grief. I spent many a night reminiscing and crying after everyone else had left The Ranch. I'd set Merlin free to run around the big private arena in the back, where I also set up camp for the evening. Merlin would mill around quietly beside my lawn chair and boom box as we listened to Steve's ethereal soundscapes in the moonlight. Sometimes, I would sing to him. Merlin seemed unusually tranquil yet attentive when I changed the lyrics to the traditional love song "Black Is the Color." It seemed to be his favorite among several tunes I made up or reworked to softly serenade him when no one else was around:

> Black, black, black is the color of my Merlin's hair.
> His eyes hold mysteries to declare.
> The handsomest face and the regalest of airs.
> He has a certain wisdom there. Beyond compare.

The soulful melody and feelings of deep affection I conveyed through those simple words seemed to reach into Merlin's heart and soften his gaze. The ebony-eyed stallion would gently step forward and let me hug his big, strong neck at those times, though he just barely endured TTouches and grooming during the day.

Two decades later, when I encountered the polyvagal theory, I was intrigued to find that Dr. Stephen Porges had created some sound protocols for healing. He specified that prosodic singing, especially in the range of a woman's voice, could activate the ventral vagus nerve complex, which conveys safety through connection, jump-starting healing and restoration circuits in mammals. The almost miraculous positive feedback I got from Merlin during my singing sessions adds evidence to support this notion, but I never formalized this as a rehabilitation technique, mostly because I was too shy to serenade him with people milling around. I was a violist, yes, but I was also a music critic who knew that my voice was not of public performance quality. Merlin didn't seem to mind. When I secretly sang to him, my tone took on a soft, luminous character I was incapable of conjuring up in any other setting. We held a tentative magic together that dissipated when the hot desert sun blasted over the mountains and drove the moon away.

One scorching afternoon, a friend and colleague drove up as I was reaching for Merlin's halter. I immediately sensed "Arielle" was extremely stressed, filled with a seething combination of anger, frustration, and grief. This wasn't surprising, considering that difficulties at work had led her to resign in the midst of increasing marriage problems. The recent death of one of her own beloved horses added insult to injury. Both of us were on the edge emotionally during that tempestuous summer, each apt to dysregulate the other, even though we had successfully worked together with special needs clients at times and always enjoyed each other's company.

As we exchanged a few pleasantries that day, I felt as if the electromagnetic field around her body was vibrating uncontrollably, leaping out six feet in front of her, and punching me in the stomach. I said whatever I could to get away as quickly as possible and practically ran over to Merlin's stall. I was so stunned by the irrational sensation of being attacked that I forgot to scan my body before I led the stallion to the arena. Had Merlin refused to put the halter on, had he become unruly as we walked across the property, I surely would have recognized my state of vulnerable agitation and simply turned him out. Oddly enough, he was especially cooperative. Even trotting on the longe, he seemed to be concentrating intently — until I asked him to canter.

Merlin suddenly reacted as if *he* were being attacked. I could see the whites of his eyes, his face contorting in a look of unmitigated terror. He pinned his ears back and bucked himself into a full run, leaning against the line, spinning around me with increasing speed. I had never experienced such a longeing emergency before. If I panicked and let go of the line, the centrifugal force would throw Merlin into the fence with enough momentum to seriously injure him. Without thinking, I calmly took a step forward, shaking the line slightly so he could no longer brace against it, whereupon he turned and lunged toward me as if I were the enemy, leaping into the air, rearing and striking as if he intended to stomp me to the ground. Waving the whip like a saber, I actually cracked him on the belly in self-defense as he towered over me. The sudden sting in this vulnerable spot plunged him into an even more intense panic, but at least he wasn't leaning against the longe line. I let go, and Merlin tore around the arena looking for a way out, his movements becoming so disorganized that his back legs flew out from under him. He slid a good twenty feet before coming to a stop, finally lying, disoriented and defeated, in a cloud of dust.

I felt no fear for his safety or my own while all this was happening. The element of danger catapulted me into a calmer, clearer state of consciousness that confidently performed a series of moves beyond anything I'd learned in the past. I had tapped into what the Taoists call "true intent" as my conditioned human mind stepped back and let a wiser force take over. When Merlin stood up, dazed and panting, I walked over and stroked his neck, talking quietly to him. For some reason, I found myself drawing his attention back to the present as if he could understand my every word, letting him know that whatever it was that scared him was simply a memory, an illusion. Then I longed him at a trot and a walk to cool him down. "See," I said as he moved around me once more, "you're alive. You're safe. I'm a different person. This is a different time. Nothing can hurt you anymore."

After leading Merlin back to his stall and sponging him off with water, however, I began to shake uncontrollably. The cool, collected soul that had handled the crisis was receding. A part of me had wanted to scream and run away, and this person was experiencing the tremors Peter Levine noticed in prey animals coming out of the immobility response. That night, I was continuously jolted out of a restless sleep with images of a vengeful horse threatening to kill me playing over and over in my dreams. For the next few days, I felt extra raw and exposed. Breathing into the sensations rather than trying to make them go away, I glimpsed an unconventional interpretation of the crisis. My alignment with true intent had blown open the boundaries of a much more mundane awareness. The feeling of my friend's chaotic energy punching me in the solar plexus and the subsequent threat that Merlin posed had loosened up and then short-circuited my limited human persona, making it possible for me to embody a much larger, more courageous perspective. This alien and fully empowered person could contain the intensity of Merlin's suffering and help him process it afterward, allowing him to leave his reenactment of some terrible tragedy with a feeling of support and compassion from me, rather than the horror and betrayal I would have normally felt. *Could I tap into this higher self again*, I wondered, *and glimpse the nature of Merlin's initial trauma?*

Since I still felt an intense emotional charge around the stallion, I decided to try my little experiment at home. I knew that if, at its root, the mind really was nonlocal, I wouldn't need to be with Merlin physically to merge with his memory. I voiced my intention to connect with the supreme nonlocal Mind that creates the universe. I reached out to the powerful nonlocal aspect of myself that had appeared a few days earlier, then called in the Horse Ancestors and, finally, the nonlocal aspect of Merlin's mind. "Show me the original trauma that Merlin relives over and over again," I requested, expecting to see his first trainer beating him unmercifully and tying his head between his legs in that darkened stall.

A vague reddish haze swirled behind my eyes, revealing a monochromatic scene of unbelievable carnage. As the vision played out like the negative of an old film, I was glad my mind's eye was colorblind. A man of indeterminate age and race was galloping across a raging battlefield on his magnificent steed, hacking his way through the madness with a heavy sword. The sheer numbers of daring foot soldiers eventually overwhelmed the team, and the mounted warrior was thrown from his horse by the force of a soaring spear. The stallion screamed and reared, striking several of the men and stomping one of them into oblivion. As the furious horse continued to rear and stomp, one of the soldiers stabbed the animal in the abdomen. The stallion's back legs flew out from under him on impact, and he hit the ground with full knowledge that he would never stand or run or fight again. Tears began to spill down my cheeks as I not only witnessed this horror but felt the sense of absolute defeat and sorrow surrounding the horse and his rider.

I truly was not prepared, however, for what came next. One of the soldiers dodged spears and arrows to reach for the warrior's sword. He raised the massive weapon with all his might and cut off the horse's head. Grabbing a substantial hunk of mane, he dragged his heavy trophy behind him as he disappeared into a sea of flashing steel and falling bodies.

After the vision dissipated, I sobbed for ten minutes in shock and outrage. I realized that I had inadvertently tapped into an ancestral memory, but a part of me wondered if such a thing could have ever happened. It seemed ridiculous that a soldier would take the time to cut off a horse's head in the heat of battle. In all my historical research, I had never heard of this. Yet the picture was so clear, the emotional charge behind it so devastating. "Why in the world would anyone do such a thing?" I asked the Ancestors.

"To take the power of a great war horse," they answered.

I subsequently realized that whether I had witnessed an actual past incarnation, a genetic memory, or an event recorded in the equine morphogenetic field, Merlin's interactions with his first trainer had somehow triggered the unresolved trauma of a particularly gruesome death. Through a series of pictures, words, and feelings, the Horse Ancestors explained that the so-called civilized equestrian arts were originally designed to prepare horses for battle. The highly sophisticated protocol of dressage, for instance, emerged from formalized European drills and strategies derived from Persian and, later, Greek techniques for training war mounts. The most famous competitive dressage riders of the twentieth century were, in fact, military men who learned their craft before tanks and jeeps mercifully replaced these animals in human conflict.

From antiquity through the conquest of what are now the Americas, a meticulously schooled war horse was more valuable than a human slave. Such an animal could rear, strike, and kick out his back legs on command to intimidate and injure foot soldiers. He could leap to the side, slide to a stop, spin, and take off running without hesitation, yet he would also stand at attention in the midst of a raging battle if his master dismounted to engage in hand-to-hand combat. Advanced riders in the Olympic Games and other competitions continue to demonstrate such feats. According to the Horse Ancestors, peacetime performances can carry an intense emotional charge for horses, especially if their riders attach a life-or-death urgency to winning.

The equine morphogenetic field scintillates with the painful memories of countless immaculately trained four-legged warriors who died in battle.

After leading an idyllic existence on Shawnee Allen's farm, Merlin was suddenly thrust into an intensive training program with a woman whose competitive, uncompromising attitude toward horses was based on the militaristic mindset still dominant in the show world. Merlin thought he had been drafted. Having his head tied between his legs was nothing compared to the subconscious impression that he was headed for a much more horrifying fate if he accepted the bit and saddle with the unquestioning obedience required of a war horse. Using a modified clearing and releasing method I had learned from Patricia Hursh, I worked to remove this karmic imprint from Merlin's system, assuring him that horses were no longer employed in war and that any activities we would engage in together would thereafter be designed for our mutual empowerment — and enjoyment.

In my heightened state of awareness, the entire drama made perfect sense, but as the days and weeks wore on, a more reasonable mindset took over, and I began to question the validity of the entire experience. Once again, I found the idea of a soldier taking a stallion's head in battle ridiculous, the product of my own overactive imagination, no doubt spurred on by the intense grief I'd felt in the wake of my mother's death. Two months later, however, I had a dream that put these skeptical thoughts to rest. I was standing in Merlin's stall, only two identical black stallions were living there. A spotlight suddenly burst from the sky, illuminating the three of us as a disembodied voice pointed to the fact that Merlin was "a double" originally owned by the goddess Hera. She was pleased with the work I had done with the horse(s) and was going to send me on a three-day "literary cruise" as a reward. The dream ended with me staring down at a ticket that had miraculously appeared in my hand with the ship's name, *Lacrimae*, clearly printed at the top.

It took me exactly three days of research to decipher the dream. Thinking Lacrimae must be a mythological character, I perused every myth and legend collection I could find at the library, to no avail. I looked up references to the goddess Hera, hoping to find some mention of Lacrimae in her adventures. Though she was most often depicted as the jealous, meddling wife of Zeus (Jupiter to the Romans), several texts theorized that Hera (or Juno) was more specifically the ancient mother goddess of early Mediterranean matriarchies. Her image was later co-opted and, to a certain extent, disempowered by the emerging Greek and Roman patriarchies. This love-less marriage of convenience led to Hera's reputation as a frustrated, angry archetype forever quarreling with her husband, undermining the sky god's intercessions in human affairs whenever possible.

Back home, I searched the internet and found some sites devoted to a rock band, a Renaissance music ensemble, and several medieval music CDs using the name Lacrimae, but no mention of what the word meant or why these people had chosen it to title their various projects. Finally, I found reference to the Latin phrase *sunt lacrimae rerum*, which was apparently a famous quote from a book I had never heard of, *The Aeneid*, by the Roman poet Virgil. Back at the library, I found an entry for that quote in a literary guide. *Lacrimae* literally means "tears." The extended phrase translates vari-ously as "the tears of things" or "tears for passing things," referring to a sense of grief and compassion arising for the traumas and transience of life and the release a defeated warrior feels in finally letting those tears fall. Intrigued, I checked out a copy of the epic poem, which was written between 30 and 19 BCE. Scanning the text, I realized I was reading yet another classic from antiquity about the Trojan Wars, only from a completely different perspec-tive. Where Homer's *Odyssey* chronicled the travels of the Greek hero who sacked Troy with the wooden horse, Virgil's *Aeneid* followed the adventures of the Trojan refugee Aeneas, who led a few ships of his fellow survivors to a new life in Italy after their city was destroyed.

Why was a horse trainer living in Tucson, Arizona, guided to read about the Trojan Wars from all possible angles? *Is this another bizarre cosmic joke?* I wondered. *Or am I haunted by a frustrated classics professor?* Finding the lacrimae passage, I wanted to get a feel for the context by reading from the beginning of the section in which the phrase appeared. Nothing, not even a wry sense of humor, could prepare me for what came next.

Sailing toward the shores of Italy, Aeneas's fleet is driven to the coast of Libya by a furious storm. After much complaining, the frustrated hero re-ceives counsel from the goddess Venus, who admonishes him for playing the downtrodden victim and not trusting in the wisdom of the gods. "Whoever you may be," she says,

> I hardly think the heaven-dwellers
> hold a grudge against you: the breath of life is yours,
> and you are near a Tyrian city. Only make your way
> until you reach the palace of the queen.

Gathering his wits about him, Aeneas hikes inland to ask for assistance in the Phoenician settlement of Tyre. As Virgil writes:

> Just at the center of the city stood
> a thickly shaded wood; this was the place
> where, when they landed, the Phoenicians first —
> hurled there by whirlwind and wave — dug up
> an omen Queen Juno had pointed out:
> *the head of a fierce war stallion* [emphasis mine]. This had meant
> the nation's easy wealth and fame in war
> throughout the ages. Here Sidonian Dido
> was building a stupendous shrine for Juno.

As Aeneas wanders through this elegant sanctuary, he finds a magnificent depiction of the Trojan Wars painted on the walls. He cries:

> Where on this earth is there a land, a place
> that does not know our sorrows? . . .
> Here, too, the honorable finds its due
> and there are tears for passing things; here, too,
> things mortal touch the mind. Forget your fears;
> this fame will bring you some deliverance.

"With many tears and sighs," Virgil reveals, Aeneas "feeds his soul on what is nothing but a picture."

The Deeps Are Rising

At first I had no idea how to process this potent synchronicity. I could only marvel at how a dream had given literary confirmation that a stallion's head might very well have been taken in battle. I was also struck by Virgil's profoundly lucid insight into a defeated warrior's moment of healing. The tears of Aeneas were released through his recognition that others remembered the battles he and his comrades had endured. Regardless of who had won or lost, who had lived or died, these events were deemed important enough to acknowledge in the shrine of a goddess. Aeneas fed his soul on what was "nothing but a picture" memorializing the suffering of men on both sides, allowing the weary and embittered warrior to witness his trials from a more exalted perspective. This, it seemed to me, was the reason the works of Virgil and Homer had endured, why they were still relevant today, why I had been drawn to them by ethereal influences I still didn't understand. People and, curiously enough, horses were experiencing the subconscious effects of past and present, actual and symbolic wars. The way through this misery required more than simply gathering up the pieces and starting a new life somewhere else. Like Aeneas getting blown off course to Libya when his sights were set on Italy, many of us needed to take a cruise on *Lacrimae*, a ship navigating the tempestuous seas of the collective unconscious, propelling us toward mythical shores where the sorrows of the world were recorded in magnificent mosaics. These artistic renderings had the potential to uplift us, allowing us to not simply wallow in despair but to mourn the past from a perspective capable of putting our sufferings into context. Only then could we sail into the future with a clean slate.

The human morphogenetic field contains the experiences of so many cultures defeated, enslaved, and assimilated against their will. What happens to the systemic memories of those whose ways of life were eradicated? What becomes of their forbidden stories and suppressed philosophies? Do their descendants occasionally tap into hidden currents of sorrow never acknowledged, never grieved?

In his extensive history *Black Sea*, Neal Ascherson uses this enigmatic body of water to symbolize the psyche's toxic reaction to unresolved ancestral pain. On the surface, the Black Sea has always seemed a place of almost monstrous abundance. Salmon and sturgeon crowded up its five tributaries to spawn, making caviar so plentiful that it was considered the food of the poor in fourteenth-century Byzantium. Yet below a fluctuating depth of 150 to 200 meters, the Black Sea is not only dead, it is filled with poison. This small, landlocked reservoir of salt water suffers from too much input. While only three rivers flow into the far bigger Mediterranean, the Black Sea receives five: the Kuban, the Don, the Dnieper, the Dniester, and the Danube. As Ascherson explains:

> It is these rivers, source of so much life, which over tens of thousands of years extinguished life in the Black Sea depths. The inrush of organic matter from the rivers was too much for the bacteria in sea water which would normally decompose it. They feed by oxidizing their nutrients, using the dissolved oxygen normally present in sea-water. But when the organic inflow is so great that the supply

of dissolved oxygen is used up, then the bacteria turn to another biological process.

The bacteria effectively create a residual gas, hydrogen sulfide, one of the deadliest substances in the natural world. A single breath of this invisible poison can kill a human being. When agitated by a particularly brutal storm or disturbed by efforts to drill for oil, the toxic currents can suddenly rise, killing everything in their path.

Postconquest civilization's compulsion to conquer and pillage without restraint, ceaselessly assimilating other cultures into its own tiny, disconnected, landlocked perspective, has created its own fatal version of the Black Sea in the collective unconscious. The descendants of subjugated societies still carry the genetic memories of their forefathers and mothers, people who were brutally murdered or mercilessly enslaved to build all those gleaming cities. Ascherson's tales of conflict brewing along the Black Sea mirror the seemingly senseless pockets of violence that erupt all over the world: "As individuals, 'the others' are not strangers but neighbors, often friends," he writes.

> But my sense of Black Sea life, a sad one, is that latent mistrust between cultures is immortal....It is true that communal savagery — pogroms, "ethnic cleansing" in the name of some fantasy of national unity, genocide — has usually reached the Black Sea communities from elsewhere, an import from the interior. But when it arrives, the apparent solidarity of centuries can dissolve within days or hours. The poison, upwelling from the depths, is absorbed in a single breath.

Suddenly, the Nazis are sacrificing Jews as scapegoats for a nameless angst, Yugoslavia erupts into a war no one else can seem to fathom, Israel and Gaza explode with incomprehensible violence, and growing numbers of teenagers wielding bombs and automatic weapons lay waste to US schools, killing innocent teachers, peers, and young children.

Like Merlin blindly trying to stomp me to the ground after showing so much promise, a simple gesture or pattern of behavior in peacetime taps the emotions of ancestral war, and something just snaps. Without warning we're reliving the unresolved conflicts and injustices of faceless wraiths whose names and causes long ago fell into historical obscurity. We may have no idea who our ancestors were, yet we find ourselves wincing from their pain and fighting their battles. Wholly rational explanations for these outbreaks of violence are shortsighted and ultimately ineffective at imagining a solution, because the postconquest mind has lost contact with the breadth and depth of human existence.

"We forced nature to reveal its secrets," asserts Jean Houston in her audio program *Myths for the Future*, but in the process we became profoundly, pathologically detached. In the name of conquest and commerce, she says, we surrendered

> our capacity for communication with the inner life of the natural world, such as the Aboriginal and indigenous people display, as well as the inner life of ourselves. Nonmythic, nonstoried folk are always [hopelessly disconnected], for they have lost their capacity for communion as well as communication. Instead we flail about in half-hearted measures to save the planet from ourselves. And I really wonder if anyone probing the inner life can really be successful without being in communion with the depths of nature.

Houston echoes the work of Carl Jung and Joseph Campbell when she discusses the dangers of repressing or simply ignoring the wisdom contained in myths, ancestral legends, and other archetypal narratives. The winged horses, centaurs, gods, and goddesses of antiquity were archetypes, "primary forms and constellations of energy that govern the psyche or that inner self we sometimes call the soul." Quintessentially, Houston explains, "archetypes are about relationship, and the impetus behind relationship, and connectedness for the way things evolve, grow, complexify, and ultimately become more integral." When repressed in the individual or the culture, "all kinds of alienation emerges, and one is cut off from nature, self, society, and spirit with consequences seen all over today's world. This alienation has gained considerably from the mechanistic view of the world, which has touched virtually every level of modern life." As nonmaterial patterns of existence, archetypes can hide out indefinitely in the depths of the collective unconscious, but they can't be suppressed forever. They reappear through the "other great bleed-through realms of human experience: dreams, religious knowings, visions, art, ritual, love, and madness. Sometimes they occur in their archaic forms bearing the accoutrements of earlier cultures, but they ask to be seen in fresh ways. They ask to be regrown."

Yet like the poisonous gases of the Black Sea, the reemergence of any archetype can have a potent shadow side, especially for people indoctrinated in the postconquest mindset. "If perceived through the lens of alienated nature and consciousness," Houston cautions, these primordial energies can "appear as warped, even demonic versions of what they truly are.... Thus we saw how in Hitler's Germany they utilized the archaic strata of Teutonic and Scandinavian myth and archetype as refashioned, and it can be argued, rendered racist, in the Wagnerian mythic opera... as [the Nazi regime] organized its own alienated purposes around these stories and this music." Even so, such images "announce a time of change and deepening" whenever they appear. "So potent are these archetypical dimensions that in order to have any continuity and comprehension in this world, they often have to be encoded in myth." Houston defines myth as "something that never was, but is always happening. It's the coded DNA of the human psyche.... Myth waters our every conscious act and is the very sea of our unconscious life."

Mythic messages evolve over time, dressing themselves up in the customs of different eras, drawing attention to destructive patterns of thought and behavior while offering solutions through symbols of transformation. Perpetually looking for an in to our world, they search for a receptive audience among artists, dreamers — and, occasionally, people who work with horses.

Around 20 BCE, Virgil observed that at Juno's urging, the head of a fierce war stallion was dug up and brought to the light of day. A temple to the queen of the gods was built on the resting place of those bones, one that memorialized distant battles and provided sanctuary for defeated warriors to weep, remember, and finally transform their grief into a source of empowerment. Two thousand years later, Carl Jung was captivated by a young theology student's dream of a black mare escaping from the tomb of an ancestral princess, leading a magician with vision and endurance to the lost keys of paradise. In the 1970s, the Greek centaur Chiron emerged from historical obscurity to usher in the era of the wounded healer. These archetypal images infused my interactions with living, breathing members of the herd in myriad ways — while ceaselessly pointing back to their origins in myth, literature, and history.

First there was Rasa, the black mare whose wounded knee led me through a series of adventures that took me from alienation to authenticity, helping me reawaken the feminine gifts of intuition and sociosensual awareness, skills that allowed me to collaborate with both horses and humans at a deeper level. Then Midnight Merlin and I relived the drama of a far more ancient crisis, motivating me to engage a nonlocal state of awareness to tap the long-buried memory of a war horse's head being taken in battle. My ability to weep for the stallion's mythic ancestral double seemed to diffuse that pain and free Merlin from the tyranny of the past. When I later questioned the validity of the entire experience, I received a dream cruise on *Lacrimae* from the goddess Hera, which in turn pointed me toward Virgil's reference to a myth that was seeping into my own life with increasing regularity.

Later that spring, a particularly intuitive client who knew little of Merlin's history said she thought she heard him speaking to her as she walked by his stall. "What did he say?" I asked.

"It makes no sense," she replied, "but it seemed to be so clearly coming from him. He said, 'To know is to weep.'"

"Oh, it makes sense all right," I said. "Perfect sense."

Something was continually rising from the depths of the collective unconscious, something that associated the horse with the resurrection of an archaic form of feminine wisdom and the resurrection of that wisdom with the power to move both species out of disconnection, strife, and suffering, in part through the long-overdue releasing of all those "tears for passing things."

Beyond Words

After my heightened experiences with Merlin and Rasa, I became interested in the phenomenon of animal communicators. The field, which is dominated by women, relies primarily on emotional resonance, clairsentience, and nonlocal mind to determine what animals are thinking and feeling. Initially considered a curiosity at best and a form of trickery at worst, the practice has gained a certain respect in recent years. Sharon Callahan, for instance, a communicator based in Mount Shasta, California, spent seven hours a day five days a week assessing the physical, mental, and emotional needs of various species, working almost exclusively on referrals from veterinarians. Most of these conversations took place over the phone as Sharon engaged a nonlocal state of consciousness while talking with the animal's owner.

"With any animal that we love and live with for a long time, there's a merging of energies that occurs," she explained during a conversation we had in the late 1990s. "I'm able to transfer my attention to the animal through the voice of the person. I loosely listen to what they're telling me, trying to get an attunement to the animal, like dialing a radio station. It comes in a little fuzzy at first, and then I've got it. When I have that connection, I will begin speaking for the animal, usually in first person. Many animals communicate with me in visual images in the form of little vignettes, almost like a movie playing in my head. Sometimes, it's more like a direct transfer of thought, a block of information, or a story they're telling that comes fully formed from their consciousness to mine."

Penelope Smith shared a similar perspective in *Animals: Our Return to Wholeness*, while Nicci Mackay chronicled her intuitive exchanges with horses in *Spoken in Whispers*. Skeptics abound, of course, but people seem much more tolerant of the idea than they were back in 1975, when English horse trainer Henry Blake went out on a limb to discuss equine extrasensory perception in *Talking with Horses*. While much of the book concentrated on body language signals and behavior modification, Blake insisted on devoting several chapters to telepathy, clairsentience, and empathic exchanges between horses and humans, despite warnings from his peers that "entry into so highly contentious an area" could "devalue" his work on other aspects of horse communication. "I have often been told that while our work on signs and sounds is far in advance of anything anybody else has done," he wrote, "our involvement with animal extrasensory perception makes us suspect — even puts us in the same class as charlatans and music-hall acts!" Even so, he decided to take a chance, feeling that "to carry out research into equine communication without taking into account e.s.p. and telepathy would be equivalent to trying to study English by studying only the nouns and the verbs and pretending that adverbs and adjectives did not exist."

Blake must have received some flack for discussing the phenomenon, however; his subsequent books, like *Horse Sense*, revert almost entirely back to behaviorist notions of training. Still, the adventurous theories presented in *Talking with Horses* coincided with many of the conclusions I came to through my own extrasensory encounters with horses. Blake's foray into the world of intuitive communication stemmed from experiences with clairsentience and emotional resonance. One night he woke with a powerful feeling that something was wrong and went out to check the animals. He says he was "subconsciously drawn" to where a cow was having trouble calving. "This started me thinking in a new direction and, step by step, I came to the somewhat startling conclusion that I could feel the moods of the horses rather than see or hear them." In developing this skill, he later found himself receiving sensual and even visual impressions from the horses over long distances, especially during emergencies.

Curious if members of his herd communicated regularly with each other in this fashion, he devised a series of experiments where he would, for example, leave a mare resting calmly in her stall with an observer while he stimulated various emotional states in one of her equine companions a quarter of a mile away. If the mare began to demand food while her counterpart was being fed, if she suddenly became energetic while her counterpart was being exercised, or if she became frightened and agitated while the other horse was feeling fear, Blake considered this a "positive result," indicating some form of extrasensory communication between the two. Out of 119 experiments, he reported positive results in 81 cases, a marginal result in 12 or more, and a possible result in 11 cases, which he translated as an overall success rate of 67.5 percent. The key, at least in the unnatural context of a controlled experiment, was to use "empathetic pairs," two horses exhibiting a strong emotional bond. "The point is that any horse cannot communicate mentally with any other horse," he concluded, "just as any human being cannot communicate mentally with any other human being. It is only if you are very close to someone that you may be able to sense what they are feeling without seeing them and talking to them. When two horses are mentally and emotionally on the same wavelength, then they too can sense what the other is thinking and what the other is doing." He subsequently used the example of two tuning forks resonating sympathetically to illustrate how the phenomenon might work.

Blake also discussed the species' gift for sociosensual awareness and their ability as sensitive, highly social mammals to coregulate each other (though he didn't use these terms) to explain why he employed older, calmer horses to help him gentle young, flighty colts, a principle horse trainers have been using for centuries. Finally, he described how human beings could tune themselves to the equine frequency by living with a herd and mimicking horse behavior patterns, moving when they move, resting when they rest, eating when they eat, playing when they play. Time and time again, Blake cited empathy as the primary entry point into extrasensory perception, a state of heightened awareness that begins with feeling what a horse feels and eventually blossoms into the ability to see what she sees — even, in some cases, actually receive telepathic communications that translate themselves into human language.

While this capacity often develops through close association with a particular horse, people who immerse themselves in equestrian pursuits or are particularly intuitive to begin with sometimes find they can pick up messages from just about any member of the species, often inadvertently. The student who heard Merlin say, "To know is to weep" had no idea of my experiences with him, and she certainly hadn't developed a close rapport with the stallion. She was, however, a gifted empath and bodyworker who could sense energy fluctuations in her human clients and was interested in studying with my herd to further develop these abilities. In *Talking with Horses*, Henry Blake described his unexpected connection with a horse named, curiously enough, Weeping Roger, whose desperate call for help couldn't be ignored. At an auction, he remembered, "I was just having a look, and talking to a friend of mine, when suddenly behind me I could feel dejection invading my mind and body as if someone or something was screaming 'for God's sake get me out of here.' I turned around, and there was a horse just waiting to go into the ring, a dirty-brown lop-eared half-starved sixteen-two thoroughbred" — whom Blake ended up taking home as a result.

When pressed, horse lovers who would never promote themselves as animal communicators admit to similar incidents. An amateur equestrian helping to round up cattle at a local ranch told me he was mystified when the owner's daughter "Kelly," who was riding along with this group of cowboys during spring break, pointed to a distant rise in the landscape and said, "There's a steer and a calf on the other side of that hill under a tree." When asked how she knew this, she said simply, "My horse told me." Everyone was skeptical until they rode over and found, much to their surprise, the pair she had described resting in the shade of a mesquite.

An even more amazing incident involved two Epona colleagues, Dana Light and Julia Standish. Dana, a talented equine massage therapist, trainer, and anatomy specialist, was helping Julia with a horse who was having some mild lameness problems. At the end of the session, Julia asked Dana to take a quick look at her other horses to see if they had any areas of soreness that might be alleviated before escalating into more serious problems. In evaluating Cookie, Julia's accomplished twenty-one-year-old lesson horse, Dana could feel the gelding was happy in his work and closely bonded to his owner. "But," she says, "as I was talking about the various issues involved, I started saying, 'There's not much time. He has a lot to teach, but there's not much time; there's not much time.' I kept repeating this phrase in an entirely different rhythm than my normal way of speaking. I really didn't understand what it meant, but it seemed to be coming from the horse, and it had a sense of real importance about it." Three weeks later, Cookie suddenly colicked without warning. Julia urged him onto the trailer and drove him to the vet.

"Through the whole ordeal, I kept getting this overwhelming feeling that Cookie was angry with me," Julia remembers, "but at first I thought it was because he was in so much pain. The vet told me Cookie had to go into surgery immediately or be put down — that's how bad it was. They actually had him on the operating table when I remembered what Dana kept saying. 'There's not much time.' I realized why Cookie was so mad. It was time for him to die, and I was forcing him into surgery. I was able to let him go that day because of what Dana had said, and I was able to see the whole experience as not so much a tragedy, something unfair that had happened to me. Instead I felt it had been an honor to know this incredible horse and to be the one chosen to help him through that transition."

The incident with Cookie and the intuitive message Kelly received from her cow horse illustrated not only telepathic communication between people and horses but the seemingly easy access the equine mind has to forms of awareness transcending time and space. My first experience with the Los Angeles–based animal communicator Tamara Solange had a similarly non-local feel to it. Tamara came to Tucson at the invitation of "Allison," one of the trainers on Epona's referral list. When Allison told Tamara I was writing a book dealing in part with some strange experiences I'd had with the horses, she agreed to spend an afternoon at The Ranch coaching me in some of her techniques. "Noche has something he wants to tell you," she said. "See if you can pick it up." I closed my eyes and concentrated intently as Allison and Tamara stood quietly beside Noche. An angry chestnut horse with a white blaze on his face came into view, striking and pawing at the ground. When I described this to Tamara, she not only validated the image, she insisted Noche thought the animal was extremely dangerous. "You don't know this horse," she said, "but somehow he's a threat, and Noche is trying to warn us about him." Later that evening, Allison arrived back at her training facility to find her partner Mary had been rushed to the hospital with a broken nose. Right around the time Allison, Tamara, and I were interacting with my herd, Mary had been evaluating a problem horse for a client ten miles across town, a chestnut gelding with a blaze who maliciously ran her into a tree. Noche had picked up on a crisis about to happen to a colleague who was not present, and Tamara and I had both tapped into this vision.

These experiences point to an expanded view of what Stephen Porges calls "neuroception." His polyvagal theory asserts that the conscious mind plays only a minor role in evaluating potential threats in the environment and in relationships. From "an adaptive survival perspective," he writes in *A Pocket Guide to the Polyvagal Theory*, "'the wisdom' resides in our body and in the structures of our nervous system that function outside of the realm of awareness."

Porges emphasizes that *neuroception* is unconscious, in contrast with *perception*, which brings cognitive functions into play. In my own experience, I've come to realize that neuroceptive and perceptive functions can interact in oddly creative ways. For example, the urge to protect my herd has elevated my neuroception for rattlesnakes to an uncanny level. I have several intriguing stories, but the first and most impressive incident took place during one of my hikes with Rasa.

As mentioned previously, I would often let her explore the desert off lead as we strengthened our bond through the relaxed, expanded awareness resonating between us. On one particularly tranquil day, I sat down and leaned against a rock as she meandered through a luxurious patch of fresh grass. The sun's warmth lured me into a semidrowsy state. I sighed, closed my eyes, and felt the outlines of a dream. Suddenly, I saw a detailed representation of the entire landscape: a luminous, pulsating, three-dimensional portrait of the mountains cradled a monsoon pasture oscillating with subtle energy. The image somehow conveyed a graceful sense of urgency without escalating into panic.

Fifty feet from a depiction of Rasa grazing among shimmering strands of green, the vibrational intensity increased, taking on a serpentine shape. I opened my eyes. Rasa was indeed nibbling in the exact spot my mind had predicted. Curious, I stood up and walked toward the highlighted area, unable at first to see anything of interest in the knee-high grass. A good twenty steps deeper into the field, however, I noticed the previously hidden form of a large rattlesnake enjoying an afternoon nap — lying in the same position as in my scintillating vision. Had Rasa wandered over without sensing his slumbering presence, she would have startled him. Two miles from the barn (with no cell phone at the time), the encounter could have been fatal, especially if he had bitten her on the nose. I could have just as easily stepped on him, but a silent visionary warning kept all three of us safe. Moving ever so gently away from the sleeping rattler, I walked casually over to Rasa, attached the lead rope to her halter, and quietly directed her back down the trail.

I was amazed. My body's nonverbal radar didn't generate vague feelings of fear that sent me into flight or fight. It devised a clever way to send the details to my mind. In doing so, my autonomic nervous system conveyed a neuroceptive message encouraging me to calmly investigate the situation and avert possible disaster.

When it comes to relationship challenges, Porges also asserts that "our body functions like a polygraph (i.e., lie detector)" capable of sensing and evaluating others' intentions and emotional states. As illustrated in previous chapters, horses are exceptionally talented in this regard, but the plot thickens when we add nonlocal awareness to the mix. In discussions with Tamara Solange, I realized that some of her intuitive interactions paralleled my more adventurous experiences in the field of equine-facilitated therapy and experiential learning. Not only did the horses she worked with seem to know a great deal about their owners' personal lives, they incessantly mirrored suppressed emotions and unresolved issues, putting Tamara in the position of crisis counselor to equestrians around the country who called her to communicate with their "problem horses."

One woman couldn't understand why her beloved mare "Star" was acting tired and sullen. When the horse started limping for no apparent reason, she realized the situation was escalating. After running a series of tests, her vet couldn't explain the behavior or the lameness, yet Star seemed to be getting worse. "Shelly" was despondent. She had always imagined that the star emblazoned on the mare's forehead was the light that guided their feet in the woods where they walked together. Now her companion was unable to leave the barn. In desperation, Shelly called a trainer friend who worked with show horses. The woman gave her Tamara's phone number, explaining that she had a certain intuition for finding out what was wrong and offering effective, often unconventional solutions.

After communicating with the mare, Tamara suggested that Star wouldn't be able to walk until the woman dealt with a particularly abusive relationship. Shelly began to cry, admitting that she had been keeping a horrible situation quiet, that it was crippling her emotionally.

"*Crippling*," Tamara emphasized to me. "That was the word Shelly used, and that was what her mare was trying to show her." Tamara performed some energy-clearing exercises on both the horse and the woman to jump-start the healing process. "Then Shelly promised us both that she would work through her destructive relationship with the proper help. At that moment, her mare let out a shrill whinny and became bright-eyed with excitement, trotting off as if she had never taken a bad step. I was as amazed as everyone else was. Never before had I seen something correct so quickly. Then I thought I heard the mare say something, and I blurted it out before I could come to my senses and stop myself because it sounded so New Age. The mare said, 'Our journey is a bright one. Your child is with us in the woods when we walk. I am your light. I am your friend.'"

Shelly burst into a barrage of tears and laughter. "I lost a child," she explained to Tamara, marveling at this unsolicited insight. "I've been so afraid to even talk about it. I found this horse after the baby died. I felt so at peace with her when I went for a trail ride that I decided to buy her. Nothing made me feel so wonderful and calm since losing the baby until that first quiet ride in the woods. At the funeral the preacher said, 'Death is difficult; it feels so lonely, so dark. But if we look hard within and then around, we can find what we need spiritually. Find it. Let it be your light; let it be your friend.'"

Glimpses of the Otherworld

Over time, I realized that the horse's legendary facility for traveling between the spirit and material realms was not a metaphor. Therapeutic riding instructor Laura Brinckerhoff is a certified addictions counselor and mental health professional. Her ability to lead people out of the downward spiral of drug dependency stems from her own experiences with drug and alcohol abuse in high school and college. Yet it was a memorable encounter with a horse, in addition to her work in recovery, that allowed her to tap into the higher power that helped her conquer her addictions.

Growing up in Tucson, Laura was heavily involved in the equestrian arts. She and her little chestnut quarter horse, Rusty, won numerous competitions, including an Arizona State Championship in the pony hunter division. "I rode him three hours a day, every day of the week," she says. "We used a saddle in lessons, but I rode him saddleless and bridleless all over the desert. We even went trick-or-treating together."

By the age of sixteen, Laura had physically outgrown Rusty. She bought a larger, more powerful horse and leased Rusty to another young girl. "I pretty much ignored him for a while," she remembers. "A part of me didn't feel like sharing him, and I really couldn't ride him effectively in shows anymore." A year later, Laura went to college in California. A few days before her father flew in for parents' weekend, she had a dream: "I was standing on this beach, and Rusty came galloping toward me. He stopped right in front of me, reared up on his hind legs, and wrapped his front legs around my shoulders. He said into my ear, 'I want to go home now.' I remember being amazed in the dream that he spoke in a human voice, in words that I could understand. I told him, 'OK.' Then this truck and trailer appeared, and I helped him into the trailer like I had always done before a show, just opened the door and he jumped in. Then the truck took off, and I watched it drive up and over a mountain. He was whinnying as they drove away, which made the significance of those few words he spoke all the more powerful."

She recorded the dream in her journal the next day. That weekend, her father took her out to dinner. "I can just picture us sitting in this seafood restaurant," she remembers, "when he said he needed to tell me about Rusty. It turned out my horse had died a few days earlier. He colicked, which was surprising because he was only fifteen years old and had never been lame or sick in his life. I immediately started to cry. Dad reached over to comfort me, but I wasn't crying from sadness. It was this incredible affirmation of his life and our connection that he could actually come to me and say goodbye, that he could let me know it was his time. It was also an incredible confirmation that he had a soul. It was something I had believed all along, but it was so much more real for me after that. It was a truth with a capital T that we are all spiritual beings, that part of us continues on and can do amazing things. More than anything, it was my dream of Rusty and all its implications that allowed me to reconnect with the spiritual base so necessary in recovery."

A similar brush with life after death came to Julia Standish and me when her horse Wally passed away. The former show horse had been donated to Julia's lesson program after his retirement. Unfortunately, Wally's career on the professional hunter-jumper circuit had taken its toll, not only on his front legs but on his digestive system. Though Julia was able to work through his lameness by giving him some time off and slowly bringing him back to arena work, Wally would occasionally colic. The anti-inflammatory drugs that had kept him jumping all those years were known to damage the intestines. During one particularly serious bout of colic, I attended to Wally while Julia got some sleep after staying up with him all night. It was a heart-wrenching experience to see him in so much pain, and after another day of his suffering, Julia finally agreed with the vet: Wally was too weak to go on. He needed to be euthanized.

The sleepless night after his death, I felt his presence in the room and finally fell into a dream. Wally was standing on a flatbed trailer with flowers all around him. Every rider he had ever known, every student he had ever taught was there to see him off. Rasa and Noche, who had lived with Wally at Timothy Graham's ranch, fell into line behind the others. Suddenly, a horse named Harvey came racing up to join the procession, leaping over the high fences surrounding the property. I had occasionally ridden this regal dressage horse, across town at Cathy Schreiber's barn, but his sudden appearance seemed a nonsensical addition to the dream. I told Cathy about it when I took my lesson later that week. "Didn't you know?" Cathy asked, amused and surprised. "Harvey and Wally were stablemates at a farm on the east side of Tucson years ago. They were very close."

The dream surprised and comforted Julia as well. A few weeks later, she had her own otherworldly encounter with Wally. "I was doing my morning meditation," she says, "trying to deal with the grief I was still feeling, when I started having this waking vision. I was sitting at the kitchen table with my sister Fran, telling her that I could still feel Wally around, like he hadn't made the transition. Fran suggested I try to connect with Wally's spirit. All of a sudden, I was walking through this beautiful field of grass with a single tree. The image went from normal to sepia tone, and I saw a chestnut horse grazing in the distance. Someone was walking with me; it felt like my spirit guide. I said to this person, 'Is that Wally? It must be; his coat is so shiny.' Wally looked up and recognized me. I could see he was wearing the halter I had gotten for him. He came cantering toward me and said, 'Is this the new place where you're boarding me?' I said, 'No, Wally, you've died. You don't have to wear that halter anymore.'"

The halter unclasped and fell off by itself. Wally bowed and trotted off happily toward the horizon. As the vision faded, Julia heard her guide explaining the rhythms of the soul's journey through life and death in a way that suggested this world, the one we believed to be so solid and stable, was really the dream.

CHAPTER FOURTEEN

THE ART OF FREEDOM

As a symbol, the horse is often associated with freedom and power. Before human beings learned to ride these fleet-footed creatures, there was little interaction between distant settlements. Horses enabled people to explore the world, expand their perspectives, and liberate themselves from the constraints of their own community value systems. The simple act of sitting astride one of these animals raised mortal men and women above the mundane and enhanced their sense of personal authority. After the Industrial Revolution, horses were limited to recreation, but their ability to infuse riders with feelings of freedom and vitality remained a significant part of the appeal. It didn't take long for the field of therapeutic riding to recognize that horses were miracle workers when it came to restoring mobility, self-esteem, and a spirit of adventure to persons with disabilities, as well as to people who felt defeated by life's struggles.

When David Trexler woke up in a Japanese hospital during his second tour of duty in Vietnam, he couldn't imagine how he'd ever be of use to anyone again. The doctors told him his Jeep had run over a land mine. Both his legs had been amputated at the knee. His face and arms were severely burned. The physical pain eventually subsided, but the scars he wore on the outside only served to remind him of the despair growing inside. As an active and adventurous young man, he had volunteered for the service. Lying helplessly in bed, he couldn't understand why his unit had bothered to save him. By the time he was transferred to a Denver army hospital, it seemed that no one would be able to draw him out of a debilitating depression.

David stared blankly out of his hospital room window and watched the days go by. Then a curious spectacle caught his interest. A lady drove up with a horse trailer and led a feisty bay Morgan out to the lawn as several veterans in wheelchairs rolled up to meet her. A couple of male nurses lifted one of the patients onto the saddle and secured a special belt around his waist. The young man took off at a gallop, whooping and hollering. No one seemed concerned that he didn't have any legs.

Eventually David worked up the courage to ride that mare himself. A few years later, he was competing in shows and training cutting horses. Al-Marah Arabians hired him to help manage the farm, and he was later elected to the board of the North American Riding for the Handicapped Association. "Those horses gave me back my freedom," he says. "I could go places my wheelchair would never be able to take me, and I was traveling faster than I ever could on my own two legs. I can't imagine what state I'd be in now if I hadn't been able to ride."

Psychologically, however, this particular path to freedom isn't always smooth or inherently pleasant. Horses demand authenticity every step of the way. To be effective, riders must develop an alert, expansive, meditative state of mind, creative approaches to problem-solving, and an ability to set long-term goals without lapsing into impatience with the challenges that arise or holding an attachment to preconceived notions of how success will be attained. Horses respond to personal integrity, thoughtful leadership, mental and physical balance, emotional congruency, flexibility, receptivity, clear intent, and sophisticated energy management. They reward their riders for even the most subtle approximations of these virtues through increased attention, cooperation, and affection, acting as unbiased barometers in the work of human development.

The problem is that many equestrian operations still treat horses as purely instinctual beings. Riding instructors advise their students to "leave your emotions at the gate" and "be the alpha of your two-member herd." These habits lead to horses acting out the suppressed emotions of their handlers — and getting punished for it. What's more, trainers lack understanding of the polyvagal nervous system, which encourages mammals to coregulate each other, communicating safety through connection to support health, restoration, and growth. Treating these animals as biological machines inspires aloof, superficial, disconnected interactions that increase stress and inhibit learning, leading to dangerously dysregulated behavior in both species.

Many professional animal communicators, including Penelope Smith, Tamara Solange, and Sharon Callahan, find these conventional attitudes grossly counterproductive. Sharon designates three levels of communication in her practice. There's the body level, useful in diagnostic work for veterinarians. "At times I will pick up the area of discomfort in my own body," she told me. "In other cases, I will receive an image of the animal in my mind's eye with the area of discomfort highlighted in some way. In still other cases, I simply know that it's in the kidneys, heart, or intestines." Then there's the personality level, which Sharon describes as "superficial conversation. The information comes as actual words back and forth. Certainly the animal is not speaking in the way that you and I do, but I translate the animal's thoughts and feelings in a present-time way." Finally, there's the soul level, where "you get amazing information about the animal's life purpose — why it's with this particular person, the lessons it has to teach.

"I like to go straight to the soul level," she explained, "which has evolved into a reading of the entire situation, including the animal and the family members, because I've found that seems to be the most useful. When an animal has difficulty, whether it's an emotional or physical problem, it's usually trying to say something about the person's overall life situation. Animals have their own agenda and their own way of ordering things in importance to them, which is usually more profound than the way the person is looking at it. Certainly each animal has its own reason for incarnating, its own path of learning, but I also feel on a soul level they all come to show us something very, very profound about ourselves. They draw attention to things. As they help us, they also grow and evolve on that level, so it's a real symbiotic thing."

One of the animals Sharon has increasingly declined to work with is the horse. "I love horses," she says, "but I find most horse people really hard to take. I had so many horse clients for a number of years, I just found it too devastating. Somehow, I feel that of all animals, horses are the least understood by people, and they've been the most poorly treated historically. I take on horses selectively, by veterinary referral, and have acquired a group of very conscious horse owners I do communication for, but as a rule, I find that working with horses can leave me with a painful residue that lingers for hours or days. I also feel horses need hands-on help, whereas I can help dogs and cats and even larger captive wild animals adeptly from a distance and in a shorter period of time. With a lot of my horse clients, I wish I could be there in person to observe a lot more of what's happening."

Part of this discrepancy stems from the fact that people don't saddle up their cats, dogs, or tigers. Trainer-authors like Mary Wanless and Peggy Cummings emphasize that human discomforts and tensions are transferred

physically to their horses through the act of riding. It takes a relatively confident and enlightened person to admit she's part of the problem.

In suppressing the horse's spirit to use him like a machine, the human
race eventually forgot the animal had a mind at all. The challenge, it seemed,
was to dig up that long-buried knowledge, to put the stallion's head back on
his body, and to begin to collaborate with him as a soulful sentient being.

Tamara Solange admits this is challenging for many equestrians. "While
I've had some incredible results from the intuitive work alone," she says,
"I'm not quite so willing to base a session exclusively on what you would call
'animal communication' anymore. The horses adapt very quickly to working
at this soul level, but quite often their owners aren't ready to deal with an
intelligent, fully empowered animal."

Sharon Callahan echoes these concerns. "Even with the most well-
meaning horse owners, it seems to be so difficult for them to shift from having the horse operate as some form of ego extension. Working with horses
is an art in itself, and that's where the field of equine-facilitated therapy
comes in. It's really an area in which the horses will be healed, allowing them
to engage with people on the deep soul [and] emotional level rather than
functioning exclusively as beasts of burden. I also feel that certain behaviors in animals and certain illnesses won't clear up completely until human
consciousness has changed. Therapeutic work is really an exalted thing for a
horse to do, to be treated as an equal in the healing process. The experience
of being able to help people, and in turn resolve their own issues, goes back
into the horse collective, and the whole horse collective is elevated."

On her website, which has become inactive in recent years, Sharon
posted an impressive collection of original interviews with such influential
thinkers and spiritual teachers as Matthew Fox, Andrew Harvey, and Rupert
Sheldrake dealing specifically with the transformational value of human-
animal relationships. Sheldrake's theory of morphogenetic fields coincides
with Sharon's observations of how the "group soul" of each species affects
the individual. When I mentioned my experiences with the Horse Ancestors,
she immediately understood the implications. She also related to the Ancestors' persistent request that I "tell the story."

"I've found that animals are more connected to the group soul or collective unconscious of their species than human beings are," she says. "When
you engage in a spiritual relationship with an animal, it not only creates a
shift on the personal level, it has universal consequences as well. People can

make a difference even if they have only one animal, because that animal is connected to and communicates with all the others. And, of course, it works in reverse: negativity can be transferred too. This is why we see an increasing rise in what's termed 'nonspecific anxiety' among beautifully cared for, adored animals that have never known moments of abuse. Animals absorb and reflect the fears of the collective."

During our conversation, she shared examples of this collective effect: "As the big cats are driven to the brink of extinction, it makes perfect sense that house cats are increasingly suffering from anxiety. As the wolf continues to be persecuted in many areas of the world, more and more dogs are developing neurotic behaviors. The good news is that as more people increase their understanding of themselves, their animals, and our greater purpose together, at some point, we'll override all the horrible things that have been done. With each act of kindness, with each loving thought, and with each prayer, the world is lifted closer to a state of grace for all beings."

Sharon often accessed images of ancestral trauma in her sessions, ancient pockets of unresolved fear and grief that influence the behavior of living members of each species. "I don't really feel that it matters whether the information arises from the animal's personal past-life experience, whether it's something the animal draws out of the collective unconscious, or whether it's just a story," she explained. "Each of us taps into the collective at a certain level. I try to define it as little as possible — as long as what's presented gets the animal's story across and the results lead to an observable change in behavior."

Sharon also understood the healing power of symbolic narratives and myths. Sometimes, she would ask the animal to tell their person a story, "like a fairy tale, and we all know ahead of time that it's a story. But stories are incredibly therapeutic and often profoundly transformative. I find that with animals who are fearful, just like children who've been through a traumatic experience, sometimes it's too raw and scary to talk about in a direct way. But if we allow the animal to tell a fairy tale, all the information gets communicated without overwhelming the animal. I also find that when animals are elderly or dying, they sometimes want their person to tell them a story.

"Stories are incredibly important," she emphasized. "They can heal the past. They can resolve the present situation, and they can look to the future in a beautiful way. I feel that horses have lots of stories, and we're just beginning to listen. They need us to tell their stories — to give them a voice."

Dharma

It was, in fact, the story of a horse named Darma that brought me into contact with Sharon Callahan. Kim McElroy, a well-known horse artist who often consults Sharon on matters related to her pets, fell in love with this beautiful bay thoroughbred while visiting a racetrack. Her rapport with the mare was so strong, she told the owners that if they ever wanted to sell Darma, she would find a way to take her. Six months later, Kim received a phone call that Darma was lame, making the mare available for an affordable price, though the vet doubted Kim would ever be able to ride her. This made no difference to an artist whose magnificently detailed paintings of horses in their natural, unbridled state convey the emotional and spiritual impact these animals have on people. Many nonequestrians buy Kim's work, visit her website (SpiritofHorse.com), and sign up to receive her inspirational images and writings. In 2007, the two of us created a deck of horse wisdom cards and guidebook titled *Way of the Horse: Equine Archetypes for Self-Discovery*. We made sure to include a card and essay inspired by the ex-racehorse's presence in Kim's life, and many of her subscribers have responded to an ongoing series of articles describing her sometimes heart-wrenching experiences with the mare.

Kim had never actually owned one of these magnificent animals. As a three-year-old racehorse who had been trained to run fast in one direction, Darma turned out to be quite a handful. "I would try longeing her, and she would drag me across the arena," Kim remembers. "If I asked her to step away from me or pick up a foot, she would often freeze and refuse to move."

Finally, Kim called Sharon Callahan. "There was this whole beautiful scenario of Darma's situation overlapping with Kim's situation," Sharon told me, "a kind of family dynamic keeping Kim from moving to the next level in her artwork and her life. As I helped her become more independent and more outspoken about her needs, Kim's relationship with Darma deepened and improved."

"Darma really needed my strength," says Kim, "and my strength had been compromised by my fear of moving forward with my life. I was stuck for a long time, just as Sharon pointed out that Darma would often plant herself and refuse to move forward when she was unsure. Most importantly, Sharon confirmed and supported my connection with Darma, giving me the faith that I would be able to take on the challenge of being a new horse owner." A period of improvement, however, suddenly turned sour after a freak accident involving Kim and Darma.

"She fell to her knees abruptly while playing," Kim reveals. "In trying to get up, she slammed into me. I flipped over and broke my foot. The accident seemed to trigger a whole new level of fear in her. Once I was better and leading her again, she reacted to everything in extreme states of panic. I could barely lead her in a straight line, she spooked so much. The first three months she was like a wild horse. I could barely touch her. I tried massage therapists and TTouches, but I couldn't even do TTouches on her, she was so uptight."

Finally she decided to send Darma off to a trainer, "Collin," who had a similar approach to Monty Roberts: doing liberty work, using horselike body language. "Darma would eventually do what he wanted, but there was a lot of resistance," Kim remembers. "I saw her get into a fight with him once, and it really frightened me, yet there was a part of me that said, 'He's the authority; he knows what he's doing.' He was teaching me to be firm and assertive, to be the boss with her, in some ways to my detriment because I kept persevering. But Darma was not gaining any confidence. She was absolutely terrified, even after six months of training."

During this time, Kim began attending classes in self-empowerment and intuitive communication. The key, Kim told me, was to treat the horse "as a conscious being who has interpretations of events beyond instinctual behavior. Most trainers are focused on instinctual descriptions, like, 'He thinks you're a mountain lion climbing on his back.' The horse whisperer I went to had very strong ideas about how horses think at this elemental level. Collin's theories seemed so intelligent and he was such a charismatic person that I was really enamored with him for quite some time."

One day, she says, a friend accompanied her to one of Collin's clinics. "He was doing this demonstration, making the horse stand in the back of the stall, pushing the animal around and slapping him when he got too close," Kim recalls. "I realized this was the real Collin, that he was performing for this crowd, showing everyone that he was boss, and the horse didn't know what was expected of it. After that, I realized all he ever achieved was compliance. He was treating these animals as a collection of behaviors, like Pavlov's dog. In his mind, they made no real choices, had no individual interpretations, no soul." No wonder his work with Darma was ineffective. "I suspect that many of these horses, like Darma, reverted to their old behaviors when they went back to their owners because the real issues had not been addressed. Collin had some good instincts around horses, but he didn't believe they were capable of real insight or emotion. At one point, he mentioned something like, 'You only give to the horse when it gives to you.' My friend asked, 'Well, where does love fit into this?' He said, 'There is no love. Horses don't love. They're not capable of it.' To which she exploded, 'Love is the driving force of the universe' and then said no more because she realized it was useless arguing with him."

But Kim's perceptions were aligned with those of her friend. "I don't know why my mare's original owners named her Darma, but I guess it was my spiritual path, what the Buddhists call 'dharma,' to realize that love, intelligence, beauty, choice, and freedom are very much a part of every creature's journey on this earth — and beyond," she speculates. "Anyone who tries to obscure those principles with fancy arguments about human superiority, about our role as the boss of all other life-forms, can't possibly be working in my best interest, or anyone else's for that matter. I'm learning to trust my heart and stand up for what I really believe, regardless of what some 'authority' says, and the adventures I've had with Darma since then have brought this home to me time and time again."

The Promise of Freedom

Shortly after establishing my fledgling training business in the mid-1990s, I too realized it was useless to take on horses without the owner's commitment to be a part of the process. Most people who wanted me to "break" their colts and "fix" their problem horses were hoping for the perfect equine machine. Not wanting to face their own fears and vulnerabilities, they were reluctant to establish a relationship with an empowered mount. They wanted a defeated, dissociative animal to order around. In trying to grasp the implications, I realized that many of my human clients didn't know how to be free themselves, much less deal with an animal capable of asserting her own will and vision.

As I developed proficiency in equine-facilitated therapy and experiential learning, I used many of these techniques to help equestrians make the personal changes necessary to enter into an authentic, collaborative partnership with their horses. Sometimes, I simply created a safe space where people could explore new ways of being, where they were allowed to make mistakes, cry, and even throw temper tantrums as long as they weren't directing their anger toward the horse. In the process, they learned how to renegotiate standard equestrian activities to enhance consensual decision-making between horse and rider. As I adapted a number of intuitive communication and mindfulness practices to the riding arena, I also realized how talented horses were in teaching the skills usually associated with meditation.

In 1999, I developed what later became an international program to teach life-enhancement skills to riders and nonriders alike. These private or group lessons and workshops draw on mindfulness practices and stress-reduction, intuitive communication, leadership, and emotional/social intelligence skills from a variety of traditions without promoting a particular religion or belief system. I chose methods for their affinity with the natural wisdom of the horse and their proven effectiveness in helping people reach higher consciousness and greater fulfillment in life and work. Starting with the first session, students learn to assess their own physical, emotional, mental, and energetic states from moment to moment. While this multilevel awareness is crucial to safe, productive interactions with horses, it's also the same ability taught through the Buddha's Four Foundations of Mindfulness: mindfulness of the body (in which breathing and bodily sensations become the objects of meditation), mindfulness of feelings (meditation on the pleasant and unpleasant aspects of bodily experience), mindfulness of thought and emotions (observing how much our routine thought patterns are rooted in the repression of uncomfortable emotions), and, finally, mindfulness of mind (in which we reach a nonhabitual state of clarity, free from projection, avoidance, or attachment).

These steps toward greater peace and self-knowledge require significant fortitude in the sitting, standing, or walking postures associated with traditional forms of meditation. Many people lose interest when they reach an impasse that requires changes in attitudes and behaviors so ingrained they're barely detectable. Horses quite naturally bring these issues to the surface, mirroring difficulties that other human beings might not notice. These animals act as highly sensitive biofeedback agents for students, facilitating breakthroughs that allow people to move forward in their mindfulness practices, in their equestrian pursuits, in their interactions with others, and, perhaps most importantly, in their relationship with themselves.

I'm constantly inspired by the many ways that horses and people uplift one another when the humans embrace past traumas and unexpected

challenges thoughtfully and compassionately. Those obsessed with performance and perfection try to hide their wounds, tears, and uncertainties, yet
wearing a mask of confidence and well-being creates disconnection, making
it difficult to access internal psychological and physiological resources for
healing, restoration, and growth. Paradoxically, acknowledging our "imper-
fections" opens us to a wider view of our potential, to the love and acceptance available to us all. The universe no longer feels cold, cruel, and exacting
but filled with adventures designed to expand consciousness and connection.
Still, what psychologist and author Marion Woodman called an "addiction
to perfection" is one of the most common issues I encounter with high-
functioning clients who attend workshops designed to help people excel in
life.

The first time I met "Janelle," I was most certainly impressed. Tall, slim,
graceful, almost regal, she had the optimal conformation for riding. And
indeed she often won high-level dressage and hunter-jumper classes. She
brought one of her students to a workshop covering leadership, nonverbal
communication, mindfulness, and emotional/social intelligence skills. I
could tell "Amber" thought the world of her teacher, for good reason. Janelle
was that rare riding instructor interested in a holistic approach beyond herbal
supplements and chiropractic care, one that included the mental, emotional,
and spiritual aspects of the horse-human connection. It was no stretch for her
to treat the animals as sentient beings worthy of respect and collaboration.

After teaching some mind-body awareness tools, self-regulation/coreg-
ulation skills, and protocols for mutual respect, I invited participants to put
all those pieces together on day two of a four-day workshop through an
activity called Exploring Connection. Many people have deeply moving and
insightful experiences during these interactions with a loose horse. As an
experienced trainer, Janelle had spent thousands of hours with the animals,
so I figured it would be a piece of cake for her. In fact, I hoped she wouldn't
be bored. So when it was her turn, I was surprised at how stressed she looked.

Part of the process involves leading people through a body scan. By consciously connecting with and naming sensations occurring in the moment,
clients become aware of postures, areas of tension and relaxation, heart rate,
breathing, and so forth — nonverbal cues that most participants ignore or
try to fix without understanding the meaning behind them. This multifaceted protocol coincides with three of the Buddha's Four Foundations of
Mindfulness: mindfulness of the body, mindfulness of feelings, and, quite

often, mindfulness of thoughts and emotions. It's also incredibly practical for riders and trainers in all disciplines.

With only 10 percent of human communication in the verbal range, many people are completely unaware of what they're conveying to horses through that other 90 percent. For instance, the body scan helps an equestrian realize that she's collapsing and leaning back when she *thinks* she's acting assertively. When a person unconsciously assumes this submissive stance, just about any horse will move into her space, no matter how stern her voice becomes. Beyond the mindfulness aspects of the tool, the body scan also offers a technique for getting information from sensations. The key is not to relax out of the feeling or try to become grounded right away, but to focus on a posture or area of tension, sending it oxygen, awareness, and curiosity while asking for *one message at a time.* This is counterintuitive for most people, especially massage therapists, chiropractors, athletes, and equestrians who are used to making adjustments in response to pain or in relation to postures that are not considered optimal for the task at hand.

Because emotions and sensations are contagious, we also use the scan to help people learn how to differentiate between what they're feeling and what others are feeling. For this reason, I had Janelle stand with her back to the horse to check in with her own body before turning around and exploring connection with her equine partner.

Janelle's face was pale, her jaw tight, her shoulders bunched up to her neck. She looked like she wanted to run. Without drawing attention to what I was doing, I shifted my breathing to coregulate her nervous system, not to encourage her to relax out of what she was experiencing but to nonverbally help her avoid panic and stay present long enough to decipher what her body was so obviously worried about. This also kept me from catching *her* tension, allowing me to adopt facial expressions and a vocal tone conveying authentic curiosity and support.

Janelle described a variety of chaotic sensations during her initial scan. I asked her to pick the one that stood out to her the most. Her hands immediately clasped her neck.

"It seems like there's a lot going on in your neck," I acknowledged, "but I want you to make a deal with your body: tell it you'll listen to what it wants to say, but only if it releases the information one piece at a time. Like when you have a corral full of feisty horses. You halter the one closest to the gate and take one horse out at a time. You don't open the paddock and let them all run over you."

I suggested that she imagine breathing into the cacophony of sensations in her neck without trying to change anything, visualizing that a light in her conscious mind was following that breath, illuminating her neck. "It's like creating an email connection between your thinking brain and your neck," I explained. "Ask for one piece of information and be open to how your body might speak to you. It may send you a color, an image, a memory, a cliché, a completely irrational phrase, or even a fragment of a song. The message may not make sense right away, because the body tends to speak more like an artist or a poet than a scientist. Just tell me the first thing that comes to your mind."

The act of breathing into a sensation is a form of creative visualization with a self-regulation component, allowing people to coax their nervous system toward a more centered state while interacting with the body as a source of intelligence. It conveys curiosity and acceptance of the body's concerns instead of enacting rigid attempts to force the body into suppression and compliance.

Janelle closed her eyes and let her hands drop to her sides. "I don't know," she said after a few moments of deep breathing. "I'm not getting anything. It just feels like a vice around my neck getting tighter."

"The image of a vice *is* the message," I assured her. "Great. Now, most people at this point would be tempted to find a way to release the vice, to get rid of it and relax. But over the years, I've learned it's more productive to find out why it's there first. So I invite you to breathe into the sensation again and ask, 'What is the purpose of the vice?'"

Janelle concentrated silently for a moment and then opened her eyes thoughtfully, like it suddenly made perfect sense to her. "It's there to hold feelings and information down. It seems to be suppressing stuff my brain doesn't want to deal with."

I asked Janelle to check back in with the sensation in her neck, to see if it had changed in some way.

"Yes," she marveled. "It relaxed slightly, like it was satisfied that I was finally listening to it. Strange."

"Horses will sigh and lower their heads when a person becomes congruent *even if the emotion is still there*," I reminded her. "The body does the same thing. Your body is the horse your mind rides around on. It's a sentient being, not a machine. Of course, you can beat it into submission, ride it hard, and put it away wet, but you and I both know that cooperation with the horse is much more effective."

Janelle nodded pensively.

"You can either ask for another message or you can just move forward," I offered. "The deal we made was to get one piece of information at a time. It's not necessary to solve every last issue you've been suppressing to move forward with your day. It's important that the body learns how to titrate the information, to bring it forward in small pieces, so we don't get our circuits blown."

Looking more thoughtful, Janelle wanted to see if the vice would let just one feeling through without overwhelming her with all the material she had been holding down for years. "But which one should I choose?"

"Remember the corral of horses?" I asked. "If the herd is racing around, you don't jump in and try to grab the rearing stallion at the back. Just imagine picking the message closest to the surface, the horse closest to the gate, so to speak."

Janelle closed her eyes, concentrating. "The feeling is fear."

"What's the concern?" I asked.

"Jeez, I don't know. I think it might be —"

"Don't think," I said. "Go back to your body. Let it speak. Breathe into the sensation and ask, 'What's the concern?'"

"Rejection," she said emphatically, her eyes widening with surprise. "Wow, I really didn't expect that."

I reminded this supremely experienced horsewoman that the goal of the exercise was not *achieving* connection but *exploring* connection. "There is no right or wrong here. We are interested in when you start to feel connected and if the horse's behavior changes in some way. Maybe the horse will walk over to you, or follow you, or allow you to approach and pet her. Maybe something in the environment will suddenly attract her attention away from you, and you'll discover a new way to regain the connection."

Janelle nodded tentatively.

I directed the much more centered woman to stay in contact with her body as she turned toward the mare. "Does anything change in your body when you look at Blanca?"

"I feel much more relaxed," she replied.

"Just for fun, let's continue the conversation with your body. As I say the goal out loud, notice where it's activated in your body or simply where your attention is drawn. The goal is to explore connection with Blanca."

"My heart," she said confidently after a moment of concentration.

"Breathe into your heart, creating that mind-body connection," I said. "Ask what advice your body has for exploring connection with Blanca today."

"Breathe and be," she replied. Janelle opened her eyes with a quizzical look. "Wow, I don't think I would have come up with that. I would have tried something more active."

"Well, see what happens if you just go in there and follow your body's advice. In this way, we are inviting your 'horse,' the one your mind rides, to have a say, to share its wisdom."

Janelle liked that idea. Upon entering the corral, she barely took two steps before Blanca turned and walked up to her. The woman rested her right hand gently on the gray mare's shoulder. I could see her breathing deeply and evenly. A minute or two later, Blanca's daughter Cloud, who had been nibbling fallen mesquite leaves in an adjoining corral, lifted her head as if she'd heard someone offering carrots and made a beeline toward Janelle. Without having to adjust her position, she reached her left arm through the fence and was able to rest this other hand on Cloud's soft neck. The three of them stood silently for ten minutes, breathing and being, in what looked to those of us watching outside like a timeless experience of profound connection. A feeling of ecstasy seemed to expand outward in concentric waves, opening the hearts and expanding the minds of everyone witnessing the quiet yet riveting event.

We all had tears in our eyes as Janelle emerged, sat down with the group, and let out a long, pensive sigh. It took her a moment to speak.

"When I was in there, I understood more about that feeling of fear," she said. "It wasn't about being embarrassed if I failed to connect. It was more dire than that. I was deeply afraid of a *soul-level rejection*."

Janelle explained that Blanca and Cloud helped her realize that she somehow unconsciously believed that she would receive love in direct proportion to how much she excelled — in school, in sports, and in the equestrian arts. "I don't know where I got that idea, really. My family was always supportive. But I guess it's something implied in our culture. My parents' and teachers' eyes would light up when I got straight A's, or won an award, or brought another first place trophy home from a major competition. I guess I never conceived what it would feel like to be loved and accepted for just, well, being me. Cloud and Blanca gave me a gift that no one had ever been able to give me before. I feel more solid somehow and at the same time, lighter, happier, *free*."

Janelle articulated a dilemma everyone in the group related to: appreciating others as soulful beings, outside the realm of practicality and achievement, is a challenge for modern humans, whether they're buying a horse as a show prospect or finding their own self-worth, daily, among members of their own kind.

Soul Friends

Since *The Tao of Equus* was first published in 2001, I've met numerous people whose stories have mirrored my own, and I'm pleased to hear the book gave them comfort in times of uncertainty. For many equestrians, it takes a "problem horse" to awaken them to a deeper relationship with these profound and benevolent beings. Sarah V. Barnes, founder of Anam Cara Equestrian, began working as a trainer and riding instructor in the early 2000s. She also competed for over a decade in eventing, the triathlon of equestrian sports. In 2013, following what seemed like a minor slip in the barn aisle, her competition prospect, a five-year-old mare named Okotillo (Tio), became unrideable. Despairing but determined not to give up on the young horse, with whom she'd developed a close bond, Sarah set out on a journey that led her away from competition and toward the heart of authentic connection. She still works as an instructor, teaching riding as a meditative art, and now writes historical fiction, including the trilogy *She Who Rides Horses: A Saga of the Ancient Steppe*, which, as I mentioned earlier, tells the story of the first person to ride a horse.

"*Anam cara* means 'soul friend' in Gaelic," Sarah explains. "Around the time of Tio's injury, I renamed my teaching business Anam Cara Equestrian to reflect the different direction in which she was leading me in regard to my own relationship with horses and also what I wanted to model for my students. *The Tao of Equus* was very helpful to me during that time. I'd always loved horses and considered myself a kind rider, but Tio taught me so much more about building a relationship, in and out of the saddle, based on listening to the horse as a teacher, guide, and spiritual companion. She led me down a path of personal growth that I never would have traveled on my own." Because of Tio's physical issues, she says, "I learned invaluable lessons about human and equine biomechanics and neuroscience, to be sure, but she also revealed the hidden realms of ancestral trauma and shamanic healing. By opening my heart, she transformed my way of being in the world. Although she passed away in 2021, she is still with me, always and forever my anam cara. Her legacy lives on in the way I try to show up in my life, as well as at the barn."

Sarah finds that "remaining authentic" around other horse people can be a challenge, however. "In many equestrian programs across the country, the old adage of 'Show the horse who's the boss, otherwise they'll take over' still applies," she observes. "Even among followers of so-called natural horsemanship, there's a persistent belief that the human must be the alpha leader, even though we now understand that horses don't operate according to the principles of hierarchy," she points out. While the teachings of people she considers "more enlightened advocates of the horse," such as Mark Rashid and Manolo Mendez, have gained a considerable following in the last couple of decades, such views have not permeated everywhere. "Harsh equipment and short-cut training techniques designed to achieve extravagant but superficial results are still prevalent, sometimes at the highest levels of equestrian sport. Similarly, while huge advances have been made in conventional veterinary diagnostic and treatment protocols, along with the use of alternative modalities, these are often employed to do whatever is necessary to allow the horse to get back to work as soon as possible, without regard to the possibility of underlying issues impacting the horse's well-being on a holistic or even spiritual level. For someone who wants to be part of the wider equestrian community without sacrificing their relationship with their horse, the way forward can be hard to discern."

Sarah boards her horses at a public facility where most of the other riders and trainers focus on upper-level dressage. "Imagine big, fancy, sometimes expensive horses and riders who hold themselves and their equine partners to very high standards," she continues. "My horses and I are fortunate that, for the most part, our community is made up of equestrians who have not lost touch with the love of horses that brought them to the sport in the first place. Despite pressure to perform and succeed in the show ring, the horses at our barn are generally not treated as disposable tools for the gratification of the human ego, as can still be the case in many competition settings."

Several of her fellow boarders are well-versed in equine neuropsychology, as well as in the latest in alternative and integrative health practices, but still, "even among the most well-meaning horse people, unexamined habits can linger," Sarah says. "Something as simple as requiring a horse to stand in crossties — a necessity in a crowded grooming area — or dismissing a horse's attempt to communicate discomfort with a casual 'Oh, he always makes that face but I've checked him for ulcers, and the saddle fits, so it must just be what he does' can cause me to pause and ask myself if we are really doing our best for our equine friends." She's the first to admit that dealing with horses can be "incredibly frustrating and discouraging, *especially* when you are trying to be conscious and conscientious — and also ride. How do we honor our horses as fully sentient beings, yet at the same time require them to live in our world and conform to our desires?"

It's a question that my colleagues, my students, and I myself continue to ask daily. Collaborating with other conscientious equestrians is essential to reimagining how the two species can evolve together to tap the full, as yet unrealized potential of the horse-human bond.

One valid answer, Sarah notes, is to not ask them to conform, at least not to the extent that many of us do. "For me personally, however, if I am to share my life with horses, some other solution is required. Riding is my passion. The shared movement — the deep physical connection — feeds my soul. Riding, for me, represents a quest for communion, a challenge to become the softest, most attuned, most balanced partner for my horses that I can possibly be." Sarah considers issues such as "How can I help them to move with ease and grace under saddle?" and "Is it possible for them to revel in their own beauty and power while carrying me?" If the animals aren't enjoying the process, she says, then neither can she. "Perhaps I'm naïve to aspire to ride in a way that honors the soul of the horse, but the alternatives — either riding with force and leverage in the way I was originally taught or not riding at all — are equally unacceptable," she explains. "The former option is simply not who I want to be as a rider. The latter path leads to a grief so crushing that it seems to carry the weight of generations of horse-crazy girls who never got the chance to fulfill their dreams of galloping across the pasture on the back of a magic steed."

Admittedly, Sarah sets her aspirations high. "Being part of the world of equestrian performance sport while at the same time staying committed to being with horses in a way that honors who they are — fully sentient beings, wise beyond human understanding — is a constant challenge," she concedes. "I have a new young horse. Every day, someone at the barn asks if

I'm planning to compete with him and when I'm going to start riding him more. '*Maybe*,' I reply, 'when he's ready.' Doubt creeps in. Who am I to attempt this reconciliation of opposites? But then I remind myself that we are just getting to know one another. Someday, if I'm worthy, he will become my next partner. And then, perhaps, if we both choose, we will dance down the centerline together. In the meantime, he reminds me each time I go to the barn of who I want to be, both as a rider and a friend."

The potential of a soulful approach to the equestrian arts is vast — and life-changing. Horses live in the moment, and their influence keeps riders from becoming mired in projections and tricks of the mind. Their nomadic nature encourages a fluidity of thought, emotion, and behavior that sedentary life subconsciously discourages. The simple act of grooming or riding puts people in a state of relaxed heightened awareness conducive to creativity and intuition. Horses also communicate important nuances of emotion through the quality and frequency of their breathing. Students learn to calm a nervous animal or move from a walk to a trot through cues given by the breath alone, reawakening and strengthening empathy and sociosensual awareness along the way.

This ambitious approach to collaborating with horses can't help but take on the patina of a spiritual practice. Riding consciously demands some facility in reaching the Buddha's fourth and final Foundation of Mindfulness: the mindfulness of mind practice. Students learn to direct the energy of a thousand-pound creature through mental focus, creative visualization, and clear intent, while remaining open to the horse's input. But it is the equine talent for teaching the art of freedom through relationship that may very well be the horse's greatest gift to us in the twenty-first century. In helping people reconnect to nature, to their bodies, to the authentic self, to ancestral wisdom, to the herd, and to the community, equine-facilitated studies create an experience of consensual liberation unavailable to the lone wolf, social outcast, or rugged individualist.

After establishing my Eponaquest Worldwide practice, touring, and communicating with people on six continents who had similar interests, I became aware of consciousness-expanding programs sprouting up internationally. EFMHA cofounder Barbara Rector created a special division of her Adventures in Awareness program called Journey Ride, which, she says, "incorporates a wellness perspective, mindful meditation, sensory integration, and equine movement to produce different states of consciousness."

Barbara cites the integrative medicine and wellness expert Andrew Weil,

MD, who speaks of the link between spontaneous healing occurrences and altered or shifted states of consciousness. "Many of the experiences I had working with the horses over the years seemed to naturally tap into a deeper layer of consciousness," she reveals. "I don't know what the mechanism is, but the horse facilitates those who are ready to enter this shift. I'm absolutely convinced there are certain horses, like people, who've stepped up to the plate, ready to coevolve [to] a different level of being for humans and animals, but I can never predict where a Journey Ride will take someone. The internal director of the participant decides how the work will proceed, and the horse will just go with it."

In her many years of facilitating equine-assisted therapy and experiential learning sessions, she learned to trust the process. "When you set out to engage the universe, which is totally benign and loving, you have an unconscious or conscious agreement to accept what is. While the feelings that come through may not be joy, joy is always behind it. At the end of a Journey Ride, I have yet to know someone who hasn't tapped in, just a little bit closer, to that spark of creative fire that connects us all."

Clean Slate

My own journey rides with Rasa took me places I never could have imagined when I met her in Phoenix in 1992. Her wounded stifle prevented us from pursuing my initial dream of endurance racing, but the mental, emotional, and spiritual terrain we covered turned out to be much more expansive in comparison. When I was on Rasa's back or simply lounging next to her in the shade of a big mesquite, time seemed to stand still. As I stared into her eyes, I saw other worlds reflected.

Six months to the day after my mother passed away, I met her spirit in a dream. She was young and beautiful and full of life. "I miss you so much, Mom," I said, "and I can't thank you enough for your faith in me. I wish you could have held my book in your hands." She smiled and nodded as we walked over to a grove of oaks, their leaves shimmering in the light of a brighter sun. There, Rasa waited for us both, and her gaze was absolutely electric. "I want you to consider my horses as your horses," I told my mother. "When you're ready, Rasa can take you anywhere you want to go."

"I'm ready now," she said simply, joyfully. I helped her climb onto Rasa's back. The two lifted into the air and soared past the horizon.

The next day Rasa seemed different in some way. There was a glow about her I had never noticed before, a peaceful, knowing look in her eyes, like the past had no influence and the future was unlimited.

"You've come into your power now, haven't you?" I asked her. Rasa nuzzled my ear and let out a gentle sigh. We stood there in silence for a while. I held up her halter, and she lowered her head in response. Then I unlatched the gate and headed for the open desert.

ACKNOWLEDGMENTS

This book would not exist without the soulful support of my husband, Steve Roach, whose music and life continually reflect the hero's journey through darkness and light and all the poignant shadows in between. He never flinches in the face of authenticity, and he knows me better than any two-legged creature alive. Many times, I've broken through the scourge of writer's block by resonating with his uncompromising soundscapes and the ineffable insights they convey.

I couldn't imagine a more sensitive and empowered editor than Jason Gardner, a man who was willing to embrace my most challenging ideas and experiences, questioning yet supporting me every step of the way. Editor Diana Rico took the revised and expanded version of *The Tao of Equus* to a whole new level in 2023, helping me to better define new research and anecdotes and to refine many insights from the first edition. I cannot thank my agent, Felicia Eth, enough for believing in this project and helping me focus my ideas way back when I was writing a book proposal for what was, in the late 1990s, an ambitious approach to exploring the transformational potential of the horse-human bond.

I wish my mother, Martha Kohanov, could be here to hold this book in her hand. She never doubted that it would be published, and she believed in me when no one else understood what I was trying to accomplish — though I never managed to get her on the back of a horse.

Eternal gratefulness to my father, Nicholas Kohanov, who through compassion, vision, and personal sacrifice held back the poisonous waters of the "Black Sea" to transfer the wisdom of the Horse Ancestors to me through his tempestuous genetic line.

Much appreciation for the faith my sister Kathryn Vrabel, her husband Myron, their daughter Brianna, and my aunt Kathryn Jones invested in this project, sometimes obscuring the intensity of my marathon writing sessions with that Patterson sense of humor. Best wishes to my niece, Reimi, who carries the wisdom of Chinese sages in her blood.

Special thanks to the enlightened riders and trainers who helped me launch Epona Equestrian Services: Julia Standish, Paula Frey, Cathie Hook, Stacey Kollman, Dana Light, Shelley Rosenberg, and Cathy Schreiber. Thanks to Buck and Dana Light for sharing their stories and wisdom over marvelous dinners at the working cattle ranch in southern Arizona. Linda Zimmerman and Georges Sarah, owners of The Ranch in Tucson, went above and beyond the call of duty to support me in so many ways during the writing of this book.

I'm especially grateful to my mentors in the fields of equine-facilitated therapy and animal communication, professionals who respected my original vision while freely sharing their hard-won wisdom: Laura Brinckerhoff, Barbara Rector, Maureen Fredrickson, Dianna Hine, Sharon Callahan, and Tamara Solange. Special thanks to Patricia Hursh, Kathleen Barry Ingram, Dr. Rebecca Bailey, and Dr. Ann Baldwin, whose insights took me to a new level in my work and in my life. Thanks to Dr. Lewis Mehl-Madrona for that single potent session. I'd also like to thank horse artist and writer Kim McElroy for continuing inspiration, Sarah V. Barnes for her historical research and soulful insights, and horse artist Judy Delano for much initial inspiration — as well as for helping dream Rasa to safety. Much gratitude to my Eponaquest Worldwide staff: Elysa Ginsburg, Sue Smades, Nyla Schaffner, Kris Kramer, Jennifer Ybarra, Callie Varney, Frank Schaffner Jr., Aiden Aguilar, and Arianna Ybarra. Their care of the horses and our clients has been essential and exemplary. Much appreciation to Nelda and Karl Buckman, Jenn and Eric Freeman, and the staff at Nelda Studios for bringing my work to a wider audience through online courses at LindaKohanov.com, where the equine teachers who changed my life continue to share their wisdom through photos and videos.

There's no doubt I learn as much from my students as they learn from me. Heartfelt thanks to Hope Crabtree, Betty Franklin, Ernestina, Joshua and Linda, the Florez family, Bianca, Autumn and Ellen, Jillian Lessner, Jess DeVaney, Lori and Ken Shaver, and the numerous people who allowed me to share their stories under pseudonyms. Special thanks to the two courageous women whose parallel lives merged in the case study of "Joy." Endless apples and carrots to my four-legged students, who were undoubtedly my greatest teachers.

I'd like to thank my first husband, K., with whom I explored so many of the questions. There was great wisdom hidden in our moments of imperfection.

Special thanks to the late Minnesota-based poet and essayist J. Otis Powell for continuous encouragement, artistic inspiration, and heated debates. He was one of the few city dwellers I've met with the nerve and tenacity to ride Tabula Rasa into his own potent, ever-evolving "Theology." I realized he'd gotten the big hit of horse knowledge when I read the ending to his poem "It's All Dat: Photographs of Tucson":

> Wild horses of our desire
> tumble through a mountain wind
> and ride away with our sanity.
> For fun.
> Just for fun.

Eternal gratefulness to my own herd for doing just that.

NOTES

Introduction

p. 3   *They "approach you, slowly"*: David S. Whitley, *Cave Paintings and the Human Spirit: The Origin of Creativity and Belief* (Amherst, NY: Prometheus Books, 2009), 75.

p. 3   *"animal bones excavated"*: Whitley, *Cave Paintings*, 31.

p. 4   *stated "unequivocally" that "non-human animals"*: Philip Low, "The Cambridge Declaration on Consciousness," ed. Jack Panksepp, Dianna Reiss, David Edelman, Bruno Van Swinderen, Philip Low, and Christof Koch (declaration presented at the Francis Crick Memorial Conference on Consciousness in Human and Non-Human Animals, Churchill College, University of Cambridge, July 7, 2012).

p. 4   *"neural networks aroused during affective states"*: Low, "Cambridge Declaration."

p. 4   *Statistics from the American Horse Council*: American Horse Council, "2017 EIS Facts: Economic Impact of the United States Horse Industry," https://horsecouncil .org/resources/2017-economic-impact-study-facts/.

p. 4   *"A 2023 article by the World Animal Foundation"*: Talitha Van Niekerk, "How Many Horses Are There in the World?," World Animal Foundation, October 11, 2023, https://worldanimalfoundation.org/advocate/how-many-horses-are-there/.

p. 8   *"know the yang, but keep"*: Hundreds of English translations exist of the Tao Te Ching, all with slightly different twists of phrase. This is the first line of chapter 28 in any translation of the Tao Te Ching. Here I have used two of the most common, straightforward interpretations. Though this ancient Chinese text is credited to Lao-tzu, there are several different spellings of the name. There is also considerable controversy as to whether Lao-tzu was an actual individual or the pen name chosen by a group of anonymous sages.

Chapter Three: Voices from the Ancestors

p. 53   *"A savage blast of thunder"*: Linda Kohanov, liner notes for Steve Roach, *Origins*, Fortuna Records 17081-2, 1993, compact disc.

p. 56   *"The title of supreme rule"*: Neal Ascherson, *Black Sea* (New York: Hill and Wang, 1995), 8–9.

p. 58   *"The Cossacks were not capable"*: Ascherson, *Black Sea*, 110.

p. 62   *"which until then had led"*: Ascherson, *Black Sea*, 81.

p. 63   *"devoted to survival, intelligence"*: Patrick Wright, quoted in Ascherson, *Black Sea*, 55–56.

p. 63   *"Here is a technique"*: Ascherson, *Black Sea*, 56.

p. 65   *"a ruthless mental dynasty"*: Ascherson, *Black Sea*, 49.

p. 74   *"Each kind of natural system"*: Rupert Sheldrake, *The Presence of the Past* (Rochester, VT: Park Street Press, 1988), xviii–xix.

p. 74   *"Natural systems, such as termite"*: Sheldrake, *The Presence of the Past*, xvii.

p. 75   *"Shamanism is a disciplined way"*: Michael Harner, quoted in Tom Soloway Pinkson, *The Flowers of Wiricuta* (Rochester, VT: Destiny Books, 1995), 13.

Chapter Four: Mind under Matter

p. 85   *Carl Jung cites water*: C. G. Jung, *The Archetypes and the Collective Unconscious*, 2nd ed. (Princeton, NJ: Princeton University Press, 1968), 18.

p. 85   *"an affair of the cerebrum"*: Jung, *The Archetypes and the Collective Unconscious*, 20.

p. 85   *"only as something to be found"*: Jung, *The Archetypes and the Collective Unconscious*, 19.

p. 85   *"a refuge for all those timorous souls"*: Jung, *The Archetypes and the Collective Unconscious*, 19.

p. 86   *"Whoever looks into the mirror"*: Jung, *The Archetypes and the Collective Unconscious*, 20.

p. 88   *"Water is the fluid"*: Jung, *The Archetypes and the Collective Unconscious*, 19.

p. 95   *"the neural pathways of social support"*: Stephen W. Porges, *A Pocket Guide to the Polyvagal Theory: The Transformative Power of Feeling Safe* (New York: W. W. Norton, 2017), 100.

p. 95   *"rapidly regulates cardiac output"*: Ann Baldwin, *The Vagus Nerve in Therapeutic Practice: Working with Clients to Manage Stress and Enhance Mind-Body Function* (London: Handspring Publishing, 2024), 16.

p. 97   *"Mirror neurons have particular importance"*: Daniel Goleman and Richard Boyatzis, "Social Intelligence and the Biology of Leadership," *Harvard Business Review*, September 2008, https://hbr.org/2008/09/social-intelligence-and-the-biology-of-leadership.

p. 98   *"In effect, the delivery"*: Goleman and Boyatzis, "Social Intelligence and the Biology of Leadership," 3.

p. 100   *"this ultra rapid connection"*: Goleman and Boyatzis, "Social Intelligence and the Biology of Leadership," 4.

p. 103   *Sorenson has developed a theory*: Christian de Quincey, "Consciousness: Truth or Wisdom?," *Noetic Sciences Review* 51 (March–June 2000): 13, 44. All E. Richard Sorenson material that follows is from de Quincey.

p. 105   *"The selfless unity that seemed"*: Sorenson, quoted in de Quincey, "Consciousness: Truth or Wisdom?," 45.

p. 105   *"epidemic sleeplessness, frenzied dance"*: Sorenson, quoted in de Quincey, "Consciousness: Truth or Wisdom?," 45.

p. 105   *"a transmodern spiritual or mystical"*: de Quincey, "Consciousness: Truth or Wisdom?," 45.

p. 105   *"Reason doesn't have to decimate"*: de Quincey, "Consciousness: Truth or Wisdom?," 46.

p. 106   *"one other thing that makes"*: Ray Hunt, quoted in Linda Boston, "Ray Hunt: A Legend in His Own Time," *Ranch and Country* 3, no. 4 (August/September 1977): 9.

p. 106   *"glad [this] one thing couldn't"*: Boston, "Ray Hunt: A Legend in His Own Time," 9.

p. 107   *"Only if we listen"*: Dietrich von Hopffgarten, "The Magic Connection," *Dressage & CT* 92, no. 255 (May 1994): 12–14.

p. 108   *"Interconnected feelings and altered states"*: de Quincey, "Consciousness: Truth or Wisdom?," 45–46.

p. 108   *"There's a thin line between psychotics"*: Jonathan Cott, "Deepak Chopra: God, Man, and the Media," *Rolling Stone*, September 28, 2000, 51.

Chapter Six: The Politics of Intelligence

p. 155   *"a relatively large brain"*: Stephen Budiansky, *The Nature of Horses* (London: Weidenfeld & Nicholson, 1997), 84–85.

p. 155   *"exceptionally large and well developed"*: Leslie Skipper, *Inside Your Horse's Mind: A Study of Equine Intelligence and Human Prejudice* (London: J. A. Allen, 1999), 69.

p. 156   *"Suppose you are a process worker"*: Skipper, *Inside Your Horse's Mind*, 71.

p. 159   *"Sadly…children emerging"*: Dianna Hine, *The Baby Bond* (Prescott, AZ: Cocoon Books, 1999), 15.

p. 160   *"such as when they are"*: Hine, *The Baby Bond*, 16.

p. 160   *"At the end of the school year"*: Larry Dossey, *Recovering the Soul: A Scientific and Spiritual Search* (New York: Bantam Books, 1989), 93–94.

p. 161   *"whose trainers believed them"*: Dossey, *Recovering the Soul*, 94–95.

p. 162   *"Too many stress hormones"*: Hine, *The Baby Bond*, 17–18.

p. 164   *"Think of the body-mind"*: Candace Pert, *Your Body Is Your Subconscious Mind: New Insights into the Body-Mind Connection*, Sounds True AW00451D, 2000, 3 compact discs.

p. 164   *"I remember marveling"*: Candace Pert, *Molecules of Emotion* (New York: Touchstone Books, 1997), 33.

p. 169   *"creative indolence"*: John Briggs, *Fire in the Crucible: The Alchemy of Creative Genius* (New York: St. Martin's Press, 1988), 204.

p. 170   *"the creative state of mind"*: Briggs, *Fire in the Crucible*, 203.

Chapter Seven: Horse Whisperings

p. 174   *"The seemingly simple change"*: Sam Powell with Lane Carter, *Almost a Whisper: A Holistic Approach to Working with Your Horse* (Loveland, CO: Alpine Publications, 1999), 103.

p. 183   *"interact with, to survive"*: Stephen W. Porges, *A Pocket Guide to the Polyvagal Theory: The Transformative Power of Feeling Safe* (New York: W. W. Norton, 2017), 99.

p. 187   *"to make the mustangs worth more"*: Monty Roberts, *The Man Who Listens to Horses* (New York: Random House, 1996), 14.

p. 187   *"A large number of the riders"*: Mary Wanless, *For the Good of the Horse* (North Pomfret, VT: Trafalgar Square, 1997), 12–13.

p. 188   *"He believed that the human"*: Linda Tellington-Jones, *An Introduction to the Tellington-Jones Equine Awareness Method* (Millwood, NY: Breakthrough Publications, 1988), xii.

p. 189   *"As you explore Connected Riding"*: Peggy Cummings with Diana Deterding, *Connected Riding: An Introduction* (Gaithersburg, MD: Primedia Equine Group, 1999), 10.

p. 190   *"You've got to have your act together"*: Pat Parelli, *Natural Horse-Man-Ship* (Salt Lake City: Western Horseman, 1993), 16.

p. 190   *"To date…I have never met"*: GaWaNi Pony Boy, *Of Women and Horses: Essays by Various Horsewomen* (Irvine, CA: BowTie Press, 2000), 54.

p. 197   *"My pulse rate is always low"*: Monty Roberts, quoted in Jackie Budd, *Reading the Horse's Mind* (New York: Howell Book House, 1996), 69.

p. 201   *"At the moment of contact"*: Peter A. Levine with Ann Frederick, *Waking the Tiger: Healing Trauma* (Berkeley, CA: North Atlantic Books, 1997), 15–17.

p. 202   *"As in the Greek myth"*: Levine, *Waking the Tiger*, 20.

p. 203   Woody Allen quips: Levine, *Waking the Tiger*, 136.

p. 203   *"The shock produced a stupor"*: David Livingstone, quoted in Levine, *Waking the Tiger*, 137.

p. 204   *"The best way to define"*: Levine, *Waking the Tiger*, 137–38.

Chapter Eight: Four-Legged Therapists

p. 207   *"Men made all the decisions"*: Matthew Mackay-Smith, "A Change for the Better," *Equus* 277 (November 2000): 77.

p. 208   *"riders who partnered"*: Mackay-Smith, "A Change for the Better," 77.

p. 214   *"Achieve without trying to achieve"*: Lao-tzu, *The Illustrated Tao Te Ching*, translated by Man-Ho Kwok, Martin Palmer, and Jay Ramsey (Rockport, MA: Element, 1993), 153.

p. 214   *"There are too many laws"*: Lao-tzu, *The Illustrated Tao Te Ching*, 35.

p. 214   *"Desiring nothing for himself"*: Lao-tzu, *The Illustrated Tao Te Ching*, 38.

p. 215   *"Thirty spokes on a cart wheel"*: Lao-tzu, *The Illustrated Tao Te Ching*, 46.

p. 215   *"comes from the virtue"*: Lao-tzu, *The Illustrated Tao Te Ching*, 163.

p. 215   *"tries to help us be true"*: Lao-tzu, *The Illustrated Tao Te Ching*, 163.

p. 217   *"The mind-body fracture"*: Don Hanlon Johnson, *Body: Recovering Our Sensual Wisdom* (Berkeley, CA: North Atlantic Books, 1983), 133.

p. 217   *"the physiological anchor"*: Wilhelm Reich, quoted in Johnson, *Body*, 141.

p. 221   *"Authorities in every kind"*: Johnson, *Body*, 140.

p. 222   *"Whether as prostitute, goddess"*: Octavio Paz, quoted in Johnson, *Body*, 134.

Chapter Nine: The Stallion Factor

p. 233   *"emotions have a mind of their own"*: Daniel Goleman, *Emotional Intelligence* (New York: Bantam, 1995), 20.

p. 234   *"method of comparison is associative"*: Goleman, *Emotional Intelligence*, 21.

p. 244   *"the stop sign of the soul"*: Karla McLaren, *Becoming an Empath* (Boulder, CO: Sounds True, 2000).

p. 245   *"The connections between the amygdala"*: Goleman, *Emotional Intelligence*, 27.

p. 245   *"they make disastrous choices"*: Goleman, *Emotional Intelligence*, 28–29.

p. 246   *"inability to notice our true feelings"*: Goleman, *Emotional Intelligence*, 43.

p. 246   *"The time has come"*: Howard Gardner, quoted in Goleman, *Emotional Intelligence*, 37.

p. 247   *"Marshaling emotions in the service"*: Goleman, *Emotional Intelligence*, 43.

p. 248   *"the fundamental 'people skill'"*: Goleman, *Emotional Intelligence*, 43.

p. 249   *"The art of relationship"*: Goleman, *Emotional Intelligence*, 43.

Chapter Ten: The Wounded Healer

p. 254   *"between the eccentric, unpredictable"*: Eric Francis, "Holistic Astrology: An Introduction to Chiron," Star IQ, http://www.stariq.com/Main/Articles/P0000866.HTM (site discontinued).

p. 254   *"as the basis for understanding"*: "Chiron — the Wounded Healer," Chiron Centre for Body Psychotherapy, http://www.chironcentre.freeserve.co.uk/abt_appr.htm (site discontinued).

p. 254   *"The archetype of the 'wounded healer'"*: Chiron Centre for Body Psychotherapy (site discontinued).

p. 256   *"Practitioners are trained to imitate"*: Don Hanlon Johnson, *Body: Recovering Our Sensual Wisdom* (Berkeley, CA: North Atlantic Books, 1983), 157.

p. 257   *"All strong souls first go"*: Clarissa Pinkola Estés, from the poem "Abre la Puerta," in *Theatre of the Imagination*, quoted on Estés's official website, https://www.clarissa pinkolaestes.com.

p. 258   *"The daimon remembers what is"*: James Hillman, *The Soul's Code: In Search of Character and Calling* (New York: Random House, 1996), 8.

p. 258   *"in terms of very large ideas"*: Hillman, *The Soul's Code*, 5.

p. 259   *"as eccentricities, compacted with"*: Hillman, *The Soul's Code*, 5.

p. 259   *"strike like an annunciation"*: Hillman, *The Soul's Code*, 3.

p. 269   *"This was the thought"*: Eckhart Tolle, *The Power of Now* (Novato, CA: New World Library, 1999), 1–2.

p. 270   *"fresh and pristine, as if"*: Tolle, *The Power of Now*, 4.

Chapter Eleven: Nekyia

p. 278   *"far best of all men"*: Homer, *The Odyssey*, quoted in Seth L. Schein, "Introduction," *Reading the Odyssey* (Princeton, NJ: Princeton University Press, 1996), 11.

p. 279   *"I have been and am still"*: Hermann Hesse, *Demian*, quoted in Larry Dossey, *Recovering the Soul: A Scientific and Spiritual Search* (New York: Bantam Books, 1989), 80.

p. 279   *"The mind is in the blood"*: Dossey, *Recovering the Soul*, 81.

p. 279   *"the new understanding of the role"*: Dossey, *Recovering the Soul*, 81.

p. 280   *"The present does not come"*: Dossey, *Recovering the Soul*, 201.

p. 282   *"DNA, by providing the code"*: Rupert Sheldrake, quoted in Dossey, *Recovering the Soul*, 198–99.

p. 283   *"in an energetic state"*: Gary E. R. Schwartz and Linda G. S. Russek, *The Living Energy Universe* (Charlottesville, VA: Hampton Roads, 1999), xv.

p. 283   *"The nonsystemic (reductionistic) story"*: Schwartz and Russek, *The Living Energy Universe*, 89.

p. 284   *"One way is through"*: Schwartz and Russek, *The Living Energy Universe*, 55.

p. 284   *"What Tesla realized was"*: Schwartz and Russek, *The Living Energy Universe*, 55.

p. 285   *"If universal living memory"*: Schwartz and Russek, *The Living Energy Universe*, 172–73.

p. 285   *"then how… can we tune into"*: Schwartz and Russek, *The Living Energy Universe*, 172–73.

p. 285   *"Narby suggests that DNA"*: Schwartz and Russek, *The Living Energy Universe*, 98.

p. 289   *"The feeling was attached"*: Jerome Bernstein, "On the Borderland," *Noetic Sciences Review* (September–November 2000): 10–13, 44–46.

p. 290   *"experience and incarnate these new"*: Bernstein, "On the Borderland," 44.

p. 290   *"a transmodern spiritual or mystical"*: Christian de Quincey, "Consciousness: Truth or Wisdom?," *Noetic Sciences Review* 51 (March–June 2000): 45.

p. 292   *"help explain co-species healing"*: Allen M. Schoen, *Kindred Spirits: How the Remarkable Bond between Humans and Animals Can Change the Way We Live* (New York: Broadway Books, 2001), 164.

p. 293   *"the neural pathways of social support"*: Stephen W. Porges, *A Pocket Guide to the Polyvagal Theory: The Transformative Power of Feeling Safe* (New York: W. W. Norton, 2017), 100.

p. 293   *"If there is an aspect"*: Dossey, *Recovering the Soul*, 2.

p. 294   *"that a kind of collective"*: Dossey, *Recovering the Soul*, 101–2.

p. 294   *"The animal with which the shaman"*: Mircea Eliade, quoted in Dossey, *Recovering the Soul*, 102.

p. 294   *"in the nonlocal, collective"*: Dossey, *Recovering the Soul*, 105.

Chapter Twelve: Sacrifice and Communion

p. 297   *"Why, we are ones who could tell"*: Aboriginal woman, quoted in Jean Houston, *Myths for the Future*, Sounds True, 1995, audiocassette.

p. 297   *"All stories are true"*: John Edgar Wideman, *The Stories of John Edgar Wideman* (New York: Pantheon Books, 1992), 3.

p. 299   "Blessed are those who hunger": Matt. 5:6, *The Holy Bible: New International Version* (Grand Rapids, MI: Zondervan Publishing House, 1994).

p. 299   "the great historical religious figure": Gary E. R. Schwartz and Linda G. S. Russek, *The Living Energy Universe* (Charlottesville, VA: Hampton Roads, 1999), 37.

p. 303   "be surprised if the Taliban": Thomas J. Barfield, email message to author.

p. 307   "For millennia Semitic peoples": Jim Corbett, *Goatwalking* (New York: Viking, 1991), 83–84.

p. 307   "Settled people work relentlessly": Corbett, *Goatwalking*, 83.

p. 308   "In a society at war": Corbett, *Goatwalking*, 14.

p. 308   "To choose freedom is to cease": Corbett, *Goatwalking*, 25.

p. 308   "The souls of the people": Linda Schierse Leonard, *Creation's Heartbeat: Following the Reindeer Spirit* (New York: Bantam Books, 1995), 11–12.

p. 311   "In these dark times": Leonard, *Creation's Heartbeat*, 37.

p. 311   "Today we search for sacred spaces": Leonard, *Creation's Heartbeat*, 28.

Chapter Thirteen: Mystics with Tails

p. 326   "I hardly think the heaven-dwellers": Virgil, *The Aeneid of Virgil*, trans. Allen Mandelbaum (New York: Bantam, 1971), 14.

p. 327   "Just at the center": Virgil, *Aeneid*, 16.

p. 327   "Where on this earth": Virgil, *Aeneid*, 17.

p. 327   "With many tears and sighs": Virgil, *Aeneid*, 17.

p. 328   "It is these rivers": Neal Ascherson, *Black Sea* (New York: Hill and Wang, 1995), 4.

p. 329   "As individuals, 'the others'": Ascherson, *Black Sea*, 9.

p. 330   "We forced nature to reveal": Jean Houston, *Myths for the Future*, Sounds True, 1995, audiocassette. This and all other quotes from Houston in the current chapter are from side 1.

p. 333   "entry into so highly contentious": Henry Blake, *Talking with Horses* (North Pomfret, VT: Trafalgar Square, 1975), 84.

p. 333   "I have often been told": Blake, *Talking with Horses*, 84.

p. 333   "This started me thinking": Blake, *Talking with Horses*, 83.

p. 334   "The point is that any horse": Blake, *Talking with Horses*, 86.

p. 335   "I was just having a look": Blake, *Talking with Horses*, 91.

p. 337   "an adaptive survival perspective": Stephen W. Porges, *A Pocket Guide to the Polyvagal Theory: The Transformative Power of Feeling Safe* (New York: W. W. Norton, 2017), 43.

p. 338   "our body functions": Porges, *A Pocket Guide to the Polyvagal Theory*, 45.

INDEX

ABOUT THE AUTHOR

Linda Kohanov is an internationally recognized author, speaker, musician, and educator who has written five books on the healing and transformational potential of the horse-human bond. In 1997, she founded a southern Arizona–based collective of educators, coaches, counselors, and horse professionals. The organization, Eponaquest Worldwide, has grown to serve clients on six continents.

Linda is considered one of the founders of the field of equine-facilitated experiential learning, which teaches people how to excel in life by practicing innovative leadership, relationship, nervous system regulation, nonverbal communication, and emotional and social intelligence skills through safe, engaging, nonriding activities with horses. She has also worked with psychologists in the field of equine-facilitated psychotherapy and regularly collaborates with Dr. Rebecca Bailey to teach workshops and private sessions in Connection Focused Therapy®, a polyvagal-informed equine-facilitated model created in 2013.

Over the past two decades, Linda has appeared at numerous conferences, universities, and retreat centers throughout the world. Her seminars attract business leaders, entrepreneurs, educators, scientists, mental health professionals, artists, clergy, and social activists. Starting in 2002, she began training instructors capable of leading their own seminars in the Eponaquest approach, Connection Focused Therapy, and the Master Herder leadership model. Over three hundred Eponaquest instructors from six continents have graduated from this highly successful in-depth apprenticeship program.

She lives in Arizona with her husband, musician Steve Roach, and her horses.

Eponaquest.com • LindaKohanov.com • MasterHerder.com

NEW WORLD LIBRARY is dedicated to publishing books and other media that inspire and challenge us to improve the quality of our lives and the world.

We are a socially and environmentally aware company. We recognize that we have an ethical responsibility to our readers, our authors, our staff members, and our planet.

We serve our readers by creating the finest publications possible on personal growth, creativity, spirituality, wellness, and other areas of emerging importance. We serve our authors by working with them to produce and promote quality books that reach a wide audience. We serve New World Library employees with generous benefits, significant profit sharing, and constant encouragement to pursue their most expansive dreams.

Whenever possible, we print our books with soy-based ink on 100 percent postconsumer-waste recycled paper. We power our Northern California office with solar energy, and we respectfully acknowledge that it is located on the ancestral lands of the Coast Miwok Indians. We also contribute to nonprofit organizations working to make the world a better place for us all.

Our products are available wherever books are sold.

customerservice@NewWorldLibrary.com
Phone: 415-884-2100 or 800-972-6657
Orders: Ext. 110
Fax: 415-884-2199
NewWorldLibrary.com

Scan below to access our newsletter
and learn more about our books and authors.